Who Gets Ahead?

WHO GETS AHEAD?

The Determinants of Economic Success in America

BY

CHRISTOPHER JENCKS

SUSAN BARTLETT · MARY CORCORAN

JAMES CROUSE · DAVID EAGLESFIELD

GREGORY JACKSON · KENT McCLELLAND

PETER MUESER · MICHAEL OLNECK

JOSEPH SCHWARTZ · SHERRY WARD

JILL WILLIAMS

Basic Books, Inc., Publishers   *New York*

Library of Congress Cataloging in Publication Data

Jencks, Christopher.
  Who gets ahead?

  A revised version of The effects of family back-
ground, test scores, personality traits, and schooling
on economic success by C. Jencks and L. Rainwater
published by the National Technical Information Service,
1977.
  Bibliography: p. 379
  Includes index.
  1. Success. 2. Education—Economic aspects—
United States. 3. Students' Socio-economic status—
United States. I. Title.
HF5386.J39   331.1   78–19809
ISBN: 0–465–09182–2

CONTENTS

TABLES AND FIGURES

Tables and Figures

Tables and Figures

PREFACE

This book grew out of the controversy that followed the publication of *Inequality: A Reassessment of the Effect of Family and Schooling in America* in 1972. In that book Jencks and seven colleagues at Harvard's Center for Educational Policy Research investigated the relationships among various kinds of inequality in America. They concluded, among other things, that disparities in adult occupational status and earnings were not primarily attributable to the fact that workers came from different family backgrounds, had different cognitive skills, and had spent different amounts of time in school.

Inequality relied on what seemed to be the best evidence available at the time, but it contained a number of potentially serious gaps. About a year after its publication we initiated a systematic effort to close some of these gaps. *Who Gets Ahead?* describes the fruits of that effort. But because it involved a different group of investigators with different backgrounds and interests, and because five years of data analysis altered our thinking in many respects, *Who Gets Ahead?* is a very different book from *Inequality*.

First, *Who Gets Ahead?* is primarily concerned with the determinants of individual success within the existing economic system, not with the determinants of the level of inequality in that system. Second, *Who Gets Ahead?* presents the evidence on which it bases its conclusions in far more detail than *Inequality* did. Third, *Who Gets Ahead?* does not devote much space to problems of public policy. Its conclusions are largely descriptive. Finally, *Who Gets Ahead?* is a more fully collaborative effort than *Inequality* was. Each of the coauthors listed on the title page either took primary responsibility for analyzing one of the surveys on which this book is based or else took primary responsibility for writing one or more of the chapters.

Who Gets Ahead? tries to assess the impact of family background, cognitive skills, personality traits, years of schooling, and race on men's occupational status, earnings, and family income. To accomplish this, we looked at eleven different surveys. Because each of these surveys had its own peculiarities, and because our reading of previous research suggested that casual use of unfamiliar data had often led to disastrous errors, every member of the project but Schwartz and Corcoran assumed responsibility for learning as much as possible about one or more of the surveys. Each of us eventually wrote a detailed comparison of "our" sample with others of nominally similar character. We also produced statistical tables describing each sample in a "standard" form that we had jointly agreed upon in advance.

Every member of the project but Eaglesfield and Ward also took responsibility for preparing one or more chapters on a substantive problem. These chapters tried to synthesize all the evidence from the sample descriptions that was relevant to a specific issue. Each chapter also required additional analyses aimed at clarifying problems that had not been apparent when we did our sample descriptions. Each chapter thus rests partly on data analyzed by its author and partly on data analyzed by others.

We completed drafts of these chapters in the winter of 1977 and circulated them to a number of potential critics. After mulling over the critics' comments, we made some revisions and submitted both our substantive analyses and our sample descriptions to the funding agencies that had supported our work. Our report, *The Effects of Family Background, Test Scores, Personality Traits, and Schooling on Economic Success,* is available from the National Technical Information Service, Springfield, Virginia, 28151. We will refer to this publication simply as the *Final Report.*

The present volume is a considerably revised version of the *Final Report.* We have eliminated some of the obscurities and errors that mar the *Final Report,* clarified a number of ambiguities by further analysis of our data, and added a new conclusion comparing our findings to those in *Inequality.* We have also cut out a substantial amount of material justifying our methodological choices, although we have retained references to this material for aficionados.

While this is a joint effort, we are not all equally responsible for every word that appears here. Lest anyone be blamed for what he or she could not prevent, it seems wise to record who worked on what.

Christopher Jencks initiated, planned, and supervised the project. He was thus largely responsible for deciding what each chapter would cover and what it would ignore. He wrote chapters 1 and 2, which describe our aims and methods, and chapter 12, which compares our findings to those in *Inequality.* With Corcoran, he wrote chapter 3, which analyzes the effects of family background on economic success. He was primarily responsible for analyzing the Veterans Survey, which he describes in Appendix G of the *Final Report*. Finally, he edited the entire manuscript, often heavily. He is therefore deeply implicated in whatever stylistic and substantive deficiencies remain.

Susan Bartlett analyzed changes in the effects of education and experience on men's income, using 1940, 1950, 1960, and 1970 Census data. Her findings appear in the Summer 1978 issue of the *Journal of Human Resources*, and we have not reprinted them here. Her description of the 1970 Census results, written jointly with Jencks, constitutes Appendix A of the *Final Report*.

Mary Corcoran shared responsibility with Jencks and Eaglesfield for investigating the effects of family background. She and Jencks wrote chapter 3. She also wrote chapter 8, which summarizes our findings about the determinants of individual success.

James Crouse wrote chapter 4, which analyzes the relationship between test performance and economic success. He also took primary responsibility for analyzing our Project Talent data, except for that dealing with personality traits. His description of the Talent samples appears in Appendices H and I of the *Final Report*.

David Eaglesfield was responsible for analyzing the NORC Brothers Survey. His description of this survey appears in Appendix E of the *Final Report*. He also estimated a large number of alternative models of the effects of family background. This work appears in his doctoral dissertation, "Family Background and Occupational Achievement," done for the Harvard Department of Sociology in 1977. Chapter 3 relies on these estimates at several points.

Gregory Jackson wrote chapter 10, which examines the degree of comparability between our four major national surveys. He also took primary responsibility for analyzing the Occupational Changes in a Generation Survey. His description of this survey appears in Appendix B of the *Final Report*.

Kent McClelland wrote chapter 11, which examines the effects of variation in individual research style on findings about the relationship between education and earnings. An earlier version of this chapter appears in his doctoral dissertation, "How Different Surveys Yield Different Results: The Case of Education and Earnings," done for the Harvard Department of Sociology in 1976. He also analyzed the Productive Americans Survey, which he describes in Appendix C of the *Final Report*.

Peter Mueser analyzed Project Talent's data on personality traits and wrote chapter 5, which summarizes the effects of adolescent personality traits on later success in the Talent and Kalamazoo surveys. He also took primary responsibility for analyzing the Panel Study of Income Dynamics, which he describes in Appendix D of the *Final Report.*

Michael Olneck wrote chapter 6, which describes the effects of educational attainment on economic success. He was also responsible for conducting the Kalamazoo Brothers Survey, which he describes in detail in Appendix I of the *Final Report* and in his doctoral dissertation, "The Determinants of Educational Attainment and Adult Status among Brothers: The Kalamazoo Study," done for the Harvard Graduate School of Education in 1976.

Joseph Schwartz and Jill Williams wrote chapter 7, which compares the determinants of earnings among whites and nonwhites. Schwartz also wrote chapter 9, which analyzes the relationship between earnings and family income.

Sherry Ward was primarily responsible for analyzing the National Longitudinal Survey's data on older men. Her description of her findings appears in Appendix F of the *Final Report.*

Several other individuals played vital roles in the project. Jan Lennon administered the project for the Center for the Study of Public Policy and typed dozens of draft chapters and thousands of tables for us. Without her, our work would have taken even longer than it did. Irene Goodsell typed the final manuscript.

David Featherman and Robert Hauser provided us with a copy of the 1962 Occupational Changes in a Generation data tape and generously authorized David Bills to make tabulations for us from the 1973 replication of that survey. The Survey Research Center at the University of Michigan provided well-documented copies of the Productive Americans and Panel Study of Income Dynamics data. William Mason gave us a copy of the U.S. Current Population Survey's 1964 survey of veterans. Project Talent gave us access to selected data from their files. Olneck also shared his Kalamazoo data unstintingly.*

Susan Bartlett, Jill Williams, and Marianne Winslett did most of Jencks's computer work for him, leaving him free to send memos suggesting additional work for everyone else. Zvi Griliches, Andrew Kohen, and Paul Taubman provided valuable criticisms of a draft of the *Final Report* while Bill Bielby did the same for a draft of the book.

The National Institute of Education and the Employment and Train-

---

* In this connection we are especially grateful to Dr. David Bartz and Dr. William Coapes of the Kalamazoo Public School System for permitting Olneck to use their archives, and to Dr. Stanley Robbin of the Center for Sociological Research at Western Michigan University for allowing Olneck to use the Center's facilities while he was resurveying the Kalamazoo respondents.

ing Administration of the U.S. Department of Labor supported our work through a grant to Christopher Jencks and Lee Rainwater for work at the Center for the Study of Public Policy, a nonprofit research organization in Cambridge. The Department of Health, Education, and Welfare's Office of Income Security Policy also made a much larger grant to Lee Rainwater at the MIT–Harvard Joint Center for Urban Studies. This grant was primarily to support work on the relationship between different sources of family income, but some of the funds were used to support our work on the determinants of male earnings.

Tradition usually dictates a discrete silence about the actual amount of such support, since researchers rightly assume that readers will be appalled by the expense involved in producing a single book. But such reticence reinforces the illusion that one "should" be able to do large-scale research on a shoestring. This is just not true.

The NORC Brothers and Kalamazoo Brothers surveys were financed by Harvard's Center for Educational Policy Research, using funds granted by the Carnegie Corporation of New York. The NORC Survey cost about $13,000. The Kalamazoo Survey cost about $25,000. Grants from the National Institute of Education and the Department of Labor provided about $100,000 for data analysis, while HEW's Office of Income Security Policy provided another $100,000. Crouse's work on the effects of cognitive skills was partially supported by the Graduate College at the University of Delaware and by National Science Foundation Grant G–OC–7103704 to Donald T. Campbell. Olneck's analysis of the Kalamazoo data was supported by a doctoral fellowship from the U.S. Department of Labor's Employment and Training Administration and by a Ford Foundation grant to Samuel Bowles and Herbert Gintis at the Harvard Center for Educational Policy Research. The Institute for Research on Poverty at the University of Wisconsin supported much of Olneck's work on chapter 6. The Carnegie Corporation of New York supported Jencks during the summer of 1977, when he was editing the final manuscript.

All told, we received about $300,000 for our work. In addition, the authors all spent substantial amounts of time on the project for which they were not paid. The true cost of our work, after allowing for this form of self-exploitation, was probably at least $400,000.

Who Gets Ahead?

CHAPTER 1

Introduction

This book investigates the relationship between personal characteristics and economic success among American males aged 25 to 64. It does not try to provide a complete picture of the determinants of individual success. Rather, its aim is to assess the effects of a man's characteristics when he enters the labor market on his subsequent success. The book focuses on four kinds of personal characteristics: family background, cognitive skills, personality traits, and years of schooling.*

When we launched this project in 1973 we were concerned with three major deficiencies in earlier work (including our own) on these issues:

1. Previous investigators had seldom had adequate measures of family background, cognitive skills, or personality traits for representative national samples.
2. Previous investigators had often made simplifying assumptions about the ways family background, cognitive skills, and educational attainment affected success without testing these assumptions empirically.
3. Previous investigators had often reached contradictory conclusions, even when asking apparently similar questions and using apparently similar data.

We set out to assemble better samples, to analyze these samples more thoroughly, and to explain the discrepancies we found. We have not achieved any of these objectives fully. We have, however, made some progress in each area. This chapter summarizes what we have accom-

Christopher Jencks wrote this chapter.
* We did not investigate the effects of changes in these characteristics after men enter the labor market. Nor did we analyze the effects of geographic mobility, marital status, fertility, or on-the-job training, all of which can change after entering the labor market, partially as a result of prior economic success.

3

plished. It begins by describing our samples and the measures we derived from them. It also summarizes very briefly how these new measures changed our understanding of the determinants of economic success. Then it briefly describes our statistical methods, again explaining how they altered our understanding of the determinants of economic success. Finally, it notes the major sources of noncomparability between our findings and the findings of other investigators. With this background readers should be able to read subsequent chapters in whatever order they want, skipping chapters that are irrelevant to their interests.

The plan of the rest of the book is as follows. Chapter 2 describes our methods in more detail. It also summarizes the effects of some of our procedural decisions, such as restricting our sample to 25- to 64-year-olds. Chapters 3 through 6 present our findings regarding the effects of family background, cognitive skills, personality traits, and educational attainment. Chapter 7 compares the effects of family background and educational attainment on the earnings of whites to their effects on non-whites. Chapter 8 summarizes our findings about the determinants of individual economic success. Chapter 9 investigates the relationship between male earnings and family income. Chapter 10 assesses the degree of comparability between our surveys, while chapter 11 looks at the effects of different analytic techniques on results from the same survey. Chapter 12 compares our results to results presented seven years ago in *Inequality*.

1. THE CHARACTER OF THE EVIDENCE

The Surveys. We will look at five national surveys of 25- to 64-year-old men:

1. The 1962 Occupational Changes in a Generation (OCG) sample collected by the U.S. Current Population Survey (CPS). This sample has been extensively analyzed by Blau and Duncan (1967); Duncan, Featherman, and Duncan (1972); and Featherman and Hauser (1976a, 1976b, 1978).
2. The 1965 Productive Americans (PA) sample collected by the University of Michigan Survey Research Center (SRC).
3. The 1970 Census of Population's 1/1,000 Public Use sample.
4. The 1971–72 wave of the Panel Study of Income Dynamics (PSID), collected by SRC. This sample has been extensively analyzed by James Morgan and his collaborators (1974–78).

5. The 1973 CPS replication of OCG. David Featherman and Robert Hauser (1976a, 1976b, 1978) have analyzed this survey. The original data were not available to other users until after we finished our work, but Featherman and Hauser provided us with means, standard deviations, and correlations among key variables for a sample similar to the one we used from the 1962 OCG.

We will also look at six special-purpose samples that cover more restricted populations but provide data not available in the five surveys listed above:

6. The 1973–74 NORC Brothers sample. This survey was conducted at our request and has not previously been analyzed in any detail.
7. The 1966–67 wave of the Census Bureau's National Longitudinal Survey of Older Men (NLS). Herbert Parnes of Ohio State University has been the principal investigator concerned with these data.
8. The 1964 CPS Veterans sample. This sample is restricted to veterans under the age of 35. It has been analyzed by Duncan (1968) and Griliches and Mason (1972).
9. Project Talent's 1960–72 representative subsample. This subsample from the full Talent sample covers students who were in eleventh grade in 1960 and who were followed up intensively in 1972. It has not been previously analyzed.
10. Project Talent's 1960–72 brothers sample. This subsample includes pairs of brothers enrolled in grades 11 and 12 in 1960 who returned a mail-back questionnaire in 1971 or 1972. It has not been previously analyzed.
11. Michael Olneck's 1928–74 Kalamazoo Brothers sample. This sample covers men who were sixth graders in Kalamazoo, Michigan, between 1928 and 1950, who had brothers in these same schools, and whom Olneck followed up in 1973–74.

For reasons we will describe later, we tried to restrict all these samples to men who were not in school, in institutions, or in the military, and who had positive earnings in the relevant year. Table 1.1 summarizes each sample's most salient characteristics. Taken together, they provide a more complete picture of the relationship between men's characteristics in youth and their subsequent success than has previously been available.

Unfortunately, these surveys tell us far less about women than about men. The Census and Project Talent were the only two of our surveys to collect comparable data on both women and men—and the Census provides very limited information on its respondents, while Talent covers only quite young respondents. In light of these data limitations we reluctantly decided to restrict all our analyses to males. Fortunately, other investigators with more suitable data have done an excellent job of analyzing the effects of sex on economic success (see e.g. Treiman and Terrell,

TABLE 1.1

Characteristics of Subsamples from Eleven Surveys

Survey name[a]	OCG	PA	Census	PSID	OCG-II
Survey organization[a]	CPS	SRC	Census	SRC	CPS
Year of initial survey	1962	1965	1970	1968	1973
Initial age	25-64	25-64	25-64	22-61	25-64
Year of follow-up	–	–	–	1972	–
Age at follow-up	–	–	–	26-65	–
Percent nonresponse[b]	17	16	3+	38	12
Percent with partial data[e]	20[k]	15	30	25	NA
N with complete data	11,504	1,188	25,697	1,776	15,817
Sample restrictions					
Positive earnings	YES[h]	YES	YES	YES	YES[h]
Nonmilitary	YES[h]	YES	YES	YES	YES
Household heads only	NO	YES	NO	YES	NO
Nonstudent	NO	YES	YES	YES	NO
Had a brother	NO	NO	NO	NO	NO
Test-score floor	NO	NO	NO	NO	NO
Education floor	NO	NO	NO	NO	NO
Variables measured[i]					
Race	D	D	D	D	D
Region of upbringing	D	D	D	D	D
Father's education	G	G	–	G	G
Father's occupation	D	–	–	G	D
Number of siblings	D	G	–	G	D
Father absent at 16	D	–	–	–	D
Adolescent personality	–	–	–	–	–
Adolescent test score	–	–	–	–	–
Early adult test score	–	–	–	–	–
Adult test score	–	–	–	G	–
Years of education	G	G	D	G	G
Degrees	–	G	–	G	–
Occupation	D	G	D	G	D
Earnings	G[h]	D	D	D	G
Weeks worked	–	G	G	D	–
Brother's education	G	–	–	G	G
Brother's occupation	–	–	–	–	–
Brother's earnings	–	–	–	–	–

[a]Abbreviations for organizations and surveys are defined in the text.

[b]This is the ratio of "nonrespondents" to "potential respondents." A "nonrespondent" is any individual who could not be located or refused the interview at *either* the initial interview *or* the follow-up. Note that this nonresponse rate is for the entire target population of the original survey, not for our target population of men 25-64 who were not in school, military service, or institutions.

[c]NORC used a block-quota sample, so the nonresponse rate is indeterminate. After detailed analysis of the General Social Survey, which has been conducted using both block-quota and probability samples, NORC has concluded that block-quota samples yield virtually the same results as full-probability samples.

[d]This is a nonresponse rate for individuals, not pairs. The exact nonresponse for individual Talent brothers is unknown, because we only retrieved individuals with a sibling who had returned follow-up data. The estimate in the table is the individual response rate for the entire eleventh-grade sample in the 1972 follow-up. The estimated nonresponse for Talent brothers is higher than for the "representative" Talent sample because Talent had made no special effort to locate individuals in our subsample of brothers who had failed to return the mail-back follow-up, whereas it did make such an effort for our "representative" sample.

[e]This is the ratio of respondents with incomplete data on one or more of the variables that interested us to all respondents with any data in *our* target population.

| NORC Brothers | NLS | Veterans | Talent | Talent Brothers | Kalamazoo Brothers |
NORC	Census	CPS	Talent	Talent	Olneck
1973-74	1966	1964	1960	1960	1928-50
25-64	45-59	30-34	16±	16-17	11±
–	1971	–	1972	1971-72	1973-74
–	50-64	–	28-29	28-29	35-59
NA^c	16	11	12	72^d	55^d
45^f	40	21	39	65^f	45^f
150^g	2,580	803	839	99^g	346^g
YES	YES	YES	YES	YES	YES
NO	YES	YES	YES	YES	YES
NO	NO	NO	NO	NO	NO
YES	YES	YES	YES	YES	YES
YES	NO	NO	NO	YES	YES
NO	NO	YES	NO	NO	NO
NO	NO	NO	YES	YES	YES
D	D	D	D	D	NV
–	D	D	D	D	NV
D	G	D	G	G	D
D	D	D	G	G	D
D	–	–	D	D	D
D	D	D	D	D	D
–	–	–	D	D	G
–	–	–	D	D	D
–	–	G	–	–	–
–	–	–	–	–	–
D	D	G	G	G	D
–	–	–	D	D	–
D	D	D	G	G	D
G	D	G	D^j	D^j	G
–	D	–	–	–	–
D	–	–	–	G	D
D	–	–	–	G	D
G	–	–	–	D^j	G

^{f}"Partial data" for brothers includes failure to provide sufficient information on one's brother for the survey organization to locate the brother. It also includes the second brother's refusal to be interviewed. In Talent, it includes respondents who responded themselves but whose brothers did not. While Talent made no special effort to locate brothers, men whose brothers returned the mail-back follow-up were more likely than most to return it too.

^{g}Number of *pairs* with complete data.

^{h}Our 1962 OCG tape had income but not earnings. It grouped men with negative incomes and men with $1-499 together. We eliminated men with zero income. We used the same definition in our analyses of OCG-II. The complete data sample also eliminates men without occupations. This presumably eliminates virtually all zero earners. It retains self-employed men who lost money. Due to an error, we did not eliminate military personnel from the basic OCG sample, but we did eliminate them from the complete data sample.

^{i}Variables recorded in detailed categories are denoted by a "D." Variables collected or recorded in broad categories are denoted by a "G." Variables not measured, or not measured in a form we could use, are denoted by a dash (–). Variables with no variance are denoted "NV." For a description of "detailed" and "broad" categories, see chapter 2.

^{j}Talent allowed respondents to report earnings on an hourly, weekly, or annual basis. We reduced all these reports to an hourly basis.

^{k}Percentage does not include those respondents who are excluded because CPS did not ask them their income.

1975). Nonetheless, this limitation is both serious and regrettable, since sex is one of the most important single factors affecting earnings.

All of these surveys measured both the respondent's occupation and his earnings. Unlike most previous investigators, we did not concentrate on one of these measures to the exclusion of the other. Instead, we looked at both and tried to contrast results obtained using occupational status to results obtained using earnings.

Occupational Status. We measured occupational status using Duncan's (1961) Socio-Economic Index. An occupation's Duncan score depends on the percentage of men working in the occupation who had completed high school and the percentage with incomes of $3,500 or more in 1950. Featherman, Jones, and Hauser (1975) and Featherman and Hauser (1976c) have demonstrated that this scoring system captures both inter- and intragenerational occupational stability better than any other system in common use.

Since an occupation's Duncan score depends on its educational requirements, education inevitably influences a man's score. This is not just a methodological artifact; it reflects a real social phenomenon. The average education of men in a given line of work is closely related to the cognitive complexity and desirability of the work. It affects not only the social position of those who engage in the work (Duncan, 1961), but their children's life chances (Klatzky and Hodge, 1971), independent of both the individual's own education and his earnings from his work (Sewell and Hauser, 1975; Bielby et al., 1977).

The Duncan scale runs from 0 to 96. To get some sense of the significance of a one-point difference in Duncan scores, we looked at Rainwater's 1971–72 Boston Area Survey. Rainwater had asked respondents to rank 120 hypothetical individuals in terms of their "general standing" in their community. Each of these 120 hypothetical individuals had a different combination of education, occupation, and income. A one-point change in a man's Duncan score had the same effect on his "general standing" as a 1.3 percent change in his income.[1]

Earnings. Except in Project Talent, we measured earnings on an annual, rather than a weekly or hourly, basis. We tried three different procedures for scaling earnings. First, we looked at actual earnings, measured in dollars. Second, we looked at the natural logarithm of earnings (ln earnings). This allows us to estimate the percentage change in earnings associated with a unit change in any other trait. Third, we looked at the determinants of the cube root of earnings (earnings$^{1/3}$). There is some evidence that subjective well-being ("utility") is more nearly a linear function of earnings $^{1/3}$ than of either earnings or ln earnings.[2] These three alternative measures of earnings yield essentially similar results, though earnings $^{1/3}$ is slightly more predictable than either earnings or ln earnings.[3] However, ln earnings has two advantages over earnings and earnings $^{1/3}$. First, ln earnings is especially sensitive to variations near the bottom of the earnings distribution. This coincides with the emphasis of public policy since 1964, which has focused on altering the bottom of the earnings distribution. Second, ln earnings yields coefficients that are easier to compare across time. Most of our analyses therefore concentrate on ln earnings.

Economists usually think of annual earnings as depending on two factors: hourly wages and hours worked per year. Chapter 9 shows that the determinants of wages are not the same as the determinants of hours, although each may influence the other. Ideally, then, we should investigate the determinants of wages and hours separately. Unfortunately, many of our surveys did not collect information on hours (or even weeks) worked during the previous year. The surveys that did collect such information often grouped it into broad categories. This means that we could not estimate the respondent's average hourly or weekly wage accurately. We therefore decided not to try to disentangle the factors that influence wages from those that influence hours in most of our analyses. Chapter 9, however, does do this for the PSID data.

The reader may also wonder why we looked only at earnings, ignoring other sources of income. The main reason is simplicity. Chapter 9 shows that among families with a "head" 25- to 64-years-old, male earnings explain 82 percent of the variance in total family income. Some families receive substantial income from female earnings, but since few females have high earnings and many have none at all, female earnings contribute far less than male earnings to the overall variance of family income. A few families also receive substantial income from dividends, interest, or rent, but such income also explains a relatively modest fraction of the variance in total family income. Transfer payments, such as welfare and social security, are even less important. The principal problem posed by concentrating on male earnings is that we completely ignore families with no male earner at all. This problem is not as serious as it seems, however, since we can predict family income quite accurately if we know that the family in question has no male earner. Such families' total income is almost always low.

Family Background Measures. We define family background as everything that makes men with one set of parents different from men

9

with a different set of parents. Most previous investigators have measured family background in terms of what we will call "demographic" advantages. By this we mean such readily measurable background characteristics as race, place of birth, father's education, father's occupation, number of siblings, and whether the respondent lived with both parents while he was growing up.[4] One can obviously augment this list by including mother's education, mother's occupation, parental income, parental ethnicity, parental religion, and the like. But no such list is ever complete. Thus while analyses of this kind can set a lower limit on the overall impact of family background, they can never set an upper limit. To get around this difficulty we have used an alternative measure of familial influence, namely the degree of resemblance between brothers. Such resemblance can be due to common genes, common environment, or the influence of one brother on the other. But unless brothers deliberately become unlike one another, resemblance between siblings sets an upper limit on the explanatory power of their common environment and common genes. (Resemblance between siblings does *not* allow us to estimate the effects of genes alone.)

Contrary to what Jencks et al. argued in *Inequality*, background characteristics seem to exert appreciable effects on both occupational status and earnings even among men with the same test scores and education. The background characteristics that exert these effects are not primarily the "standard" demographic measures of parental advantages, such as father's occupation and parental income. Rather, some set of as yet unmeasured background characteristics makes brothers more alike than we would expect on the basis of their test scores and education. The unmeasured background characteristics that affect economic success appear to be different in kind from the background characteristics that influence test scores and educational attainment. Taking account of these unmeasured influences increases the apparent importance of growing up in the "right" family. Chapter 3 explores these effects in detail.

Cognitive Measures. Almost all investigations of the effects of cognitive skills on economic success have relied on a single cognitive test, usually designed to measure academic "aptitude" or "intelligence." [5] Project Talent, in contrast, administered cognitive tests covering 60 different areas to a national sample of high school students in 1960. In 1972 Talent recontacted a relatively representative subsample of former eleventh graders, most of whom were then 28 or 29 years old, and obtained data on their education, occupational status, and earnings. The Talent data therefore allow us to explore the effects of different adolescent cognitive skills in far greater detail than previous investigations have. Chapter 4 shows that tests of academic aptitude and skills predict economic success better than did Talent's other tests (e.g. "creativity," "clerical checking," "abstract reasoning"). Within the academic domain no one general area is clearly more important than others. The best predictors are those that test a wide range of verbal and quantitative skills.

Test performance in sixth grade seems to predict subsequent success as accurately as test performance later in school or in adulthood. This implies that changes in test performance after sixth grade have little impact on adult success. If this is the case, it is the "aptitude" component of test performance that affects success, not the "achievement" component. The evidence for this interpretation is by no means conclusive, however, and some Swedish data contradict it (Fagerlind, 1975). If confirmed, this finding would imply that *changing* a student's relative test performance, at least after sixth grade, has little effect on his life chances.

With the exception of Taubman and Wales (1974), most previous investigations of the relationship between adolescent cognitive skills and later economic success have measured workers' success when they were still quite young. Our Talent respondents are also young, but Olneck's Kalamazoo sample is 35- to 59-years-old. Since Olneck's data cover brothers, they also allow us to distinguish the effects of cognitive skills from the effects of family background more adequately than previous research. Chapter 4 analyzes the effects of cognitive skills in detail.

Personality Measures. Most previous research on the effects of personality traits has relied on cross-sectional data. This makes it very difficult to say whether "favorable" personality traits cause economic success or vice versa. The Talent and Kalamazoo surveys probably provide the best longitudinal data on adolescent personality traits now available. The Kalamazoo schools collected teacher ratings of tenth graders' personality traits. Project Talent collected a wide range of self-assessments from its high school respondents. It also asked respondents to describe their high school behavior. Variations in such behavior presumably reflect personality differences to some extent.

No one personality measure predicts success in maturity as well as test scores do. When we combine a number of different adolescent personality measures, however, their combined effects are as strong as the combined effects of different adolescent cognitive tests. Furthermore, personality traits affect earnings in ways that are largely independent of background, test scores, and educational attainment. Overall, then, our data suggest that personality traits are considerably more important than earlier data implied. The best predictor of economic success appears to be what Talent labeled "leadership" and Kalamazoo teachers called "executive ability." Chapter 5 analyzes the effects of these traits in more detail.

Education. Like most previous investigators we were primarily concerned with estimating the economic effects of the amount of time respondents had spent in school, but none of our surveys asked how many years students had actually spent in school. Instead, our surveys asked the respondent the highest grade of school or college he had completed. Like previous investigators we used highest grade completed as a proxy for time in school. Our estimates of the economic benefits of schooling do not, then, differ from those of previous investigators because we measured respondents' educational experience differently but because we had more measures of respondents' characteristics *before* they were exposed to different amounts of schooling. Chapter 6 shows that improved measurement of respondents' initial characteristics somewhat reduces the apparent benefits of school attendance. The reduction is larger for secondary school than for higher education, and larger for earnings than for occupational status.

While our primary concern was estimating the effects of time spent in school ("quantity"), we also devoted some attention to differences in respondents' experiences while they were enrolled in school ("quality"). The Talent and Veterans surveys asked respondents what kind of curriculum they had pursued in high school and found that those who had completed a college preparatory curriculum were somewhat better off economically than those who had completed a nonacademic curriculum. But as chapter 6 notes, this difference is entirely attributable to the fact that enrolling in a college preparatory curriculum increases a student's chance of attending college. When we compared students who had the same amount of schooling, we found no evidence that either the subject matter or the attitudes acquired in a college preparatory curriculum were more valuable economically than those acquired in other curricula.

Talent also collected data on the subjects its respondents had studied in college and on the institutions they had attended, but we have not yet analyzed these data. The only other survey we analyzed that recorded data on college quality was the Productive Americans (PA) survey. The PA survey reported the "selectivity" of the last college or graduate school a respondent had attended and showed that respondents who had attended selective institutions earned more than those who had attended unselective ones. But since PA did not collect data on students' abilities or aspirations before they entered college, it does not allow us to say how much of the economic advantage enjoyed by the alumni of selective colleges is due to their college experiences per se.

2. STATISTICAL METHODS

In considering the association of workers' characteristics with one another, we asked three questions:

1. *How strong is the observed relationship between any given worker characteristic and economic success?* We were not satisfied with merely establishing the *existence* of a relationship. Rather, we tried to determine the *size* of the relationship. The size of a given relationship depends on the population one studies, the way in which one asks and codes questions, and the statistics one uses to describe the results. One must devote considerable attention to technical details in order to make meaningful statements about the size of relationships.

We did not assume that the relationships between worker characteristics and economic success were necessarily linear. Chapter 2 describes how we tested for nonlinearities. Nonlinearities proved unimportant when estimating the effects of family background and test scores. But a year of higher education raises occupational status by two or three times as much as a year of elementary or secondary education. A year of higher education also raises earnings by a larger dollar amount, though not by a larger percentage, than a year of elementary or secondary education. The first and last years of high school and college are associated with larger percentage increases in earnings than the intervening years. This could be due to institutional selection, self-selection, or "credential effects."

2. *How much of a trait's observed relationship to economic success is a by-product of the fact that both the trait in question and economic success depend on causally prior traits?* If we want to assess the true "effect" on economic success of, say, staying in school rather than dropping out, we must compare groups of respondents who had the same characteristics in adolescence but who then got different amounts of schooling for some unknown reason. We use multiple regression equations to make such comparisons. To assess the effect of schooling on occupational status, for example, we regress occupational status on schooling while

controlling all worker characteristics that are causally (i.e., temporally) prior to leaving school. These traits include family background, adolescent test scores, and adolescent personality traits.

We did not restrict ourselves to controlling causally prior variables that we could measure directly. By looking at differences between brothers, we were also able to control the unmeasured family background characteristics that make brothers alike. This allowed us to isolate the effects of cognitive skills and education more precisely than most previous investigators.[6] Furthermore, the fact that some of our surveys contained measures of both adolescent test scores and adolescent personality traits allowed us to estimate the extent to which ignoring these factors biases other estimates of the economic benefits of schooling. Chapter 6 shows that controlling all aspects of family background plus adolescent test scores substantially reduces the estimated returns to schooling.

We retained nonlinear education measures throughout our analyses. This turned out to be quite important. Chapter 6 shows that controlling family background and cognitive skills lowers the estimated economic benefits of elementary and secondary education more than it lowers the estimated benefits of higher education.

We also investigated whether the effect of one worker characteristic depended on the value of another. Chapter 2 describes our procedures for detecting such interactions. In general, they did not appear to be very important. Chapter 6 shows, for example, that returns to education do not depend on initial ability. Similarly, chapter 7 shows that, contrary to much previous research, percentage returns to education are not consistently higher for whites than for nonwhites. It would be wrong, however, to say that interactions are *never* important. Chapter 7 shows that race affects returns to different *levels* of education, with whites generally receiving higher returns to the first 15 years of schooling and nonwhites gaining more from the 16th year. Chapter 6 shows that men with white-collar fathers obtain a greater occupational payoff from elementary and secondary schooling than men with farm fathers, but the pattern is reversed for higher education. Such interactions are atypical, however.

3. *What are the mechanisms by which a given characteristic exerts its influence on economic success?* To answer this question we augment our regression equations by including worker characteristics that are causally subsequent to the characteristic under study. Thus, if we want to say *how* education affects economic success, we control test scores in maturity, years of labor-force experience, or other traits that depend on education.

As we add each of these "intervening" variables to our equation, the coefficient of education changes. If we could identify all the relevant intervening variables and could measure them correctly, the coefficient of education might fall to zero. If we cannot identify (or properly measure) all the relevant intervening variables, the coefficient of education will remain positive. The ratio of the coefficient after controlling an intervening variable to the coefficient with only causally prior variables controlled tells us how much of the effect of education depends on the fact that education affects this intervening variable. According to sociological convention, the effects of one variable on another that are not explained by intervening variables are known as "direct" effects, while the explained effects are known as "indirect." The magnitude of the "direct" effects is, of course, a function of the investigator's choice of "intervening" variables.

3. RECONCILING DISCREPANT FINDINGS

One major advantage of our investigation was our simultaneous use of many different surveys. These surveys often yielded apparently inconsistent results. This made us unusually sensitive to the many sources of noncomparability in social science research. It also led us to investigate some of these sources of noncomparability in a systematic way.

Chapter 10 shows that even when we made a systematic effort to eliminate all differences between our major national surveys, irreducible "survey organization effects" remained. Specifically, we found that Michigan's Survey Research Center interviews fewer unskilled and semiskilled workers than the Census Bureau. SRC may also get higher quality income data from the people it interviews.

Chapter 11 shows how various "arbitrary" decisions that researchers make in the course of analyzing their data affect the apparent distribution of both education and earnings in the 1970 Census and in the 1970 wave of the PSID. It also shows that with one major exception these decisions do not appreciably alter the estimated value of an extra year of school. The exception is the treatment of respondents without earnings. Our work focused exclusively on individuals with positive earnings. Some other investigators include respondents with zero earnings. If one is predicting dollar earnings and is looking only at men aged 25 to 64, including nonearners makes little difference. But if one is predicting the logarithm of earnings, as economists usually do, one must assign men without earnings some arbitrary value. Most economists choose $1. Even when the overwhelming majority of respondents have earnings, this has disastrous effects. Including nonearners and assigning them $1 dramatically increases the apparent variance of earnings. It also means that one's equations primarily describe the determinants of labor-force participation, not the determinants of relative earnings among participants. Studies that use this method cannot be compared to studies like ours that do not.

Chapter 2 discusses several other issues that affect the comparability of results from different studies. Age restrictions appear to be the most important source of noncomparability. Samples that include men under 25 (e.g., Mincer, 1974) yield very different results from samples that include only older men. Even samples of 25- to 34-year-olds differ in important respects from samples of older men. This means that we cannot generalize with much confidence from our Talent samples to all men aged 25 to 64.

As the foregoing summary indicates, our research took us in a variety of different directions. The result is a long book. In order to facilitate selective reading, we tried to make each chapter as self-contained as possible. This leads to a certain amount of repetition. To prevent such repetition from becoming unbearable, we decided *not* to make each chapter methodologically self-contained. Instead, we grouped almost all our methodological material in chapter 2. Later chapters assume familiarity with this material. Readers with limited time or trusting dispositions can therefore skim chapter 2 and then turn to the substantive chapters that particularly interest them.

CHAPTER 2

Methods

This chapter describes how we analyzed our eleven samples and provides some of the technical information needed to assess the plausibility of our results. Section 1 describes the questions different surveys asked and how we coded the responses. Differences between surveys account for some of the inconsistencies in our subsequent numerical estimates.

Section 2 discusses associations among pairs of variables. We begin by discussing unstandardized linear coefficients (i.e., correlations). Then we present the usual formula for estimating standardized linear coefficients (i.e., correlations). Then we discuss the interpretation of such unstandardized coefficients when the dependent variable is the natural logarithm of earnings. We conclude by discussing our procedures for identifying nonlinear relationships (i.e., quadratic terms and comparison of eta ^{2} with R ^{2}) and for summarizing such nonlinearities in regression equations (i.e., orthogonal quadratic terms, splines, and dummies). Readers with economic training will find nothing new here, except perhaps for our discussion of orthogonal nonlinear terms. Sociologically trained readers should also peruse the discussion of semilog equations. Readers who do not use statistics on a daily basis may want to read the whole section.

Section 3 discusses multivariate relationships. It begins by describing how we estimated the "effect" of one trait on another, as distinct from the association, by controlling causally prior traits. It also discusses how

Susan Bartlett, James Crouse, David Eaglesfield, Gregory Jackson, Christopher Jencks, Kent McClelland, Peter Mueser, Michael Olneck, Joseph Schwartz, Sherry Ward, and Jill Williams all contributed to this chapter. Jencks wrote the text.

we controlled unmeasured background characteristics by estimating "difference equations" for brothers. Then it discusses how we investigated the mechanisms through which a trait affected economic success by controlling "intervening" variables. It concludes by discussing our search for nonadditive relationships, which we tried to identify both by splitting each sample into subsamples and by including orthogonal multiplicative terms in our equations. Statistically sophisticated readers will find nothing new here except for our discussions of difference equations and orthogonal multiplicative terms.

Section 4 discusses measurement error. It presents evidence on the likely size of such errors in various samples and gives simple formulas for estimating the effect of random errors on bivariate associations.

Section 5 gives some rules of thumb for estimating the significance of differences obtained from weighted samples and for calculating the significance of differences between pairs of regression coefficients. Readers familiar with these problems should skip this section.

Section 6 discusses the effects of eliminating students, soldiers, inmates, and respondents with incomplete data. It also presents data on the effects of age restrictions. This discussion should help explain some of the apparent discrepancies between samples discussed in later chapters. Section 6 also discusses the biases introduced by estimating returns to schooling with experience rather than age controlled.

1. QUESTIONS AND CODING

We habitually describe the men who interest us as "respondents." In a number of instances, however, our information about these men comes from someone else, whom we might call an "informant." In OCG, for example, information on the respondent's education and occupation came from a March 1962 CPS interview which was conducted with the most knowledgeable adult who happened to be at home when the interviewer reached a given household. OCG's income data came from similar interviews in February. Women are at home more often than men, so most of these data probably come from wives. The PA and PSID tried to get data from men whenever they could, but they did not always succeed. The Census asked "the householder" to fill out the questionnaire for everyone in his or her household but did not say who the householder was. The other surveys obtained virtually all their data directly from the respondents. Chapter 11 concludes that PSID wives' estimates of their husband's earnings were about as accurate as the husbands' estimates, but this may not hold for other surveys or traits.

Race. The Census Bureau and the Survey Research Center (SRC) told interviewers to guess the informant's race, using whatever visual or verbal clues the interviewer thought appropriate. When the informant was not the respondent, both the Census Bureau and SRC assumed that the respondent was of the same race as the informant. The NORC Brothers Survey told interviewers who had any doubt about the respondent's race to ask the respondent, "What race do you consider yourself?" The 1970 Census and Project Talent relied largely on mail questionnaires and asked all respondents to report their race for themselves.

We assigned "white" respondents a score of 1 on this variable. We assigned all others 0. This variable's coefficient therefore measures the benefit of being white rather than nonwhite.*

Father Absent. The NLS, Veterans, and NORC Brothers surveys asked, "With whom were you living when you were 15?" OCG and Kalamazoo asked, "Were you living with both your parents most of the time up to age 16?" Talent asked eleventh graders, "With whom are you now living?" The PA, Census, and PSID did not ask this question. In analyzing the PSID we assumed that respondents who reported neither their father's education nor his occupation had not grown up with their fathers.†

Father's Education. The Census did not ask about father's education. Talent asked "What is the highest grade of school or college your father reached?" All other surveys substituted "completed" for "reached." All surveys but the PA and PSID asked respondents who were not living with their father when they were 15 or 16 (or when they were "growing up") to report on the individual who "headed" their household. Between 7 and 20 percent of all respondents reported on someone other than their father, with the percentage varying by age and geographic location. The NLS, NORC Brothers, and Kalamazoo surveys recorded the exact number of years completed. The OCG, PA, Veterans, PSID, and Talent surveys grouped responses into categories like "some high school," "high

---

* Tables A2.1 and A2.5 treat PSID's "Spanish American" respondents as "nonwhite." Chapter 7 treats Spanish American respondents as white, in order to increase comparability with our other surveys, which did not distinguish Spanish Americans from other respondents.

† This coding procedure means that the coefficient of the PSID variable is not comparable to the coefficient of the father absent variable in other samples and should not be given any substantive interpretation. Its only purpose is to avoid eliminating men who knew nothing about their fathers.

school graduate," "some college," and so forth. We used 1970 Census data to estimate the mean number of years of school completed by men in each category and assigned all respondents the estimated mean of their category. Grouping makes the observed variance slightly less than the true variance.

The PA and PSID surveys asked respondents who did not know their father's education whether he could read and assigned those who could not read to the category "0 to 5 years of school." Neither PA nor PSID retained flags for these assigned values, so we could not eliminate them. The PA and PSID did not ask how many years of school fathers had completed beyond high school. Instead, they asked whether the father had attended college, whether he had earned a bachelor's degree, and whether he had earned a graduate degree. We estimated years of school from these data.

There was a serious nonresponse problem among men who said their father was not living at home when they were "growing up" or when they were 16. We assigned such men the survey mean if they did not report their father's education and relied on the dummy variable for father absent to capture differences in economic success between men with no father at home and the rest of the sample.

Father's Occupation. The OCG, Veterans, NLS, and Kalamazoo surveys asked respondents what kind of work their fathers did when they were about 15 or 16 years old. The NORC Brothers Survey asked what the father "normally" did when the respondent was "growing up." These surveys also asked who the respondent's father worked for, if anyone. They classified the resulting replies using Census three-digit occupation and industry codes and then assigned them Duncan scores.

The PSID asked about the father's "usual occupation" when the respondent was "growing up" and coded replies into eight categories that correspond roughly to broad Census occupational groups. Talent asked its eleventh-grade respondents which of seventeen occupational categories "comes closest to describing your father's work." Talent provided a minimal description and a few examples for each category. We assigned the PSID and Talent categories an approximate Duncan score, based on Duncan's (1961) data on workers in the relevant category. Grouping reduces the measured standard deviation of father's occupation by about a seventh in the PSID. There is no apparent reduction in Talent.

OCG, Veterans, NLS, Kalamazoo, and Talent asked respondents who were not living with their fathers to report on the individual who headed their household when they were 15 or 16. PSID did not ask whether the father was absent. Nor did it ask for data on the person who headed the household if the father was absent. The PA and Census did not ask about the father's occupation.

Father Foreign. The PA and PSID asked respondents where their father grew up. The OCG, NLS, and Kalamazoo surveys asked where he was born. The Census also asked where the father was born, but we did not utilize this question in our Census analyses. The Veterans, Project Talent, and NORC Brothers surveys did not ask about the father's place of birth.

Siblings. The OCG, PA, PSID and NORC Brothers surveys asked about the number of brothers and the number of sisters the respondent had. OCG asked respondents to include stepsiblings, adopted siblings, and siblings who had lived but were now deceased. PSID added that foster siblings should not be included. NORC said nothing about foster siblings but qualified OCG's list with "if you grew up with them." Talent asked how many living children there were in the respondent's family. Kalamazoo asked separately the number of older and younger "children [who] grew up in your family." The Veterans, NLS, and Census surveys did not ask about siblings.

Nonfarm Upbringing. NLS asked, "When you were 15 years old, where were you living?" and included "rural farm" as a possible answer. OCG asked a similar question but allowed respondents to answer, "The same place I do now." The Census Bureau coded OCG respondents who gave this answer as having grown up on a farm if they were living on a farm in 1962. There is no way to identify OCG respondents who grew up on a farm, no longer lived on one in 1962, but still lived in the same community.* PA and PSID asked, "Where did you grow up? Was that on a farm, in a city or what?" Veterans asked "In what kind of place did you live most of the time up until you were 15?" NORC Brothers did not ask such a question, so we assumed that men whose fathers were "normally" farmers or farm laborers grew up on farms. We could have done this in Talent as well, but we did not. Kalamazoo respondents all lived in the city of Kalamazoo when they were in sixth grade, so the question seemed redundant. The Census did not collect any information on whether the respondent grew up on a farm.

Non-South Upbringing. OCG, NLS, and Census asked where the respondent was born. The Veterans Survey asked where the respondent lived "most of the time" up to age 15. PA asked where he "grew up

---

* We could have treated such respondents as having grown up on a farm if they said their father worked in farming, but this is not quite the same thing. Some men work on farms without living on one. Others live on farms while working primarily in some other, more lucrative occupation.

(from about ages 6–16)." PSID merely asked, "Where did you grow up?" We defined the South as including all states south of the Mason-Dixon line and the Ohio River, plus Arkansas, Louisiana, Oklahoma, and Texas. We coded everyone else as nonsouthern. We did not code this information in Talent. We did not collect it from NORC or Kalamazoo Brothers.

Test Score. Talent administered a large battery of tests to eleventh graders. Kalamazoo administered the Terman or Otis Group IQ test in sixth grade. The Veterans Survey retrieved men's AFQT scores at the time they entered military service. The PSID administered a thirteen-item sentence-completion test in 1972. The other samples have no test-score data. We scaled all these tests using an "IQ" metric, in which the population mean is 100 and the standard deviation is 15.[1]

Age. PA, PSID, OCG, Census, Veterans, Talent, and NLS asked respondents how old they were, with OCG and Census specifying "on your last birthday." The Census also asked for date of birth. NORC Brothers asked, "In what year were you born?" Kalamazoo obtained the birth year from school records. Since all Talent respondents were in eleventh grade in 1960, variation in their age is mainly due to variation in the age at which they started school and the number of grades they skipped or repeated. With test score controlled, age did not affect success in Talent, so we ignored it.

Education. OCG and Census asked for the highest grade the respondent had attended and whether he had completed that grade. Veterans, NLS, and Kalamazoo asked for the highest grade completed. PA and PSID asked about grades attended through high school and whether high school graduates had started or completed college or graduate school. In addition, PSID asked whether respondents had any trouble reading. Talent asked whether respondents had obtained a high school diploma and how much college and graduate schooling they had completed. NORC asked about both years of schooling and degrees obtained.

Census, NLS, Kalamazoo, and NORC Brothers recorded the highest grade in single years. OCG, Veterans, PA, and PSID recorded responses in broader categories. This reduces the standard deviation of education slightly. The 1975 wave of the PSID, which became available after our analyses were complete, asked respondents how many years of education they had completed and recorded exact years. This measure correlated 0.976 with the grouped PSID measure based on degrees. Neither education measure predicts economic success consistently better than the other in PSID, so we ignore the distinction.

Experience. We defined "experience" as the number of years the respondent had been out of school since the age of 14. For this purpose we assumed that every respondent entered first grade when he was six and advanced one grade per year. It follows that:

$$\text{Experience} = \text{Age} - (\text{Education} + 6) \text{ if Education} \geqslant 8$$
$$= \text{Age} - 14 \text{ if Education} \leqslant 8$$

Of course not all men enter first grade when they are 6 years old, and not all advance one grade per year.* Furthermore, many of our surveys did not ask exactly how many years of school respondents had had, especially if they had attended graduate school. Our estimates of experience therefore contain a fair amount of error.

Note that this variable does not measure experience since school completion. Many men leave school, work for a few years, and then return to school. Our variable includes experience prior to reentering school. Note, too, that our variable does not measure *work* experience. Many respondents work while they are in school. Many others do not work even while they are out of school. And finally, our variable does not measure on-the-job training. We have no data regarding such training.

Occupation. OCG, Census, NORC, and Kalamazoo asked, "For whom do you work?" "What kind of business or industry is this?" and "What kind of work are you doing? (Please describe duties as specifically as possible)." They coded responses into three-digit Census occupational categories and then recoded to Duncan scores. Veterans and NLS merely asked, "What kind of work are you doing?" and coded it similarly. PA and PSID asked, "What is your main occupation?" and classified responses into broad Census categories, to which we assigned Duncan scores. Talent assigned respondents to one of 181 occupational categories. We tried to match these Talent categories with those used by the Census Bureau and then estimated each category's Duncan score.

Earnings. We defined earnings as income from wages, salaries, and self-employment. OCG, PA, NLS, PSID, and the Census asked respondents to report income from wages and salaries, nonfarm self-employment, and farming separately. Unfortunately, our OCG tape did not record these separate responses. Instead, it recorded total income from *all* sources, including assets and transfer payments. Most respondents underreport their asset and transfer income to the Census Bureau, so the distortion is not as serious as it might be. For Census respondents with a current occupation, 95 percent of all reported income is from earnings. Chapter 11 shows that substituting income for earnings raises the estimated returns to schooling by about 1 percent in the Census but has

* OCG asked about age at school completion, but the responses contain so many oddities that we did not try to use them.

23

no effect in the PSID. The difference is smaller if one restricts the analysis to men with a current occupation, as we do. We therefore treat results for income and earnings as interchangeable.*

The OCG, PA, NLS, Census, and NORC Brothers surveys asked respondents to report their earnings or income for the calendar year prior to the survey. This means that the earning year does not coincide with the survey year, and that some respondents reported a current occupation different from the occupation they engaged in when they earned the amount reported.† PSID also asked respondents about their earnings during the previous calendar year, but because the survey was repeated at one-year intervals we were able to ascertain both occupational status and earnings for the same year (1971). Some Kalamazoo Brothers were surveyed near the end of 1973 and were asked how much they *expected* to earn during that year. The rest were surveyed in early 1974 and were asked how much they had actually earned in 1973. Veterans were asked how much they expected to earn in 1964. Responses to this question appear to be about as accurate as responses to questions about actual earnings for the previous calendar year. Talent respondents were asked their hourly, weekly, or monthly earnings at the time of the survey. We reduced all the Talent responses to an hourly value, since we did not know how many hours respondents had worked during the previous year.

The OCG, Veterans, NORC, and Kalamazoo surveys grouped responses into quite broad categories. This compresses the variance of earnings. It also increases the correlation of earnings with other traits, since the traits we measured did not explain much of the variation within the top or bottom categories. As a result, grouping earnings slightly increases standardized coefficients while leaving unstandardized coefficients almost unchanged (see chapter 11).

Family Income. We defined family income as the sum of the respondent's earnings, his income from assets and transfer payments, and the income from all sources of all other family members. This measure is available for the Veterans, PA, NLS, Census, PSID, Kalamazoo, and

---

* PSID did not record total self-employment income. Instead, it divided such income into "labor" and "asset" income, and grouped the latter. We reconstructed the approximate amount of PSID self-employment income using other data. For details on this problem see *Final Report*, Appendix D and chapter 16.

† Tables dealing with occupational status ordinarily indicate the year of the survey, while tables dealing with earnings indicate the earning year. This means that the same survey is identified in different ways in different tables. When we refer to *both* occupational status *and* earnings we often identify a survey as covering a two-year interval: "the 1961–62 OCG data," for example.

NORC Brothers samples, but we did not use it in our Veterans or Census analyses.

As the foregoing discussion indicates, there is no professional consensus on how best to measure standard "demographic" concepts. As a result, every investigator feels free to "improve" previous investigators' measures. In most cases these "improvements" have no effect. But there is seldom any simple way to be sure of this, since those who improve their predecessors' measures rarely bother to try both approaches and compare the results. Thus when we obtain different results from different samples we rarely know precisely why. Furthermore, whether or not an "improvement" actually "works" (e.g. by predicting an outcome of interest more accurately than alternative measures), most investigators give their new measures the same verbal label as older ones. This creates the illusion of greater comparability than really exists. This is one reason why knowledge in the social sciences is so seldom cumulative. We have tried to be sensitive to this danger in our own analyses, but we have not completely avoided it.

Table A2.1 in the Appendix shows the mean and standard deviation of each variable for each sample of respondents with complete data. Table 10.1 in chapter 10 shows frequency distributions for OCC, PA, Census, and PSID samples that have been modified slightly to make them more nearly comparable to one another. Chapter 10 also discusses some of the reasons for differences among our samples.

2. BIVARIATE RELATIONSHIPS

Unstandardized Coefficients.   One way to estimate the association between two worker characteristics is to write an equation relating them to one another. Suppose, for example, that we want to relate education (U) to earnings (Y). If we use the subscript i to designate any randomly selected individual, the coefficient B_0 to designate the expected earnings of individuals with no schooling, and the coefficient B_1 to designate the average increase in earnings associated with the average year of schooling, we can write:

(1) $$Y_i = B_0 + B_1 U_i + E_i$$

where E_i is an error term, equal to the difference between the ith individual's actual earnings (Y_i) and the value predicted on the basis of the equation $(\hat{Y}_i)$. This predicted value is simply $B_0 + B_1 U_i$. If we estimate B_1 using conventional least squares regression, E will be uncorrelated with U. Taking the variance of both sides of equation 1 then yields:

(2) $$s^2_Y = B^2_1 s^2_U + s^2_E$$

where s^2_Y, s^2_U, and s^2_E are the variances of Y, U, and E respectively. Since $\hat{Y}_i = B_0 + B_1 U_i$ it follows that $s^2_Y = B^2_1 s^2_U$ and equation 2 can be reduced to:

(2a) $$s^2_Y = s^2 \hat{Y} + s^2_E$$

We designate $s^2 \hat{Y}$ as the "explained" variance. It follows that $s^2 \hat{Y}/s^2_Y$ is the percentage of the total variance in Y "explained" by variation in U. We designate this percentage as R^2. (Since the observed value of R^2 tends to be slightly higher than the true value, especially in small samples, we sometimes report a "corrected" value of R^2, denoted as $\overline{R}^2$).

Standardized Coefficients. Measures like test scores and occupational status have no "natural" metric. Even when a measure has a natural metric, as education and earnings do, it is often convenient to "standardize" it for comparability with other measures with different metrics. To accomplish this we subtract a variable's mean $(\overline{Y}$ or $\overline{U})$ from all observations and then divide by the standard deviation $(s_Y$ or $s_U)$. Every standardized variable's mean is therefore zero, with a standard deviation of 1.000. If we denote these standardized measures with lowercase letters, we can show that:

(3) $$y_i = r_{YU} u_i + e_i$$

where r_{YU} is the correlation between Y and U, and $e_i = E_i/s_Y$. We can also show that:

(4) $$B_1 = \left(\frac{s_Y}{s_U} \right) r_{YU}$$

Squaring both sides and rearranging gives us:

(4a) $$\frac{B^2_1 s^2_U}{s^2_Y} = \frac{s^2 \hat{Y}}{s^2_Y} = r^2_{YU}$$

The correlation coefficient therefore has a double meaning. Suppose, for example, that $r_{YU} = 0.40$, a fairly typical value. Equation 3 then tells us that two individuals who differ by one standard deviation on education can be expected to differ by 0.40 standard deviations on earnings. Equation 4a tells us that the ratio of explained to total variance in earnings is equal to $r^2_{UY} = 0.16$. Tables A2.2–A2.12 in the Appendix display the correlations among the principal variables in our complete data samples. One can combine these correlations with the standard deviations in table A2.1 to obtain unstandardized regression coefficients.

Logarithmic Coefficients. If we want to estimate the *percentage* increase in earnings associated with an extra year of education, we use the natural logarithm of earnings (i.e., the log to the base e, where $e \sim 2.71828$) as the dependent variable. Then we estimate:

$$(5) \qquad \qquad \ln Y_i = B_0 + B_1 U_i + E_i$$

Taking the antilogarithm of both sides, we have:

$$(5a) \qquad \qquad Y_i = e^{B_0} e^{B_1 U_i} e^{E_i}$$

A one-year increase in education (U) thus multiplies earnings by e^{B_1}. Suppose, for example, that $B_1 = 0.10$. Since $e^{0.10} = 1.1052$, each extra year of school multiplies earnings by 1.1052, an increase of 10.52 percent. The following table of equivalents is likely to be useful for interpreting logarithmic coefficients:

$e^{.00} = 1.000$	$e^{.10} = 1.105$	$e^{-.10} = .905$
$e^{.01} = 1.010$	$e^{.20} = 1.221$	$e^{-.20} = .819$
$e^{.05} = 1.051$	$e^{.50} = 1.649$	$e^{-.50} = .607$

These calculations show that logarithmic coefficients between 0 and 0.10 approximate percentage effects quite closely. Even when the coefficient is as large as 0.20, the upward bias can usually be neglected. For values above 0.20, the percentage effect should be calculated directly by taking the antilog of the coefficient and subtracting 1.000. Note that when the logarithmic coefficient is negative, it *under*estimates the percentage reduction in the dependent variable associated with a one-unit change in the independent variable. This discrepancy between the logarithmic coefficient and the percentage effect is larger if the independent variable changes by more than one unit and smaller if it changes by less than one unit. If, for example, $\ln Y = 0.10X$, a five-unit increase in X will multiply Y by a factor of $(1.105)^5 = e^{(5)(0.10)} = 1.649$. Conversely, an 0.10 unit increase in X will raise Y by a factor of $(1.105)^{0.10} = 1.010$. Thus, for sufficiently small changes in X the logarithmic coefficient will always equal the percentage effect, while for large changes the logarithmic coefficient will always underestimate the percentage effect.*

Nonlinearities: Eta² The bivariate coefficients in tables A2.2–A2.12 measure the linear association of every trait with every other. The values of B_1 in equation 1 may, however, vary as U varies. In that case a plot of $\overline{Y}$ for various values of U will not be linear. To test this hypothesis we divided each continuous worker characteristic into six to ten categories and calculated the percentage of the total variance in education, occupational status, and earnings, attributable to variation in the means of the categories. This percentage is known as eta². Eta² is equal to the value of R^2 we would obtain if we treated each category of the independent variable as a dichotomous variable, assigned each respondent a value of 1 if he fell in the category and 0 if he did not, and then regressed economic success on these dummy variables. Since no association is perfectly linear eta² always exceeds the bivariate r^2.† The discrepancy is usually too small to deserve attention, but when eta² was appreciably larger than r^2, we looked for the simplest nonlinear specification that would capture the deviations from linearity.

Orthogonal Quadratic Terms. Except in the case of education, we found that we could capture virtually all significant deviations from linearity by assuming that the regression slope was a parabola instead of a straight line, i.e., that B_1 in equation 1 was a linear function of U. When we regressed our measures of economic success on test score and test score² or on father's occupation and father's occupation², for example, the value of R^2 was extremely close to our "target" eta². The assumption that nonlinearities were parabolic allowed us to keep the total number of independent variables relatively modest. In analyzing a given sample we included the quadratic term only when its coefficient was statistically significant.

Linear and quadratic terms tend to be highly correlated with one another. Thus, when we add the quadratic term, the standard error of the linear term rises sharply. This makes it hard to tell when the linear coefficient differs significantly across samples. Furthermore, if the

---

* The logic of the semilog coefficients is analogous to that of compound interest. The logarithmic coefficient estimates the implied return over an infinitely short period. The longer the period over which these returns compound, the larger the discrepancy between the implied rate of return and the ratio of total returns to initial investment.

† When the independent variable had more than ten categories, we grouped it into ten or fewer. Although this slightly reduces eta², the reduction is never appreciable. In such cases, however, r^2 will *exceed* eta² if the relationship is perfectly linear.

Tables 10.2–10.6 in chapter 10 show the means and standard deviations of education, occupation, and income for each category of father's education, father's occupation, siblings, and education.

quadratic term is insignificant in only one of the two samples and is therefore omitted from one but not the other, the two linear coefficients are no longer at all comparable. To facilitate comparisons between samples we therefore wanted squared terms that captured only the deviations from linearity. If the distribution of the trait (T) is symmetrical around the mean, the squared deviation from the mean, $(T - \overline{T})^2$, is uncorrelated with T and captures only deviations from the linear slope. But since distributions are seldom perfectly symmetrical, we had to develop a more general procedure for isolating the nonlinear component of the quadratic relationship. To eliminate the linear component of T^2 we first regressed T^2 on T, obtaining:

$$(6) \qquad T^2_i = B_0 + B_t T_i + E_i$$

where B_0 is a constant, B_t is the increase in T^2 associated with a unit increase in T, and E is the usual error term. If we subtract $B_t T$ from both sides, we obtain:

$$(7) \qquad T^2_i - B_t T_i = B_0 + E_i$$

We call the left side of equation 7 the "orthogonal squared term" and denote it as T^2_0.

In order to see how the use of these orthogonal terms affects our results, consider what happens when we regress a measure of economic success (Y) on T and T^2_0.
We begin with:

$$(8) \qquad Y = B_0 + B_1 T + B_2 T^2_0 + E$$

Substituting $T^2 - B_t T$ for T_0 gives us:

$$(9) \qquad \begin{aligned} Y &= B_0 + B_1 T + B_2 T^2 - B_2 B_t T + E \\ &= B_0 + (B_1 - B_2 B_t)T + B_2 T^2 + E \end{aligned}$$

Since T^2_0 is uncorrelated with T, the coefficient of T controlling T^2_0 is the same as the coefficient we would obtain if we regressed Y on T alone. The coefficient of T^2_0 is the same as the coefficient of T^2 controlling T. The coefficient of T controlling T^2_0 is not, however, the same as the coefficient we would obtain if we controlled T^2. Substituting T^2_0 for T^2 reduces the coefficient of T by $B_2 B_t$ (compare equations 8 and 9).

Orthogonalization has three important virtues and one important vice. The first virtue is that it facilitates comparisons between samples, since linear coefficients from equations that do not control nonlinear effects because they are statistically insignificant mean roughly the same thing as linear coefficients from equations that do control such effects. The second virtue is that since the orthogonal squared term is independent of the linear term, squaring the standardized coefficient of the orthogonal term yields the percentage of the total variance explained by the nonlinear quadratic effect. The third virtue is that orthogonal terms reduce the danger of serious rounding errors—a nontrivial hazard in most standard computing packages.

The major drawback of orthogonalized terms is that they make it harder to estimate the marginal change in Y associated with a given change in T. If we want to know the change in Y associated with an increase of T from 6 to 7, for example, we must calculate the first derivative of Y with respect to T when T = 6.5. Using equation 9, this is:

$$(10) \qquad \frac{dY}{dT} = 2B_2T + B_1 - B_2B_t$$

We cannot evaluate this unless we know the value of B_t used in constructing the orthogonal squared term.[2]

Splines and Dummies. Quadratic terms do not adequately capture the nonlinear effects of education. Nor do they provide a theoretically satisfying representation of the effects of different levels of education. After much experimentation, we settled on three variables to represent the effects of education. We called the first of these three variables "years of education." It is equal to the highest grade of school or college the respondent completed. We called the second "years of higher education." It is a "spline" variable and is equal to o for those with twelve or fewer years of education and to years of education – 12 for those with thirteen or more years of education. We called the third "college graduation" or "BA." It is a "dummy" variable and is equal to 1 if the respondent completed sixteen or more years of school, o if he did not. When we include all three variables in a single equation, the coefficient of years of education measures the average change in the dependent variable associated with an extra year of elementary or secondary education. The coefficient of years of higher education measures the difference between the change associated with an extra year of elementary or secondary education and the change associated with an extra year of higher education. The overall effect of a year of higher education is thus the sum of the coefficient of years of education and the coefficient of years of higher education. The coefficient of college graduation then represents the additional increment associated with completing the sixteenth year of school, over and above the increment predicted by summing the coefficients of years of education and years of higher education. While this specification is not ideal, especially for predicting occupational status, it works better than a simple linear specification. Chapter 6 discusses it in more detail.

3. MULTIVARIATE RELATIONSHIPS

Effects vs. Associations. While we are sometimes concerned with the observed association between pairs of worker characteristics, we are more often concerned with the extent to which the association persists with other traits controlled. To estimate these "partial" associations we estimated multiple-regression equations. Suppose, for example, that we wanted to know the association between education and earnings among men from similar demographic backgrounds. If we had only one demographic measure (X) we would estimate:

$$(11) \qquad Y = B_0 + B_1X + B_2X^2 + B_UU + e$$

where U again represents education. If the effects of X were either linear or quadratic, as this equation assumes, B_U would represent the average change in earnings associated with an extra year of education among men with the same value of X. One can easily expand equation 11 to include more Xs or to include nonlinear measures of U.

When we have controlled *all* the measured worker characteristics that influence both education and earnings, it becomes natural to think of the remaining association as causal. Thus, when we have controlled all available Xs we habitually interpret B_U as the "effect" of a one-year change in education attainment on an individual's earnings. Experience suggests, however, that the reader should treat such language with extreme caution. Our equations never include all the potentially relevant control variables. B_U is therefore likely to be biased, usually upward. This means that raising a random individual's educational attainment by one year is unlikely to change his earnings by an amount equal to B_U. This caveat probably applies with even greater force to changing test scores, personality traits, or background characteristics. Furthermore, even if our equations were perfectly specified, so that changing a few random individuals' test scores or education produced the expected effect on their occupational status or earnings, it would be rash to assume that changing *all* workers' test scores or educational attainment would change their *mean* occupational status or earnings by the expected amount. The mean level of economic success would only change by the expected amount if changing individual characteristics changed the overall occupational structure and national income by exactly the same amount that it changed individuals' relative positions. This would only happen if macroeconomics were a branch of microeconomics.

Controlling Unmeasured Characteristics with Difference Equations. When we try to assess the effects of a trait like education on economic success, we would like to control not only measured background characteristics like father's occupation, but unmeasured background characteristics like parental values and attitudes. One way to do this is to compare pairs of brothers. This will not control every conceivable family influence, since families do not treat all their sons exactly alike. But it will control more aspects of family background than merely controlling demographic background. It will also control roughly half the influence of genotype, since brothers share approximately half the genes that vary among individuals.

In order to compare brothers, we estimate a "difference equation." If Y denotes the first brother's earnings and Y′ the second brother's earnings, and if U denotes the first brother's education and U′ the second brother's education, we define ΔY as $Y - Y'$ and ΔU as $U - U'$. We then estimate:

$$(12) \qquad \Delta Y = B_{\Delta U} \Delta U + E_{\Delta Y}.$$

Comparing $B_{\Delta U}$ to the value of B_U in a simple bivariate equation tells us how much of the association between education and earnings is due to the effects of shared family background on both education and earnings. We can easily extend this approach to take account of nonlinearities and to include several independent variables.*

Intervening Variables. Suppose we know that individuals who get an extra year of education earn 5 percent more as a result. Our next ques-

---

* All pairs of brothers appear twice in our data files with their order reversed. This is a constrained equivalent to ordering pairs randomly. It makes the correlations between brothers symmetric (i.e., $r_{UY'} = r_{YU'}$). When this is done, $B_{\Delta U} = (s_Y/s_U)(r_{YU} - r_{YU'})/(1 - r_{UU'})$. This means that if one has the symmetrical matrices of correlations among the traits of both individuals and their brothers, one can estimate the difference equations without recourse to the raw data. The relevant data appear in tables A2.6, A2.10, A2.11, and A3.4. A derivation of the above equation appears in figure 3.1. Note that the equation does not require $r_{YY'}$. Thus, if we have, say, education data on both brothers but economic data on only one, as in OCG, we can still estimate $B_{\Delta U}$ if we are willing to assume that the observed matrix estimates the symmetrical matrix obtained by entering all pairs twice with order reversed.

tion is likely to be why. We answer this question by controlling "intervening" variables that depend on education.

One standard hypothesis, for example, is that education provides men with useful cognitive skills. To test this claim we might measure such skills after school completion and denote them as Q. We would then estimate an equation that included not only causally prior Xs (X_1, X_2, . . . , X_n) but also Q:

$$(13) \qquad Y = B_0 + B_1X_1 + B_2X_1{}^2 + \ldots + B_nX_n{}^2 + B_UU + B_QQ + E_Y$$

B_U now estimates the difference in earnings between respondents who differ by one year on education attainment, who have the same characteristics prior to school completion (i.e., the same Xs), and who have the same cognitive skills after school completion. If B_U remained the same in equation 13 as in equation 11, we would conclude that education did not pay off because it taught men cognitive skills. If, on the other hand, B_U were zero in this equation, we would conclude that education paid off entirely because it provided general cognitive skills. Once again, we can extend this logic to any number of intervening variables.

Nonadditive Effects: Split Samples. Suppose that after controlling adolescent test scores, a one-year increase in education is associated with a 5 percent increase in earnings. Up to now we have talked as if the earnings of men with high and low scores would both increase by 5 percent. This implies that the effects of test scores and education are independent, and hence additive.* In some cases, however, the effects of one variable depend on the value of the other. When this is the case, we say there are interactions. We tried to detect these interactions by separating whites from nonwhites, by separating men with white-collar, blue-collar, and farm fathers, and by separating men with high, medium, and low test scores. We found no consistent differences between men with high, medium, or low scores. The only consistent differences between men with white-collar, blue-collar, and farm fathers were in returns to education (see chapter 6). Race had complex and changing effects on the coefficients of background characteristics, education, and experience (see chapter 7).

* The fact that *effects* are independent does not necessarily mean that the *levels* are independent. Educational attainment, for example, clearly depends on test performance. But the *benefits* of education do not increase as test scores increase.

When we predict ln earnings, the additive model assumes that the *percentage* effects of different traits are independent. This means that the *dollar* effects cannot be independent. The semilog model does not, however, imply that the effects of the independent variables are *multiplicative,* as the double-log model does.

Orthogonal Multiplicative Terms. Our second strategy for identifying interactions was to multiply selected worker characteristics by one another and enter the products in our regression equations. If the effect of a characteristic changes in a consistent direction as another trait rises or falls, the product terms will have significant coefficients even with their linear components controlled. Because there were so many possible product terms, we only included those that were statistically significant. In order to maintain the comparability of results from samples where the product terms entered with results from samples where the product terms did not enter, we made the products orthogonal to their linear components. To accomplish this we regressed the product term (X_1X_2) on its components, so that:

$$(14) \qquad X_1X_2 = B_1X_1 + B_2X_2 + E$$

Subtracting $B_1X_1 + B_2X_2$ from X_1X_2 leaves the orthogonal component of the multiplicative interaction. Orthogonalization has precisely the same virtues and vices here as it did with nonlinearities.

We found no multiplicative interactions that were consistently significant in different surveys. Indeed, none had consistent signs in different surveys. We will therefore spend very little time discussing these results.[3]

4. MEASUREMENT ERROR

Measurement errors fall into three broad categories. The most serious and intractable errors are conceptual. If we treat a short-term memory test as an adequate proxy for a respondent's other cognitive skills, for example, we will systematically underestimate the importance of cognitive skills in determining economic success. Likewise, if we assume that the status of a father's occupation is an adequate proxy for the family's overall economic position, we will underestimate the effect of economic background on children's life chances. The bias can, of course, also work the other way. If we treat a vocabulary test as a measure of short-term memory, for example, we will overestimate the importance of memory. These problems have no easy solutions. Readers will have to judge for themselves how well our measures correspond to the labels we use to describe them.

A second type of error arises when respondents make consistent reporting errors. A respondent may, for example, always say that his father was a factory manager, because that is the impression his father gave him, even though the father was in fact a foreman. Or a boy's teachers may all report that he is unusually diligent in doing his homework, when in fact his parents do it for him. Conventional reliability studies cannot detect errors of this type, because conventional methods rely on inconsistency to detect error. If an error recurs over and over, conventional methods will assume that it is the truth. We have no way of knowing how important such errors are.

What we usually call "measurement error" arises when a respondent describes his family background, educational attainment, or economic position differently in different surveys; gets a different score on two different cognitive tests that purport to measure the same thing; or describes his aspirations in different ways on different days. Coders also make random errors, both in transcribing clear-cut responses and in classifying ambiguous ones. Available evidence suggests that errors of this kind are independent of one another (Bielby et al., 1977; Olneck, 1976).

The best evidence regarding the reliability of our measures of economic success comes from matching respondents' answers to different surveys. Since different surveys seldom use the same methods, their reliabilities are seldom the same. CPS, for example, uses face-to-face interviews, mostly with wives, while the Census relies mainly on a mail-back questionnaire. If errors were strictly random, we could assess the relative quality of two matched surveys by comparing their variances. But when we make this assumption, all kinds of anomalies appear. In the case of income, for example, this assumption implies that CPS reports contain less error than Census reports and no more than tax returns.[4] We do not believe that CPS income data are really as accurate as tax returns. Rather, we believe that CPS reports contain more error, but that these errors are negatively correlated with true values, keeping the measured variances the same. Presumably men overestimate their income if it is low and underestimate it if it is high.[5] Once we allow for such patterns, we cannot estimate error variances with any confidence. We can, however, make rough estimates of the "reliability" of different measures, i.e., the correlation between two independent estimates of the same underlying trait.

Table A2.13 in the Appendix gives reliabilities of this kind for occupational status and earnings from various surveys. If we eliminate men without earnings and take logarithms, two independent measures of income or earnings in the same year correlate between 0.93 and 0.84.

This suggests that between 7 and 16 percent of the measured variance cannot possibly be explained by our independent variables. The analogous figures for occupational status are between 4 and 14 percent. Reporting errors of this sort lower the standardized regression coefficients of independent variables as well as R^2. To correct R^2, one divides the observed R^2 by the estimated reliability. To correct the standardized regression coefficients, one divides by the square root of the estimated reliability. This will raise the standardized coefficients by 2 to 9 percent. If errors in the dependent variable are completely random, they will not affect the unstandardized regression coefficients. If errors are negatively correlated with true values, they will lower the unstandardized regression coefficients.

Table A2.14 in the Appendix gives estimated reliabilities for education, father's education, father's occupation, and family size. Chapter 4 discusses the reliability of test scores. The reliability of a variable is a function of the true variance as well as the amount of error. Thus, the fact that education reports from the matched CPS–OCG-II sample are less reliable ($r = 0.85$) than reports from the matched CPS–Census sample ($r = 0.89$) does not imply that OCG-II respondents made larger errors than Census respondents. The difference may be due to the fact that the observed variance is larger in the Census sample. The ratio of error variance to total variance would therefore be lower.

Yet even after correcting for differences in the measured variances, the estimated error variances for father's education and occupation depend heavily upon the estimation procedure. OCG-II reinterviewed the same respondent and obtained high reliabilities. Indeed, if one believes the OCG-II data, sons' reports on their fathers are more accurate than their reports about themselves. This seems unlikely. Presumably, sons reinterviewed about their fathers tend to make the same errors as in the initial interviews, whereas they change their reports about themselves.[6] This hypothesis is supported by the Kalamazoo results, which use brothers to get two independent estimates of the father's education. Our OCG results, while more conjectural, also imply that there is more error in reports of father's education than in self-reports. The same holds for father's occupation. Corcoran's (1979) PSID analysis, which uses *both* fathers' self reports *and* sons' retrospective reports about their fathers, also implies far more error in sons' reports than Bielby et al. (1977) found. Thus, despite Bielby's findings, we are inclined to believe that sons' retrospective reports about their fathers contain substantially more error than fathers' self-reports, with reliabilities of around 0.75 for representative samples.

The reader can in theory use the data in tables A2.13 and A2.14 to correct observed correlations. If r_{XY} denotes the observed correlation between two traits, r_{XY} denotes the true correlation, r_{XX} denotes the reliability of X, and r_{YY} denotes the reliability of Y, one can show that:

$$(15) \qquad r_{XY} = \frac{r_{XY}}{(r_{XX}r_{YY})^{1/2}}$$

Thus if we have plausible reliability estimates for two measures in a particular sample, we can estimate their true correlation. We cannot estimate unstandardized regression coefficients unless we also know the true standard deviations.

If we had reliability measures for all our independent variables, we could take this logic a step further by correcting entire correlation matrices. This would allow us to estimate the true standardized regression coefficients in multivariate equations. But we do not have all the relevant reliabilities, and if we correct some variables but not others, we can easily obtain more biased results than if we make no corrections at all. The reader can, however, set an approximate upper bound on the true coefficient of a given trait (X) when predicting Y by multiplying the observed coefficient by $(1/r_{XX}r_{YY})^{1/2}$. If the independent variables are highly correlated with one another, as they often are, this correction will often be too large. If the reliability of X is high while the reliability of other measures that correlate with X is relatively low, the true coefficient of X may actually be smaller than the observed coefficient. But when all variables have roughly equal reliabilities, as they do in our data, corrections of this sort will suffice for virtually any practical purpose. Indeed, uncorrected data will suffice for most purposes, and that is what we will usually present.

5. SAMPLING ERROR

Weighted Samples. In the Census 1/1,000 sample, every individual in the covered population has an equal chance of appearing. Self-weighting samples of this kind are very expensive. OCG, Veterans, PA, NLS, and PSID therefore used clustered samples that included several respondents from the same neighborhood. Since people living in the same neighborhood tend to have the same characteristics, measurements obtained in such samples are not completely independent. This makes the sampling errors larger than they would be in a strict probability sample of similar size.

Since there is more nonresponse in some neighborhoods than in others, clustered samples also weight respondents in underrepresented areas more heavily than respondents in overrepresented areas to make the sample more representative of the target population. OCG, Veterans, and PSID also weighted respondents unequally to compensate for differential attrition after the first interview. These unequal weights further inflate the standard errors of all estimates.

The PSID and NLS samples were also stratified so as to oversample poor and black respondents. This kind of stratification yields more stable estimates at one extreme of most distributions, lowering most standard errors, but it provides slightly less stable estimates at the other end of most distributions.

One can think of weighting as affecting the "efficiency" of a sample. Thus, if there are 10,000 individuals in a truly random sample, the sampling error of an observed mean will be $(1/10,000)^{1/2} = 1$ percent of the standard deviation for all individuals in the covered population. If the sample is weighted, the sampling error of the mean might rise by 50 percent. The observed sampling would thus be equivalent to what one would expect in an unweighted sample $10,000/(1.50)^2 = 4,444$ individuals. The "efficiency" of this sample design is thus only 44 percent of that in an unweighted design.

Unfortunately, samples seldom have a single, uniform efficiency for all purposes. A sample may be 90 percent efficient for estimating the percentage of blacks in the target population, but only 70 percent efficient for estimating the returns to graduate education. Making efficiency estimates is expensive and time consuming. We therefore adopted a less precise approach. We calculated standard errors as if the sample were unweighted, by making the mean weight 1.00. This underestimates most standard errors. If a difference is more than twice its estimated standard error using this procedure, we call it "significant." A difference of this size would arise by chance in about one random sample out of twenty. It would be in the expected direction by chance in about one random sample out of forty. In weighted samples like OCG, Veterans, PA, NLS, and PSID, such differences are more common. As a rough rule of thumb, the reader might expect 10 rather than 5 percent of all differences to exceed twice their estimated standard error by chance in these samples. About 5 percent of all such chance differences should also be in the expected direction.

We did not weight our NORC Brothers, Kalamazoo, or Talent samples. The initial NORC Brothers sample was based on block quotas, so there was no simple way of estimating the effects of nonresponse among initial respondents. We could have weighted initial respondents unequally to correct for differential response rates among these initial respondents' brothers, but we chose to investigate the effects of fraternal nonresponse directly.[7] Olneck made the same decision in his Kalamazoo sample.[8] The initial Talent sample was stratified by school size, but we did not weight our final results to compensate for this.* Nor did we weight our Talent samples to compensate for nonresponse, which was low in the "representative" sample but high for the sample of brothers.

Differences between Regression Coefficients. The difference between two regression coefficients from independent samples is likely to be roughly normally distributed, with a sampling variance equal to the sum of the separate sampling variances of the two coefficients. Thus if B_1 and B_2 are two coefficients from different samples and s_{B1} and s_{B2} are the sampling errors of these coefficients, we can test the significance of the difference between B_1 and B_2 for large samples by using:

$$(16) \qquad t = \frac{B_1 - B_2}{(s^2_{B1} + s^2_{B2})^{1/2}}$$

For reasons indicated above, *t*-statistics from weighted samples should be interpreted conservatively.

6. SAMPLE RESTRICTIONS

Inmates. Inmates of institutions constituted 1.2 percent of all male Census respondents aged 25 to 64 in March 1970. Of these, 20 percent reported 1969 earnings to the Census. These individuals had worked an average of 31.3 weeks during 1969. None of our other surveys covered inmates. We excluded them from our target population partly to achieve consistency, partly because we doubted the accuracy of data on inmates' earnings for the previous year, and partly because we assumed that most inmates had been institutionalized during at least part of 1969. We saw no good way of estimating a man's economic status during weeks he was institutionalized.

* As a check, we compared the unweighted Talent correlation matrix to the weighted matrix. The two were virtually identical.

Soldiers. Members of the military constituted 2.0 percent of all male Census respondents aged 25 to 64 in 1970. Of these, 94.9 percent reported earnings for 1969, compared to 94.7 percent of all other 25- to 64-year-old men who were not inmates or students. Soldiers with 1969 earnings reported having worked an average of 49.6 weeks, whereas men with earnings who were not soldiers, inmates, or students reported having worked 48.2 weeks. There is, then, no prima facie reason for excluding soldiers, at least if they were serving voluntarily, as they usually were if they were over 25. But our other surveys did not cover soldiers living on bases. We therefore excluded soldiers from our target population to achieve consistency. In addition, we felt that soldiers' earnings could be misleading, since soldiers receive an unusually large part of their compensation in kind rather than in cash.

Students. According to the Census, 2.4 percent of all men aged 25 to 64 were enrolled in school in March 1970. Of these, 91.5 percent reported 1969 earnings. Students who had worked during 1969 reported an average of 43.6 weeks of employment.* Students often receive room, board, tuition, or money from their parents, the college they attend, or the government. In most cases this income is only available so long as they remain students. From the student's viewpoint, then, such income is virtually equivalent to regular earnings. Our surveys did not collect information on such income. As a result, they systematically underestimate the economic status of students.† We eliminated full-time students whenever we had the necessary information. When we could not distinguish full-time from part-time students, we eliminated both. In OCG we eliminated neither.

Missing Respondents. The Census Bureau claims to have located 98 percent of all males aged 25 to 64 living in the Unites States, and to have obtained at least partial data from 97 percent. Our other surveys did less well (see table 1.1). Olneck got data from only 45 percent of the original Kalamazoo sample, and Talent got data from only about 28 percent of all brothers. Some surveys tried to compensate for missing respondents by differential weighting of those who remained. Unfor-

---

* Not all these men were students throughout 1969, so it would be a mistake to assume that students work as much while enrolled in school as these figures imply.

† Another widely cited reason for eliminating students from analyses of this type is that students' current status underestimates their eventual status. This is true, but irrelevant. The coefficients from our equations estimate effects of specific traits averaged over a specific forty-year age interval. These averages are depressed by all sorts of individual decisions, from going to school to becoming a drunk (or a poet). While it would be instructive to analyze a sample in which everyone was maximizing his current occupational status or earnings, this is not feasible. But eliminating some non-maximizers while retaining others yields estimates with *no* clear meaning.

tunately, we can never be sure how well such weighting has worked. One way to estimate the sensitivity of statistics to sample attrition is to compare weighted to unweighted results. We did this for several samples. Weighting did not affect regression coefficients in any consistent way.

We also compared results from samples with high attrition rates to results from samples with low attrition rates. Chapter 11 shows that the 1970 Census, which obtained data from 97 percent of its target population, differs in several respects from the 1970 wave of the PSID, which obtained data from only 62 percent of its target population. But chapter 10 shows similar differences between the 1962 OCG, in which 83 percent of the target population is represented, and the 1964 PA, in which 84 percent is represented.* Read together, chapters 10 and 11 suggest that there are systematic differences between CPS and SRC sampling frames or survey methods. They do not suggest that differential response rates have any predictable effect.

Men with Partial Data. Even when respondents agree to be interviewed and return their questionnaires, they seldom provide complete data. Item nonresponse of 15 percent is quite common in our data, and in some cases it is even higher.

The Census Bureau usually assigns nonrespondents the value reported by the last previous respondent who resembles the nonrespondent on some presumptively relevant set of traits, such as sex, race, age, and the like. If the Bureau used *all* the respondent's known characteristics to allocate missing values, and if nonrespondents were like respondents with similar measured characteristics, this procedure would reproduce the multivariate distributions for the population as a whole. But it is seldom possible to find another sample member who resembles the nonrespondent in *every* respect. The Census Bureau does not even try to do this. As a result, retaining men with allocated values usually depresses correlations slightly (see chapter 11). We eliminated men with allocated values whenever we could.

Some investigators (e.g., Duncan et al., 1972) compute every statistic for all individuals reporting the necessary data and then assume that these individuals are representative of the entire sample. If this assumption is correct, one can treat all the observed means, standard deviations, and correlations as if they applied to the full sample and can use them to compute regression equations for the full sample. If the assumption is incorrect, one can easily get results that do not apply to

---

* CPS may, however, have done better at weighting OCG to compensate for nonresponse than SRC did with PA.

any population. If, for example, poor people fail to report their occupations, while rich people fail to report their incomes, a "pairwise present" correlation matrix involving education, occupation, and income will end up using some data for the rich, some data for the poor, and some data for both. The results are unpredictable.

Another strategy, which appears preferable in almost every respect to the preceding one, is to use only individuals with complete data. These individuals constitute our "complete data" samples. These samples typically exclude something like a third of the initial respondents. We compared each univariate and bivariate statistic for the complete data sample to the analogous statistic for everyone in the full sample with relevant data to see if they differed to any appreciable degree.[9] The complete data sample yields essentially the same regression results as the full sample in almost every case. The Veterans sample was the main exception. There, highly educated men were often missing AFQT scores, and the pairwise sample overestimated the effect of controlling AFQT on the coefficient of education when predicting earnings.

Age. We restricted our analyses to men between the ages of 25 and 64. We had two reasons for doing this. First, we were interested in the effects of personal characteristics on individuals' "potential" status or earnings if and when they worked for pay. To make such estimates, we must make some assumption about the potential status and earnings of those who chose *not* to work for pay during the period under investigation. Other things being equal (which they seldom are), individuals with high potential status or earnings are more likely to work for pay than individuals with low potential status or earnings. Looking only at individuals who chose to work will therefore lead us to underestimate the impact of personal characteristics on economic success, because it will eliminate a disproportionate number of individuals whose personal characteristics have had unusually large negative effects on their potential status or earnings. The simplest way to minimize this bias is to look at a group in which labor-force participation is nearly universal. Since our 1970 Census sample indicated that 95 percent of males aged 25 to 64 had worked for pay during 1969, compared to 65 percent of males aged 14 to 24, 31 percent of males aged 65 to 99, and 49 percent of females aged 14 to 99, we decided to concentrate on males between 25 and 64.*

---

* Techniques are now available for estimating the degree of bias introduced by nonparticipation (Heckman, 1974). These techniques require assumptions that are hard to test, however, and in any event they were not available when we chose our target population.

Our second reason for concentrating on men between the ages of 25 and 64 was that such men are less likely than others to be trading status or earnings for other objectives, such as leisure. We can see this most clearly in the case of earnings. An individual's standard of living depends largely on his or her family's total income, not on his or her personal earnings. An individual whose family income depends largely on his or her personal earnings is therefore under more pressure to maximize such earnings than an individual whose family's income comes largely from other sources. Since women's earnings are lower and less variable than men's, variation in wives' earnings explains only 9 percent of the variation in 25- to 64-year-old couples' total family income. Variation in husbands' earnings explains more than 84 percent of the variation in such couples' total family income (see Table A9.1). We have not calculated analogous statistics for men of other ages, but a priori reasoning certainly suggests that the link between individual earnings and family income is closer for men 25 to 64 than for younger or older men. Young men often live with their parents, which means that their standard of living depends to a significant extent on their parents' income, not their own. Men over 65 often receive substantial pensions and Social Security benefits, which again weakens the link between their earnings and their standard of living. Of course even men between 25 and 64 usually have other goals in addition to maximizing their earnings. This means that when we estimate the effect of a personal characteristic like education on all 25- to 64-year-old men's earnings, we inevitably underestimate its effect on those 25- to 64-year-olds who are most concerned with maximizing their earnings. We decided to concentrate on men between 25 and 64 simply because we assumed that this problem would be less serious for them than for other groups.

Five of our samples cover only part of our target population of 25 to 64 year olds. Our two Talent samples cover men who were almost all 28 or 29. Our Veterans sample covers men between 30 and 34. The NLS sample covers men between 45 and 59. The Kalamazoo sample covers men between 35 and 59. We cannot assess all the consequences of such age restrictions, since we do not have samples of 25- to 64-year-olds with all the information that these restricted samples provide. (If we did, we would not use the restricted samples.) We can, however, show how age alters the economic benefits of race, region of birth, and education, since the Census Bureau collects information on these three traits from men of all ages.

Table 2.1 breaks down Census occupational statistics by age for men who were not in school, in the military, or in institutions in 1970. Since

TABLE 2.1

Relation of Occupational Status to Race and Education, by Age[a]

Age	N	Occupational Status		Bivariate Regression Coefficients			
				Race		Education	
		Mean	SD	B	beta	B	beta
14-19	917	22.06	14.59	4.5	.096	1.96	.254
20-24	2,947	33.00	21.23	10.2	.143	4.39	.480
25-29	3,748	40.77	24.17	13.2	.161	5.34	.636
30-34	3,375	42.12	24.75	12.9	.147	4.83	.630
35-39	3,361	43.49	25.19	16.0	.177	4.62	.647
40-44	3,602	42.27	24.66	17.1	.186	4.32	.629
45-49	3,633	41.05	24.64	18.8	.205	4.32	.614
50-54	3,201	39.76	23.97	16.5	.181	4.09	.591
55-59	2,749	37.48	23.72	16.4	.172	4.08	.624
60-64	2,028	37.22	24.46	16.6	.178	4.11	.625
65-69	1,005	35.79	24.41	18.1	.210	3.75	.619
70-74	417	34.80	25.42	16.2	.162	3.56	.579
75+	208	38.78	26.72	17.5	.165	3.30	.541
27-29 & Education ≥ 11							
	1,799	45.85	24.23	11.6	.129	6.57	.618

[a] 1970 Census 1/1000 sample of men not in school, institutions, or the military in 1970, reporting positive 1969 earnings and reporting all other relevant data.

men keep entering the labor force in large numbers up to the age of 25, these cross-sectional data do not describe the life cycles of individuals over time. Table 2.1 implies, for example, that mean occupational status rises by 11 points between the ages of 14 to 19 and 20 to 24. But retrospective Census data on 20- to 24-year-old men who report having had an occupation in 1965 show that their mean status increased only 6 points during this five-year interval. Similarly, the mean status of 25- to 29-year-olds was 8 points higher than that of 20- to 24-year-olds, but 25- to 29-year-olds who worked in 1965 only gained 4 points between 1965 and 1970. The "unexplained" gains were due to the fact that young men who entered the labor force between 1965 and 1970 entered higher-status occupations than men who were already working. This follows from the fact that a year of schooling raises occupational status more than a year of labor-force experience. This problem becomes negligible once men pass about 25.

One could tell a long story about table 2.1, but our only concern here is with how restricting samples to men aged 25 to 64, or to a subset of such men, is likely to affect conclusions about the determinants of occupational status. The most obvious effects are as follows:

1. Most workers under 25 are in low-status jobs, regardless of their race or education. Eliminating such men increases the apparent importance of race and education in determining status. OCG data on 20- to 24-year-olds suggest that this generalization also holds for other aspects of demographic background. The Veterans and Talent surveys suggest that it also holds for cognitive skills.

2. The variance of education is smaller for men 25 to 34 than for older men, but most of the variance for 25- to 34-year-olds is at the postsecondary level, where it has a large effect on occupational status. Among older men, most of the variance is at the elementary and secondary level, where it has relatively little effect on occupational status. The net result is to make the unstandardized coefficient of education (β) higher for 25- to 34-year-olds than for older men, but to leave the standardized coefficient (β) about the same.

3. The difference between 25- to 34-year-olds and their elders is a cohort difference, not a matter of age per se. Retrospective Census data indicate that for men over 25 in 1965, the effect of education on occupational status was virtually the same in 1970 as in 1965. This means that the effects of education on status do not change appreciably with age. The differences between 25- to 34-year-olds and their elders are attributable to changes in the distribution of education and in the occupational structure the 25- to 34-year-old cohort confronted when it entered the labor market.

4. Both the standardized and unstandardized effects of race on status are larger for the cohorts born before 1936 and hence over 35 in 1970. The effects of race have traditionally increased with age up to about 30, because whites advanced more than blacks did as they got older. In addition, affirmative action has been more beneficial to younger cohorts of blacks than to their elders. One cannot separate these age and cohort effects with data such as that in table 2.1.[10]

Table 2.2 shows the mean and standard deviation of ln earnings, along with its regression on race, education, and experience for men of various ages. Mean earnings rise up to about the age of 42 and then decline. This is partly because older men have less schooling. With schooling controlled, the coefficient of experience does not become significantly negative until men pass 55.

The standard deviation of ln earnings declines until about the age of 30, partly because young men often work only part of the year and therefore have very low annual earnings. The standard deviation increases again after 30. The very large standard deviations for men over

TABLE 2.2

Relation of Ln Earnings to Race, Education, and Experience, by Age[a]

Age	Ln Earnings		Coefficient of Race[b]		Coefficient of Education				Coefficient of Experience[d]	
					Age Controlled[c]		Experience Controlled[c]			
	Mean	SD	B	beta	B	beta	B	beta	B	beta
14-19	7.304	1.085	.248	.071	.044	.076	.252	.439	.375	.299
20-24	8.316	.831	.424	.152	−.003	−.007	.098	.273	.128	.322
25-29	8.807	.648	.345	.157	.040	.177	.072	.320	.035	.162
30-34	8.999	.616	.359	.165	.061	.322	.075	.394	.015	.080
35-39	9.070	.669	.501	.209	.075	.397	.077	.405	.002	.009
40-44	9.094	.693	.594	.230	.078	.404	.077	.399	−.001	−.005
45-49	9.068	.712	.620	.234	.080	.394	.076	.375	−.004	−.021
50-54	9.005	.754	.474	.181	.089	.408	.089	.410	.001	.003
55-59	8.943	.762	.552	.181	.085	.403	.067	.321	−.020	−.092
60-64	8.786	.873	.408	.122	.084	.357	.048	.203	−.043	−.173
65-69	8.148	1.194	.488	.116	.090	.304	−.002	−.007	−.116	−.353
70-74	7.778	1.326	.539	.103	.083	.257	.043	.133	−.052	−.141
27-29 and Education ≥ 11										
Annual	8.923	.608	.213	.094	.027	.099	.050	.187	.023	.093
Hourly[e]	5.157	.632	.174	.074	.031	.113	.043	.155	.012	.045

[a]1/1000 Census sample of men not in schools, institutions, or the military in 1970, reporting positive 1969 earnings and reporting all other relevant data.

[b]No controls.

[c]Race, region of birth, and race × region also controlled.

[d]Race, region of birth, race × region, and education controlled.

[e]Estimated hourly earnings. Estimate derived by dividing total 1969 earnings by weeks worked in 1969 to get 1969 weekly earnings, and then dividing by hours worked in last week of March 1970 to get mean hourly earnings in 1969. This introduces an unknown but probably substantial amount of error.

60 are again partly due to increased variation in weeks worked. But average weekly earnings also vary more for men under 25 and over 60 than for men aged 25 to 60.

The effects of race are larger for older men, though the increase is not perfectly monotonic. Restricting samples to 25- to 64-year-olds therefore increases the estimated effect of race, regardless of whether one uses standardized or unstandardized coefficients.

The effects of education also appear to vary with age. The apparent direction of the change depends on whether, within a given age group, one controls age itself or experience. Columns 6 and 7 show the coefficients of education with age controlled. These coefficients are larger for older men, implying that an extra year of school is worth more to older men. Columns 8 and 9 show the education coefficients with experience, rather than age, controlled. These coefficients decline as men get older, implying that the value of schooling declines as men get older.

The most plausible explanation of this apparent contradiction is that the effects of education are actually quite stable over the life cycle. According to this hypothesis, the changes in table 2.2 derive from the fact that it controls either age or experience when it should control both.

For illustrative purposes, consider the way in which table 2.2 estimates the value of the last year of high school. Ignoring nonlinearities and interactions, the equation for 14- to 19-year-olds implies that a 19-year-old with twelve years of school earns 4.4 percent more than a 19-year-old with eleven years of school. But a 19-year-old with eleven years of school is likely to have two years of labor-force experience, whereas a 19-year-old high school graduate is only likely to have one year of experience. Since the first few years of experience are worth a lot more than later ones, the earnings differential at 19 will underestimate the likely differential when the two men have, say, twenty-one and twenty-two years of experience respectively. This explains the apparent increase in returns to schooling as men get older. Mincer (1974) argues that the right way to solve this problem is to control experience instead of age. When we do this, we are in effect estimating the value of twelfth grade by comparing the earnings of 19-year-old high school graduates with those of 18-year-olds who finished eleven years of school. Again ignoring nonlinearities and interactions, our equations imply that the earnings differential between these two groups averages $e^{0.252} - 1 - 29$ percent. They also imply that this differential declines to only 7 percent by the time these men are 28 and 29 respectively. The most reasonable explanation is that a large part of the difference between the 18- and 19-year-olds was due to age, not education, and that the effects of age diminish after men pass about 25.

We see the same problem in reverse when we look at men over 55. If we control only age, returns to education look quite stable from 55 to 75. If we control experience, returns fall precipitously. When we control experience, however, we are comparing 64-year-olds with eleven years of school to 65-year-olds with twelve years of school. Because physical aging reduces both weeks worked and weekly earnings after the age of 55, such a comparison implies lower returns to schooling than would a comparison of men who were the same age.

The inference we draw from these data is that age per se has important effects on earnings up to about 25 and after 55. Experience, however, also has important effects on earnings. An ideal specification would therefore control both age and experience.[11] One can only do this, however, if one has some good basis for distinguishing the two, which we do not. We therefore decided to focus our analyses on a relatively homogeneous age group, where we thought physical aging would have minimal effects. We chose 25- to 64-year-olds to maintain comparability with earlier work and with published Census data. The data in table 2.2 suggest that 30- to 55-year-olds might have been a better choice, but the differences are not great.

Within the 25- to 64-year-old group, the coefficient of education is more stable with experience controlled than with age controlled. This does not necessarily mean that experience has more effect on 25- to 64-year-olds' earnings than age does. But if we want to estimate the effect of education on lifetime earnings and we have only data on relatively young men, as we often do, table 2.2 suggests that we may do somewhat better with equations that control experience than with equations that control age. This generalization does *not* hold, however, for men under 25 or over 55. Table 2.2 suggests that neither specification is adequate for these men.

Finally, it is worth noting that since each extra year of education means a year less experience, the net benefit of education at a given age is equal to the coefficient of education minus the coefficient of experience. But extra education is associated with higher labor-force participation, longer life, and slightly later retirement, so highly educated men end up working as many years as poorly educated men. Thus if one is concerned with lifetime earnings differentials, equations that control experience are likely to yield better estimates than equations that control age.[12]

Education Restrictions. The Kalamazoo sample includes only individuals who reached sixth grade. This restriction does not seem serious, since almost all Kalamazoo children got at least six years of schooling after World War I. The Veterans sample systematically undersamples both highly educated and poorly educated men, as well as men who scored below the tenth percentile on the AFQT. These restrictions introduce all sorts of complex biases.[13] The full Talent sample includes only those who reached eleventh grade, and the Talent Brothers sample includes only those who reached eleventh grade and had a brother who reached twelfth grade (or vice versa). This restriction excludes about 15 percent of the cohort.

Since the Talent data play a crucial role in our analyses of cognitive skills and personality traits, we were quite concerned about the likely effect of this restriction. Tables 2.1 and 2.2 provide some summary data on the determinants of economic success among Census respondents aged 27 to 29 with at least eleven years of school. Looking first at the results for occupational status in table 2.1, we see that eliminating men with less than eleven years of school lowers the standardized coefficient of education but raises the unstandardized coefficient. This is what we would expect, given the underlying nonlinearity of the association. The effects of race also fall slightly. Turning to table 2.2, we see that eliminating men with less than eleven years of school substantially reduces the estimated effects of both race and education on ln earnings. This is partly because returns to postsecondary education are usually lower than returns to secondary education for young men. Table 2.2 also shows coefficients when the dependent variable is hourly, rather than annual, earnings. The Census results suggest that race, education, and experience generally have less effect on hourly earnings than on annual earnings.* This is relevant because our Talent analyses predict hourly rather than annual earnings.[14]

Conclusions about Sample Restrictions. Our data suggest that it makes little difference whether we include or exclude individuals in institutions, in the military, or in school when studying 25- to 64-year-old males. Nor does nonresponse at the individual or item level appear to affect our regression results. Samples selected on the basis of education, test scores, or family background will usually yield different results than more representative samples, but we can predict the direction of these differences with some confidence on a priori grounds. Samples selected on the basis of age will also yield different results than samples without age restrictions. We cannot predict the character of these differences with confidence using a priori reasoning. We can predict some of them using existing data, but in other cases no relevant data exist. Generalizing from a narrow age range to a broader one is therefore quite risky.

* The Census asked about annual earnings in 1969. To estimate hours worked in 1969, we multiplied grouped data on weeks worked by the number of hours the respondent was said to have worked in the last week of March 1970. This introduces an unknown amount of random error. These errors should inflate the observed variance, lower R^2, and lower the standardized coefficients. They should not affect unstandardized coefficients. But there may also be some nonrandom errors. The estimation procedure probably overestimates the 1969 hours of highly educated men who left school during 1969. The unstandardized coefficient of education when predicting ln hourly earnings may therefore be too low, while the unstandardized coefficient of experience may be too high.

CHAPTER 3

The Effects of Family Background

This chapter assesses the effect of "family background" on men's expected economic success. We define the effects of family background as including all the potentially predictable consequences of having one set of parents rather than another. To see what this means, imagine two parents with an infinite number of sons. If their sons earned an average of $16,000 while the average man earned $12,000, we would say that having these particular parents was worth an average of $4,000. This advantage would, of course, reflect not only the effects of the parents themselves, but the effects of the neighborhood in which the parents raised their sons, the schools to which they sent their sons, the economic opportunities available to men in the parents' community (to which the sons would have an "irrational" attachment), the genes the parents passed on to their sons, and many other "nonparental" influences. Still, we could plausibly say that the overall effect, direct and indirect, of being born to this pair of parents was to raise a man's expected earnings by $4,000.

This definition poses two major problems. The first is theoretical. It is not clear what specific factors account for the influence of what we label "family background." It subsumes some but not all of the effects of an individual's genes, since brothers share about half the genes that ordi-

Mary Corcoran and Christopher Jencks wrote this chapter. Zvi Griliches and Paul Taubman made helpful criticisms of an earlier draft.

narily vary from one individual to another. It also includes some but not all of the effects of environmental influences, since parents, teachers, and neighbors treat brothers more alike than random individuals.

These theoretical difficulties are not, however, unique to our definition of family background. They are equally applicable to concepts like "father's occupation," "socioeconomic status," and "class origins," all of which affect life chances because they are proxies for many other unmeasured traits.

The second problem is practical. Families are not infinitely large. Indeed, we usually sample only two sons from a given family. As a result, we cannot determine the mean status or earnings of all conceivable brothers raised in a given family. All we know is the mean for some specific pair of brothers raised in the family. Fortunately, sampling theory tells us how much these pair means are likely to deviate from the hypothetical family mean if the family had an infinite number of sons. If we subtract the variance of pair means due to sampling error from the total variance of the pair means, we can estimate the likely variance of family means if each family had an infinite number of sons. Comparing this estimate to the total variance of individual success gives us the percentage of the total variance attributable to what we call family background. This percentage is equal to the correlation between pairs of brothers.*

This chapter is divided into three parts. First, we estimate the likely degree of economic resemblance between brothers aged 25 to 64 who have been raised in "representative" American homes. Then we try to identify the characteristics that make brothers alike. Finally, we look at the extent to which background affects economic success by affecting cognitive skills, personality traits, occupational aspirations, and educational attainment.

---

* If we had an infinite number of pairs and arranged them randomly, the product-moment correlation would estimate the variance ratio. In finite samples we can achieve the same result by entering all pairs twice, with the order reversed. Product-moment correlations for such samples are equal to intraclass correlations. For a more detailed explanation, see Snedecor and Cochran (1967). Brittain (1977) also discusses the relationship between variances and correlations, but we are unable to follow his argument.

1. ECONOMIC RESEMBLANCE BETWEEN BROTHERS

Data Quality. Four of the five brothers surveys discussed in this chapter started with a list of known siblings and traced each individual. Many members of the target population were not found. Since a respondent's estimate of his brother's occupational status or earnings is not very accurate,* one can only use pairs in which *both* members were located. The proportion of pairs with usable data is thus even smaller than the proportion of individuals. Because of high attrition, these four samples underrepresent poor respondents. The five samples we will examine are as follows:

1. *Olneck's Kalamazoo Brothers sample.* This sample began with 2,782 brothers from 1,224 families, all of whom had attended sixth grade in the Kalamazoo schools between 1928 and 1950. Out of 1,408 "independent" pairs of brothers, Olneck obtained complete data on 346 independent pairs. This means that 25 percent of all potential pairs were both interviewed.
2. *The Talent Brothers sample.* This sample includes 198 brothers from 99 families who were enrolled in grades 11 and 12 of Project Talent high schools in 1960 and who returned complete follow-up data in 1971–72. We do not know the exact number of potentially eligible pairs, but judging by results for twins, we believe that about 20 percent of all eligible pairs returned follow-up data. Of these, about a quarter provided incomplete data. We therefore assume that our final sample includes about 15 percent of all potentially eligible pairs.
3. *John Brittain's "Cleveland" sample.* This sample includes 151 individuals from 66 families in which one of the parents died in the Cleveland area in 1964–65. Brittain does not report the response rate for pairs. The response rate for individuals was 60 percent, implying a response rate of at least 36 percent for pairs.
4. *Paul Taubman's Twin sample.* This sample includes 1,926 pairs of MZ and DZ twins born between 1917 and 1927. The sample includes only pairs who both served in the armed forces, i.e., about 30 percent of all pairs born in the relevant years. Taubman obtained usable data from about a sixth of all living pairs with military records, i.e., about 5 percent of all

* Of the 279 NORC respondents aged 25 to 64 who reported having a 25- to 64-year-old brother, 93 percent estimated his educational attainment, but only 77 percent could describe his occupation, and only 67 percent were willing to estimate his earnings. NORC was able to verify about two-thirds of these estimates by telephone or mail. The correlation between the initial respondent's estimate and his brother's report was 0.86 for education, 0.77 for occupational status, and 0.65 for earnings. Olneck (1976a) reports similar results for the Kalamazoo sample. The education correlation implies that respondents' reports on their brothers are almost as reliable as self-reports. The occupation and earnings correlations imply that a respondent's estimate of his brother's economic position is far less reliable than a self-report (compare table A2.13).

pairs born in the relevant years. Unfortunately, Taubman's occupational data are very peculiar, so we analyze only his earnings data.[1]

5. *The NORC Brothers sample* was created using a different method from the other four samples. NORC screened its fall, 1973, Amalgam survey for 25- to 64-year-old men who reported having a 25- to 64-year-old brother. NORC asked these men about their brother's education, occupation, and earnings. (If men had more than one brother, NORC asked about the oldest.) NORC also asked respondents for their brother's address and telephone number. Some respondents were unwilling or unable to provide NORC with enough data to locate their brother. Others had brothers who refused to be interviewed. But 63 percent of all brothers were located and interviewed. After eliminating another 9 percent of the original respondents because they or their brother had incomplete data, we had complete data on 54 percent of all potentially eligible pairs. In terms of both target population and response rate, then, the NORC sample is likely to be more representative of economically active 25- to 64-year-olds, than the other four samples. But the NORC sample includes only 300 individuals from 150 families.[2]

One possible source of bias in all these sibling studies deserves comment. Every survey but Talent relies at least in part on one brother to help trace the other. One might plausibly expect brothers to stay in closer touch with one another if they were economically similar than if their fortunes had diverged. If this happens, our surveys will overestimate the degree of resemblance between brothers in general. The NORC Brothers Survey suggests that this problem is not serious with respect to occupational status, but it may be of some importance for earnings.*

Table 3.1 compares our five sibling samples to one another and to the 1973 OCG-II survey of 25- to 64-year-old men. We present the OCG-II baseline data in two forms. Column 1 uses the full list of OCG-II background measures and the most precise available coding of income. Column 2 excludes background measures not available in the NORC Survey and groups income in much the same way that the NORC and Kalamazoo surveys group earnings. We will begin by discussing the results for occupational status and then turn to income.

Occupational Resemblance. NORC and OCG-II respondents have

---

* The NORC Survey asked the initial respondent about his brother's education, occupation, and earnings. The correlation between initial respondents' occupations and their estimate of their brother's occupation was 0.35 for respondents in our final sample of brothers. It was 0.34 for respondents who did not end up in the final sample, either because NORC could not trace the brother or because of incomplete data. For earnings, the correlations were 0.21 for men in the final sample vs. 0.06 for men not in the final sample. While this difference is not statistically significant, it is not trivial. It may mean that brothers who ended up in the final NORC sample are more alike with respect to earnings than brothers who had lost touch with one another. Alternatively, respondents who have lost touch with their brother may simply make larger random errors in estimating his earnings. Many did not even try.

TABLE 3.1

TABLE 3.1

Resemblance Between Brothers on Occupational Status and Earnings

	OCG-II		NORC Brothers	Talent Brothers	Kalamazoo Brothers	Taubman DZ Twins	Taubman MZ Twins	Brittain Brothers
Survey year	1973		1973-74	1971-72	1973-74	1974	1974	1965-66
Age	25-64		25-64	28-29	35-59	47-57	47-57	42±10[l]
N	15,817		300	198	692	1,814	2,038	151
Background measures[a]	1, 3, 4, 5, 6, 7, 8, 9, 10, 11	1, 3, 4, 5, 8, 9, 10	1, 3, 4, 5, 8, 9, 10	1, 3, 4, 9, 10	(1), 2, 3, 4, 5, 6, (7), (8), 9, 10	(1), 3, 4, 6, 7, 8, 9, 12		1, 3, 4, 9, 11, 12
Duncan score								
Mean	40.10	40.10	40.10	49.60	49.91	49.8[f]	50.4[f]	NA
SD	25.40	25.40	24.90	25.64	23.16	21.1[f]	21.7[f]	NA
R^2 with background measures	.226	.208	.189	.141	.125	.09[m]	.09[m]	.288[g]
Sibling r	–	–	.371	.321	.309	.20[f]	.43[f]	.407[g]
(SE)			(.08)	(.10)	(.05)	(.03)	(.03)	(.12)
Ln earnings								
Mean	9.17[b]	9.18[i]	9.19[c]	1.48[d]	9.63[e]	9.64	9.67	9.10[h]
SD	.774[b]	.684[i]	.870[c]	.406[d]	.446[e]	.57	.53	.485[h]
R^2 with background measures	.089[b]	.092[i]	.045[c]	.029[d]	.080[e]	.11[m]	.11[m]	.120[h]
Sibling r	–	–	.129	.207	.220	.30	.54	.436
(SE)	–	–	(.08)	(.10)	(.05)	(.03)	(.03)	(.12)
$s_{\hat{Y}}$[j]	.231	.207	.220	.069	.126	.189	.176	.168
$s_{\hat{Y}(sib)}$[k]	–	–	.312	.185	.209	.312	.389	.320

Note: OCG-II, NORC, Talent, and Kalamazoo samples are restricted to men with complete data.

[a] 1 = white, 2 = father born in U.S., 3 = father's education, 4 = father's occupation (Duncan scale), 5 = father white collar, 6 = mother' education, 7 = son's region of birth or upbringing, 8 = son raised on a farm, 9 = number of siblings, 10 = father absent when son 15 or 16 11 = parental income or wealth, 12 = religion. Variables in parentheses have no variance due to sample restrictions.
[b] Covers total income, not earnings.
[c] Initial respondent's earnings reported in 12 categories. Brother's earnings in 9 categories. Men without earnings were grouped wit men earning "under $1,000." To eliminate nonearners we dropped men with no current occupation. This may retain a few men with n earnings during the previous year, inflating the variance.
[d] Covers hourly, not annual, earnings.
[e] Grouped into 15 categories (see *Final Report*, Appendix I).
[f] All data from Taubman (1976a). See note 1, p. 362, for limitations.
[g] Occupations grouped into seven categories, scaled 1 to 7.
[h] Family income, not earnings. In the NLS sample of men 45 to 59, In family income had a 1966 mean of 8.96 and an SD of 0.74
[i] Covers total income (not earnings) grouped using 1961 OCG categories (see chapter 10), inflated to 1972 equivalents.
[j] $s_{\hat{Y}}$ = SD of predicted values from regression of Ln earnings on variables listed in row 4.
[k] $s_{\hat{Y}(sib)} = (r_{sib})^{1/2} s_{\hat{Y}}$
[l] Britain (1977) reports that the median age of his sample was 42, that the SD was "less than 10 years," and that 97 percent of th sample was between the ages of 25 and 64.
[m] R^2 from pooled MZ and DZ twin samples.

about the same mean status, since excluding men without brothers reduces the NORC mean, while excluding men with untraceable brothers increases it. The other four sibling surveys have higher means than OCG-II or other representative samples because they undersampled poor respondents. Setting aside Taubman's twins, the variances are quite similar.

Although each survey measured different demographic background characteristics, the overlap among these characteristics is quite high. As a result, R^2 is not very sensitive to the inclusion or omission of any specific background characteristic. When we restrict the list of background characteristics in OCG-II to those available in the NORC survey (see column 2), R^2 is 0.208 in OCG-II vs. 0.189 for NORC Brothers. As we shall see, this discrepancy is probably due to the fact that men with brothers come from less varied backgrounds than men in general. Apparently neither random sampling error nor sample bias has appreciably distorted the NORC regression results for occupational status. R^2 in Kalamazoo is lower than in OCG-II, primarily because father's occupational status has a very modest effect in Kalamazoo. This difference is too large to attribute solely to sampling error. R^2 in Talent is also lower than in OCG-II, probably because all the Talent respondents had at least reached eleventh grade. R^2 in Brittain's sample is much higher than in OCG-II, presumably because of random sampling error.[3]

Other things being equal, sibling correlations should be higher in samples where demographic background explains a large percentage of variance. The correlations between brothers' occupational statuses follow this pattern. The sibling correlations exceed the R^2 obtained by regressing occupational status on measured background by 0.18 in the Talent, Kalamazoo, and NORC surveys and by 0.12 in the Brittain Survey.

Judging both by the character of the target population and the explanatory power of demographic background, the NORC sample appears likely to give us a relatively unbiased estimate of the correlation between the Duncan scores of all brothers aged 25 to 64. In what follows we treat the NORC correlation (0.37) as the best available estimate of the correlation between 25- to 64-year-old brothers' occupational statuses.

Earnings Resemblance. What we call "earnings" is not really comparable from sample to sample, since each sample uses a different measure (see table 3.1). When we compared the earnings distribution for the NORC Brothers to the Census and PSID distributions, we found

that there were too many NORC Brothers with earnings under $1,000.*
When we compared the distributions for the other four samples of
brothers to analogous Census and PSID distributions these four brothers
included too many high earners and too few in the lower brackets. As
a result, the standard deviation of ln earnings is inflated in the NORC
Brothers sample and restricted in the other four brothers samples.

Table 3.1 shows that demographic background explains very different
percentages of the total variance in different samples. This is not because one sample measures hourly earnings, another measures annual
earnings, another measures annual personal income, and still another
measures annual family income.† It may, however, be partly because
some samples group the income data while others do not. Experiments
with OCG-II, the Census, and PSID indicate that grouping income or
earnings, as NORC and Kalamazoo did, typically raises R^2 by a fifth to
a third, though grouping does not change the absolute amount of variance explained. Sampling only older respondents, as Brittain, Taubman, and Kalamazoo did, increases both R^2 and the absolute amount
of variance explained. Restricting the list of independent variables lowers R^2. Finally, NORC's oversampling of low earners is likely to lower
R^2.‡ All these sample differences are likely to affect correlations between
brothers in much the same way they affect R^2.

The explanatory power of demographic background in our samples
is inversely related to the amount of variance to be explained. This
suggests that the absolute effects of demographic variation may be relatively similar in different samples, even though the total variance of income differs. The standard deviations of predicted annual earnings $(s\hat{y})$
range from 0.13 in the Kalamazoo sample, where there is the least variation in demographic background, to 0.23 in the OCG-II sample, where

---

* NORC did not distinguish men without earnings from men earning $1–999 or
men who lost money as a result of self-employment. We assigned all these men $500.
Since the earnings question covered the year in which NORC ascertained the respondent's occupation, we tried to eliminate men without earnings by restricting the
sample to men who reported a current occupation. But 97.8 percent of all NORC's
25–64 year old respondents reported a current occupation, whereas only 94.5 percent
of all Census respondents reported 1969 earnings. We infer that some of those classified as earning less than $1,000 may have reported an occupation from which they
currently received no money. Alternative explanations are (a) random sampling error
and (b) NORC's use of a block quota sample, which overrepresents those who
happen to be at home and hence, perhaps those not in the labor force.

† Neither chapters 2, 9, and 11 nor tables A2.2–A2.12 in the Appendix show consistent differences in correlations as one moves from hourly earnings to annual earnings to personal income to family income. Furthermore, the correlation between
brothers' family incomes is −0.02 in the NORC Brothers sample and 0.218 in the
Kalamazoo Brothers sample.

‡ Eliminating NORC respondents who earned less than $1,000 raised the correla-
tion between brothers to 0.17.

both variation in background and the number of background measures are largest. Unlike the discrepancies in R^2, these discrepancies in s_Y make intuitive sense. The much lower standard deviation of predicted hourly earnings in the youthful Talent sample also makes sense. The same pattern holds when we look at brothers. The standard deviations of the predicted family means, assuming that each family had an infinite number of sons ($s\hat{Y}_{sib}$), are 0.21 in Kalamazoo, 0.31 in the NORC sample, 0.31 for Taubman's DZ twins, and 0.32 in Brittain's "Cleveland" sample. The low standard deviation for the Kalamazoo sample is what we would expect if Kalamazoo families were more alike than American families generally.

If the line of reasoning suggested above is correct, the standard deviation of predicted family means for ln earnings should also be about 0.31 in a large representative sample of 25- to 64-year-old brothers. The standard deviation for individuals in such a sample is about 0.75 using ungrouped data (see the Census and PSID results in table A2.1). The implied correlation between brothers is thus about $(0.31/0.75)^2 = 0.17$. Grouping should raise the correlation slightly. Undersampling low earners should raise it substantially.

We do not have great faith in this estimate. We could, after all, have made a good theoretical case for expecting the *within*-family variance to remain constant across samples, while the *between*-family variance differed. Correlations between brothers would then have been higher in samples with large variances. The inverse relationship of correlations to variances in our samples may just be an accident. In what follows we will treat 0.17 as the best available point estimate of the correlation between 25- to 64-year-old brothers, but we will assume that the value could fall anywhere between 0.12 and 0.28. We regard 0.12 as a plausible minimum because demographic background alone explains almost 12 percent of the variance in recent representative samples. We regard 0.28 as a plausible maximum because it is almost as large as the value Taubman obtained for DZ twins, and the correlation between ordinary brothers should be somewhat lower than that between DZ twins.

If these estimates were correct, if brothers were representative of all men, if our measures of economic success were accurate, and if brothers did not influence one another, we could conclude that family background explained about 37 percent of the variance in occupational status and 12 to 28 percent of the variance in ln earnings among 25- to 64-year-old men. But brothers are not typical of all men, and our data are not entirely accurate, so further adjustments are necessary.

Brothers vs. Other Men. Family size is the only background characteristic likely to affect whether a respondent has a brother. This means that restricting our samples to men with brothers is not likely to affect the variance of unmeasured background characteristics that vary independently of family size. Restricting our samples to men with brothers is therefore likely to lower the explanatory power of family background by the same amount that it lowers the explanatory power of demographic background. In OCG this reduction is from 24.2 to 20.4 percent for occupational status and from 16.5 to 14.4 percent for ln income.* Thus if family background explains 37.1 percent of the variance in 25- to 64-year-old brothers' occupational statuses, it should explain about $37.1 + (24.2 - 20.4) = 40.9$ percent of the variance for all men aged 25 to 64. Likewise, family background should explain 14 to 30 percent of the variance in ln earnings for all men aged 25 to 64 who work.

Reliability Corrections. Self-reports of occupational status appear to have reliabilities of about 0.86. The value for ln earnings appears to be between 0.86 and 0.93. This implies that if we eliminated random error, and if brothers did not influence each other, family background would explain $0.409/0.86 = 48$ percent of the variance in occupational status and between $0.14/0.93 = 15$ and $0.30/0.86 = 35$ percent of the variance in ln earnings.

2. SOURCES OF RESEMBLANCE BETWEEN BROTHERS

The most obvious source of resemblance between brothers is the fact that they come from the same demographic background. As we shall see, however, this is not the whole story. In addition, brothers share somewhat more than half the genes that ordinarily vary from one individual to another. This appears to be important. But unmeasured aspects of their home environment may also make brothers alike. Finally, brothers may influence one another. We will consider these explanations in turn.

Demographic Influences. We investigated the influence of thirteen demographic characteristics on men's occupational status and earnings. These traits were:

* The explanatory power of some aspects of demographic background fell between the time of the OCG and OCG-II surveys, but this was not true for family size.

1. Race (white/nonwhite)
2. Father's birthplace (U.S./other)
3. Father's education (highest grade completed)
4. Father's occupation (Duncan score)
5. Father white collar (yes/no)
6. Mother's education (highest grade completed)
7. Son's region of birth (South/other)
8. Son raised on a farm (yes/no)
9. Number of siblings
10. Father absent when son was fifteen or sixteen (yes/no)
11. Parental income (1967 dollars)
12. Religion (Catholic/Jewish/Protestant)
13. Ethnicity (Irish/Italian/Polish/French/German/Slavic/Spanish/British/ Jewish/Black/Other)

No one survey provides data on all thirteen of these traits. Tables A3.1 and A3.2 in the Appendix present the standardized equations we obtained when we regressed occupational status and earnings on the traits that were available in our eight largest samples.[4] These tables support the following conclusions:

1. A comparison of OCG to OCG-II indicates that the effects of demographic background on both occupational status and ln income declined between 1961–62 and 1972–73. This also holds for the unstandardized equations.[5] The same trend emerges when we compare the 1964–65 SRC sample (PA) to the 1971 SRC sample (PSID), though this trend is somewhat obscured by the fact that the 1971 equation includes more background measures than the 1964–65 equation.

2. Demographic background explained less of the variance in occupational status and more of the variance in ln earnings in the Survey Research Center samples (PA and PSID) than in the Census Bureau samples surveyed at about the same time (OCG and OCG-II). The depressed R^2 for occupational status in the SRC surveys presumably reflects the fact that SRC grouped occupations into broader categories than the Census Bureau did. The inflated SRC R^2 for earnings probably relates to the fact that SRC has fewer low earners, though SRC may also get higher quality data from its respondents.

3. Demographic background explains more of the variance in occupational status than in earnings or income for every sample except the PA. If we were to construct a single index of demographic advantages, its correlation with occupational status would be between 0.4 and 0.5 in our large national samples of 25- to 64-year-old men, whereas its correlation with ln earnings or ln income would be between 0.3 and 0.4 in these same samples.

4. Being white, having a father or mother with a lot of schooling, having a father with a high-status occupation, having parents with high incomes, and coming from a small family all enhance a son's economic prospects.

5. Being raised outside the South increases a man's expected earnings but not his occupational status. OCG shows that men born in the North only earn more if they remain there. Southerners who move to the North are no worse off than native northerners once we control for other advantages.[6]

6. Growing up on a farm lowers a man's expected status and earnings even more than one would expect on the basis of the fact that most men who grew up on farms had fathers with low Duncan scores. This disadvantage arises largely because men who grew up on farms continue to live in smaller than average communities, where mean status and earnings are below the national average. It virtually disappears once we control current community size in OCG.

7. Having a native-born father provides no occupational advantage and is associated with slightly *lower* earnings. This disadvantage is reduced but does not quite disappear in OCG when we control for the fact that men with native-born fathers are more likely to live in rural areas and small towns.

8. Our principal surveys had no measures of parental ethnicity.* We therefore consulted Andrew Greeley, who has collected a large number of national surveys that asked about both religion and ethnicity during the 1960s. Greeley assigned respondents to one of thirteen ethnic/religious groups: Blacks, Jews, French Catholics, German Catholics, German Protestants, Irish Catholics, Irish Protestants, Italian Catholics, Polish Catholics, Slavic Catholics, Hispanic Catholics, British Protestants, and "American" Protestants. A simple white/nonwhite dichotomy accounted for 5 percent of the variance in both occupational status and family income in Greeley's samples.† Ethnic/religious differences among whites explained another 3 percent of the variance in both occupational status

---

* PSID asked if the respondent was Catholic, Jewish, or Protestant. We did not analyze this variable, but Greg Duncan found that after controlling most of our other demographic measures, it raised R^2 for ln earnings by 0.017 for 25- to 54-year-old PSID men. Most respondents probably belong to the same major religious group as their parents, so this is probably a true "background" measure.

† Greeley's surveys did not ask about individual earnings. Part of the ethnic variation in family income could be due to differences in savings rates and female labor-force participation, rather than male earnings. Greeley also found appreciable variation in status and income among Protestant denominations. But since the surveys all asked about the respondent's denomination rather than his parents' denomination, and since economically mobile Protestants often switch denominations, we cannot necessarily impute these economic differences to differences in *parental* religion.

and family income with nothing but race controlled. Ethnicity presumably correlates with father's and mother's education, father's occupation, parental income, and region of birth. We therefore doubt that ethnicity and religion would boost R^2 by more than 0.02 if we controlled our other demographic background measures.

9. The nonlinear effects of our background measures are sometimes significant but seldom large enough to be substantively interesting.[*] There is no evidence that men born at the very bottom of the distribution are consistently worse off than a linear model implies. A few multiplicative interactions are significant, but none is consistently significant across samples or across different measures of economic success. Indeed, none has a consistent sign in different samples. Positive interactions do not outnumber negative interactions, so we cannot argue that those with multiple handicaps are worse off than an additive model implies.[7] The linear, additive model therefore seems satisfactory for our purposes.

Explanatory Power of Demographic Background. OCG-II is our most recent sample and has the most extensive list of background measures. Its ten measures explain 22.6 percent of the variance in occupational status and 8.9 percent of the variance in ln income. We could not investigate nonlinearities or interactions in OCG-II, but quadratic nonlinearities and multiplicative interactions only raised R^2 by 0.003 for occupational status and 0.001 for ln income in OCG. The increases in R^2 are similar in our other large samples, so we assume they would be similar in OCG-II. Greeley's data imply that measures of parental ethnicity and religion would probably raise R^2 by about 0.02 for both occupational status and income. Eliminating errors in measuring occupational status should raise R^2 by another 0.04, while eliminating errors in measuring ln income should raise its R^2 by 0.01 or 0.02. If Bielby et al.'s (1977) estimates of the accuracy of OCG-II respondents' reports on their parents' characteristics are correct, eliminating this source of error would probably raise R^2 by about 0.03 for occupational status and 0.01 for ln income. If one makes what we regard as more realistic assumptions about the accuracy of respondents' reports on their parents' characteristics, the increase in R^2 could be as large as 0.12 for occupational

---

[*] The squared terms in tables A3.1 and A3.2 are constructed so as to be orthogonal to the analogous linear terms. This makes them virtually orthogonal to the other linear terms as well. As a result, their contributions to R^2 closely approximate the squares of their coefficients. We included an orthogonal quadratic term in these equations if it had been significant in a bivariate regression that controlled only the linear term. Quadratic terms that were tested but insignificant at the bivariate level are denoted with "NS." Terms not tested are denoted with a dash. For more details on nonlinear effects, see chapter 10.

status and 0.06 for ln income.[8] Taking all these adjustments together, we obtain the following expected values for R^2:

	Occupation	Ln Income
Race, father's education and occupation, intactness of family, mother's education, family income, number of siblings, region of birth	.226	.089
Nonlinearities and interactions	.003	.001
Religion and ethnicity	.02	.02
Total for measured background	.25	.11
Errors in measuring success	.04	.01-.02
Errors in measuring background	.03-.12	.01-.06
Estimated true R^2	.32-.41	.13-.19
Estimated true correlation between brothers raised in representative homes	.48	.15-.35

These calculations imply that if brothers came from precisely the same demographic backgrounds, our thirteen demographic measures would explain 55 to 85 percent of the resemblance between their occupations and earnings.[9] But brothers' demographic backgrounds are not precisely the same. A family's size, structure, place of residence, and economic position all change over time. These changes occur when brothers are different ages, and they could have different effects on each brother's life chances. If a family's fortunes rise between the time one brother finishes high school and the time the next one finishes, for example, the younger brother may find it easier to attend college than the older one did. If this happened, some of the variance explained by parental income would be variation within families rather than between them. Our demographic measures would then explain less than two-thirds of the resemblance between brothers than the foregoing calculations imply.

To see if this was a problem, we examined the Kalamazoo survey in more detail. Each Kalamazoo brother reported his father's occupation when he was 15. Since brothers were typically born about five years apart, an appreciable number of fathers changed occupations during the interval. These changes did not affect the sons' life chances. If we use brothers' reports to estimate each father's occupation before or after the respondent was 15, we find that the father's occupation when a son was older or younger than 15 predicts his life chances as well as the father's occupation when the son was 15.*

If changes in family characteristics while children are growing up do not affect children's life chances, we are probably underestimating the effects of demographic background on life chances. Our Kalamazoo results imply, for example, that a son's economic position depends on his father's average occupational status throughout the years when the son is growing up, not on the father's status at a single arbitrarily selected point in time. If we calculated each father's mean status from the time his son was born until the son left home, this mean would probably correlate no more than 0.90 with the father's status when his son was 15. Thus, if the father's status when his son is 15 correlates 0.36 with his son's status, the correlation between the father's *mean* status and his son's status might be as high as $0.36/0.90 = 0.40$. This same logic may apply to other family characteristics that change over time. Nonetheless, conventional demographic measures are unlikely to account for the entire resemblance between brothers. We must therefore ask why brothers might end up more alike than random individuals from the same demographic background.

Genetic Resemblance between Brothers. A mother passes along half her genes to each of her children, but she does not necessarily pass on the same half to any two children. The same holds for a father. Thus, if parents married randomly, full brothers would share half the genes that ordinarily vary from one individual to another. But parents do not marry randomly. They tend to choose spouses who resemble them genetically—

---

* As a further test of the effects of demographic changes on brothers' life chances, we looked at the effects of birth order. Oldest children spend the first few years of their lives in smaller families than younger children do. If unadulterated parental attention is helpful in early childhood, oldest children should end up better off than others. But youngest children typically spend their late adolescence in a smaller family than their elders did. So if unadulterated parental attention were helpful in adolescence, younger children should end up better off. (In addition, younger children often enjoy economic advantages denied to their older siblings, partly because parents have more money when they are older and partly because the older siblings cease to make claims on the family's resources.) Middle children should end up worse off than either their elders or their juniors.

The OCG data support these expectations, but very modestly. The more older siblings men had, the worse off they were economically in 1962. But this relationship virtually disappeared once we controlled overall family size. Within families of any given size, men without older siblings scored only one point higher on the Duncan scale than men with one older sibling. Men with two older siblings were also better off than men with only one older sibling, but the advantage was less than half a point on the Duncan scale. Each subsequent "demotion" in ordinal position raised expected occupational status by another half point. These effects explain only 0.2 percent of the variance in occupational status. The effects on income follow the same pattern but are not statistically significant. Either birth order is not closely related to changes in families' demographic characteristics, or else demographic changes do not explain much of the variation among men reared in the same home.

except, of course, with respect to sex. Whites tend to marry whites, tall women tend to marry tall men, and so forth. As a result, brothers share more than half the genes that ordinarily vary from individual to individual.

In discussing the effects of genetic resemblance between brothers, it is important not to fall into the trap of trying to separate the effects of heredity from the effects of environment. One of the primary mechanisms by which heredity is likely to influence a man's economic success is by influencing his environment. To begin with, a man's genes are likely to influence the environments he selects for himself. Tall men are more likely to try out for the basketball team, for example. This means that tall men have a better than average chance of acquiring the skills needed to become professional basketball players. In addition, a man's genes are likely to affect the environment others create for him. Basketball coaches are likely to spend more time with tall players than with short ones, for example. This means that we cannot separate resemblance between brothers into "genetic" and "environmental" components. We can, however, try to estimate the *overall* impact of genetic resemblance, assuming that it may work either through the environment or in other ways. We can then ask how much of the resemblance between brothers remains unexplained. This nongenetic residual is the expected degree of resemblance between pairs of genetically unrelated men reared in the same home.

Our only direct quantitative evidence regarding genes' contribution to economic resemblance between brothers comes from Taubman's twin survey. His identical twins' earnings correlate 0.54, while his fraternal twins' earnings correlate 0.30. The correlation for fraternal twins is thus 56 percent of the correlation for identical twins. We know from genetic theory that fraternal twins and ordinary siblings share more than half the genes that ordinarily vary from one individual to the next. Taubman's results are therefore compatible with the hypothesis that genes explain the entire resemblance between twins' earnings and that common home environment is of no importance.[10]

There are, however, several alternative explanations for Taubman's findings. First, the fact that identical twins have the same genes may lead other people to treat them as a single social unit. Second, identical twins may have more influence on one another than fraternal twins or ordinary siblings. Third, interactions among genes, or between genes and environment, may inflate the resemblance between identical twins. In order to rule out these hypotheses, we would need additional data of a kind not currently available.[11]

Indirect evidence does, however, raise serious doubt about the hypothesis that genes explain the *entire* resemblance between brothers. For this to be true, the effects of demographic background would also have to be traceable to the fact that demographic background is correlated with genotype. This is clearly true in some cases. Race, for example, predicts economic success partly because it is correlated with skin color, facial features, and other genetically determined traits. These genetically determined traits affect the value many employers place on an individual's services. Other demographic characteristics may operate in the same way.

It seems less likely, however, that traits like father's and mother's education and occupational status are simply proxies for parental genes. They may affect a son's life chances partly because genes affect parental success and parents pass on their genes to their children, but it is hard to believe this is the whole story. In order to assess the extent to which father's education and father's occupation affect a son's life chances by affecting the son's genotype, we looked at OCG data on sons who were raised in a family with a male head other than their natural father. About 3 percent of all OCG respondents reported that their household was headed by a male other than their natural father when they were 16 and also reported this head's education and occupation. Some of these nonpaternal heads were presumably uncles, grandfathers, or other relatives who shared some genes with the respondent. Others were presumably stepfathers, who would also tend to have more genes in common with the respondent than with random individuals because of assortative mating. Nonetheless, if a household head's education and occupation affect a son's life chances exclusively because they are proxies for genotype, the effects should be attenuated when the household head is not the respondent's natural father. Yet in our OCG sample, a nonpaternal head's characteristics had about four-fifths as much effect on his son's occupational status and income as when the head was the respondent's natural father. This difference was not statistically significant. Furthermore, a nonpaternal head's characteristics had slightly *more* effect on a son's educational attainment than a paternal head's characteristics. All in all, then, our OCG data do not support the view that parental status affects a son's life chances primarily because it is a proxy for parental genotype.[12]

Our other demographic measures are even less likely to correlate with genotype. Family size does not seem to depend on the parents' genes, but even if it did, not many of the genes affecting fertility are likely to affect economic success. Region of birth is also unlikely to be a proxy for genotype. All things considered, we doubt that there is much overlap between the variance attributable to demographic background and the variance attributable to genes. If we are right about this, the fact that demographic background explains at least two-thirds of the resemblance between brothers implies that genes are unlikely to explain much more than a third of such resemblance.

Other Unmeasured Background Characteristics. In order to get more clues about common influences that make brothers alike, it is useful to ask whether the same traits explain resemblance on different outcomes. If the same background characteristics explain resemblance on test scores, education, occupational status, and earnings, it is tempting to think of these traits as proxies for global concepts like "socioeconomic status" or "native ability." If different background characteristics affect different outcomes, we need a subtler vocabulary.

We began by asking whether the same *demographic* characteristics affected different outcomes. To answer this question, we compared the relative size of each trait's coefficients when predicting test scores, education, occupational status, and earnings. We found a number of modest differences. Race, for example, usually had a larger relative weight when predicting test performance than when predicting educational attainment. Parental income had a larger relative weight when predicting earnings than when predicting educational attainment. Father's education had a larger weight when predicting a son's education than when predicting his occupation. But no demographic trait that helped consistently in one area was consistently harmful in another. Thus when we combined demographic measures into a single index of demographic advantage, the index that best predicted one outcome correlated better than 0.85 with the index that best predicted the other three outcomes. For most purposes, then, it is reasonable to talk about demographic advantages as if they had uniform effects on all outcomes.

If we extend this logic to include all the other unmeasured factors that produce resemblance between brothers, the picture changes. Imagine regressing two different outcomes like test scores (Q) and education (U) on a comprehensive set of background measures that includes all relevant nonlinearities and interactions. If brothers have no effect on one another, these common background measures must explain the entire resemblance between brothers. Next, imagine an index of background characteristics in which each characteristic receives the same weight it had in our hypothetical regression equation. Let us denote the index for predicting test scores as F_Q and the index for predicting education as F_U. The correlation between the index predicting test performance and actual performance will then be:

(1)
$$r_{FQ,Q} = r_{QQ'}{}^{1/2}$$

where $r_{QQ'}$ is the correlation between the two brothers' test scores. We can write analogous formulas for calculating the correlation between any other outcome and the index predicting that outcome. We can also calculate the correlation between the index that best predicts test scores and the index that best predicts education:

(2)
$$r_{FQ,FU} = \frac{r_{QU'}}{(r_{QQ'}r_{UU'})^{1/2}}$$

where the primes again denote the second brother's traits.[13]

TABLE 3.2

Estimated Correlations Among Sets of Background Characteristics
Influencing Different Outcomes

	Background Characteristics Influencing:		
	Test Scores and Education	Test Scores and Occupation	Test Scores and Ln Earnings
Kalamazoo Brothers[a]	.788	.788	.526
Talent Brothers[b]	.801	.822	.623
	Education and Occupation	Education and Ln Earnings	Occupation and Ln Earnings
Kalamazoo Brothers[a]	.918	.774	.836
Talent Brothers[b]	.983	.625	.479
NORC Brothers[c]	.906	.655	1.051[f]
Taubman DZ Twins[d]	.882	.721	.776
Taubman MZ Twins[d]	.770	.624	.560
OCG[e]	.970	.886	.925

[a]Derived from correlations in tables A2.11 and A3.4.
[b]Derived from correlations in tables A2.10 and A3.4.
[c]Derived from correlations in tables A2.6 and A3.4.
[d]Derived from correlations in Taubman (1976a).
[e]Estimates are for *demographic measures only*, and are derived by correlating values predicted for education, occupation, and ln earnings using independent variables listed in tables A3.1 and A3.2.
[f]The population value cannot exceed 1.00. The estimate can exceed 1.00, due to sampling error.

Table 3.2 shows the correlations between the background characteristics that affect different outcomes in each sample of brothers. These correlations are almost all lower than the correlations between demographic background traits predicting the same outcomes in OCG. Not surprisingly, the indices that predict highly correlated outcomes, like education and occupational status, are more highly correlated than the indices that predict poorly correlated outcomes, like earnings and test scores. Table 3.2 suggests that we will be seriously misled if we think of the unmeasured family characteristics that make brothers alike as being the same for all outcomes. We should not, for example, think that the unmeasured "ability" factors affecting education and earnings are exactly the same.[14] Nor can we invoke a one-dimensional notion of class background to explain resemblance between brothers.[15] Rather, we need to imagine genetic or nongenetic influences that affect some outcomes without affecting others. A family's values regarding the relative importance of ideas, status, and money might, for example, operate in this way.

Do Brothers Influence One Another? Another possible explanation of resemblance between brothers is that they influence one another. There is no general way to test this hypothesis without quasi-experimental data. We can, however, ask whether the pattern of resemblance between brothers is consistent with specific hypotheses about how brothers might influence one another.

Our first hypothesis was that older brothers might serve as models for their younger brothers, especially when the younger brother was deciding whether to remain in school. If this hypothesis were correct, we would also expect older brothers to partially displace fathers as role models. (The more accessible models the respondent has, the less crucial any one should be.) We assessed the father's importance as a role model by looking at the effect of his education on his son's education and the effect of his occupation on his son's occupation with all other aspects of demographic background controlled. When we made such comparisons for OCG men from intact families, we found no significant differences between oldest sons and younger sons. We also looked at the effects of father's education and occupation on men with different numbers of older brothers and sisters. Again, there was no significant reduction in the effects of the father's characteristics as the number of alternative role models increased.*

---

* The multiplicative interactions of father's education and occupation with both the number of older brothers and the total number of older siblings never approached significance in predicting either the respondent's education or his occupation. The multiplicative interaction between father's education and number of *younger sisters* was significant ($t = 3.3$) when predicting respondent's education. Each younger sister reduced the estimated effect of father's education by about 5 percent. The multiplicative interaction between father's occupation and *total* number of siblings was significant ($t = 2.6$) when predicting respondent's occupation. Again, each extra sibling reduced the effect of father's occupation by about 5 percent. If one allows for the effects of weighting and the large number of interactions we tested, these results might conceivably be due to chance. We certainly cannot explain them otherwise.

Our second hypothesis was that younger brothers might arbitrarily select *one* older brother as a model, either because he was the most successful or for other reasons, and that this might happen without diminishing the father's influence. If this were the case, the correlation between the respondent's characteristics and his oldest brother's characteristics should diminish as the number of older brothers increased. Yet once we controlled other background characteristics, the partial correlation between the respondent's education and his oldest brother's education in OCG did not vary significantly with either the number of older brothers or the total number of older siblings the respondent reported.*

Our third hypothesis was that brothers might affect one another's cognitive skills or personality traits. If this were the case, we would expect brothers born close together to influence one another's development more than brothers born many years apart, since brothers born close together spend more time together. To test this hypothesis we correlated the absolute age difference between brothers with the absolute difference in their educational attainment, occupational status, and earnings in the NORC, Kalamazoo, and Talent samples. The correlation was both positive and significant for education in NORC and for occupational status in Kalamazoo. It was positive but insignificant in most other cases. It was never significantly negative.† But even if brothers born close together end up more alike, this need not mean that brothers influence one another, since brothers born close together are also treated more alike and are more likely to attend the same schools,

* There is a significant *positive* interaction ($t = 4.6$) between brother's education and *total* number of older siblings until we add the interaction between brother's education and number of younger sisters. With the latter interaction included ($t = 3.9$), the t-value for the former is only 0.25. We have no explanation for this finding.

† In the NORC sample, a one-year increase in the absolute age difference is associated with an 0.13-year increase in the absolute educational difference ($t = 3.2$). The t-statistics for occupational status and ln earnings are 0.5 and −0.2.

In Kalamazoo, Olneck (1976b) reports that brothers born within three years of one another had Duncan scores that correlated 0.469, while those born more than three years apart correlated only 0.181. The education correlation was insignificantly larger for men born within three years of one another, while the earnings correlation was insignificantly smaller.

Our Talent brothers were all born very close together, so for this purpose we used a larger sample of Talent siblings in grades 9–12 followed up five years after high school (Jencks and Brown, 1977). Age difference was not significantly related to education difference in this sample ($N = 817$).

The number of intervening siblings is also a partial proxy for the age difference between an OCG respondent and his oldest brother. Once other aspects of background are controlled, the partial correlation between the respondent's education and his oldest brother's education does not depend on the number of intervening siblings (see previous footnote). This may, however, merely mean that intervening siblings are a poor proxy for age differences.

grow up in the same neighborhood, and enter the same labor market.

Since we found no support for our first two hypotheses about the likely character of brothers' influences on one another, and since brothers born close together may end up more alike because they encounter more similar environments, we cannot confidently attribute resemblance between brothers to the fact that brothers influence one another. Yet the fact that brothers born close together end up slightly more alike on some outcomes means that we cannot rule out reciprocal influences either. This is doubly true for reciprocal influences exerted after both brothers enter the labor market. If brothers *do* influence one another, our estimates of family background's impact on economic success will be too high.* If brothers influence one another more on some outcomes than on others, our earlier conclusion that family background is multi-dimensional may also be wrong.

3. MECHANISMS BY WHICH BACKGROUND
AFFECTS ECONOMIC SUCCESS

Family advantages seem to affect economic success in at least five conceptually distinct ways:

1. Men from advantaged backgrounds have cognitive skills that employers value.
2. Men from advantaged backgrounds have noncognitive traits that employers value.
3. Among men with similar cognitive and noncognitive traits, those from advantaged families have more educational credentials. Employers appear to value these credentials in their own right, even when they are not associated with measurable skills, attitudes, or behavior.
4. Among men with similar skills and credentials, those from advantaged families seek jobs in higher-status occupations than those from disadvantaged families.

---

* Given our uncertainty about reciprocal influences, the reader may wonder why we have not defined the problem out of existence by asserting that "family background" includes the influence of brothers as well as parents. The difficulty with this definition is that it prevents us from using resemblance between brothers as a measure of family background's explanatory power. Let Y = one brother's measured success, Y' = the other brother's success, F = an optimally weighted sum of background characteristics other than the brother's success, and assume $Y = aF + bY' + e_Y$ and $Y' = aF + bY + e_{Y'}$. If brothers do not affect one another, $b = O$ and $r_{YY'} = a^2$. If we redefine F to include Y' for the first brother and Y for the second, a is indeterminate, unless we know b, which we do not.

5. Even among men with similar skills and credentials who enter the same occupation, employers seem to pay men from advantaged families slightly more than men from disadvantaged families.

Researchers have traditionally investigated the relative importance of these influences by measuring family advantages directly. They have then asked whether the apparent effects of a given family advantage (e.g., a highly educated mother) persisted when they controlled the respondent's own characteristics (e.g., his education). We will do this too, but we will also extend the analysis by using our more comprehensive definition of family background, namely everything that makes brothers alike. We label this "shared" or "common" background to distinguish it from the narrower concept of "demographic" background. We then ask, in effect, how much of the resemblance between brothers on our measures of economic success derives from the fact that brothers have, say, similar cognitive skills or similar educational attainments. Ideally, we would like to do this for personality traits and aspirations as well, but the samples of brothers with relevant data were too small to justify such analyses.

If we want to assess the extent to which shared background affects earnings by affecting an intervening variable like test scores, we need a model with two distinct indices of background characteristics. One index (F_Q) must explain resemblance between brothers' test scores. The other (H_Y) must explain resemblance between brothers' earnings, over and above the resemblance expected on the basis of their test scores. The second of these indices (H_Y) will be somewhat different in character from the index that explained overall resemblance of brothers' earnings (F_Y), since the relative importance of specific background characteristics will change when we control test scores. A father's cognitive skills, for example, are likely to influence his son's earnings largely by influencing his son's test performance. A father's race will affect his son's earnings even with test scores controlled. Figure 3.1 displays such a model visually and gives the equations for estimating its parameters. Comparing the standardized coefficient of H_Y in figure 3.1 to the zero-order correlation of F_Y with Y tells us how much of shared background's overall effect on earnings operates independently of test performance.

To estimate the extent to which strictly demographic advantages affect earnings by affecting test scores, we calculated the economic advantage enjoyed by someone who was one standard deviation above the mean on all the background characteristics measured in a given survey. We then reestimated this advantage with test scores controlled.

FIGURE 3.1

Family Effects on Test Scores (Q) and Earnings (Y)

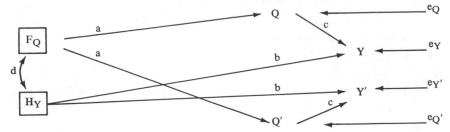

Standardized Structural Equations

1. $Q = aF_Q + e_Q$
2. $Q' = aF_Q + e_{Q'}$
3. $Y = b(H_Y) + cQ + e_Y$
4. $Y' = b(H_Y) + cQ' + e_{Y'}$

Normal Equations

5. $r_{YQ} = c + abd$
6. $r_{YQ'} = r_{QY'} = cr_{QQ'} + abd$
7. $r_{QQ'} = a^2$
8. $r_{YY'} = c\,r_{YQ'} + b^2 + abcd$

Solutions

9. $a = (r_{QQ'})^{1/2}$

10. $c = \dfrac{r_{YQ} - r_{YQ'}}{1 - r_{QQ'}}$

11. $b = r_{YY'} - 2cr_{YQ'} + c^2 r_{QQ'}$

12. $d = \dfrac{r_{YQ} - c}{ab}$

Note: For estimates of a and b, see table 3.3. For estimates of c, see chapter 4. For estimates of c with schooling substituted for test scores, see chapter 6.

An individual who ranks one standard deviation above the mean on *all* demographic measures is considerably more advantaged than an individual who ranks one standard deviation above the mean on a composite index of advantages, so we cannot compare the absolute effects of demographic measures to the effects of the index that explains resemblance between brothers.* We can, however, ask how much controlling test scores reduces the estimated benefits of demographic background,

* In order to compare the two sets of results, we would need what Heise (1972) calls a "sheaf" coefficient. Chapter 5 uses this coefficient. Our method here is cruder but serviceable. We simply add the standardized regression coefficients in a given equation, ignoring the covariances among background variables.

and we can compare these percentages to percentage reductions in the estimated effect of all aspects of "shared" or "common" background.

Cognitive Skills. Conservatives have traditionally argued that disproportionate numbers of men from privileged backgrounds end up in privileged positions themselves because men from privileged backgrounds are more likely to have personal characteristics that society needs and values. Since World War II America has increasingly seen itself as a "meritocracy" in which "intelligence" is the key to advancement. Conservatives have therefore been increasingly inclined to argue that men from privileged backgrounds end up in good jobs because they are smarter than other people. In its "strong" variant, this theory claims that men from privileged backgrounds inherit more than their share of the genes that facilitate cognitive development. In its "weak" variant, the theory merely claims that men from privileged backgrounds grow up in homes that facilitate cognitive development, and that early experiences are so important that these men's initial advantage persists throughout their lives.

In principle, the PSID, Veterans, Kalamazoo, and Talent samples are all suitable for testing this claim, since these four surveys all include a measure of cognitive skill. The PSID test was administered long after most men had entered the labor force, however, so a man's score could be a result of his labor market position as well as a cause of it. In addition, the PSID test is not very reliable and may not measure the same skills as most general purpose cognitive tests. The Veterans, Kalamazoo, and Talent tests were all given before men had acquired any appreciable labor force experience, and all appear to measure general cognitive skills quite reliably. These three samples include fewer men over 35, men from disadvantaged backgrounds, men with low test scores, and men with low educational attainment than our national samples of men aged 25 to 64. As a result, the overall association of demographic background with economic success is weaker in these three samples than in our national samples of 25- to 64-year-olds. Nonetheless, these three samples tell a relatively consistent story. We are therefore inclined to believe that the same story applies to all men aged 25 to 64.

Table 3.3 shows that 46 to 63 percent of demographic background's effect on Kalamazoo and Talent men's occupational status and earnings derives from its effect on their cognitive skills before they enter the labor market. Among Veterans, the figures are only 40 percent for occupational status and 28 percent for earnings. These results support the conservative view that general cognitive skills play a significant role in the transmission of privilege from one generation to the next. They obviously say

TABLE 3.3

Percentage of Background's Effect on Occupational Status and Ln Earnings Attributable to Background's Effect on Test Scores and Education

		Coefficients Controlling:			Percent Reduction in Coefficient Controlling:		
	Nothing	Only Test Score	Test Score + Education	Only Education	Only Test Score	Test Score + Education	Only Education
Occupational status							
(Total effect using brothers)							
Kalamazoo	.556[a]	.418[b]	.246[c]	.273[b]	25%	56%	51%
Talent	.574[a]	.409[b]	.133[c]	.141[b]	29%	77%	75%
NORC	.609[a]	–	–	.361[b]	–	–	41%
(Summed coefficients of demographic variables)[d]							
Kalamazoo	.448	.240	-.043	.002	46%	110%	100%
NORC	.702	–	–	.297	–	–	58%
Talent (full)	.543	.199	.150	–	63%	72%	–
Veterans	.568	.339	.198	.239	40%	65%	58%
PSID	.688	.530	.159	.212	23%	77%	69%
OCG	.879	–	–	.381	–	–	57%
PA	.662	–	–	.229	–	–	65%
NLS	.656	–	–	.185	–	–	72%
OCG-II	.723	–	–	.300	–	–	59%
Ln earnings							
(Total effect using brothers)							
Kalamazoo	.469[a]	.399[b]	.353[c]	.325[b]	15%	25%	31%
Talent	.456[a]	.358[b]	.346[c]	.357[b]	21%	24%	22%
NORC	.359[a]	–	–	.276[b]	–	–	23%
Taubman's DZ Twins	.543[a]	–	–	.403[b]	–	–	26%
Taubman's MZ Twins	.738[a]	–	–	.662[b]	–	–	10%
(Summed coefficients of demographic variables)[d]							
Kalamazoo	.336	.177	-.023	.046	47%	107%	86%
NORC	.214	–	–	-.100	–	–	147%
Talent (full)	.277	.140	.130	.157	49%	53%	43%
Veterans	.589	.426	.377	.418	28%	36%	29%
PSID	.664	.445	.235	.338	33%	65%	49%
OCG	.768	–	–	.481	–	–	37%
PA	.739	–	–	.421	–	–	43%
NLS	.690	–	–	.350	–	–	49%
OCG-II	.513	–	–	.247	–	–	52%

[a] Estimated as $(r_{DD'})^{1/2}$ or $(r_{YY'})^{1/2}$.

[b] Estimated as b from figure 3.1.

[c] Estimated from extended version of figure 3.1. See Eaglesfield (1977).

[d] Sum of standardized coefficients in table A3.1 or A3.2, omitting orthogonal squared terms and reversing signs of father absent and siblings.

nothing about whether men from privileged backgrounds do better on standardized tests for genetic or for nongenetic reasons.

The picture looks somewhat different if we consider the overall effect of family background rather than just the effect of demographic advantages. Whereas sixth grade IQ scores accounted for 46 and 47 percent of demographic background's impact on occupational status and earnings in Kalamazoo, they account for only 25 and 15 percent of family background's overall impact. The unmeasured background characteristics that affect Kalamazoo men's life chances must, then, differ in some important way from the demographic background characteristics measured in the Kalamazoo survey, since they exert far less of their impact via cognitive skills. The same holds in Talent. Thus if we are interested in all the ways in which parents affect their children's life chances, concentrating exclusively on parents with demographic advantages will lead us to exaggerate the importance of cognitive skills as an intervening variable. Most of us, however, are primarily concerned with the mechanisms by which *demographic* advantages affect children's life chances. The mechanisms by which different families with the same demographic characteristics exert different effects on their children are of far less political concern.

Personality Traits. "Intelligence" is not the only virtue that all members of society value, though it has certainly been the most widely publicized. When the Kalamazoo high school asked its tenth grade homeroom teachers to rate students' noncognitive traits, it constructed a list of virtues that almost all Kalamazoo parents probably wanted their children to have: cooperativeness, dependability, executive ability, emotional control, industriousness, initiative, integrity, and perseverance. The only trait on the Kalamazoo list that might now seem problematic to a significant number of people is "appearance." While these ratings probably have quite low reliabilities and validities, chapter 5 shows that they do predict economic success to some extent.

Conservatives have often argued that one reason men from privileged backgrounds are especially likely to succeed economically is that they are more likely than men from less privileged backgrounds to display the kinds of virtues measured in Kalamazoo. The Kalamazoo data offer little support for this view. Demographic advantages explain only 2 to 7 percent of the variance in teacher ratings on these nine traits, and the trait most strongly related to earnings, namely "executive ability," has the weakest relationship to background. As a result, teacher ratings of these traits explain a negligible fraction of the association between demographic background and economic success among Kalamazoo men.

The Talent sample provides no teacher ratings, but it does provide both self-assessments and measures of students' behavior in high school. Like the Kalamazoo teacher assessments, Talent's noncognitive measures have a moderate effect on economic success (see chapter 5). But they account for a negligible fraction of the association between demographic background and economic success. The "sheaf" coefficient of the demographic background measures that best predict occupational status in the Talent sample is 0.39 with no controls and 0.24 with eleventh grade test scores controlled. Adding the Talent measures of noncognitive traits to this equation only lowers the coefficient of background to 0.19. This means that Talent's measures of noncognitive traits explain only $0.05/0.39 = 13$ percent of demographic background's effect on occupational status. The sheaf coefficient of demographic background when predicting hourly earnings is 0.23 with no controls, 0.17 with test scores controlled, and 0.15 with test scores and noncognitive traits controlled. Talent's noncognitive measures thus explain even less of demographic background's impact on earnings than on occupational status. Again, these results do not provide much support for the view that men from privileged backgrounds end up in good jobs because their parents instill noncognitive virtues that either employers or society as a whole value.

The idea that noncognitive traits play an important role in the transmission of privilege from one generation to another is not, of course, confined to conservative defenders of the status quo. Liberals and radicals (Kohn, 1969; Bowles and Gintis, 1976) have also espoused such theories. Their argument has been that work is organized hierarchically, and that different positions in this hierarchy demand different attitudes towards conformity and authority. According to this view, parents try to socialize their children in ways that would ensure success at whatever level in the job hierarchy the parents occupy. To the extent that parents succeed, they increase their children's chances of ending up in jobs like those the parents held. Unfortunately, our data are not really suitable for testing this theory. First, we have no good measure of parents' place in the work hierarchy, though the father's occupational status is a crude proxy. Second, and more crucial, our noncognitive measures do not really allow us to distinguish students who have adopted a "working class" mode of conformity from students who have adopted a "middle class" mode of conformity. One could perhaps argue that students rated high on "cooperativeness" and "dependability" were likely to fit into low level jobs more easily than students rated high on "initiative" and "executive ability", but since ratings on *all* these traits correlate positively with one another and with eventual economic success, this argument is difficult to sustain. Alternatively, one could argue that all nine Kalamazoo ratings measure virtues that are increasingly valuable as one moves up the job hierarchy. This is consistent with the finding that students from middle-class backgrounds rank somewhat higher on all nine measures, and that those who rank high on these measures are somewhat more successful economically when they grow up. Nonetheless, Kalamazoo teacher ratings account for a negligible fraction of the association between a father's occupational status and either his son's status or his son's earnings. While we regard this as evidence against Kohn's hypothesis about the transmission of privilege from generation to generation, we do not regard it as strong evidence.*

Aspirations. If men from privileged backgrounds were more concerned about maximizing their occupational status and earnings than men with similar skills from less privileged backgrounds, this would help explain why men from privileged backgrounds ended up better off. Project Talent asked eleventh graders to rate the attractiveness of 112 different occupations on a five-point scale. We assigned each occupation a Duncan score and used the respondent's assessment of occupations at various levels to estimate his level of aspiration. When we control this index of occupational aspirations along with cognitive and noncognitive traits, the "sheaf" coefficient of the family background measures falls from 0.19 to 0.16 when predicting occupational status at age 28, and from 0.15 to 0.13 when predicting hourly earnings at 28.[16] This suggests that differences in eleventh-grade aspirations play a very limited role in explaining demographic background's effects on occupational status and earnings.

We have no way of knowing what jobs our respondents actually applied for, or what promotions they sought, so we cannot rule out the hypothesis that some of the unexplained economic advantage enjoyed by men from advantaged backgrounds derives from differences in the jobs they eventually seek.

---

* As a further test of Kohn's hypothesis, we looked at the correlations between the 105 pairs of brothers who both had ratings on these traits. These correlations range from a low of 0.24 for "executive ability" to a high of 0.47 for "perseverance." This suggests that family background as a whole plays a major role in determining such traits, even though demographic advantages of the kind we measured are not very important. This is consistent with Kohn's view that the parents' position in the work hierarchy is critical. But the family background characteristics that promote the nine noncognitive virtues measured in Kalamazoo are not the same as the family background characteristics that promote later economic success. The coefficient of the trait with the largest effect on occupational status, namely "industriousness," actually *increases* when we control all aspects of family background by looking at differences between brothers. Such an increase implies a negative correlation between the set of background characteristics affecting "industriousness" and the set affecting occupational status with "industriousness" controlled (See equation 12, figure 3.1).

Education. Men from advantaged families succeed economically partly because they obtain more education than most people. This is particularly true when we measure success in terms of occupational status. For reasons discussed earlier, we believe that the NORC data on brothers' occupations are more representative than the Kalamazoo or Talent data. Controlling education explains 41 percent of shared background's effect on occupational status in the NORC sample. Background characteristics have less impact in Kalamazoo, and education explains slightly more of their effect. Among the handful of Talent brothers, all of whom finished high school, education explains 75 percent of background's effect on status. Education and test scores together explain little more of shared background's effect in Talent and Kalamazoo than education alone. Nor is the pattern very different when we look only at demographic background than when we consider all aspects of shared background.

Education explains only a quarter of shared background's effect on brothers' earnings, compared to almost half its effect on occupational status. Education explains 40 to 50 percent of demographic background's effect on earnings, compared to 60 to 70 percent of its effect on occupational status. With education controlled, background's effect on earnings is about as large as its effect on occupational status.

The role of education in transmitting occupational status cannot be fully explained by the fact that men who had more education had unusual cognitive or noncognitive traits before they finished school. In the Talent sample, for example, adding education to an equation that controls cognitive and noncognitive traits plus occupational preferences in eleventh grade lowers the coefficient of background from 0.16 to 0.10 in the occupation equations.

Education plays a far smaller role in helping advantaged parents boost their sons' earnings than in helping them boost their sons' occupational status. The coefficient of background in the Talent hourly earnings equations is 0.12 with test scores, noncognitive traits, and occupational preferences controlled. It is still 0.12 with education also controlled. One finds much the same pattern in the earnings equations from most other samples. Except in PSID, controlling education as well as test scores explains only a little more of background's effect on earnings than controlling test scores alone.

Discrimination. Race, ethnicity, father's occupation, farm upbringing, and southern birth affect economic success even with education controlled in both OCG and OCG-II. The effects of farm upbringing and southern birth derive largely from their influence on current place of residence. The effects of race, ethnicity, and father's occupation require more careful scrutiny.

Race directly affects occupation and earnings in all our large national surveys of 25- to 64-year-olds. This is also true in most of the surveys that control test scores. Talent is the only survey where race has no independent effect, perhaps because of the high nonresponse rate in Talent's nonwhite sample. Of course, none of these surveys controls every worker characteristic that affects employers' willingness to hire or promote whites. These unmeasured worker characteristics could account for at least part of the white/nonwhite difference. Our data only indicate that economic differences between whites and nonwhites persist even when they have the same amount of schooling and the same scores on cognitive tests. Nonetheless, this creates a strong prima facie case for assuming that on the average, and despite affirmative action, nonwhites suffer from discrimination based on skin color.

Our data do not allow us to analyze the effects of ethnicity in any detail. Greeley (1977) found that Jews enjoyed occupational statuses about a third of a standard deviation higher than those of other white males with the same schooling and parental education, even after taking account of the fact that they mostly live in the urban North. Among gentiles in the urban North, white Anglo-Saxon Protestants and German Catholics ranked about a sixth of a standard deviation above the level expected on the basis of their demographic background and schooling, while Italian and "French" (mostly French Canadian) Catholics and Irish Protestants ranked about a sixth of a standard deviation lower. Most Catholic ethnic groups earn 10 to 20 percent more than we would expect on the basis of their background, education, and place of residence. The same held for Jews.*

Father's occupation directly affects both occupation and income in OCG and OCG-II, but its effects are insignificant and occasionally have the wrong sign in NLS and PSID. The PSID result may reflect the cruder measurement of the father's occupation in that survey, but the NLS measure is identical to OCG's.

One way in which a father's status could affect his son's status independent of the son's schooling or ability would be if sons inherited

---

* Greeley's occupational rankings are based on the NORC prestige scale. His income data cover family income, not earnings, and his income equations either have no controls or control both education and occupation. The statements in the text are thus approximations.

farms, small businesses, professional practices, or union memberships directly from their fathers. To test this hypothesis we reestimated the 1962 OCG equation for a sample that included only sons who worked in a different Census occupational category from their father. With education controlled, this sample change lowered the standardized coefficient of the father's occupational status from 0.103 to 0.061 in the occupation equation and from 0.071 to 0.068 in the income equation. Direct inheritance of occupations is thus a small part of the story.

The OCG equations do not control test scores, personality traits, aspirations, or such "skills" as having a middle-class accent.[17] With test scores and aspirations as well as education controlled, a father's occupational status has virtually no effect on either occupational status or earnings at age 28 in the Talent sample. But father's occupation is not as well measured in Talent as in OCG, and its bivariate relationship to economic success is weaker in Talent than in an OCG sample of the same age.[18] In the Veterans sample, where father's occupation is better measured, its effects persist with both test scores and education controlled. The same is true in the Wisconsin sample (Sewell and Hauser, 1975). All in all, while test scores, personality traits, aspirations, and education *may* explain the apparent effects of father's occupation, we cannot rule out the possibility that employers discriminate on the basis of parental status, or at least on the basis of traits that serve as proxies for parental status, such as speech patterns.

Unmeasured family characteristics also exert substantial effects on sons' occupations and earnings with both test scores and education controlled. This is true even in the NORC and Kalamazoo samples, where demographic background has no effect on earnings with test scores and education controlled. It is tempting to suppose that these unmeasured characteristics are unmeasured aspects of socioeconomic status. But the unmeasured family characteristics that affect a son's earnings with cognitive skills controlled are completely uncorrelated with the family characteristics that affect cognitive skills.* Likewise, the family characteristics that affect earnings with education controlled are not the same as the family characteristics that affect education itself. Indeed, they are not even consistently correlated with the factors that

* In figure 3.1, $r_{FQ.HY} = -0.018$ in Kalamazoo and -0.085 in Talent. If we extend figure 3.1 to include education as well as test scores, and redefine H_Y as the weighted sum of the family characteristics that influence earnings independently of *both* test scores *and* education, $r_{FQ.HY} = -0.213$ in Kalamazoo and -0.016 in Talent. These low correlations are not a methodological artifact. If, for example, one performs the same calculations using occupational status rather than earnings as the dependent variable, $r_{FQ.HY} = 0.575$ and 0.602 for the two-variable model and 0.379 and 0.607 in the three-variable model for Kalamazoo and Talent respectively.

make brothers alike on occupational status.* Thus, while we cannot identify the unmeasured family characteristics that affect sons' earnings, we can reject candidates that would affect a wide range of outcomes rather than just affecting earnings.

CONCLUSIONS

We began this chapter by asking how much effect family background had on economic success. After allowing for differences between men with brothers and men in general, and after correcting for random measurement error, we concluded that family background as a whole explained about 48 percent of the variance in occupational status and 15 to 35 percent of the variance in earnings among men aged 25 to 64 in the early 1970s. These estimates imply that those who do well economically typically owe almost half of their occupational advantage and 55 to 85 percent of their earnings advantage to family background.†

We investigated thirteen demographic characteristics that explained at least two-thirds of the overall impact of family background on both occupational status and earnings. Other unmeasured background characteristics that vary among families with similar demographic profiles seem to account for significant amounts of variance in occupational status and earnings. These unmeasured characteristics differ from most conventional measures of socioeconomic status in that we cannot classify them as "advantages" or "disadvantages" for a wide range of purposes. Rather, they seem to be "advantages" for one purpose (e.g., earnings) but not for

* If one substitutes education (U) for test scores (Q) in figure 3.1, $r_{FU,HY} = 0.409$ in Kalamazoo, 0.085 in Talent, −0.179 in NORC, 0.382 for Taubman's DZ twins, and 0.497 for Taubman's MZ twins. For occupational status (D), the analogous values are 0.587 for Kalamazoo, 0.657 for Talent, and 0.701 for NORC. In the three-variable model, $r_{HU,HY} = 0.286$ in Kalamazoo and − 0.097 in Talent, while $r_{HU,HD} = 0.489$ in Kalamazoo and 0.522 in Talent. In a three-variable model that treats education and occupational status as intervening variables between family background and earnings, $r_{HD,HY} = 0.367$ in Kalamazoo, −0.685 in Talent, and 0.872 in NORC. These estimates have *very* large sampling errors, so there is no necessary inconsistency between samples.

† If we express all values as deviations from the mean, the fraction of the average individual's earnings advantage or disadvantage attributable to family background is the expected ratio of an individual's actual advantage or disadvantage (Y) to the advantage or disadvantage expected on the basis of an individual's background ($\hat{Y}$). If $\hat{Y}$ explains 48 percent of the variance in Y, then $r_{\hat{Y}Y} = S_{Y}/S_{\hat{Y}} = 0.48^{1/2} = 0.69$. The expected value of $\hat{Y}$ for a given value of Y is equal to the regression coefficient of Y in an equation predicting $\hat{Y}$, i.e., $(r_{\hat{Y}Y})(S_{\hat{Y}}/S_{Y}) = 0.48$.

others (e.g., test performance). These family characteristics could be genetic. Alternatively, they could involve subtle differences in the habits and values that parents inculcate in their children. Or they could involve local differences in intellectual or economic opportunity. Or brothers could influence each other on some outcomes but not others.

The fact that demographic background affects cognitive skills and educational attainment explains more than half its effect on occupational status and earnings in recent surveys (PSID and OCG-II). The unmeasured background characteristics that make brothers' earnings more alike than we would expect on the basis of their common demographic background do not seem to exert as much of their influence via test scores and education as demographic traits do. Only a quarter of the overall impact of shared background on earnings is traceable to its impact on test scores and education.

The fact that demographic background affects personality traits and occupational aspirations in high school also explains some of its effect on the economic success of Talent 28-year-olds. We could not assess the contribution of such traits to economic resemblance between brothers.

Southern and farm upbringing depress a man's chances of economic success, largely because they often affect where he lives as an adult. Father's occupation usually affects economic success even with education controlled. This effect is reduced but not eliminated when we eliminate men who work in precisely the same occupation as their father. We cannot say for sure whether it would persist with test scores, personality traits, and aspirations controlled. Race has a large effect on both occupational status and earnings with everything else controlled.

If we define "equal opportunity" as a situation in which sons born into different families have the same chances of success, our data show that America comes nowhere near achieving it. If, for example, an omniscient social scientist were to predict the economic standing of sons from different families, he would find that sons from the most favored fifth of all families had predicted Duncan scores of about 64, while sons from the least favored fifth of all families have predicted scores of about 16.* This is the difference between a social worker or the manager of a hardware store (both 64) and a construction painter (16), a farmer (14), or an auto mechanic (19). If we rerank families in terms of their sons' predicted earnings, the sons of the most advantaged fifth could

---

* If family background explains 48 percent of the true variance, Duncan scores have a mean of 40 with an SD of 25, and the extreme quintiles average 1.4 SD's from the mean, their predicted scores are $40 \pm (1.4)(25)(0.48)^{1/2} = 40 \pm 24$ points. This calculation assumes that the *predicted* values are normally distributed. The *observed* values are skewed, with a long tail to the right.

expect to earn 150 to 186 percent of the national average, while the sons of the least advantaged fifth could expect to earn 56 to 67 percent of the national average.*

But relatively few people seem to care whether sons born into different families have different chances of success. This becomes an issue only if the reasons for such differences are judged "unfair" or "unjust." At least in contemporary America, this means that inequality between families or individuals is acceptable so long as it derives from "merit" of some sort. We doubt that merit runs in families to anything like the extent necessary to reconcile our results with "meritocracy." But our data do not speak to this issue directly.

We have shown, for example, that a nontrivial fraction of background's effect on success derives from the fact that background affects cognitive skills. But it is not clear that cognitive skills are, or should be, synonymous with "merit." A large vocabulary seems to help a man get through school, and getting through school clearly helps him enter a high-status occupation and earn more money than most men do. But this does not prove that a man "needs" a large vocabulary in order to perform competently in most highly paid jobs. Furthermore, even if such jobs *do* demand a large vocabulary, it does not follow that this is either technically inevitable or morally desirable. The same logic applies to educational attainment. Educational credentials are essential for obtaining some lucrative jobs. But it does not follow that educational credentials *ought* to be essential for these jobs. If what we want is competence, for example, we might be better off dispensing with academic credentials and setting up on-the-job selection procedures for identifying incompetents. We cannot draw any firm moral or political conclusions about the legitimacy or inevitability of the processes by which parents enhance or diminish their children's life chances simply by knowing that they depend on test scores or educational attainment.

We cannot even draw clear moral or political conclusions from the fact that family background affects life chances independent of test scores and education. Elitists have traditionally argued, for example, that family background affects economic success partly because those who are "properly" brought up have the "right" attitudes and values for top jobs. Our surveys do not measure these attitudes or values. But even if attitudes and values were to explain the "direct" effects of family background on

---

* These estimates assume that the SD of ln earnings is 0.75, that the top and bottom quintiles average 1.4 SD's from the mean, that family background explains 15 to 35 percent of the variance in ln earnings, and that the distribution of predicted values for ln earnings is normal.

economic success, what would we conclude? The answer would depend on whether the attitudes or values that explained the success of men from privileged backgrounds were ones that we thought essential to maintaining the overall quality of life, or whether they were simply the hallmarks of some clubby snobbery. Without evidence on this, our data constitute neither an indictment nor an endorsement of the status quo.

CHAPTER 4

The Effects of Academic Ability

Men who score well on cognitive tests usually obtain higher-status jobs and earn more money than lower-scoring men.[1] Nonetheless, policy analysts of different political persuasions interpret the relationship of test performance to adult success quite differently.[2] Liberal interpretations stress that low test scores often result from poor schooling. They also stress that the tests themselves measure assimilation of "middle-class" culture and are therefore more difficult for children from working-class or lower-class backgrounds. Conservative interpretations stress that school failure may result from poor heredity, and that one cannot have a technically advanced society without "middle-class" skills and values. Our results do not speak directly to these interpretations, but they do bear on the social and economic significance of test performance. In brief, our findings are as follows:

1. Tests of academic ability predict economic success better than other tests. Tests that do not correlate highly with academic ability correlate poorly both with one another and with later educational and economic success. Tests covering a wide range of academic abilities predict economic success better than tests covering a single ability.

2. Tests given as early as sixth grade appear to predict educational

James Crouse wrote this chapter. Lee Cronbach, Arthur Hoerl, Arthur Jensen, Andrew Kohen, Jon Magoon, Victor Martuza, Robert Stump, and Paul Taubman made critical comments on earlier drafts.

attainment, occupational status, and earnings as well as tests given later. This suggests that it is not cognitive skill per se that affects later success. Rather, the stable motivations and aptitudes that lead to the development of cognitive skills also affect later success. A test's predictive power appears to derive in large part from its relationship to these stable underlying factors.

3. The correlation of test scores with educational attainment, occupational status, and earnings appears to have remained fairly stable in the United States since shortly after the turn of the century. If test scores measure "merit," our data offer no evidence that the U.S. has grown more "meritocratic."

4. The apparent economic benefits of ability exceed the actual benefits. Adolescents with more ability are successful partly because they possess family advantages that affect both their ability and their adult success. Some of these advantages are probably genetic.

5. Adolescents with greater academic ability succeed economically to a considerable degree because they are selectively encouraged to have higher aspirations and to attend school longer. This may be because they learn more in school, because they possess other characteristics that lead to educational success, or because they benefit from irrational prejudices on the part of teachers and employers.

6. Even among men whose background, personality, and schooling do not differ, those with high test scores are worth somewhat more to employers who hire, fire, and pay them. This may be because they are more productive or because employers prefer workers with high scores for noneconomic reasons and are willing to pay modest amounts to indulge this prejudice.

This chapter is divided into six sections. The first section describes the relative importance of different cognitive abilities and skills and describes the tests used in the later sections. Section 2 looks at changes in the relationship between ability and adult success when ability is measured at different ages, while section 3 examines historical trends in the association between test scores and success. Section 4 estimates the effect of adolescent cognitive skills on education with family background controlled and analyzes some of the mechanisms by which cognitive skills affect educational attainment. Sections 5 and 6 investigate the effects of adolescent cognitive skills on occupational status and earnings.

1. THE RELATIVE IMPORTANCE OF DIFFERENT SKILLS

Project Talent is the only national sample that provides data on the relationship of many different adolescent abilities to subsequent education, occupation, and earnings. Talent gave a two-day battery of 60 tests to high school students in 1960. The Talent tests covered a wide range of information and skills. Our data come from 839 male Talent students who were tested in eleventh grade. Talent ascertained their education, occupation, and earnings in September 1972, when they were about 28 years old.

One problem is how to classify these tests. One common approach is to assume that if two tests are highly correlated they measure similar abilities. But this is not necessarily so. Knowledge of Latin and knowledge of geometry have no logical relationship to one another, for example, yet because of the way American high schools are organized, students who have studied Latin are also likely to have studied geometry. As a result, knowledge of the two subjects is likely to be highly correlated, at least among American high school seniors. Rather than grouping tests on the basis of their intercorrelations, we therefore began by grouping them on the basis of what they purported to measure.

We divided the tests into four a priori categories: academic subjects, nonacademic subjects, aptitude and ability, and rote memory. The classification is based on the subject matter of the tests. It is not meant to suggest that performance on the "academic subject matter" tests is independent of ability or rote memory, or even that the "aptitude and ability" tests measure aptitude better than other tests. Nor is the "aptitude and ability" label meant to imply that either of these tests measure stable traits or that a student's performance on these tests is unaffected by the kind of school he attends or by kinds of formal instruction he gets. A test of "reading comprehension," for example, presumably measures a student's ability to read and understand English prose. Most students acquire this ability in school and lose it if they do not use it. To call it an "ability" is not to say that its development depends on factors that are fundamentally different from the factors affecting, say, knowledge of English literature.

Table 4.1 shows correlations between thirty different Talent tests and later success. Information in academic areas predicts success better than information in nonacademic areas, but the differences are not large. The differences disappear almost entirely when the correlations are corrected

TABLE 4.1

Correlations of Thirty Project Talent Tests with Later Education, Occupational Status and Earnings[a]

Type of Test	Talent Designation	Number of Items	Reliability[b]	Observed Correlations				Correlations Corrected for Unreliability of Test (But Not Outcome)			
				Education	Occupation	Hourly Earnings	Ln Hourly Earnings	Education	Occupation	Hourly Earnings	Ln Hourly Earnings
Academic subjects											
English	R-230	113	.921	.471	.423	.164	.173	.491	.441	.171	.180
Literature	R-103	24	.817	.510	.439	.162	.162	.564	.486	.179	.179
Social Studies	R-105	24	.835	.499	.436	.176	.172	.546	.477	.193	.188
Mathematics information	R-106	23	.892	.550	.495	.219	.206	.582	.524	.232	.218
Arithmetic computation	R-410	72	NA	.338	.316	.166	.164	NA	NA	NA	NA
Arithmetic reasoning	R-311	16	.779	.425	.338	.148	.152	.482	.383	.168	.172
Introductory mathematics	R-312	24	.893	.516	.421	.191	.189	.546	.446	.202	.200
Advanced mathematics	R-333	14	.773	.474	.360	.176	.148	.539	.409	.200	.168
Physical science	R-107	18	.848	.454	.364	.131	.123	.493	.395	.142	.134
Biological science	R-108	11	.665	.381	.315	.107	.095	.467	.386	.131	.116
Mean of the ten correlations[c]				.462	.391	.164	.158	.523	.439	.180	.173
Nonacademic subjects											
Music	R-104	13	.749	.459	.399	.180	.183	.530	.461	.208	.211
Art	R-131	12	.678	.381	.357	.182	.185	.463	.434	.221	.225
Home economics	R-114	21	.512	.217	.180	.125	.116	.303	.252	.175	.162
Law	R-132	9	.574	.377	.314	.107	.116	.498	.414	.141	.153
Health	R-133	9	.625	.367	.361	.101	.103	.464	.457	.128	.130
Architecture	R-135	6	.415	.325	.309	.078	.071	.504	.480	.121	.110

	R-number	Reliability[b]	N								
Photography	R-148	.240	3	.235	.199	.107	.114	.582	.406	.218	.233
Theater	R-150	.598	8	.369	.320	.148	.152	.477	.414	.191	.197
Farming	R-113	.635	12	.160	.143	.060	.055	.201	.179	.075	.069
Mean of the nine correlations[c]				.326	.287	.121	.122	.447	.389	.164	.166
Aptitude and ability tests											
Reading comprehension	R-250	.919	48	.489	.405	.178	.176	.510	.422	.186	.184
Vocabulary	R-172	.849	30	.482	.428	.184	.191	.523	.465	.200	.207
Creativity	R-260	.799	20	.352	.311	.130	.117	.394	.348	.145	.131
Mechanical reasoning	R-270	.852	15	.256	.247	.122	.111	.277	.268	.132	.120
Abstract reasoning	R-290	.744	15	.361	.354	.153	.162	.419	.410	.177	.188
Visualization	R-282	.796	16	.268	.256	.125	.119	.300	.287	.140	.133
Table reading	R-420	NA	72	.003	.054	.087	.109	NA	NA	NA	NA
Clerical checking	R-430	NA	74	.051	.054	.092	.107	NA	NA	NA	NA
Object inspection	R-440	NA	40	−.006	.014	.023	.042	NA	NA	NA	NA
Mean of the nine correlations[c]				.251	.236	.122	.126	.404	.367	.163	.161
Measures of rote memory											
Memory for sentences	R-211	.613[d]	16	.095	.171	.040	.037	.121	.091	.051	.047
Memory for words	R-212	.824[d]	24	.282	.228	.103	.107	.311	.251	.113	.118
Mean of the two correlations[c]				.189	.150	.072	.072	.216	.171	.082	.083

[a] Sample includes 839 Talent males with complete data.
[b] Split-half reliabilities reported in table 4-7 of Shaycoft (1967).
[c] Since all correlations were less than 0.60, the means were calculated arithmetically rather than with the Z transformation.
[d] Kuder-Richardson reliabilities (KR-21) reported in table 2-5 of Flanagan, et al. (1964). KR-21 sets a lower bound for reliability, so its use in correcting correlations for unreliability could result in some upward bias in the corrected correlations.

for unreliability.° As we shall see, students who are informed in academic areas tend to be informed in nonacademic ones as well. But the correlation between academic and nonacademic performance is far from perfect.

The aptitude and ability tests differ considerably in their prediction of success. The reading comprehension and vocabulary tests correlate as highly with success as any academic subjects. But skills like table reading, clerical checking, and object inspection, in which schools seem to have little interest, have almost no correlation with success.

Tests like "memory for sentences" and "memory for words" have sometimes been considered measures of an individual's "learning quotient."[3] But rote memory does not predict later success at all well, even after correction for attenuation. This suggests that a student's "learning quotient" is of little economic importance. Insofar as these tests measure rote memory, the small correlations with educational attainment are also hard to reconcile with critiques of schooling that claim schools only reward rote memory.†

In order to get a better sense of the relative importance of the Talent tests, we factor analyzed the tests covering academic subjects and used the first principal component as an index of academic ability. We did the same thing for tests that had a "verbal" label, a "quantitative" label, and a label stressing rote memory. The first principal components account for between 63.0 and 76.4 percent of the variance in these four groups of tests. Part of the variance that is not explained by the first principal components is due to random measurement error. In order to estimate the percent of stable nonerror variance explained by the factors, we corrected the correlations for test reliability and recomputed each factor analysis. When this is done, each of the four factors explains 80 to 95 percent of the stable nonerror variance in the tests used to construct it. The four factors therefore seem to capture the skills measured by these thirty tests quite adequately.‡

The academic ability factor explains 34.2 percent of the variance in

---

° Computed as $r_{q*s} = r_{qs}/(r_{qq})^{1/2}$, where r_{q*s} is the corrected correlation between test performance and success, r_{qs} is the observed correlation, and r_{qq} is the estimate of reliability in table 4.1. We did not attempt to correct the measures of success for measurement error.

† "Memory for sentences" and "memory for words" together explain only 7.2 percent of the variance in Talent respondents' average grades in English, history and social studies, math, science, and foreign language courses.

‡ We corrected the correlations by assuming $r_{q1*q2*} = r_{q1q2}/(r_{q1q1}r_{q2q2})^{1/2}$, where r_{q1*q2*} is the corrected correlation between the two tests, r_{q1q2} is the observed correlation, and r_{q1q1} and r_{q2q2} are the reliabilities for the two tests. The reliabilities were taken from table 4.1. We corrected the diagonal elements of each correlation matrix by inserting the test reliabilities. This obviously introduces some random error, since the reliabilities were not estimated from the present sample. Table A4.1 summarizes our results.

education. In a multiple regression equation that weights the thirty separate tests so as to maximize their capacity to predict education, instead of weighting them on the basis of their correlations with one another, they explain 37.1 percent of the variance in education. This suggests that the first principal component is a fairly good proxy for the separate tests. The analogous figures are 24.0 vs. 27.0 percent for occupational status, 4.4 vs. 4.8 percent for hourly earnings, and 4.2 vs. 5.1 percent for ln hourly earnings. No single test predicts success quite this well. This suggests that the tests typically used in survey research somewhat underestimate the relationship between test performance and adult status.

The academic ability factor predicts men's education, occupation, and earnings better than do any of the other tests, factors, or composites. Verbal and quantitative factors are next in importance. There is no striking evidence that one is more important than the other.[4] Rote-memory tests are again the least important predictors of later success. Talent also computed a priori academic, verbal, and quantitative composites. The correlations of these composites with success are similar to the correlations of the analogous factors with success.

The academic, verbal, and quantitative factors have an average intercorrelation of 0.915. Rote memory correlates poorly with these abilities and with later success. In general, tests that do not correlate well with each other do not predict economic success very well. Such tests also measure traits in which schools take little formal interest.[5] These results suggest that academic, verbal, and quantitative ability predict educational and economic success better than other kinds of information or cognitive skills. Academic, verbal, and quantitative skills are highly correlated. Common sense suggests, however, that they are quite different. Having a large vocabulary is different from being able to solve quadratic equations. The three kinds of tests presumably correlate because they have common causes. They also seem to have similar effects, at least on economic success. For studies of stratification, then, they are interchangeable.

Our findings suggest that academic ability is largely but not entirely one-dimensional, at least for the purpose of predicting life chances. "Nonacademic" tests seem to predict success only insofar as they correlate with academic tests. This does not mean that all academic skills are the same, or that they all correlate equally well with all outcomes that one might conceivably measure. It means only that their effects on socioeconomic status are similar. This is probably because they share common causes.

We also investigated nonlinearities in the relationship of test scores to success. We regressed education, occupation, hourly earnings, and ln hourly earnings on each of the thirty tests in table 4.1 and then added a test score^2 term to each regression. The test score^2 term had different signs with different tests and outcomes. It only increased R^2 by more than 0.02 for "table reading" and "clerical checking." Unlike the other twenty-eight tests, these two tests had seriously skewed distributions. We conclude that test scores' nonlinear effects on life chances are not important so long as the original scores are more or less symmetrically distributed. This conclusion could be wrong if the test score distributions are truncated and mask nonlinearities at the very top or bottom of the ability distribution. Since our Talent sample includes only those who reached eleventh grade, it cannot tell us much about the effects of very low scores. Eliminating such men led us to expect some positive skew in the Talent distributions. However, about two-thirds of the tests show both negative skewness and kurtosis. The degree of nonnormality is seldom large, although it reaches statistical significance in some instances.

The fact that two-thirds of the Talent tests have negatively skewed distributions suggests that ceiling effects may have truncated the upper end of some distributions. Very few individuals got every item right, however. This suggests that ceiling effects were not produced by a ceiling on the number of items students could possibly get correct. Rather, the tests must have contained enough very difficult items to impose an artificial ceiling above which even the most clever students seldom rose. Jencks and Brown (1975) reached a similar conclusion from their examination of longitudinal changes between ninth and twelfth grade for the Talent tests.

Deviations from normality therefore do not appear to be substantial for most Talent tests and probably can be traced to the joint effects of sample restrictions and ceiling effects. But because the range of all distributions is restricted at the lower end, and some may be restricted at the upper end, the conclusion that nonlinearities are small must be tentative.

In the analyses that follow we will use data from nine longitudinal surveys to look at the effects of test performance. Table 4.2 describes the surveys and some of their characteristics. The surveys used seven tests, all but one of which were administered to groups rather than individually. Five were administered to adolescents. Adolescents taking a given test were all enrolled in the same grade. Two of the tests were administered to adults with different amounts of formal education. The tests are as follows.

1. *The Project Talent Academic Composite.* This measure is the unequally weighted sum of a respondent's correct answers on tests of "vocabulary," "reading comprehension," "mathematics," "English," "abstract reasoning," and "creativity." Talent based its weighting scheme on a priori reasoning, not factor analysis, and this lowered the composite's predictive power slightly.[6] It would have been better to use the principal component of the academic ability tests, but this was not available when we initiated the analyses that follow. Since the a priori composite and the principal component correlate 0.95, the difference is minor. Scores on the Academic Composite have a roughly normal distribution. We rescaled them to a mean of 100 and a standard deviation of 15 for those who reached eleventh grade. The Talent staff estimates the reliability of this composite as greater than 0.97.

2. *The Henmon–Nelson Test of Mental Ability.* This test was given to Wisconsin eleventh graders in Sewell and Hauser's sample. The scores are standardized to a mean of 100 and a standard deviation of 15 for all Wisconsin high school juniors. Hauser estimates the reliability of this test to be between 0.92 and 0.95.[7]

3. *The EEO Test of Academic Aptitude.* This twenty-item test gives approximately equal weight to vocabulary and arithmetic reasoning. The test was designed for maximum discrimination between the sixth and eighth deciles of an unselected twelfth-grade population. Consequently, the mean was only 7.81 for the tenth graders in the EEO sample. Stice and Ekstrom (1964:10) estimate the reliability at 0.82 for a twelfth-grade sample. Unlike Alexander, Eckland, and Griffin (1975), we standardized the test to a mean of 100 and standard deviation of 15.

4. *The Terman or Otis Intelligence Test.* One or the other of these tests is available for all Kalamazoo sixth graders. They are primarily verbal rather than quantitative in character, and they consist of multiple-choice items. The two tests were not standardized to the same mean and variance. Olneck equalized the means, but not the variances, in his Kalamazoo sample. The two tests' correlations with other variables are similar. Their reported reliabilities range from 0.85 to 0.97. Both tests correlated 0.85 with overall scores on the Metropolitan Achievement Test in tenth grade in the Kalamazoo sample (Olneck, 1976).

5. *The Modified Hallgren Group Intelligence Test.* This is a Swedish test. Fagerlind describes it as a standardized mental ability test. It was designed especially for the Malmo study.

TABLE 4.2

Characteristics of Longitudinal Surveys that Collected Test Scores

	Talent 28- to 29- Year-Olds	Talent 22- to 23- Year-Old Identical Twins	Talent 28- to 29- Year-Old Brothers	Wisconsin
References	Final Report, Appendix H[a]	Jencks and Brown (1977)[b]	Final Report, Appendix K[c]	Sewell and Hauser (1975)[d]
Survey organization	Talent	Talent	Talent	U. of Wisconsin plus Social Security Administration
Initial survey year	1960	1960	1960	1957
Age when tested	grade 11	grades 9-12	grades 11-12	grade 11
Final survey year	1972	1965-68	1972	1967
Final age	28-29	22-23	28-29	24-28[j]
Test	Academic Composite	Academic Composite	Academic Composite	Henmon-Nelson
Year of test	1960	1960	1960	1956
Sample size	839	332	198	1,789

Note: All nonadult samples restricted to individuals who reached the grade shown in row 4. Twin and sibling samples restricted to those with a twin or sibling who also reached this grade. All samples restricted to those with complete data.

[a]Talent complete data sample (see tables A2.1 and A2.9).
[b]Includes only pairs who were *both* enrolled in grades 9-12 of a Talent school. Includes 180 females.
[c]Includes only pairs who were both enrolled in grades 11 or 12 of a Talent school (see tables A2.1 and A2.10).
[d]Male Wisconsin high school graduates in 1957 with nonfarm background, not enrolled in school and employed in civilian labor force in 1964, with nonzero earnings 1965-67.

6. *The PSID Sentence Completion Test.* SRC developed this test from the Lorge–Thorndike "intelligence" test. It correlates 0.4 to 0.6 with other IQ tests. It is the only one of our tests administered individually, but this advantage is offset by the fact that the interviewers who administered it had no psychometric training. Each item is a sentence with a missing word. The respondent is asked which of five words that might complete the sentence is "best, truest, most sensible." Many items are ambiguous. We dichotomized responses to each item into the one SRC deemed "correct" and the four SRC deemed "incorrect." "Correct" responses to some items predict economic success better than "correct" responses to others. But the differences between items are not statistically significant. Ambiguous items predict educational attainment and eco-

EEO	Kalamazoo	Malmo	Veterans	PSID
Alexander, Eckland, and Griffin (1975)[e]	Final Report, Appendix I[f]	Fagerlind (1975)[g]	Final Report, Appendix G[h]	Final Report, Appendix D[i]
ETS, IRSS	Olneck	National Archives of Sweden	CPS	SRC
1955	1928-52	1938	1964	1971
grade 10	grade 6	grade 3	19-25	25-64
1970	1974	1971	1964	1972
30-31	35-57	42	30-34	25-64
Academic	Terman/	Modified Halgran	AFQT	Sentence Com-
Aptitude	Otis	Group Intelligence Test		pletion Test
1955	1928-52	1938	1947-62	1972
538	692	707	803	1,774

[e]Restricted to men with nonfarm backgrounds in predominantly white institutions.
[f]Kalamazoo complete data sample (see tables A2.1 and A2.11).
[g]Restricted to men from Malmo, Sweden.
[h]Veterans complete data sample (see tables A2.1 and A2.7).
[i]PSID complete data sample (see tables A2.1 and A2.5). Occupation data from 1971 wave. Earnings from 1972 wave, describing 1971 earnings. Test score from 1972 wave. Age as of 1972.
[j]Wisconsin respondents reported their occupation seven years after high school graduation (roughly age 24). Their earnings were ascertained from Social Security records eight, nine, and ten years after graduation. We look exclusively at tenth-year earnings.

nomic success at least as well as unambiguous ones. We therefore decided to weight all 13 items equally and treat the total number of "correct" answers as a score.

We converted raw scores on this test to a mean of 100 and a standard deviation of 15. The distribution of these scores is severely skewed to the left, making its effects nonlinear on occupation and earnings, though not on ln earnings (*Final Report*, Appendix D).

7. *The Armed Forces Qualification Test (AFQT)*. This test is a lineal descendent of the Army General Classification Test used during World War II and Army Alpha used during World War I. It is supposed to measure a respondent's capacity to carry out the tasks normally required of an enlisted man. It is a multiple-choice, paper-and-pencil test, usu-

ally administered to large groups under less than ideal conditions. Prior to 1953, the AFQT consisted of thirty vocabulary items, thirty mathematical items, and thirty spatial-relations items. These items were very similar to those used in other group tests that purport to measure "academic aptitude" or "intelligence." From 1953 on, the AFQT included twenty-five items from each of the three original categories plus twenty-five items on the use of tools. The tool items appear to have lowered the correlation between AFQT score and educational attainment, while raising the correlation between AFQT score and efficiency ratings within the military (*Final Report*, Appendix G).

Our data tape did not include separate scores for the four AFQT subtests. Neither did it include the exact number of right or wrong answers. All we had were percentile scores, grouped in quite broad intervals. The percentile scores are relative to men mobilized in 1944. We rescaled these percentile ranks to a population mean of 100 and a standard deviation of 15, on the assumption that the underlying distribution was normal. When scaled in this way, the effects of test performance on economic success are essentially linear.

We do not know how strongly these seven tests correlate with one another. Other reliable tests of this kind typically correlate at the 0.65 to 0.85 level. Our analyses of the Talent tests show that if one extracts the first principal component from a battery of heterogeneous tests, this principal component explains almost as much of the variance in economic success as the separate tests in a multiple regression. It therefore seems reasonable to proceed on the assumption that the different tests all correlate with economic success largely because they correlate with the same underlying trait or traits, but that the different tests may not all correlate equally well with these underlying traits.

2. AGE OF TESTING

One might expect tests given close to school completion to predict subsequent success better than tests given earlier in life, but available evidence offers only limited support for this hypothesis. Jencks and Brown (1975) report, for example, that when Talent followed up a sample of students tested in ninth grade and gave them the same tests again in twelfth grade, students' twelfth-grade scores did not predict their educational attainment five years later any more accurately than did their ninth-grade scores. This same pattern holds in the smaller Fels Institute sample, which was tested repeatedly from age 3 through 18. IQ scores obtained between the ages of 3 and 6 correlated only 0.1 to 0.2 with eventual educational attainment, while IQ scores obtained between the ages of 8 and 16 correlated 0.45 to 0.50 with eventual attainment. There was no clear trend between the ages of 8 and 16, but education correlated more highly with IQ scores obtained at age 18 than with IQ scores obtained between 8 and 16. This may be because some respondents left school before the age of 18. The correlation between educational attainment and IQ at 18 may, in other words, reflect the fact that educational attainment can affect IQ at 18 as well as vice versa.[8]

Our samples also suggest that tests given as early as sixth grade have the same predictive validity as tests given later. Sixth-grade Terman or Otis scores correlate 0.541 with education for Olneck's 150 Kalamazoo men born 1934–38. Eleventh-grade Academic Composite correlates 0.561 with education for Talent men born around 1944. Education five years after high school correlated 0.567 with Talent's Academic Composite for ninth graders, 0.517 for tenth graders, 0.520 for eleventh graders, and 0.527 for twelfth graders.

The fact that tests given after sixth grade predict education no better than sixth-grade tests suggests that while abilities may develop at different rates in different individuals, the stable aptitudes measured by these tests are the ones that affect educational attainment. Apparently, the tests used in these surveys measure such stable aptitudes as well in the sixth grade as they do in the twelfth grade.

Test scores in third grade also appear to predict an individual's occupational status about as well as tests given later in school.[9] The same holds for earnings.[10] These findings are what we would expect if ability influenced men's occupations and earnings in large part by influencing their education.

Adult vs. Adolescent Scores. It is not obvious whether adult tests should predict economic success better or worse than adolescent tests. Correlations between adolescent and adult test scores are typically at least 0.80 (cf. Bloom, 1964). These correlations suggest that adult success should show much the same relationship to adult tests as to adolescent tests. However, measures of adult ability incorporate not only the effects of early ability but the effects of unequal schooling. Thus we might expect adult success to correlate higher with adult tests than with earlier tests. But the tests used to measure ability before and after school completion are seldom alike. Even when they have the same content, the tests may measure different things for adolescents and adults. Adolescents who can be located as adults may also have environments which have changed less than those of adolescents who cannot be located, so their adult success may be more predictable from early tests than is the case for those who could not be located.

We have only one survey that measures adolescent ability, adult ability, and adult economic success for the same individuals, and it was conducted in Malmo, Sweden. The Malmo study includes a measure of ability at age 10, a military test of ability at age 20 (when almost all respondents had finished their schooling), and measures of occupational status and earnings at the ages of 25, 30, 35, 40, and 43. The two tests correlated 0.745, which is lower than in most American studies of representative samples. Occupational status had an average correlation of 0.351 with test scores at age 10 and 0.486 with test scores at age 20. For income, the correlations averaged 0.274 vs. 0.333. The adult test thus had somewhat higher correlations with both occupation and income than did the earlier test. Furthermore, Fagerlind (1975) reports that those who attended a university had some of their formal education after "adult" ability was measured. His data may therefore slightly understate the difference between adolescent and adult tests. On the other hand, his test for 10-year-olds may simply have been less reliable than that for 20-year-olds.

No American studies that have both adolescent and adult test scores also follow up men's economic success. There are, however, several American surveys that measure *only* adult scores. The Veteran's survey includes AFQT scores for men tested between the ages of 19 and 25 who were followed up between the ages of 30 and 34. Some of these men had additional schooling after their military service. The PSID includes sentence-completion scores for men aged 25 to 64 who were no longer in school. The Malmo results suggest that these posteducational tests should explain more of the variance in economic success than do adolescent tests from surveys like Talent and Kalamazoo. No such pattern emerges, but this may be because of differences in sample coverage and test reliability.* The PSID sentence-completion test is far less reliable than the other three tests. The education distribution has been artificially truncated in the Veterans and Talent samples, which is likely to lower almost all correlations in those samples. The Talent respondents are also younger than the respondents in other samples, which usually

---

* When we use test score to predict occupational status, eta² is 0.143 for Veterans, 0.128 for PSID, 0.213 for Talent, and 0.154 for Kalamazoo. The bivariate regression coefficient is 0.62 for Veterans, 0.50 for PSID, 0.77 for Talent, and 0.69 for Kalamazoo. When we predict earnings, eta² is 0.081 for Veterans, 0.106 for PSID, 0.026 for Talent, and 0.111 for Kalamazoo.

lowers correlations.* Thus while adult tests do not seem to predict occupational status or earnings any better than adolescent tests do in our samples, adult tests may still have larger effects when one retests the same individuals.

3. HISTORICAL CHANGES

Education. The mean level of educational attainment has increased steadily in the United States since the turn of the century, but very little is known about whether educational attainment has become more dependent on test scores in elementary or secondary school. This is somewhat surprising in light of claims that schools are becoming more meritocratic, less meritocratic, or not changing. The topic has never been investigated in a national survey, but some local data exist.

The Kalamazoo, Michigan, public school system has preserved the results of its ability-testing program since 1928. Olneck (1976, 1977) has described these data in detail. The correlation between sixth-grade test scores and educational attainment does not appear to have changed much since the late 1920s for men raised in Kalamazoo. We examined correlations between sixth-grade Terman or Otis scores and educational attainment in cohorts of Kalamazoo men born in 1919–23, 1923–28, 1929–33, and 1934–38. There were about two hundred men in each cohort. The correlations between test scores and years of education were 0.555, 0.472, 0.616, and 0.541. These changes are not significant and do not move in any consistent direction. The lowest correlation is for men who finished high school between 1940 and 1945, the highest for men who finished between 1946 and 1950.†

* In addition, the occupation metric in PSID and the earnings metric in Talent differ from other samples. It is not clear what effect, if any, these differences have on correlations.

† The standard deviation of education has decreased since 1919 in the United States. It was smaller in Kalamazoo than in the United States in 1919, but it has not fallen much in Kalamazoo since 1919. Thus, educational attainment has become more homogeneous since 1919 in the United States, but has been relatively homogeneous all along in Kalamazoo.

The standard deviations of education in Kalamazoo are 2.54, 2.55, 3.05, and 2.77 for the 1919–23, 1923–28, 1929–33, and 1934–38 cohorts. Roughly corresponding Census values estimated by Jencks, et al. (1972) are 3.30, 3.21, 3.21, and 2.92. The Kalamazoo test score standard deviations are 14.36, 16.69, 17.01, and 13.66. The unstandardized coefficients are 0.0983, 0.0720, 0.1098, and 0.1096. The unstandardized

Taubman and Wales (1972) argue that the relationship of test scores to college entrance was higher in the 1950s than in earlier decades. This might be because test scores had less effect on whether an individual finished high school in the 1950s, forcing college admissions offices to stress test scores more in order to retain their traditional level of selectivity. Alternatively, educators at all levels may have put more emphasis on test scores in the 1950s than before. Taken in isolation, their data are inconclusive.[11]

As a further check on whether the test score–education correlation has changed, we compared Benson's (1942) sample of Minneapolis sixth graders who took the Haggerty Intelligence Examination in 1923 with the Talent eleventh graders tested in 1960. Benson reports a correlation of 0.57, which Duncan, Featherman, and Duncan (1972) reestimate at 0.542. The Talent correlation between Academic Composite and education reported earlier is 0.561. While these tests may differ in reliability, the correlations are quite similar.

All in all, there is no evidence that the correlation between elementary and secondary school test scores and eventual educational attainment changed for men born after World War I. This suggests that schools have put about the same weight on the skills these tests measure throughout the twentieth century. No data seem to exist on whether the correlation of the test performance with educational plans is changing. The unstandardized regression coefficient of elementary school test scores is probably declining, simply because the variance of educational attainment is declining. This decline in the variance of educational attainment need not, however, change the *relative* importance of test scores in determining attainment.

Occupational Status. When we correlated sixth-grade Terman or Otis IQ's with first occupation for the four cohorts of Kalamazoo men who were born between 1919–23, 1923–28, 1929–33, and 1934–38, the correlations were 0.455, 0.371, 0.523, and 0.429. The unstandardized coef-

---

coefficients rise slightly among younger men, although the differences are not significant. The education standard deviations for the older Kalamazoo cohorts are more restricted compared to the Census. This implies that the Kalamazoo data may underestimate the national correlation more for the older cohorts than for the younger cohorts. We have no evidence on the representativeness of the Kalamazoo test score standard deviations. We corrected the correlations using the Census standard deviations, assuming that:

$$r_{TE} = [r_{te}(s_E/s_e)] / [1 - r^2_{te} + r^2_{te}(s_E/s_e)^2]^{\frac{1}{2}}$$

where r_{TE} and r_{te} are the corrected and observed correlations and s_E and s_e are the Census and Kalamazoo standard deviations (McNemar, 1962: 144). The corrected correlations are 0.595, 0.526, 0.623, and 0.552. This suggests that there was little change in the relationship between test scores and education for men born between 1919–38.

ficients were 0.706, 0.504, 0.775, and 0.825. These coefficients do not differ significantly. Nor is there a consistent trend over time.*

We also correlated 1972 test scores with first occupation for PSID respondents born in 1907 to 1916, 1917 to 1926, 1927 to 1936, and 1937 to 1946. These correlations were 0.340, 0.343, 0.261, and 0.256, suggesting that test scores exerted more impact on initial status before World War II than afterward. The trend is not statistically significant, however, and the data may be contaminated if occupational status affected 1972 test scores as well as the other way around.

Taken together, the Kalamazoo and PSID data offer little support for the claim that occupational selection has become more dependent on the skills measured by standardized tests over the past half century. Unfortunately, no reliable data are available for earlier eras. Indeed, even the data for the past half century are far from conclusive, so our conclusion about trends in occupational selection must be provisional.

Earnings. Despite the importance of tests in American society, there has never been a historical study of the relationship between adolescent test scores and adult earnings. Our data show only that the correlation does not vary systematically with age, at least after men pass the age of 35. The correlations between sixth-grade IQ scores and ln earnings in adulthood for cohorts of Kalamazoo men aged 35–39, 40–44, 45–50, and 50–54 were 0.337, 0.455, 0.339, and 0.324. The unstandardized coefficients show the same pattern. The coefficients do not differ significantly from one another.

4. EFFECTS OF ADOLESCENT ACADEMIC ABILITY ON EDUCATIONAL ATTAINMENT

This section looks at the effects of academic competence prior to high school completion on the amount of education men get. We will try to determine how much of the correlation between test scores and

---

* We also correlated these same Kalamazoo men's IQ scores with their occupational status in 1973. The correlations were 0.342, 0.402, 0.488, and 0.491 for the four birth cohorts listed in the text. The unstandardized regression coefficients were 0.545, 0.546, 0.678, and 0.837. Test scores thus had appreciably less impact on current than on first occupation among men born between 1919 and 1923. (Most of these men probably entered the labor force before 1943, then served in the military, and then returned to civilian life.) Because of the difference between first and current occupations in the oldest Kalamazoo cohort, there is a consistent increase in the apparent effect of test scores on current occupation in more recent Kalamazoo cohorts. The trend is not statistically significant, however, and is not found in PSID.

TABLE 4.3

Regressions of Education on Adolescent Test Score Controlling Selected Background Variables[a]

Sample (year of test)	NONE	WHITE	POPED	POPOC	MOMED	PARINC	HEDAB	SIBS	POPED * SIBS	POPOC * TEST	ALL BKG	B	Beta	% Reduction in Test-Score Coefficient[k]	R²
Talent Representative (1960) N = 839	X											.094	.561	–	.314
			X	X	X	X		X				.079	.475	15.3	.360
		X	X	X	X	X	X					.081	.485	13.5	.366
			X	X	X	X	X	X	X			.082	.491	12.3	.379
Talent Brothers (1960) N = 198	X											.115	.632	–	.399
			X	X				X				.096	.528	16.5	.468
											X	.078	.431	31.8	NA
Talent MZ Twins (1960) N = 332	X											.128	.621	–	.385
											X	.053	.251	58.6	NA
Kalamazoo Brothers (1928-52) N = 692	X											.103	.576	–	.332
			X	X				X				.081	.456	21.4	.443
											X	.059	.331	42.7	NA
Wisconsin (1956)[b] N = 1,789	X											.053	.446	–	.199
			X	X	X	X						.043	.367	17.7	.277
EEO (1955)[c] N = 538	X											.085	.480	–	.230
			X	X	X	X[d]						.067	.378	21.1	.309
Malmo (1938) N = 707	X												.403[f]	–	.162
			X	X[e]	X			X		X			.257[g]	36.2	.410
Inequality	X												.580[h]	–	.336
			X	X									.452[h]	22.1	.430
											X		.415[i]	28.4	.630
											X		.227[j]	60.9	.564

All coefficients are more than twice their standard error.

aPOPED = father's education; POPOC = father's occupation; MOMED = mother's education; PARINC = parent's income; HEDAB = head absent; SIBS = siblings; ALL BKG = background controlled using regressions of sibling differences, i.e. regressing ΔU on ΔQ, where ΔQ is the difference between two brothers' test scores and ΔU is the difference between their educational attainments. Coefficients are standardized using s_Q and s_U, not $s_{\Delta Q}$ or $s_{\Delta U}$.

bFrom Sewell and Hauser (1975), table 4-3.

cKarl Alexander kindly supplied the correlations and standard deviations, from which we computed the full equations for the model in Alexander, Eckland, and Griffin (1975).

dThirteen-item index of possessions in respondent's household when he was in high school.

eFour-category scale based on father's occupation, 1973 family income, number of children at home, and appearances on the social welfare register of the Malmo schools.

fEducation had only four categories: $ED < 8$, $8 \leq ED \leq 10$, $11 \leq ED \leq 14$, $ED \geq 15$. Data available for 72 percent of population. Education correlated 0.814 with level of education defined as $type$ of schooling completed.

gFagerlind's variables were all defined to have a mean of 0. Father's occupation $\times$ test score had a mean of 0.257. The test-score coefficient when father's occupation is at the mean is 0.174. The test-score coefficient had a standardized coefficient of 0.174. The test-

hJencks et al. (1972), figure B-2, which is corrected for measurement error.

iUpper bound estimate from Jencks et al. (1972), figure B-7, which is corrected for measurement error.

jLower bound estimate from Jencks et al. (1972), figure B-7.

kThe percentage reductions in this and later tables in this chapter were calculated from raw coefficients with five significant digits. They differ slightly from the values one would obtain using the rounded coefficients in this table.

education is due to their both being affected by family background. We will also try to show in some detail *how* ability exerts its effects.

High-scoring individuals have greater educational opportunities than low scorers. Table 4.3 compares regression results from eight surveys. A fifteen-point test-score advantage in elementary or secondary school is associated with an educational advantage in adulthood of 0.8 to 1.9 years in these surveys, with the population value being about 1.4 years in the 1960s.*

Academic ability predicts educational attainment at least as well as measured socioeconomic background in the United States. Yet test scores alone never explain more than 40 percent of the variance in educational attainment (see tables 4.3 and A4.2).[12] This means that the standard deviation of educational attainment among those who have the same test scores averages at least 77 percent of the standard deviation for the sample as a whole. Bowles and Gintis (1976) argue that the educational system fosters and reinforces the belief that economic success depends essentially upon the possession of technical and cognitive skills. Yet educational inequality among those with the same test scores is three-quarters that for the population as a whole.

Test scores correlate with education partly because both depend on family background. The different surveys measured different background characteristics, so controlling these characteristics does not always have the same effect. Table 4.3 shows, however, that only 12 to 21 percent of the bivariate relationship between test scores and education in the United States results from higher-scoring individuals coming from families with demographic advantages.

No survey can measure all of the family characteristics that affect test scores and education. We can control family background more fully by analyzing pairs of brothers. Regressing the educational difference between brothers on the test-score difference yields test-score coefficients unbiased by factors that are uniform for the whole family. Table 4.3 suggests that unmeasured family characteristics explain another 15 to 20 percent of the correlation between test scores and education. These results imply that 57 to 68 percent of the observed correlation between test scores and education is independent of family background.†

* The estimate of 1.4 years is based on the Talent representative sample. The less representative twin and sibling surveys show stronger relationships between test scores and schooling. The weakest relationship, shown by the Wisconsin survey, probably results in part from the fact that Sewell and Hauser excluded from their sample both men who were still in school seven years after high school and men who did not reach twelfth grade.

† Jencks et al. (1972) estimated the range from 39 to 72 percent (see last two lines of table 4.3).

What are the unmeasured family characteristics that affect test scores and education? Father's education, father's occupation, and number of siblings explain about 30 percent of the variance in the weighted sum of all the shared family characteristics that affect a man's test scores and about 47 percent of the variance in the weighted sum of all the shared family characteristics that affect his education after test scores are controlled in the Talent and Kalamazoo Brothers surveys.* Thus, a family's effects on its children's ability and education vary considerably, even within groups that have similar demographic advantages.

One possible explanation is that the unmeasured characteristics are genetic, since siblings share roughly half the genes that ordinarily vary from one individual to another. Unfortunately, there is at present no way to identify most of the genes that affect test scores and education. This means we cannot identify individuals who are alike only on relevant genes. We can, of course, study identical twins, who have *all* their genes in common, but such twins almost always grow up in the same families. Separating the genetic and nongenetic components of the test score–education relationship is therefore difficult.[13]

In theory, regressing the educational difference between pairs of MZ twins on the test-score difference between the same pair of twins provides a coefficient that cannot be biased by either genes or other common background characteristics. The Talent 22- to 23-year-old sample in table 4.3 is the only one with both education and an early test score for MZ twins. Comparison of regressions from this sample with regressions from the Talent sample of 28- to 29-year-old siblings implies that genes make an important contribution to the relationship of test scores to education.

Controlling all genes and common environment reduces the coefficient of test scores from 0.128 to 0.053. This 59 percent reduction for MZ twins is considerably higher than the 32 percent reduction for Talent Brothers, for whom we can control common environment, but only half the relevant genes. It is also higher than the 43 percent reduction for Kalamazoo Brothers. If we take the Talent MZ twin results at face value, they suggest that controlling the half of all genes that siblings do not have in common reduces the effect of test score on education by $59 - 32 = 27$ percent. Controlling all genes must therefore reduce the

---

* Father's education, father's occupation, and siblings have a multiple correlation of 0.558 with the weighted sum of all family characteristics that brothers share that affect test scores in Talent. The multiple correlation is 0.702 with the weighted sum of shared family characteristics that affect education after test scores are controlled in Talent. The corresponding values are 0.532 and 0.664 in the Kalamazoo Brothers sample. Chapter 2 of the *Final Report* presents the models in more detail.

coefficient by 54 percent. Controlling those aspects of twins or siblings' common environment that act independently of genes can only reduce the test-score coefficient by $59 - 54 = 5$ percent. This suggests that 54 percent of the effect of test performance on education arises because tests are proxies for "native ability," 5 percent arises because they are proxies for home environment, and 41 percent arises because they are proxies for other traits that vary even when individuals have the same genes and the same parents (e.g., interest in schoolwork).

These inferences must, however, be treated with extreme caution. After comparing these same MZ twins to a small sample of DZ twins (instead of siblings), Jencks and Brown (1977) concluded that only a small fraction of the relationship between tests and educational attainment arose because the same genes affect test scores and education. If this were true, parents who provided their offspring with a genotypic advantage for test scores would not necessarily provide their offspring with a genotypic advantage for education. Given the small samples and large number of assumptions required to derive these results, they should all be treated with special caution. This is particularly true because we cannot say *how* genotype affects test scores or educational attainment. The Talent tests were given during high school. Genotype could easily affect both tests and education by affecting a child's home or school environment. Both sex and skin color probably work this way to some extent.

We turn now to explaining *how* ability exercises its influence on an individual's schooling. Higher-scoring individuals are treated differently than lower-scoring individuals, especially in school. Adolescents with high scores are more likely to be in a college curriculum, more likely to receive high grades, more likely to report that their parents want them to attend college, more likely to say their friends plan to attend college, more likely to discuss college with teachers, and more likely to have ambitious educational and occupational plans. It is not possible to decompose the effects of test scores on educational attainment into components uniquely associated with each of these consequences, since their causal order is unknown. But it is possible to estimate the maximum amount that ability could affect educational attainment by influencing any one of these characteristics. Table 4.4 presents the relevant regression results from three surveys.

The skills measured by test scores influence educational attainment partly because they affect a student's success in high school. Controlling high school grades reduces the coefficient for test scores 14 percent below its level with only background controlled in the Talent Survey. The

Regressions of Education on Adolescent Test Score Controlling Selected Intervening Variables

Sample (year of test)	Variables Controlled[a]										Coefficient of Test Score		% Reduction in Test-Score Coefficient	R^2
	MEASURED BKG[d]	GRADES	T-INFLUENCE	P-INFLUENCE	F-PLANS	EDPLANS	OCPLANS	EARNPLANS	HS CURRICULUM	PERSONALITY	B	Beta		
Talent Representative (1960) N = 839	X										.081	.485	—	.366
	X	X									.067	.419	13.6	.391
	X		X	X							.067	.418	13.8	.404
	X				X						.056	.358	26.2	.447
	X					X					.073	.436	10.0	.392
	X						X				.081	.485	.0	.368
	X							X			.064	.385	20.6	.395
	X								X		.079	.470	3.2	.391
	X	X	X	X	X	X	X	X		X	.053	.316	34.8	.463
	X	X	X	X	X	X	X	X	X	X	.051	.307	36.8	.476
Wisconsin (1957) N = 1,789	X										.043	.367	—	.277
	X	X[b]									.019	.164	55.2	.371
	X		X	X							.026	.221	39.7	.419
	X				X	X					.021	.181	50.6	.483
	X						X	X			.025	.208	43.4	.418
	X	X[b]	X	X	X	X	X	X			.007	.053	84.8	.541
EEO (1955) N = 538	X										.067	.378	—	.309
	X	X[c]									.041	.233	38.4	.396
	X		X	X							.058	.329	13.0	.378
	X				X	X					.057	.320	15.3	.388
	X						X				.059	.334	11.7	.351
	X	X[c]	X	X	X	X	X				.037	.211	44.3	.454

All coefficients are more than twice their standard error.

[a] PERSONALITY = self-ratings of sociability (R-601), social sensitivity (R-602), impulsiveness (R-603), vigor (R-604), calmness (R-605), tidiness (R-606), culture (R-607), leadership (R-608), self-confidence (R-609), and mature personality (R-610); HS CURRICULUM = high school curriculum; GRADES = grades; T-INFLUENCE = teacher's influence on education; P-INFLUENCE = parent's influence on education; F-PLANS = friend's educational plans; EDPLANS = educational plans; OCPLANS = occupational plans; EARNPLANS = earning plans; MEASURED BKG = father's education, father's occupation, mother's education, parental income.

[b] Rank in high school class obtained from high school records, expressed as a percentile, and transformed to produce an approximately normal distribution.

[c] Self-reported sophomore class standing in terms of quartile rank.

[d] Father's education, father's occupation, mother's education, family income.

reduction is 38 percent in the EEO and 55 percent in Wisconsin.* These estimates of how much ability affects education by affecting grades are inflated to the extent that grades depend on other high school characteristics (like curriculum assignment) that themselves affect education.

Individuals with high test scores report more discussions with teachers, more parental encouragement, and higher aspirations among their peers than low-scoring individuals. This may be partly because high-scoring individuals seek out persons who will provide encouragement, but it may also be partly because high-scoring individuals receive more encouragement than low-scoring individuals from the same people, or at least feel that they receive more such encouragement. Our estimates suggest that no more than 40 percent of the test-score effect, and perhaps as little as 13 percent, can be explained by differences in the encouragement high school students feel they get from parents, teachers, and friends.

The test-score effect among Wisconsin seniors, 26 percent for Talent juniors, and 15 percent for EEO sophomores. Students' plans conform to their actual attainment more closely as they approach high school graduation. This is probably partly due to the selective encouragement they receive.† As a result, while tenth grade educational plans explain only 15 percent of test score's effect on actual attainment in EEO, eleventh grade plans explain 26 percent of the effect in Talent, and twelfth grade plans explain 51 percent of the Wisconsin sample.

About 21 percent of the effect of test scores depends on the fact that the skills measured by test scores affect curriculum placement in the Talent sample.[14] This estimate is too high if curriculum placement also affects test scores, but most evidence suggests that it does not.[15] It is also too high if encouragement, plans, and aspirations affect curriculum placement.

Self-assessed personality characteristics explain little of the effect of

* The greater importance of grades in the Wisconsin sample could be due partly to the fact that Wisconsin grades are school reports from twelfth grade, while Talent and EEO have self-reports from the middle of eleventh and tenth grades respectively. Grades were also measured by class standing in Wisconsin and EEO, whereas Talent asked for letter grades.

† After controlling for prior variables, the standardized coefficient for educational plans is 0.160 for EEO sophomores, 0.230 for Talent juniors, and 0.331 for Wisconsin seniors. These coefficients suggest that plans for higher education become better predictors of actual attainment as men approach the transition from high school to college. This correlation probably approaches 1.00 as the time of decision approaches. Occupational plans are somewhat less important. Controlling for prior variables, the standardized coefficients are 0.072 in the EEO survey, 0.069 in Talent, and 0.066 in Wisconsin. The Talent and Wisconsin coefficients are significant, but the EEO coefficient is not.

test scores on education. Controlling them explains only 3 percent of the test score effect in Talent. Better measures of personality characteristics might explain more of the test score effect, but none of the analyses in chapter 5 suggest that test scores are simply proxies for personality characteristics.

We can also estimate how much of the effect of ability persists with *all* of these characteristics controlled. Grades, encouragement from others, and educational and occupational plans explain 44 percent of the test score effect in EEO and 37 percent in Talent. Controlling high school curriculum and personality as well as grades, encouragement, and plans lowers the coefficient by another 2 percent in Talent. The Talent and EEO values agree reasonably well. But these same intervening variables explain 85 percent of test score's effect on education in the Wisconsin Survey. This could be due to the fact that the Wisconsin Survey measured grades, plans, and influence of others in twelfth grade, whereas Talent measured them in eleventh grade and EEO measured them in tenth grade.

These results mean that adolescents with greater ability get more education partly because they are treated differently in school. They are more likely to be in the college curriculum. They also receive higher grades, talk more with teachers, have more ambitious friends, and develop more ambitious plans of their own. But we cannot say to what extent these differences arise because schools favor abler students and to what extent abler students seek out favorable environments within a given school.

Adolescents with greater ability may receive more encouragement because they learn more in school. Their higher grades suggest this. But even if they do not learn more in school, they may possess other characteristics, not measured in our surveys, that lead to selective encouragement. They may, for example, be "better" behaved or more pleasant for teachers to work with.

It is not clear that adolescents with greater ability *must* be selectively favored, or even that they "merit" the preference shown them. Bloom (1976) argues that under very favorable conditions, a large proportion of slow learners can learn as much as fast learners. When previously slow learners do succeed in reaching the same level of achievement as fast learners, he says, they appear to be able to learn equally complex subsequent ideas, their retention is equally good, and their application of newly learned ideas is equally competent. Previously slow learners' interest and attitudes toward school do not differ from those of fast learners once their achievement is similar, and the previously slow learners cease to need extra time to master new tasks. If Bloom is correct, the selective treatment given adolescents with greater ability may be irrational or simply convenient.[16] This suggests that the effects of ability on educational attainment could fall if the relationship of ability to grades, encouragement, and plans fell.[17]

We can summarize the findings in this section as follows:

First, high-scoring individuals have greater educational opportunity in the United States than low scorers. As much as a fifth of their advantage results from their coming from families that are economically more successful, more educated, smaller, and stabler. Another fifth seems to be explained by family characteristics that are not measured in our surveys. These characteristics may well involve ways of socializing children. They may also involve genetic differences among families.

Second, after controlling for family background, more than half of the observed correlation between academic ability and education remains unexplained. Adolescents with greater ability get more education partly because they are treated differently than adolescents with less ability. They may also seek out more favorable environments. This is not inevitable, and our data do not tell us whether it is desirable. Nor do our data tell us whether the relationship of ability to educational attainment conforms to meritocratic criteria. The relationship may arise partly out of convenience or from causes that are "unfair" to adolescents with low ability.

5. EFFECTS OF ACADEMIC ABILITY
ON OCCUPATIONAL STATUS

We have seen that a man's adolescent ability substantially affects his educational attainment. This section will show that academic ability also affects adult occupational status. Our evidence mostly comes from the occupations of relatively young men. But tests given early in adolescence seem to predict Kalamazoo men's occupational attainment equally

TABLE 4.5

Regressions of Occupational Status on Adolescent Test Score Controlling Selected Background Variables

Sample	Variables Controlled									Coefficients of Test Score		% Reduction in Test-Score Coefficient	R²
	NONE	WHITE	POPED	POPOC	MOMED	PARINC	HEDAB	SIBS	ALL BKG	B	Beta		
Talent Representative													
Age 28 to 29	X									.771	.474	–	.225
			X	X				X		.673	.414	12.8	.248
			X	X	X	X				.680	.418	11.9	.252
		X	X	X	X	X	X	X		.679	.418	12.0	.254
Talent Brothers													
Age 28 to 29	X									.913	.484	–	.234
			X	X				X		.748	.396	18.1	.270
									X	.559	.297	38.7	NA
Kalamazoo Brothers													
Age 35 to 59	X									.685	.453	–	.206
			X	X				X		.601	.397	12.3	.217
									X	.436	.288	36.4	NA
Wisconsin													
Age 24 to 25	X									.605	.376	–	.141
			X	X	X	X				.499	.310	17.6	.199
EEO													
Age 30 to 31	X									.550	.350	–	.123
			X	X	X	X				.414	.264	24.7	.189
Inequality	X										.440[a]	–	.193
			X	X							.317[a]	28.0	.285
									X		.297[b]	32.5	NA
									X		.198[c]	55.0	NA

All coefficients are more than twice their standard error.

[a] Derived from Jencks et al. (1972), figure B-2, which is corrected for measurement error. The uncorrected values, derived from figure B-1, are 0.380 and 0.288.

[b] Upper bound estimate from Jencks et al. (1972), figure B-7, which is corrected for measurement error.

[c] Lower bound estimate from Jencks et al. (1972), figure B-7.

well throughout their lifetimes, so findings for young men can probably be generalized to older men.*

Data on the overall effects of adolescent ability on occupation appear in table 4.5. A fifteen-point difference in adolescent test performance is associated with an occupational advantage of a third to half a standard deviation. The advantage is larger in the Talent and Kalamazoo surveys than in Wisconsin and EEO. Controlling most combinations of measured background reduces the test-score coefficient between 12 and 25 percent. Controlling all background (with sibling difference regressions) reduces the test-score coefficient by 39 percent among Talent Brothers and 36 percent among Kalamazoo Brothers.† It follows that almost two-thirds of the test-score effect arises from causes independent of family background. Unfortunately, we have no data on identical twins to check this inference.

The most important reason why individuals with high scores end up in occupations of higher status than individuals with low scores is that they get more schooling. Table 4.6 shows that controlling education alone reduces the test-score coefficient 62 percent in the Talent representative sample. All of our other surveys also show substantial reductions in the test-score coefficient with only education controlled. These results suggest that test scores affect a man's occupational status primarily by influencing his educational attainment.

High school students with higher ability also have more ambitious occupational plans than students with less ability, even when they get no more education. Our results suggest, however, that unless these students get more schooling, they derive little occupational benefit from their ability. Table 4.6 shows that controlling occupational plans reduces the test-score coefficient only 1 to 9 percent after background and education are controlled.

The findings are similar with regard to other characteristics measured in high school. Curriculum placement, grades, encouragement, plans, and personality explain why adolescents with higher ability get higher-status jobs largely because they explain why adolescents with higher ability go to school longer. After controlling education, these characteristics explain very little of the effect of ability on occupation.

---

* Olneck reports that Terman or Otis IQ scores correlate 0.475 with first occupation and 0.453 with current occupation at age 35 to 59 in his Kalamazoo sample with complete data. Fagerlind (1975) reports that group IQ tests at age ten correlate 0.277, 0.350, 0.389, 0.386, and 0.352 with occupational status at age 25, 30, 35, 40, and 43 for his sample of Swedish men.

† Jencks et al. (1972) estimated the range of likely values as 33 to 55 percent (see last lines of table 4.5).

TABLE 4.6

Regressions of Occupational Status on Adolescent Test Score Controlling Selected Intervening Variables

Sample	MEASURED BKG	ALL BKG	PERSONALITY	HS CURRICULUM	GRADES	T-INFLUENCE	P-INFLUENCE	F-PLANS	EDPLANS	OCPLANS	EARNPLANS	EDUCATION	EDPASTHS[c]	BA	EARLYOC[d]	WORKEXP[e]	Coefficient of Test Score B	Coefficient of Test Score Beta	% Reduction in Test-Score Coefficient	R²
Talent Representative																				
Age 28 to 29	X[a]																.680	.418	—	.252
	X[a]				X	X	X	X	X	X	X						.257	.158	62.2	.435
	X[a]				X	X	X	X	X	X	X						.251	.154	63.1	.435
	X[a]		X	X	X	X	X	X	X	X	X	X					.224	.138	67.1	.305
	X[a]		X	X	X	X	X	X	X	X	X	X					.207	.127	69.5	.451
	X[a]											X				X	.207	.127	69.6	.451
Talent Brothers																				
Age 28 to 29	X[b]																.748	.396	—	.270
	X[b]											X					.067	.035	91.1	.519
		X															.559	.295	—	NA
		X										X					.049	.026	91.3	NA
Kalamazoo Brothers																				
Age 35 to 59	X[b]																.601	.397	—	.217
	X[b]											X	X	X			.247	.163	58.9	.369
	X[b]											X	X	X	X		.228	.151	62.1	.410
			X														.436	.288	—	NA
			X									X	X	X			.226	.149	48.2	NA
			X									X	X	X	X		.220	.145	49.5	NA
Wisconsin																				
Age 24 to 25	X[a]																.499	.310	—	.199
	X[a]				X	X	X	X	X								.182	.113	63.6	.409
	X[a]				X	X	X	X	X	X		X					.136	.085	72.7	.424
	X[a]				X	X	X	X	X	X		X					.083	.051	83.5	.426
EEO																				
Age 30 to 31	X[a]																.414	.264	—	.189
	X[a]				X							X					[.094]	[.060]	77.3	.390
	X[a]				X					X		X					[.075]	[.048]	81.7	.402
	X[a]				X					X		X					[.048]	[.031]	88.4	.415

Coefficients less than twice their standard error are in brackets.

[a] Indicates controls for father's education, father's occupation, mother's education, family income.
[b] Indicates controls for father's education, father's occupation, siblings.
[c] Years of education beyond high school.
[d] First occupation after completion of school.
[e] Years of experience.

Olneck surveyed Kalamazoo men when they were older than Wisconsin, Talent, and EEO men. In addition to asking their current occupation, he also asked for their first occupation. Controlling first occupation as well as education reduces the test-score coefficient only 1 to 3 percent more than controlling education alone. Thus, the occupational advantage of middle-aged men with high adolescent scores over men with the same education but lower scores does not appear to depend on beginning their career at a higher level.

The effects of ability on occupation are relatively small after controlling for education. In the EEO survey, the effect of test scores on adult status does not reach significance once education is controlled. It is significant in Talent, Wisconsin, and Kalamazoo (beta = 0.11 to 0.16). We found no significant interaction between test scores and education in either the Talent or the Kalamazoo surveys.* This suggests that at least within the range of cognitive skills found in these two surveys, the occupational payoff to education is no greater for bright students than for slow learners who persist in school.

We also looked at the two samples tested *after* school completion, namely PSID and Veterans. A fifteen-point difference in adult test performance is associated with an occupational difference of 0.36 standard deviations among PSID men and 0.43 standard deviations among Veterans. Controlling measured family background reduces the regression coefficient by 14 percent in the Veterans Survey and 34 percent in the PSID. Controlling education reduces the test-score coefficient 80 percent in the PSID and 67 percent in the Veterans Survey.† These results are quite similar to those in table 4.6 where the tests were administered *prior* to school completion.

These findings lead to three general conclusions:

* We investigated twenty-eight interactions between the five background variables, test scores, grades, and education in Talent. We would expect one or two of the twenty-eight interactions to reach significance by chance alone. In fact, only two of the twenty-eight had coefficients more than twice their standard errors. The test-score coefficient also did not differ significantly in samples having blue-collar and white-collar fathers in either Talent or Kalamazoo. See Hauser and Daymont (1977) for similar evidence in the Wisconsin survey.

† The findings are shown in table A4.3. They are not modified by considering interactions among the determinants of occupation. None of the multiplicative interactions between race, father's education, father's occupation, father absent, siblings, test score, education, and experience was significant in the PSID. Nor did the test-score coefficient differ significantly for subsamples based on the respondent's race or on having a white-collar, blue-collar, or farm father. The coefficient for AFQT is significantly higher for men with white-collar fathers than for men with blue-collar fathers in the Veterans sample. The AFQT coefficient for men with blue-collar fathers is, in turn, larger than for men with farm fathers, but not significantly larger. Not much weight should be put on these interactions for Veterans, since they do not appear in the PSID, or for adolescent test scores.

First, a man's ability in sixth to eleventh grade has important effects on his later occupational status, but 60 to 80 percent of the effect is explained by the amount of schooling he gets. Academic ability's effect on schooling can, in turn, be traced largely to its effects on curriculum placement, grades, encouragement from others, and high school plans. Men who fail to convert their ability advantage into additional schooling do not have much of an occupational advantage over men with lower scores. These results suggest that if instruction were changed in schools so that the relationship of ability to educational attainment fell, adolescents with differing abilities would have more equal occupational chances as adults. This might occur if low-ability students were to learn more, receive more encouragement, have higher aspirations, and therefore attend school longer.

Second, if employers view cognitive skills as essential for high-status occupations, they impose this requirement by the relatively inefficient device of requiring educational credentials. Alternatively, employers may not see cognitive ability as a prerequisite for high-status occupations. They may believe that credentialed individuals have more suitable attitudes and values.

Third, the standard deviation of occupational status among men who have identical test scores averages at least 88 percent of the standard deviation among men in general. This suggests that the United States cannot be considered a "meritocracy," at least if "merit" is measured by general cognitive skills. Our findings offer little support for Herrnstein's (1973) arguments that the United States is rapidly approaching a hereditary meritocracy based upon the genetic transmission of IQ. Nor do they offer much support for the part of Herrnstein's syllogism which assumes that ability is an important determinant of occupational success. Thus even if test scores are entirely explained by genes, which they almost certainly are not, the genes that affect test scores have rather modest effects on occupational success.

6. EFFECTS OF ACADEMIC ABILITY ON EARNINGS

The first complication an investigator faces when analyzing the effects of academic ability on earnings is that previous investigators have measured earnings in quite varied ways. Some have looked at earnings,

TABLE 4.7

Regression of Ln Earnings and Earnings on Adolescent Test Score Controlling Selected Background Variables

		Variables Controlled									Coefficient of Test Score		% Reduction in Test-Score Coefficient	R²
	Age	NONE	WHITE	POPED	POPOC	MOMED	PARINC	HEDAB	SIBS	ALL BKG[a]	B	Beta		
Talent Representative (Ln Hourly Earnings)	28-29	X									.0055	.203	–	.041
				X	X	X	X				.0046	.167	17.6	.052
				X	X	X	X	X			.0048	.176	13.6	.057
			X	X	X	X	X	X			.0047	.171	15.8	.059
Talent Brothers (Ln Hourly Earnings)	28-29	X									.0107	.356	–	.127
				X	X				X		.0115	.385	-8.1	.147
										X	.0100	.333	6.6	NA
Kalamazoo Brothers (Ln Annual Earnings)	35-59	X									.0106	.360	–	.130
				X	X				X		.0094	.319	11.3	.144
										X	.0105	.357	0.9	NA
Malmo[b] (Ln Annual Earnings)	43	X									.0121	.396	–	.157
				X	X				X		.0091	.297	25.0	.252
Wisconsin (Annual Earnings/$7,574)[c]	27-28	X									.0039	.163	–	.026
				X	X	X	X				.0032	.137	16.1	.048
EEO (Annual Earnings/$11,303)	30-31	X									[.0019]	[.070]	–	.005
				X	X	X	X				[-.0012]	[-.045]	163.2	.092
Inequality (Standardized Annual Income)	25-64	X									NA	.314[d]	–	.098
				X	X						NA	.240[d]	23.6	.133
										X	NA	.232[e]	26.1	NA
										X	NA	.194[f]	38.2	NA

Coefficients in brackets are less than twice their standard error.

[a] Controlled using differences between brothers.

[b] Fagerlind (1975), table 9. Test scores converted to an SD of 15. Sample excludes very low earners, which probably raises all coefficients.

[c] Earnings taken from Social Security records. Values above the withholding maximum were estimated from the month in which the maximum was reached.

[d] Computed from Jencks et al. (1972), figure B-2, which is corrected for measurement error.

[e] Computed from Jencks et al. (1972), figure B-7, which is corrected for measurement error. Upper bound estimate.

[f] Lower bound estimate.

others at ln earnings. Some have looked at hourly earnings, others at annual earnings. In order to minimize the effects of these differences, we divided the coefficients in equations that predicted untransformed earnings by the sample mean. The resulting coefficient expresses the effect on earnings of a one-point change in test performance as a percentage of the mean earnings of the entire sample. These transformed coefficients were almost identical to the coefficients we obtained when predicting ln earnings in the samples for which both were available, so we will treat the two as if they were interchangeable.*

A second complication is that the effects of adolescent academic ability on earnings increase as men get older. The correlation between adolescent academic ability and earnings increases steadily up to around the age of 35.† The standard deviation of ln earnings increases steadily from the age of 25 to the age of 65, so the unstandardized coefficient of adolescent test performance continues to rise even after the standardized coefficient stabilizes.

Table 4.7 shows the effects of adolescent academic ability on earnings in various samples. In general, the effects are larger for older samples. With nothing else controlled, a one-point increase in test performance is associated with a 0.4 percent increase in Wisconsin men's earnings at 27 or 28, a 0.6 percent increase in Talent men's earnings at 28 or 29, a 1.1 percent increase in Kalamazoo men's earnings between the ages of 35 and 59, and a 1.2 percent increase in Malmo men's earnings at the age of 43. The principal exception to the pattern is the EEO sample, in which a one-point increase in test performance is associated with only a 0.2 percent increase in earnings at the age of 30 or 31.

Table 4.8 shows parallel results for adult test scores. A one-point

* After dividing by the sample mean, the coefficients of test score in Kalamazoo and Talent equations predicting earnings never differ by more than 0.0003 from the analogous coefficients in equations predicting ln earnings, and values of R^2 never differ by more than 0.003 in table 4.7. The differences are slightly larger with intervening variables controlled (see tables A4.4 and A4.5).

† Sewell and Hauser (1975) report that Wisconsin men's eleventh grade IQ scores correlate 0.096 with their earnings eight years out of high school, 0.125 with their earnings nine years out of high school, and 0.166 with their earnings ten years out of high school. Hauser and Daymont (1977) indicate that the correlation continues to rise for men eleven, twelve, thirteen, and fourteen years out of high school, although they do not report the exact values.

Fagerlind (1975) reports that a group IQ test administered at the age of 10 correlated 0.082, 0.222, 0.343, 0.333, and 0.396 with ln earnings at the ages of 25, 30, 35, 40, and 43 in the Malmo sample.

Cross-sectional results for the 1973 earnings of Kalamazoo men aged 35 to 54 show no statistically significant age trend. The correlations are 0.319, 0.476, 0.338, and 0.283 for men aged 35 to 39, 40 to 44, 45 to 50, and 50 to 54 in 1973. The pattern for the unstandardized coefficients and for ln earnings is similar.

TABLE 4.8

Regressions of Ln Earnings on Adult Test Score Controlling Selected Background and Intervening Variables

Sample (year of earnings)	NONE	MEASURED BKG	ED	EDPASTHS	BA	VOCTRAIN	WORKEXP	WORKEXP^2	JOB TENURE	INTERACTIONS	OC	Coefficient for Test Score B	Coefficient for Test Score Beta	% Reduction in Test-Score Coefficient	R^2
PSID (1971) N = 1,774	X											.01773	.353	–	.125
		X[a]	X									.01292	.257	27.1	.178
		X[a]	X	X	X	X						.00753	.150	57.5	.255
		X[a]	X	X	X	X	X					.00670	.134	62.2	.298
		X[a]	X	X	X	X	X	X	X	X[c]		.00662	.132	62.7	.334
		X[a]	X	X	X	X	X	X	X	X[c]	X	.00595	.118	66.4	.353
Veterans (1964) N = 803	X											.01224	.351	–	.123
		X[b]	X									.00920	.264	24.8	.185
		X[b]	X									.00687	.197	43.9	.196
		X[b]	X				X					.00668	.192	45.4	.202
		X[b]	X				X				X	.00563	.162	54.0	.238

All coefficients are more than twice their standard error.

[a] White, father's education, father's occupation, father white collar, father foreign, father absent, siblings, nonfarm upbringing, non-South upbringing, father's education^2, and father's occupation^2, father's occupation X father's education, siblings X white, siblings X father's education.

[b] White, father's education, father's occupation, male head absent, nonfarm upbringing, and non-South upbringing.

[c] Father absent, experience X father absent, experience X father's education.

increase in adult test scores is associated with a 1.2 percent increase in earnings among 30- to 34-year-old veterans and a 1.8 percent increase among PSID 25- to 64-year-olds. The larger coefficient in the PSID sample reflects the fact that the variance of earnings in PSID is not as restricted as in the other surveys that collected a test score. The standardized coefficient of test score in PSID is quite similar to that in our other surveys. We are therefore inclined to treat the unstandardized PSID coefficient as our best population estimate for both adolescent and adult tests, even though it may be biased downward by the unreliability of the PSID test.

The effects of controlling measured background on the test-score coefficient also vary from sample to sample. The coefficient becomes negative (but insignificant) in the EEO survey. The coefficient increases slightly in the Talent Brothers sample. This could be due to sampling error, since there are only ninety-nine pairs in this sample. The remaining samples show reductions in the test-score coefficient between 11 and 27 percent. This holds for the samples in which tests were administered after school completion as well as those where they were administered before.

The pattern is similar when one uses sibling differences to estimate the effect of unmeasured as well as measured background characteristics. The coefficients in the difference equations imply that background accounts for 1 percent of the apparent effect of test performance on earnings in the Kalamazoo Brothers sample and only 7 percent in the Talent Brothers sample.[18] The reduction with sibling controls is slightly *less* than with measured background controlled in the Kalamazoo Brothers sample but more in the Talent Brothers sample.

The overall effect of test scores on earnings with all background controlled appears to be substantively important. Each fifteen-point test-score increase is associated with a 17 percent increase in Kalamazoo Brothers' annual earnings. In the PSID, where the test is given to adults and the variance of earnings is much greater, a fifteen-point increase in test performance is associated with a 21 percent increase in earnings. The effects may be even larger than this, since the PSID test is likely to underestimate the overall effect of the cognitive skills measured by a battery of reliable tests. Nonetheless, there is still a great deal of variability in earnings among men with the same test scores.

The fact that academic ability affects educational attainment accounts for between 36 and 47 percent of ability's effect on subsequent earnings in the Talent, Wisconsin, and Kalamazoo samples (see tables A4.4 and A4.5 in the Appendix). Thus if an academically talented male fails to get more schooling than other men, he does not usually earn appreciably more, at least not up to the age of 30. Among men from the same demographic background and with the same amount of schooling, a fifteen-point advantage on a test of academic ability in adolescence is associated with an earnings advantage of only 4.6 percent among Talent 28- and 29-year-olds and 3.0 percent among Wisconsin 27- and 28-year-olds. Among EEO respondents from similar backgrounds and with the same amount of schooling, a fifteen-point test score advantage is actually associated with a 3.8 percent earnings disadvantage. The impact of academic ability independent of background and schooling does, however, seem to increase with age. Among Kalamazoo Brothers with the same amount of schooling, for example, a fifteen-point difference in sixth-grade IQ scores is associated with a 14 percent difference in annual earnings between the ages of 35 and 59. Results using adult test scores in the Veterans sample of 30- to 34-year-olds and the PSID sample of 25- to 64-year-olds are similar.*

Test scores continue to affect a man's earnings even with occupation controlled. Thus if Kalamazoo Brothers have the same education and the same occupational status but have test scores that differ by fifteen points, they differ by 11 percent in earnings. The PSID results are roughly similar.†

We found no significant interaction between test score and education when predicting earnings in the Talent or Kalamazoo sample.[19] If bright students learn more in school, and if school learning were the basis for higher earnings, we would expect a positive interaction.

These results suggest that even if men with high scores do not have high aspirations or get more schooling than average, they are worth somewhat more to employers who hire, fire, and pay them. There are several reasons why this may be true. Men with higher ability may have attitudes or personality characteristics not measured in our surveys that employers value. Early proponents of testing believed, for example, that ability affected "social character." Social character may be important, though probably not in the ways early proponents of testing claimed.[20] Men with higher ability may be more productive on the job, but we have no direct evidence for this. Men with higher ability may also

---

* Table 4.8 shows that in the PSID, using an unreliable adult score which may be affected by education, the difference is 12 percent. In the Veterans sample, with a more reliable test but a restricted variance for earnings, the difference is 11 percent.

Preliminary results from Taubman's (1977) sample of MZ twins suggest that additional controls for all common background and genes may reduce the estimated effect of adult test score below the values in the PSID and Veterans samples.

† The relevant regressions appear in tables 4.8, A4.4, and A4.5.

search more effectively for lucrative jobs. Or employers may have an economically irrational preference for workers with high scores and may be willing to pay to indulge this preference.

Our findings with respect to earnings can be summarized as follows:

First, the apparent economic benefits of ability exceed the actual benefits by about a quarter. But even controlling family background, a fifteen-point test-score difference is associated with a 17 percent difference in Kalamazoo Brothers' annual earnings.

Second, the effects of test performance on earnings increase with age.

Third, differences in education help explain why men with high test scores earn more, but nearly two-thirds of the effect of test scores on earnings is independent of men's education. Differences in adolescent plans and other measured adolescent characteristics do not explain the effects of ability on earnings among men with the same amount of education. A fifteen-point test-score difference between men with the same amount of education is associated with as much as a 14 percent difference in their annual earnings.

Fourth, the effects of test performance on earnings are not very large relative to the overall earnings gap between the rich and the poor in general. The best paid fifth of male earners earns about five times what the worst paid fifth earn, and the disparity is even greater if one compares, say, the top and bottom tenths. Our findings therefore do not characterize the United States as a "meritocracy," at least when merit is measured by general cognitive skills.

CHAPTER 5

The Effects of Noncognitive Traits

Common sense tells us that noncognitive as well as cognitive characteristics affect social and economic success. Most people assume, for example, that individuals with "ambition," "good attitudes," "high aspirations," or "good judgment" are more likely to succeed than individuals who lack these characteristics. Employers and college admissions committees reflect this belief when they seek personal interviews, letters of recommendation, and other personal evaluations, even when test scores and other measures of cognitive ability are available.

Past Research. Although most people assume that noncognitive characteristics are important determinants of life success, few studies have attempted to measure their importance.

Crockett (1962) found a positive relationship between socioeconomic mobility and an individual's "need for achievement" score on the Thematic Apperception Test (TAT). When Duncan, Featherman, and Duncan (1972) reanalyzed Crockett's data, they found that need for achievement had a small direct effect on occupational status (standardized coefficient 0.12) after controlling father's occupation and respondent's education. However, since the test was administered at the same time occupation was measured, the respondent's occupational status may have affected his TAT responses, rather than the other way around.

Peter Mueser wrote this chapter.

Elder (1968) used longitudinal data to consider the influence of high school students' noncognitive traits. He found that estimates of need for achievement based on high school TAT responses had a negligible effect on subsequent educational attainment and occupational status. But a measure of "motivation" based on observers' ratings of students' behavior in high school had appreciable effects on both educational and occupational attainment (standardized coefficients 0.236 and 0.222, controlling IQ and social class). Unfortunately, Elder's sample was small (N = 65), all white, and drawn entirely from Oakland, California, so it is unclear whether his findings can be generalized.

Featherman (1972) used longitudinal data to examine the effects of "positive orientation to work," "materialistic orientation," and "perception of personal achievements" at the age of 30 on men's occupational and economic success three to ten years later. After controlling for demographic background, education, occupational status, and income at age 30, he found that "work orientation" at age 30 had a small effect on occupational status at age 33 (standardized coefficient 0.063) but no other statistically significant effects. "Materialistic orientation" affected income three and six to ten years later (standardized coefficients 0.052 and 0.071), as did "subjective achievement" (coefficients 0.157 and 0.083).

Sewell and Hauser (1975) analyzed the effects of several social-psychological factors on Wisconsin high school seniors' educational attainment and occupational status at age 24 and earnings between the ages of 25 and 28. After controlling for socioeconomic background characteristics and academic ability, they found that students' high school grades, perceived influence from teachers, peers, and parents, and students' own educational and occupational aspirations all influenced years of education. These factors also affected occupational status and earnings, although their effects on earnings were small. Sewell and Hauser suggested that the encouragement a student receives and his level of aspirations affect his educational attainment and economic success. It is possible, however, that such measures merely reflect the respondent's own underlying motivational characteristics.

Bowles and Gintis (1976) reported that measures of rule orientation, dependability, and internalization based on sixteen peer ratings by high school students were related to grade-point average in high school after controlling measures of cognitive ability. Similar traits, based on peer ratings by Boston area workers, predicted the ratings that individuals received from supervisors on their jobs. Bowles and Gintis argue that individuals learn these noncognitive traits in high school and are later rewarded for them by employers. Unfortunately, since the data were not longitudinal, the measures they use may simply reflect behavior patterns developed in the particular setting, rather than stable personality characteristics. Thus, individuals who respond in an "appropriate" fashion in school may not be the same individuals who succeed on a job.

Andrisani and Nestel (1976) found that "internal control"—the extent to which an individual believes success is determined by personal initiative rather than external events—had a positive relationship to occupational status and earnings for NLS men over 45. They also found that this measure predicted change in earnings over the two years following the initial survey. This is consistent with theory, which suggests that internal control should affect success (see Rotter, 1966). But the direction of causation is still unclear, even in this longitudinal data. Individuals may believe they can control their lives because they face favorable circumstances, or because they possess other unmeasured characteristics that facilitate success. Nonetheless, Andrisani and Nestel's findings suggest that some aspect of personality may influence earnings.

Numerous studies have examined the relationship between personality and job success for individuals in restricted occupational groupings.[1] However, since these studies are usually limited to a single occupational grouping (e.g., salesmen, managers) and often to a single company, it is difficult to determine whether relationships found in such self-selected populations apply to representative samples. The personality measures also differ across studies, so results for different occupational groupings cannot easily be pieced together. Even if results were comparable within a wide range of occupations, they would not tell us anything about the effects of personality on occupational choice or selection. Therefore, these studies are of little help in determining the extent to which personality predicts success for the population in general.

Data and Methods. The Talent and Kalamazoo surveys provide more comprehensive data on adolescents' noncognitive traits and their subsequent economic success than any other surveys that we could find. The Talent Survey asked students to assess their own personality traits, to provide numerous details on their behavior in high school, to describe other people's attitudes toward them, and to describe their own aspirations and plans. Talent measured educational attainment and economic success twelve years after the initial survey.

Kalamazoo teachers rated tenth graders on a variety of character traits. Olneck contacted these men when they were 35 to 59 to determine their educational attainment and economic success. Both surveys also measured demographic background and cognitive ability. Since Olneck surveyed brothers, one can also control whatever unmeasured family characteristics brothers have in common when analyzing this data.

Since previous empirical evidence has not supported any particular theory in a consistent way, our analyses of these data are exploratory. We examine a large number of noncognitive variables in an effort to identify those which have predictive power. Our first concern is to answer the global question of how important noncognitive traits are in the status-attainment process, since most stratification research ignores such variables entirely. We also hope to draw conclusions about the nature of those traits that are important and thus to shed light on the mechanisms by which individuals succeed or fail in our society. Since our concern is with the possible causal role of noncognitive traits, our analyses focus on these traits' effects after controlling background characteristics.

It is worth noting that we seek to identify traits that have long-term, consistent effects on individual success. We are not concerned with traits that are valuable in one job or with one employer. A trait must be valued by enough different employers so that demand exceeds supply and men with the trait enjoy a general competitive advantage over men who lack it. If, for example, some jobs demand docility while others demand initiative, and if the frequency of the two sorts of jobs is proportionate to the frequency of the two traits among relevant workers, jobs requiring each trait will pay equally well and enjoy equal status. Observers may still attribute an individual's success or failure in a given job to docility or to initiative, but on the average neither docility nor initiative will influence status or earnings. Traits of this kind therefore have no value in predicting individuals' economic standing.

This chapter is divided into four sections. Section 1 examines the importance of ten self-assessed personality traits. Project Talent derived these ten measures from students' responses to the high school questionnaire. Since responses to individual questions are not available, the validity of these analyses depends on the validity of Talent's scales.

The second section considers more than 60 questions on the Talent questionnaire relating to student activities, behavior, and attitudes. We treat these as proxies for students' noncognitive traits and use principal component analysis to search for factors that have consistent effects on later success.

In the third section, we consider the combined effects of all the noncognitive traits measured in Project Talent, using a model that includes students' perceptions of encouragement from others as well as their explicit preferences and plans. We also look for nonlinear and nonadditive effects of personality.

In the fourth section, we use the Kalamazoo Survey to determine the importance of teacher ratings of student character for predicting students' later success. Since Olneck followed up Kalamazoo respondents when they were aged 35 to 59, his data allow us to investigate whether effects found among 28-year-old Talent men persist in later years.

1. PERSONALITY SELF-ASSESSMENTS

Talent's personality self-assessments are based on questions that require respondents to make judgments concerning their own actions, preferences, or the way others view them. The Talent staff grouped together statements which they thought described similar types of behavior, summed scores on each group of items, and gave the resulting composite a verbal label. Table 5.1 lists these composites and selected items from each. The items differ in generality. The "sociability" items, for example, range from "I am friendly" (weighted positively) to "I prefer reading a good book to going out with friends" (weighted negatively). Most items require the respondent to characterize his behavior as if it were relatively stable over time and across situations. An individual who did not believe in such stable traits could either omit the question or give the most noncommittal response. In either case, he would end up with a low score on the scale. It therefore seems fair to assume that the composites measure the extent to which the respondent believes he possesses a given set of traits.

With the possible exception of "impulsiveness," the composites measure perceived conformity to socially acceptable patterns of behavior. In a factor analysis using a Talent sample which differed from ours, Lohnes (1966) found that all the composites, excluding "impulsiveness," loaded on a single factor. He suggested that these composites were largely measuring an individual's need to conform. We coded all these composites so that the "approved" response led to a higher score than the "deviant" response. The correlations among these nine composites range from 0.28 to 0.62.

TABLE 5.1

Selected Questions from the Ten Talent Personality Self-Assessment Scales[a]

Regarding the things I do and the way I do them, this statement describes me
> A. *extremely well*
> B. *quite well*
> C. *fairly well*
> D. *slightly*
> E. *not very well*

An item is marked with a plus (+) when Talent scored options A or B as 1 and options C, D, and E as 0. The item is marked with a minus (−) when Talent scored options D and E as 1 and A, B, and C as 0. Scores on a scale are found by summing the scores on the items included in this scale. Thus scores range from 0 to the number of items in the scale.

Sociability (12 items)
> (+) *People seem to think I make new friends more quickly than most people do.*
> (−) *I prefer reading a good book to going out with friends.*
> (+) *I am friendly.*

Social sensitivity (9 items)
> (+) *I seem to know how other people will feel about things.*
> (+) *People consider me a sympathetic listener.*
> (+) *I am sympathetic.*

Impulsiveness (9 items)
> (+) *I like to do things on the spur of the moment.*
> (+) *I am impulsive.*
> (−) *It takes me quite a while to come to a decision.*

Vigor (7 items)
> (+) *I can work or play outdoors for hours without getting tired.*
> (+) *I am energetic.*

Calmness (9 items)
> (−) *People seem to think I get angry easily.*
> (+) *I am even-tempered.*
> (+) *I am usually self-controlled.*

Tidiness (11 items)
> (+) *I am never sloppy in my personal appearance.*
> (+) *Before I start a task, I spend some time getting it organized.*
> (+) *I am neat.*

Culture (10 items)
> (+) *I enjoy beautiful things.*
> (+) *I take part in the cultural activities in my community.*
> (+) *I am refined.*

Leadership (5 items)
> (+) *I am the leader in my group.*
> (+) *I am influential.*
> (+) *I have held a lot of elected offices.*
> (+) *People naturally follow my lead.*
> (+) *I like to make decisions.*

Self-confidence (12 items)
> (+) *I am confident.*
> (+) *I'd enjoy speaking to a club group on a subject I know well.*
> (−) *Being around strangers makes me ill-at-ease.*

Mature personality (24 items)
> (+) *I make good use of all my time.*
> (+) *I work fast and get a lot done.*
> (+) *It bothers me to leave a task half done.*
> (+) *I do my job, even when I don't like it.*
> (+) *I do things the best I know how, even if no one checks up on me.*
> (+) *I am dependable.*
> (+) *I am reliable.*

---

[a]For a complete list of questions in the ten scales, see *The Project Talent Data Bank: A Handbook* (1972), pp. 38-42.

While "impulsiveness" is not usually considered a socially acceptable trait, this label may not be entirely appropriate to the items included under it. One might, for example, argue that the items in this scale really measure "decisiveness" rather than "impulsiveness," and that "decisiveness" is a socially desirable characteristic. Whether for this or other reasons, "impulsiveness" correlates positively with all the other composites ($r = 0.11$ to 0.25). It also correlates positively with later success. We therefore retained the original coding rather than transforming the scale into a measure of "nonimpulsiveness."

Responses to the 108 separate questions were not available, so we could not determine whether Talent had lost important information in constructing the composites.

The ten self-assessments are not closely tied to measured family characteristics. Fourteen measures of demographic background explained less than 6 percent of the variance in "leadership" and less than 4 percent in the other nine measures.

Effects on Occupation. Table 5.2 presents zero-order correlations and standardized coefficients of the self-assessments when they are used to predict occupational status 12 years after the initial survey.* Columns 3 to 4a indicate that when the measures are considered together, "leadership," "mature personality," and "culture" have positive effects, while "social sensitivity" and "impulsiveness" have negative effects. The negative effect for "social sensitivity" in this regression contrasts with its positive coefficient when it is considered in isolation (column 2). If these composites really measure what their labels imply, we might claim that social sensitivity increases with leadership and cultural interest, but that at any given level of leadership and cultural interest, the more socially sensitive students enter lower-status occupations.

Comparisons of regressions before and after controlling test score indicate that "mature personality" has much of its effect because it reflects cognitive ability. In contrast, "culture" has most of its moderate effect independent of cognitive ability.

In order to compare the relative importance of family background, ability, and self-assessed personality, we created a variable that combined all the significant composites into a single "supercomposite." We

---

* Our sample differs from the basic Talent sample described in chapter 2 in that it does not exclude students or military personnel. Only two males with occupations or earnings report being students, however, and only five report that they are in the military, so the inclusion of such respondents will not make much difference. In addition, each analysis in this chapter eliminates men with missing data on the variables used in that analysis. This means that the sample changes from one analysis to the next.

TABLE 5.2

Standardized Regressions of Occupational Status on
Self-Assessed Personality Measures Controlling Selected Variables[a]

	Entered Separately[b]		Entered Together[c]				
	(1)	(2)	(3)	(3a)	(4)	(4a)	(5)
Sociability	.066	[.030]	[−.051]		[−.013]		[−.014]
Social sensitivity	.115	[.051]	[.070]		−.084	−.078	[−.076]
Impulsiveness	.020	[−.033]	[−.064]	−.071	[−.050]		[−.045]
Vigor	.122	.072	[.012]		[−.004]		[.000]
Calmness	.170	.112	[.057]		[.022]		[.033]
Tidiness	.127	.092	[.011]		[.010]		[.007]
Culture	.162	.104	[.055]		.096	.105	.089
Leadership	.168	.116	.090	.087	.078	.071	[.064]
Self-confidence	.137	.085	[.032]		[.006]		[.006]
Mature personality	.181	.130	[.069]	.102	[.015]		[−.022]
Controls:							
Background[d]			X	X	X	X	X	X
Test score[e]					X	X	X
Grades[e]							X
$\bar{R}^2$ with controls only			.142	.142	.255	.255	.271
$\bar{R}^2$ with self-assessments			.165	.164	.264	.267	.275
Significance of ten self-assessments			$p < .01$		$p < .05$		$p > .05$
Combined coefficient of significant self-assessments[f]				.159		.119	

Coefficients in brackets are not significant at the 0.05 level, two-tailed.

[a]Sample includes 898 Talent males with complete data on self-assessed personality measures, background, test score, grades, years of education, and occupation.

[b]Column 1 gives zero-order correlations. Column 2 gives coefficient of each trait, entered separately but with background controlled.

[c]Columns 3a and 4a include measures added in the order of their contribution to $\bar{R}^2$ until no unentered variable increased $\bar{R}^2$ significantly. Columns 3, 4, and 5 include all ten traits.

[d]Background controls include white, father's education, father's occupation, father absent, siblings, Talent's socioeconomic index and its square, socioeconomic index X siblings, white X father absent, father's education X siblings, and father absent X siblings. Together, they control for all linear, quadratic, and multiplicative interaction effects of the six background measures. Except for the socioeconomic index, these variables are defined in chapter 2. Talent constructed the socioeconomic index from student responses to nine questions on their families, including parental education, income, and material possessions. The index is fully described in *The Project Talent Data Bank: A Handbook* (1972).

[e]The test score is Project Talent's "academic composite," described in chapter 4. Grades are the average of self-reported grades in math, science, foreign languages, history, and social studies. Test score[2] and grades[2] were not significant in any regression.

[f]The combined coefficient is the coefficient of a variable constructed by multiplying each component variable by its unstandardized coefficient and summing the products. Heise (1972) discusses the computation and application of this measure.

constructed this new variable by multiplying each significant trait by its unstandardized coefficient and summing the products. Its coefficient measures the effect of having the most desirable combination of non-cognitive characteristics.[2] The bottom row of table 5.2 shows this "combined coefficient." With only background controlled, the standardized coefficient of this composite is 0.159. Controlling academic ability (equation 4a) reduces the coefficient to 0.119. Controlling high school grades as well as academic ability reduces all but one personality self-assessment to nonsignificance. The remaining effects are thus too small to construct a meaningful combined coefficient in a sample of this size.

The importance of self-assessed personality traits in explaining occupational attainment thus depends on whether personality traits affect cognitive skills and high school grades. If self-assessed personality traits affect cognitive skills but not vice versa, the standardized coefficient of 0.159 is the best measure of personality traits' combined effects. If cognitive skills and grades affect self-assessments but not vice versa, or if they all depend on the same unmeasured but causally prior traits, self-assessed personality traits have insignificant effects.

The coefficient for test scores in equation 4 is 0.373, and the multiple correlation between the demographic background measures and occupation is 0.391. These comparisons suggest that self-assessed personality is far less important than either background or cognitive skills in determining eventual occupational status.

In regressions that control educational attainment, none of the self-assessed measures of personality has a significant effect on occupational status. This suggests that among men with the same amount of education, prior personality self-assessments are not important in determining who will enter a high-status occupation. These adolescent personality traits affect occupational status largely if not exclusively by affecting education.

Effects on Earnings. When we looked at the effects of self-assessed personality on hourly earnings, the "leadership" composite had the largest effect (0.202).* With "leadership" controlled, none of the other self-

---

* Table A5.1 in the Appendix presents the relevant results. Talent asked respondents to report wages on their present job as an hourly, weekly, or monthly figure. It also asked how many hours they had worked that week and how many weeks they had worked during the previous twelve months. This allows accurate calculation of hourly earnings. It only allows accurate calculation of annual earnings if respondents had had the same hours and wages for the previous twelve months. When we estimated annual earnings on these assumptions, the results were similar to those using hourly earnings, except that the equations explained a somewhat smaller proportion of the variance.

assessments had a statistically significant coefficient. Controlling for academic ability and grades decreases the coefficient of "leadership" less than 10 percent, implying that only a small portion of the effect is due to its association with cognitive ability.

An increase of one standard deviation in the leadership measure appears to have increased a 28-year-old male's hourly earnings by about 45 cents in 1972. This return may seem modest when we consider that hourly earnings averaged $5.27, and that the standard deviation was $2.24. Nonetheless, the coefficient of "leadership" with background controlled (0.202) is larger than the combined coefficient of all the background variables with no controls (0.197). And the coefficient of "leadership" with background, test scores, and grades controlled (0.191) is nearly twice as large as the combined coefficient of test scores and grades in the same equation (0.115).

Only a small part of "leadership's" effect on earnings works through education. Controlling years of schooling, college graduation, and years in graduate school lowers the standardized coefficient for "leadership" to 0.181. The combined coefficient for the three education variables in this same equation is only 0.183 at this age.

The standardized effects of "leadership" on ln hourly earnings are about 30 percent smaller than are those on hourly earnings, although effects of family background and cognitive ability are about the same. This indicates that personality traits associated with leadership explain less of the variation near the bottom of the earnings distribution than near the top.[*]

Conclusions about Effects of Self-Assessed Personality Traits. If personality affects academic ability and high school grades but not vice versa, the effects of self-assessed personality traits on occupational status are about half as large as the effects of test scores and the effects of background. If, more reasonably, we assume that personality is codetermined with or depends on ability and grades, its effects are much smaller. Self-assessed personality affects occupational status almost exclusively by affecting educational attainment.

In contrast, self-assessed "leadership" has an appreciable effect on hourly earnings at age 28, independent of cognitive ability and grades. "Leadership" does not affect earnings primarily by influencing schooling or occupational status.

---

[*] Coefficients could also be lower because effects on ln hourly earnings conformed poorly to the linear model. However, this is unlikely, since effects of the self-assessments were seldom significantly nonlinear in regressions predicting ln hourly earnings.

Students who characterize themselves as vigorous, calm, or tidy enjoy no subsequent advantage over those who do not characterize themselves in these ways, once we control other self-assessments. Those who are more socially oriented (as reflected in the "sociability" and "social sensitivity" self-assessments) end up in lower-status occupations when we control the other self-assessed traits. This is because they obtain less schooling. This supports the notion that socially oriented individuals are less interested than others in academic work. Despite their lower occupational attainments, sociable students' wages at age 28 are not appreciably lower, perhaps reflecting the fact that many jobs require social skills.

The effects of "culture" on occupational status also work through education, but are largely independent of ability and high school grades. If "culture" measures the extent to which the student identifies with a group that values education, it may appear to influence education because it reflects the student's values.

The leadership composite is the student's perception of his peers' judgment of him. It may reflect his ability to accomplish concrete goals in a high school peer-group context. The personality factors that make up this perceived ability must be somewhat stable, since leadership exercises an appreciable effect on earnings twelve years later, even when background and intervening factors are controlled. Apparently, it measures social skills that are useful in a wide variety of circumstances.

2. INDIRECT MEASURES OF PERSONALITY

If eleventh graders have stable personality characteristics that affect later success, students' life styles and attitudes should reflect these characteristics. We selected 60 questions from Talent's high school questionnaire that seemed to describe the way the student interacted with his environment. These questions cover five broad areas: (1) study habits and attitudes, (2) participation in group activities, (3) participation in other activities, (4) attitudes, and (5) ability-related characteristics.*

We did not examine responses to all 60 questions at once, since very

---

* We also examined students' reports of height in order to test Deck's (1968) claim that height influenced salary. Height did not have a significant effect on occupation or earnings. Nor did a measure of obesity based on weight and height.

few students answered every question. To increase reliability and to aid in interpretation, we combined related questions into composites. The method was to some degree ad hoc, since we looked at questions' correlations with later success before deciding how to combine them. Once we decided to combine a set of questions, however, we used either

---

TABLE 5.3

Talent Questions on Study Habits and Best Work

For the following statements indicate how often each one applies to you. Please answer the questions sincerely. Your answers will not affect your grades in any way. Mark one of the following choices for each statement. A. Almost always, B. Most of the time, C. About half the time, D. Not very often, E. Almost never.

Study Habits is the first principal component of responses to 14 questions. We coded all 14 questions so that "approved" responses received high scores. The first principal component explained 30.8 percent of the variance in responses to these fourteen questions. The following questions are typical:

I do a little more than the course requires.

I make sure that I understand what I am to do before I start an assignment.

Lack of interest in my schoolwork makes it difficult for me to keep my attention on what I am doing.

Failure to pay attention in class has caused my marks to be lowered.

I consider a very difficult assignment a challenge to my abilities.

I feel that I am taking courses that will not help me much in an occupation after I leave school.

I don't seem to be able to concentrate on what I read. My mind wanders and many things distract me.

I keep up to date on assignments by doing my work every day.

On the average, how many hours do you study each week? Include study periods in school as well as studying done at home.
(Response categories coded in hours. Range 0-22.)

Best Work
I do my assignments so quickly that I don't do my best work.

---

the first principal component (which depends on the correlation among questions being combined) or an a priori weighting scheme.* To test whether a composite captured the effects of all the individual questions, we first regressed education, occupation, hourly earnings, and ln hourly earnings on the composite, controlling measured family background characteristics. We considered the composite adequate if none of its

---

* If an individual answered more than half of the questions, we assigned him a score based on the questions he answered. If he answered fewer than half of the questions, we assigned no score, and thus omitted him in analyses using that composite.

components added appreciably to R^2 after the composite was controlled.* No composite adequately represented certain sets of questions, so we kept these questions separate in our analyses.

We will begin by discussing the measures we constructed from the behavioral and attitude questions. Although we cite those results that bear on the validity of the measures, we will postpone a full discussion of other results until after we discuss the measures themselves.

Study habits is the first principal component of 14 questions which measure the extent to which a student says he accepts his teachers' norms regarding academic work. Table 5.3 lists the questions. Students receive a high score if they say they pay attention in class, keep up to date on their assignments, do more work in a course than is required, or spend many hours on homework. If such behavior persists when students take a job, and if employers value it, high scorers should earn more than low scorers (Bowles and Gintis, 1976).

Best work is based on a fifteenth question about study habits, namely, whether the student says he often does assignments "so quickly that I don't do my best work." Teachers presumably prefer students who never do assignments too quickly. Although this question correlated positively with study habits, its effects on outcomes were different.†

Positive affiliations and *negative affiliations* measure student participation in group activities (see table 5.4). Positive affiliations is the principal component of responses to seven questions about participation in groups that had positive effects on later success. These groups included church groups, social clubs, and clubs dealing with school subject matter. Negative affiliations is the principal component of responses to four questions about membership in groups with negative effects on later success. These groups include farm youth groups, political clubs, military or drill units, and hobby clubs. We have no convincing explanation for why the first set of group memberships aids later achievement while the second set depresses it. The two types of group membership are positively correlated with one another, suggesting that individuals

---

* We also performed this test with test score controlled. In addition, we checked for nonlinear effects after controlling the composite. Thus, if any question in a composite had a substantively important linear or nonlinear effect that was not reflected in the composite, we rejected the composite.

† Including "best work" in the "study habits" composite led to a serious underestimate of the effects of these questions. This suggests that even when different questions appear to measure the same personal trait, they may not do so. It also underlines the danger of using a priori composites without considering whether the items all measure the same underlying traits. Factor analysis alone does not suffice to answer this question. This caveat applies with special force to the analyses of self-assessed traits in the previous section, since we were not able to test the adequacy of Talent's a priori grouping of these traits.

TABLE 5.4
Talent Questions on Group Membership and Leadership

How active have you been in any one or more of the following organizations? Mark your answers as follows: A. Extremely active, B. Very active, C. Fairly active, D. A member, but not very active, E. A member but rarely active, F. Not a member of any of these organizations.

Positive affiliations
- School newspaper, magazine, or annual
- School subject-matter clubs, such as science, mathematics, language, or history clubs
- Debating, dramatics, or musical clubs or organizations
- Church, religious, or charitable organizations, such as Catholic Youth of America, B'nai B'rith Youth Organization, Protestant youth group; organized nonschool youth groups such as YMCA, YWCA, Boy's Club, etc.
- Informal neighborhood group
- Social clubs, fraternities, or sororities
- How many athletic teams have you been a member of in the last three years? Count intramural, church, school, and other teams. (Coded as number. Range 0-12.)

The first principal component explained 31.0 percent of the variance in these questions.

Negative affiliations
- Political club, such as Young Democrats or Republicans
- Military or drill units
- Hobby clubs, such as photography, model building, hot rod, electronics, woodworking, crafts, etc.
- Farm youth groups, such as 4-H Club, Future Farmers of America, etc.

The first principal component explained 39.1 percent of the variance in these questions.

Leadership roles (constructed by Talent)[a]

- How many times have you been president of a class, a club, or another organization (other than athletic) in the last three years?
- How many times in the last three years have you been captain of an athletic team?
- How many times have you been an officer or committee chairman (other than president) of a class, a club, or another organization (other than athletic) in the last three years?

[a]See *The Project Talent Data Bank: A Handbook* (1972) for exact coding.

who join the first set of groups are likely to join the second set as well. But whatever "joiners" share is either not stable or has little effect on later success.

Leadership roles is a composite constructed by Talent researchers on the basis of leadership positions the student reported he held in various student groups (see table 5.4). Given the effect of the leadership self-assessment discussed in the previous section, we expected it to have a positive effect on later achievement, especially on earnings.

Social Activities are measured by four questions on dating and involvement in social recreation. We were unable to devise a composite that captured these variables' effects, so we retained all four questions in later analyses. The four questions ask the age at which the student started dating, the number of dates he had per week, how often he had gone steady, and how many times per week he went out for recreation.* We coded each variable in its natural metric (i.e., age or number of times). For the three dating variables we also included a dummy to identify individuals with no dating experience whatever. Coleman (1961) argues that at least in the late 1950s social activity implied involvement in an adolescent subculture that discouraged intellectualism. If this were so, social activity should be negatively associated with educational attainment. Socially involved individuals might also have less taste for schoolwork. Alternatively, individuals who are less interested in school may become more involved in social activities. Later achievements are also likely to require social skills, however, so socially involved students may not suffer the same disadvantage in earnings as in educational attainment.

Student employment experience is the number of hours per week the student worked during the school year. We also considered three other measures of employment experience: the age at which the student first began working, the number of summers he had worked, and the percentage of his spending money he said he got from a job. But after we controlled hours worked, none of the other questions had a statistically significant effect on later success, so we dropped them from later analyses.

Although we might expect individuals who had held down jobs to be more oriented toward achievement, especially in nonacademic pursuits, high school employment is actually negatively associated with both educational and occupational attainment and has no effect on earnings, even after family background is controlled. The fact that other employment experiences have no impact after controlling for hours worked during the school year suggests that those who have held jobs before eleventh grade do not differ in any consistent way from those who have not held jobs. Hours worked during the school year may therefore lower educational attainment and occupational status either because students who are less concerned or interested in academic matters spend more time working during the school year, or because the student's job leaves less time for schoolwork. Hours worked during the school year may also reflect aspects of background not captured by our controls. Employment in high school does not, however, seem to imply motives or talents that facilitate later success.

Intellectual reading is the principal component of responses to four questions on the nonrequired reading done by students. These include a measure of the total number of books read, as well as measures of

---

* These and subsequent questions appear in table A5.2 in the Appendix.

reading in science, literature, politics, and history. Although we expect intellectualism to be associated with greater educational attainment, its effects on occupational status and hourly earnings are not so easy to predict. Since intellectuals prefer occupations requiring cognitive skills, and since such occupations generally have high status, intellectualism should be positively associated with status. However, intellectuals may sacrifice earnings for intellectual challenge. If so, intellectualism may not lead to high earnings.

Science fiction reading is positively associated with other nonrequired reading, but negatively associated with educational attainment. It is probably best thought of as an alternative to academic pursuits.

Student interest in high culture is ascertained from a question that asks how often the student attended *cultural events* such as concerts, lectures, plays, etc. Like the self-assessment for culture, we expected this measure to affect occupation through educational attainment, but to have little effect on earnings.

We used composites constructed by Talent researchers to measure students' interest in *hobbies* and their involvement in various *sports.*° Since preliminary analyses indicated that participation in sports had no statistically significant effects on later success after controlling family background, we omitted it from later analyses.

Importance of insurance is the student's response to a single question on the importance of life insurance. Three other questions relating to financial security (expected life insurance in terms of future salary; expected savings in terms of salary; expected investments in securities in terms of salary) had insignificant effects after controlling importance of insurance.

Education necessary is the student's view of whether it is necessary to have a college education to be a leader in the community. We also considered a question that asked students whether "girls should go to college only if they plan to use their education on a job," but found boys' answers to the question had no effect on their later success after controlling assessments of whether education was necessary for leadership.

Materialistic orientation tries to measure the extent to which the student views adult work in terms of monetary rewards. *Interest orientation* tries to measure the importance of intrinsic rewards to work. *Advancement orientation* tries to measure the value of continued promotions and raises. Each question asks how likely the student would be to quit a job

---

° We used these two composites without testing whether they adequately reflected the effects of their component questions. Effects of individual questions may therefore be hidden.

if it did not meet the particular standard. Correlations between these items range from 0.6 to 0.7, perhaps reflecting the fact that for all questions a positive answer implies taking purposive action.

Perception of ability is the principal component of six questions that ask the student to judge his own academic skills, including his reading and writing ability and his studying skills. This measure correlates only 0.38 with test scores, and it is of interest if it predicts success independently of such scores.

Students' *grades* in history and social studies courses had larger effects on all outcomes than did grades in English, mathematics, foreign language, or science courses. History and social studies grades also had a greater effect on all outcomes than did average grades in all academic subject areas.

None of the indirect measures of personality is well explained by measured family background. Background controls explain 8 percent of the variance in positive affiliations, 6 percent of the variance in cultural events and perception of ability, and less than 5 percent of the variance in the other noncognitive measures.

Effects on Occupation. Table 5.5 shows the effects of these noncognitive measures on occupational status with various controls. Column 1 shows the observed correlations. Columns 2 to 4 show each noncognitive measure's standardized coefficient when we control background, test score, and education, but not the other noncognitive measures. Columns 5 and 6 show each noncognitive measure's coefficient when we also control other *similar* noncognitive measures. Columns 5a and 6a show combined coefficients for each group of noncognitive measures. Columns 7 to 9 show each noncognitive measure's coefficient with *all* the other noncognitive measures entered. Columns 7a to 9a show combined coefficients for each group of noncognitive measures with all the others controlled.

Columns 5 and 6 allow us to consider the way that similar questions relate to occupational status when they are entered together. We can see that although "study habits" has a positive effect on occupational status, the "best work" measure has a negative effect. Those who say they often do assignments too quickly to do their best work thus have an occupational advantage over those who say they are more conscientious. Since those who say they do assignments too quickly get *less* schooling, we might take this as an indication that the pragmatist has an advantage over the perfectionist after he leaves school. Alternatively, individuals who say they never work too quickly to do their best work may have lower personal standards, so the negative sign may indicate that those who set high standards for themselves enter higher-status occupations, even when they do not obtain more schooling.

The pattern of coefficients for the three work-orientation questions confirms our expectation that individuals who are concerned only about pay and not about whether a job provides interesting work or opportunity for advancement obtain lower-status jobs (coefficient –0.086).

The coefficients in columns 5 and 6 should, however, be viewed with caution. The three social activities variables, for example, include reports of past and present dating behavior. Since the two are logically related, the standardized coefficient of one variable with the other held constant has no meaningful interpretation. Similarly, while membership in one set of groups is separable from membership in another, a person's various affiliations are probably interrelated. It may not be possible to alter an individual's membership in one group without altering his social contacts, and thus his memberships in other groups. Thus, we should not necessarily attach causal importance to one affiliation measure's coefficient while the other is controlled. The same caveat applies to the work orientation and study habits variables.

In order to provide more interpretable coefficients, we combined coefficients for groups of variables that were similar. These coefficients appear in columns 5a and 6a. With just background characteristics controlled, the three questions on dating and social behavior have a combined effect of 0.210. This is the effect of the best linear combination of the three variables.

The combined coefficients in columns 5a and 6a indicate the relative importance of different classes of variables. These combined coefficients are meaningful only if the different groups of variables measure distinct traits. We have not tried to prove that they do. Nonetheless, we will proceed as if each group label really identifies a conceptually distinct trait. Thus, column 5a implies that having the "right" response to academic demands, having appropriate dating experience, or being affiliated with certain kinds of groups plus holding positions of leadership predict eventual occupational status equally well. These traits' effects are not completely independent of one another. Column 7 shows, for example, that holding down a job during the school year depresses occupational attainment less when other noncognitive traits are controlled, suggesting that the working student suffers partly because his other noncognitive traits put him at a disadvantage.

TABLE 5.5

Standardized Regressions of Occupational Status on Indirect Measures of Personality[a]

	Personality Measures Entered Separately			
	(1)	(2)	(3)	(4)
Academic response				
Study habits	.302	.236	.143	.067
Best work	.000	[−.008]	[−.026]	[−.042]
Group activities				
Affiliations (+)	.196	.130	.134	.056
Affiliations (−)	−.127	−.085	[.010]	[.005]
Leadership roles	.186	.137	.138	.093
Social activities[b]				
Never dated	.091	.117	.077	[.030]
Doesn't date	−.010	[.014]	[−.023]	[−.051]
Times out per week	−.208	−.172	−.135	−.080
Hours per week job	−.160	−.119	−.082	[−.015]
Reading				
Intellectual reading	.134	.090	[.060]	[.022]
Science fiction reading	.010	[.008]	[.000]	[.014]
Culture and hobbies				
Cultural events	.251	.178	.137	.062
Hobbies	−.066	[−.048]	.010	[.031]
Attitudes				
Importance of insurance	.160	.111	[.044]	[.012]
Education necessary	.118	[.065]	[.017]	[−.013]
Work orientation:				
Material	.056	[.031]	[−.004]	[−.006]
Interest	.119	.075	[.005]	[−.022]
Advancement	.113	.080	[.034]	[.007]
$\bar{R}^2$				
History/social studies grades			.160	[.051]
Perception of ability			.082	[.031]
Controls:				
Background		X	X	X
Test score			X	X
Education				X

Coefficients in brackets are not significant at the 0.05 level, two-tailed. Values in column 5a, 6a, 7a, 8a, and 9a are combined coefficients.

[a]Sample includes 836 Talent males with complete data on background characteristics test score, high school curriculum, years of education, and occupation, as well as the 2 indirect measures of personality listed in the table.

[b]Omitted from this table were age of first date, dates per week, times gone steady, an the dummy for never having gone steady. These had no effect on occupation after co trolling other social activities variables.

	Personality Measures Entered in Groups				All Personality Measures Entered at Once					
(5)	(5a)	(6)	(6a)	(7)	(7a)	(8)c	(8a)	(9)c	(9a)
	.245		.156	.165			.110		.074
.264		.167		.172		.110		.067	
−.088		−.074		−.073		−.067		−.064	
	.223		.175		.160		.143		.084
.143		.113		.075		[.070]		[.012]	
−.156		[−.054]		−.100		[−.044]		[−.030]	
.114		.106		.111		.106		.080	
	.210		.173		.188		.165		.119
.139		.111		.133		.114		.074	
−.092		−.107		−.097		−.097		−.096	
−.171		−.142		−.148		−.130		−.092	
−.119		−.081		−.079		−.070		[−.020]	
−		−		[.028]		[.022]		[.002]	
−		−		[−.021]		[−.026]		[.000]	
	.201		.139		.124		.092		.040d
.199		.142		.109		.087		[.041]	
−.091		[−.022]		−.086		[−.054]		[−.005]	
	.130		.063d		.095d		.064d		042d
.096		[.052]		[.056]		[.037]		[.022]	
[.035]		[.011]		[.027]		[.012]		[−.007]	
−.086]		[−.046]		−.071		[−.046]		[−.005]	
.042]		[−.023]		[.002]		[−.037]		[−.052]	
.043]		[.045]		[.070]		[.063]		[.033]	
				.267		.313		.428	
						.096		.028	
						[.020]		[−.010]	
X	X	X	X	X	X	X	X	X	X
		X	X			X	X	X	X
								X	X

c All coefficients and $\bar{R}^2$ were estimated without history/social studies grades and erception of ability in the equation. The coefficients of these two variables are from a pplementary equation that also included all other variables shown in this column.

d Combined coefficients for variables that are statistically insignificant are especially :ely to be upwardly biased.

The attitude questions have small and only occasionally significant effects. If students who have appropriate attitudes are more successful than others, our measures must not capture the relevant attitudes very well. Extracurricular reading has a statistically insignificant effect after other measures are controlled.

No single noncognitive characteristic appears central in determining what kind of job an individual will obtain. Instead, many different traits have small but distinct effects. Correlations between these measures are usually positive but sometimes negative.

Columns 3, 6, 6a, 8, and 8a present effects of these same noncognitive measures under the assumption that they depend on academic ability and that one should therefore assess their effects with ability controlled. Controlling ability reduces combined coefficients by as much as 25 percent. The pattern of coefficients remains unchanged, however. These columns also present the effects of history/social studies grades and perception of ability, since these measures depend on cognitive ability. Column 8 indicates that once other noncognitive characteristics are controlled, perception of ability does not affect occupational attainment, while history and social studies grades do.

Controlling for education as well as ability (columns 4 and 9) reduces the impact of all personality measures, implying that they affect occupation partly by influencing how much schooling an individual gets. The positive effect of having good high school grades and attending cultural events, and the negative effect of holding down a job during high school, all decline by more than 50 percent. Similarly, the impact of having the right study habits and attitudes and of belonging to the right types of groups declines by more than 40 percent. However, measures of leadership and social activities have less than 30 percent of their impact on occupational status because they influence education. This is in sharp contrast to self-assessed personality traits, which exert almost all their influence on occupation by affecting education.

Background explained 12.7 percent of the variance in occupational status. The noncognitive measures raise $\overline{R}^2$ to 26.7 percent. If we enter the noncognitive measures after academic ability (column 7), $\overline{R}^2$ rises from 0.241 to 0.318, and if we enter them after ability and education, $\overline{R}^2$ rises from 0.408 to 0.428.

Effects on Earnings. Table 5.6 presents regressions of hourly earnings at age 28 on those noncognitive measures that had significant effects in preliminary analyses. "Leadership roles" has the largest effect when we

TABLE 5.6

Standardized Regressions of Hourly Earnings on Indirect Measures of Personality[a]

	Entered Separately				All Entered Together		
	(1)	(2)	(3)	(4)	(5)	(6)[b]	(7)[b]
Academic response							
Study habits	.102	[.066]	[.035]	[.006]	.100	[.072]	[.047]
Best work	-.054	[-.060]	[-.071]	-.079	-.086	-.088	-.089
Leadership roles	.134	.115	.114	.097	.096	.098	.082
Never gone steady	-.088	-.088	-.107	-.113	-.081	-.093	-.099
Intellectual reading	-.041	-.065	-.074	-.082	-.095	-.097	-.101
Attitudes							
Importance of insurance	.079	[.060]	[.041]	[.028]	[.002]	[-.011]	[-.024]
Education necessary	.092	.075	[.058]	[.050]	[.052]	[.043]	[.039]
Work orientation:							
Material	.071	[.063]	[.055]	[.051]	[-.013]	[-.003]	[.004]
Interest	.099	.089	.072	[.066]	[.063]	[.047]	[.046]
Advancement	.073	[.065]	[.053]	[.047]	[-.000]	[.001]	[.001]
$\bar{R}^2$			.101	.088	.054	.062	.079
Perception of ability						.112	.113
$\bar{R}^2$						.069	.086
Controls:							
Background		X	X	X	X	X	X
Test score			X	X		X	X
Education				X			X

Coefficients in brackets are not significant at the 0.05 level, two-tailed.

[a]Sample includes 843 Talent males with complete data on background characteristics, test score, high school curriculum, years of education, and hourly earnings, as well as the eleven indirect measures of personality listed in the table.

[b]All coefficients and the first $\bar{R}^2$ were estimated without perception of ability in the equation. The coefficient of perception of ability and the second $\bar{R}^2$ were estimated from a supplementary equation that also included all the other variables shown in this column.

consider the composites one at a time (column 2), but the coefficient is only 0.114. The other coefficients are even smaller. "Study habits" has a positive effect, and the "best work" measure a negative effect, as in equations predicting occupational status.

Never having gone steady has a negative coefficient, indicating that students who had gone steady by the time they were in eleventh grade are more successful economically 12 years later than students who had not gone steady. Controlling cognitive ability increases the positive effect of having gone steady (column 5), as does controlling education. It thus appears that students who have gone steady have slightly lower academic ability and obtain slightly less education but possess other characteristics that enhance their earnings despite these disadvantages. They may have social skills that increase their earnings. Alternatively, they may be more likely to marry young, have family responsibilities, and therefore work steadily.

The negative coefficient of intellectual reading indicates that intellectuals have lower earnings at age 28. This may be because intellectuals are trading income for intellectual challenge. If so, their disadvantage may only be temporary. Alternatively, high school intellectualism may be negatively associated with later earnings because it reflects a rejection of the adolescent subculture. Following Coleman's (1961) argument, this may indicate a lack of concern for collectively pursued goals. Intellectuals may be less productive than others on jobs that require them to adopt group goals and perform in a group context. This could depress earnings later on as well.*

Doing nonrequired reading and never having gone steady both have negative effects on earnings, despite the fact that they are both positively related to socioeconomic background and academic ability. Individuals from advantaged backgrounds and with high ability thus have certain characteristics that depress their earnings, at least at the age of 28.

Comparing columns 5 and 6 indicates that noncognitive traits' effects on earnings are not generally tied to academic ability. The greatest decline is for study habits, indicating that students with good study habits have an advantage partly because they have greater academic ability.

Controlling for educational attainment further reduces the impact of study habits but has little effect on the other measures. These measures

---

* Lower earnings are not due to taking longer to complete a given level of education and thus having less work experience. When we controlled for work experience, the negative coefficient of intellectual reading declined less than 5 percent.

apparently affect economic success independent of how much schooling an individual obtains.

Entered together after background characteristics, noncognitive traits raise the explained variance in hourly earnings from 0.022 to 0.054. If we assume that academic ability precedes these measures, the contribution to explained variance remains appreciable, with $\overline{R}^2$ increasing from 0.032 to 0.062.[*]

Conclusions about Effects of Indirect Measures of Personality. High school behavior predicts occupational status and earnings at age twenty-eight even with ability and family background controlled. Behavior predicts occupational status better than self-assessed personality traits do, but it does no better in predicting earnings.

Habits and attitudes that teachers like ("study habits") help students get higher-status jobs by helping them to obtain more schooling, but they do not raise earnings much. Similarly, at least at age 28, those who have the "right" friends in high school, as indicated by group memberships, obtain more schooling but have little economic advantage independent of their schooling.

Leadership behavior correlates only 0.37 with self-assessed leadership, but the two measures predict economic success in much the same way. Individuals who hold positions of leadership, like those who see themselves as leaders, obtain greater earnings even when they neither have a lot of schooling nor enter high-status occupations.

Although those who have gone out for dates or other social recreation enter lower-status occupations, those who have gone steady make more money. While it is not clear what these measures mean, the pattern suggests that different mechanisms determine what kind of occupation an individual enters and how much money he makes once he enters it.

Attending cultural events correlates only 0.28 with the culture self-assessment, but both influence occupational status, primarily through education.

Although student attitudes toward financial security, education, and jobs usually have the effects predicted by conventional wisdom, these effects are small and decline further after controlling ability and behavioral measures of personality. This suggests that student behavior predicts future success better than attitudes do.

---

[*] Regressions which predict ln hourly earnings are very similar to those predicting hourly earnings. $\overline{R}^2$ with background controls is 0.003 less. $\overline{R}^2$ adding noncognitive characteristics is 0.004 less. There are no important substantive differences.

3. COMBINED EFFECTS OF DIFFERENT PERSONALITY TRAITS

While our evidence indicates that many loosely related noncognitive traits affect individual achievement, it is also instructive to combine them into a single measure. Tables 5.7 and 5.8 present standardized coefficients for combined variables. The variable labeled "noncognitive traits" is constructed from *both* self-assessed *and* behavioral personality measures. The noncognitive characteristics embodied in this variable change from one regression to the next, since the noncognitive measures are reweighted in each regression to have maximum predictive power. Family background and education also change in this way. This means that the correlations among composite traits also change from regression to regression, though the changes are seldom large.

We have also entered several social-psychological variables similar to those used by Sewell and Hauser (1975). These include parents' educational hopes, friends' educational plans, respondents' educational plans, and respondents' occupational preferences.

Effects on Occupation. About a third of family background's effect on occupational status derives from its effect on noncognitive traits, either directly or indirectly via cognitive ability. With background characteristics but not academic ability controlled, the noncognitive composite has a sheaf coefficient of 0.418. Controlling for academic ability reduces the coefficient to 0.309, implying that one-quarter of the effect of noncognitive traits is due to their association with academic ability. If academic ability is formed before these noncognitive traits, this proportion should be considered spurious. If academic ability develops after these noncognitive traits, one-quarter of their effect is traceable to the fact that they influence ability. Whatever the causal ordering, individuals with high academic ability tend to have personality traits that help them obtain higher-status jobs, as indicated by a correlation of 0.269 between the academic composite and the noncognitive traits that affect occupation. Noncognitive traits are as important overall as cognitive skills; both have standardized coefficients of 0.31 with background controlled.

Table 5.7 also shows that even after controlling grades, the influence of parents and friends, and the student's own occupational preferences and educational plans, noncognitive traits still have a sizable coefficient (0.218). Thus we may conclude that certain noncognitive characteristics influence occupational status independent of family background, academic ability, grades, peer group pressures, educational plans, and occupational preferences in eleventh grade.

Indeed, noncognitive traits have an appreciable effect on occupational status even with education controlled (see equations 7 to 9), with standardized coefficients ranging from 0.166 to 0.186. The noncognitive traits that affect occupational status independent of education are much less closely tied to cognitive ability or family background than the noncognitive traits that work through educational attainment (correlations 0.120 and –0.001 vs. 0.269 and 0.177).

Of the social-psychological variables, only occupational preferences have an effect on occupation after education is controlled. Almost none of the posteducational influence of the other noncognitive traits on status attainment is due to the fact that these traits correlate with occupational preferences in high school. Over 20 percent of the posteducational impact of cognitive ability is attributable to the fact that ability correlates with high school occupational preferences (compare equations 8 and 9).

Effects on Hourly Earnings. Table 5.8 presents combined effects of noncognitive traits on hourly earnings. Equations 0 and 2 indicate that a sixth of the effect of background on earnings works through our measures of noncognitive traits. It appears, then, that at least among 28-year-olds, the noncognitive traits we have measured are not critical in facilitating the conversion of parental advantages into earnings.

Adding test scores to the model indicates that noncognitive characteristics do not work through academic ability either. The correlation matrix for equation 3 indicates that students who have noncognitive characteristics that boost earnings are not particularly likely to have high test scores ($r = 0.101$) or to come from more advantaged backgrounds ($r = 0.070$). This conclusion is strengthened if we consider only those noncognitive traits that exert effects independent of friends' plans and occupational preferences. The intercorrelations among the combined measures in equation 4 indicate that individuals who rank above average on these noncognitive characteristics score slightly *below* the sample mean on the Talent tests. Indeed, most of these noncognitive characteristics seem to affect wages at age 28 independent of schooling and occupational status. The total effect of noncognitive traits therefore remains appreciable (0.245) even after controlling education and occupation.*

---

* When we add work experience to the earnings equations, the coefficients for the noncognitive measures (considered one at a time) change less than 10 percent. The coefficients usually fall, suggesting that individuals with favorable personality traits have slightly more labor-force experience at age 28 than others with the same education. But this does little to explain why they make more money.

TABLE 5.7

Combined Coefficients from Regressions of Occupational Status on Family Background, Noncognitive Traits, Test Scores, Social-Psychological Measures, and Education[a]

Standardized Regression Equations

	Family Background[b]	Noncognitive Traits[c]	Test Score[d]	Grades[e]	Parents' Educational Hopes[f]	Friends' Educational Plans[g]	Educational Plans[h]	Occupational Preferences[i]	Education	$\bar{R}^2$
0)	.389									.138
1)	.239		.384							.253
2)	.266	.418								.283
3)	.195	.309	.313							.330
4)	.192	.270	.297	.117						.335
5)	.160	.218	.211	.086	[.009]	[.067]	[.058]	.150		.348
6)	.124								.607	.413
7)	.126	.186	.142	—[j]					.550	.440
8)	.105	.168							.504	.448
9)	.098	.166	.110	—[j]	[−.012]	[.035]	[.002]	.094	.473	.452

Correlations

Equation 3

	(1)	(2)	(3)	(4)
(1) Family background	1.000			
(2) Noncognitive traits	.177	1.000		
(3) Test score	.343	.269	1.000	

Equation 5

	(1)	(2)	(3)	(4)
(1) Family background	1.000			
(2) Noncognitive traits	.048	1.000		
(3) Test score	.339	.180	1.000	
(4) Grades	.146	.192	.328	1.000

	(1)	(2)	(3)	(4)
Equation 8				
(1) Family background	1.000			
(2) Noncognitive traits	−.001	1.000		
(3) Test score	.194	.120	1.000	
(4) Education	.177	.230	.557	1.000
Equation 9				
(1) Family background	1.000			
(2) Noncognitive traits	−.042	1.000		
(3) Test score	.158	.124	1.000	
(4) Education	.104	.232	.557	1.000

Coefficients in brackets are not significant at the 0.05 level, two-tailed.

[a]Sample includes 732 Talent males with complete data on all variables.

[b]Family background = combined coefficient for eleven variables used to control background (see table 5.2). Since all measures were included, regardless of significance, this coefficient overestimates the impact of family background.

[c]Noncognitive traits = combined coefficient for noncognitive measures that were tested and were found to be statistically significant. Measures tested were sensitivity, impulsiveness, leadership, mature personality, study habits, best work, affiliations (+), affiliations (−), leadership roles, never dated, doesn't date, times out per week, hours worked, cultural events, hobbies, and importance of insurance.

[d]Project Talent "academic composite" (see chapter 4).

[e]Grades = history and social studies grades.

[f]Parents' educational hopes taken from the question: "How much education do your parents or guardians want you to have?" Response coded in years. Range 11-18.

[g]Friends' educational plans taken from the question: "How much education are most of your friends planning to obtain?" Response coded in years. Range 11-18.

[h]Educational plans taken from the question: "What is the greatest amount of education you expect to have during your life?" Response coded in years. Range 11-18.

[i]Occupational Preference: Students rated 112 occupations on a five-point scale indicating how much they would like the work. We assigned estimated Duncan scores to occupations and coded occupational preference as the average Duncan score weighted by the individual's preferences. This measure had a greater effect than preference measures based on the student's most preferred occupation.

[j]Not statistically significant and therefore not entered in this equation.

TABLE 5.8

Combined Coefficients from Regressions of Hourly Earnings on Family Background, Noncognitive Traits, Test Scores, Social-Psychological Measures, Education, and Occupation[a]

Standardized Regression Equations

	Family Background	Noncognitive Traits[b]	Test Score	Parents' Educational Hopes	Friends' Educational Plans	Educational Plans	Occupational Preference	Education	Occupation	R̄²
0)	.225									.036
1)	.172		.156							.054
2)	.189	.286	.138							.108
3)	.153	.273	.090	[.018]	.105	[.044]	.103			.120
4)	.125	.242	[.058]	[.019]	.090	[.014]	-[.082]			.130
5)	.119	.245	[.042]	[.023]	.084	[.011]	[.071]	.147		.140
6)	.115	.245						.098	.142	.150

Correlations

(Column numbers (1)–(5) are positioned beneath the headers Noncognitive Traits, Test Score, Parents' Educational Hopes, Friends' Educational Plans, and Educational Plans, respectively.)

Equation 3

	(1)	(2)	(3)
(1) Family background	1.000		
(2) Noncognitive traits	.070	1.000	
(3) Test score	.265	.101	1.000

Equation 4

	(1)	(2)	(3)
(1) Family background	1.000		
(2) Noncognitive traits	-.015	1.000	
(3) Test score	.171	-.099	1.000

Equation 6

	(1)	(2)	(3)	(4)	(5)
(1) Family background	1.000				
(2) Noncognitive traits	-.015	1.000			
(3) Test score	.108	-.104	1.000		
(4) Education	.069	-.040	.306	1.000	
(5) Occupation	.083	-.047	.463	.317	1.000

Coefficients in brackets are not significant at the 0.05 level, two-tailed.

[a]Sample includes 732 Talent males with complete data on all variables.

[b]The following measures were entered in order of contribution to explained variance until no unentered measure increased explained variance significantly: leadership, study habits, best work, leadership roles, never gone steady, academic reading, and education necessary.

It is hard to predict whether the effects of noncognitive traits will increase or decrease as the sample ages.

Interactions and Nonlinearities. The analyses presented up to this point have entered squared terms to account for nonlinearities in the effects of background characteristics and cognitive ability and product terms to account for interactions among background characteristics. In contrast, we have treated the noncognitive traits as if their effects were exclusively linear and additive. To see if there were important non-linearities, we added squared terms to the linear equations. Several were statistically significant, but none altered $\overline{R}^2$ enough to be sub-stantively interesting. Since the original scaling of the noncognitive traits was arbitrary, the nonlinearities have no clear substantive interpre-tation.

The scanty available evidence (Elder, 1968; Crockett, 1962) also indi-cated that personality traits might not have additive effects. Although these studies had serious flaws, they suggested that individual motivation was more important for individuals from lower-status background. This implies a negative multiplicative interaction between family background and motivation. Gasson, Haller, and Sewell (1972), in contrast, suggested that student educational plans and occupational aspirations might inter-act positively with background and ability, since a student should have less trouble realizing his aspirations or plans if his resources were greater. Numerous other potential interactions suggest themselves. If any one personality trait either accentuates or reduces the effect of another, for example, we should find significant multiplicative interactions between the relevant personality measures. Individuals with certain personality characteristics may also realize greater returns to ability or education than others.

To test such possibilities, we added product terms involving the per-sonality measures to regressions that already controlled their additive effects. We tested more than 100 potential interactions in this way, including interactions of personality measures with background charac-teristics, cognitive ability, and education, and interactions between dif-ferent personality measures. Fewer than one in ten of the interaction terms was statistically significant at the 0.05 level. The significant inter-actions do not fit any pattern suggested by previous research. We were not even able to find any convincing explanation for the observed ef-fects, perhaps partly because more than half were due to sampling error and we had no way of knowing which half.

In addition to testing single-interaction terms, we also performed numerous experiments with groups of interactions. Their explanatory power was often greater than we would expect by chance, suggesting that interaction effects exist. The explanatory power of the interactions was invariably small, however, and their inclusion did not change the coefficients of other variables. Our investigation does not, then, support any of the obvious alternatives to a simple additive model. This does not mean that the world is "really" additive. It is not, and any theory that predicted the specific interactions we found would be far better than our additive approach. But because we lack such a theory, and because we found no empirical support for the a priori theories discussed above, we must settle for additive approximations of reality.

4. PERSONALITY ASSESSMENTS BY OTHERS

Kalamazoo's tenth-grade homeroom teachers rated their students on nine character traits: "cooperativeness," "dependability," "executive ability," "emotional control," "industriousness," "initiative," "integrity," "perseverance," and "appearance." They rated students above average, average, or below average on each trait. There is no way of ascertaining how well teachers knew the students they rated. Homeroom teachers were in charge of as many as eighty students. Although teachers had further contact with some students in regular classes, teachers' ratings of many students must have been based on second-hand information or on the student's general reputation in the school. Not only are teachers likely to have rated some students relatively inaccurately, but different teachers are likely to have interpreted the nine traits differently. Nonetheless, these ratings have the virtue of portraying students as others see them, not just as they see themselves.

For each of the nine traits, more than half the students received ratings of average. The proportion of students rated above average ranged from 32.1 percent for "cooperativeness" to 10.8 percent for executive ability. Teachers rated more students above average than below average on every trait. We coded these responses as if they represented an equal interval scale (below average = 1, average = 2, above average = 3).*

---

* We used dummies to test whether the equal-interval coding adequately represented the effects of the teacher ratings. Although deviations from linearity were consistent and often statistically significant, they were not large enough to alter substantive conclusions. We therefore retained the equal-interval coding in the analyses that follow.

Teacher ratings for different traits tend to be highly correlated, the lowest correlation being 0.4. This may be because the underlying character traits tend to vary together, because teachers tend to rate individuals consistently without regard to the actual pattern of traits, or because different ratings measure the same underlying trait. Correlations of "dependability" with "cooperativeness" and of "perseverance" with "industriousness" exceed 0.8, suggesting that these traits are perceived as very similar. The correlations of the teacher ratings with IQ scores are consistently smaller than the correlations among the ratings (0.2 to 0.3 vs. 0.4 to 0.8). If teachers are rating students largely on an underlying unitary trait, that trait is not closely associated with test performance.

Father's education, father's occupation, and family size explain less than 6 percent of the variance in any teacher rating. If these three family characteristics captured all aspects of the family that made brothers alike, the correlations between teachers' ratings of brothers would average less than 0.06. In fact, the correlations between teacher ratings of brothers range from 0.24 to 0.46. Teachers may rate a student partly on a basis of his brother's behavior. Brothers may also affect one another's behavior, making them more alike than we would expect if all they shared was a common background. It seems unlikely, however, that these factors alone explain the large sibling correlations. Genetic or environmental factors shared by brothers that operate independently of father's education, father's occupation, and family size probably have appreciable effects on students' behavior and hence on teacher ratings.

Effects on Occupation. Table 5.9 indicates that positive ratings by teachers are associated with higher-status first occupations, even after family characteristics and cognitive ability are controlled.* "Initiative" and "integrity" have negative effects, however, once we control the other significant ratings. Experiments with various forms of this regression indicate that if we omit "dependability," "integrity" no longer has an appreciable negative effect. This suggests that individuals rated as displaying integrity but not dependability suffer on the job market. This negative effect is generally hidden, since individuals are usually rated similarly on both traits. We found a similar relationship between "executive ability" and "initiative," suggesting that displaying initiative is not in itself helpful, but that it appears helpful because those who take initiative also have other virtues.

* Since cognitive ability is measured by a test administered in the sixth grade, we have assumed it is causally prior to tenth-grade teacher ratings.

TABLE 5.9

*Standardized Regressions of Initial Occupational Status
on Kalamazoo Teacher Ratings of Personality Traits*[a]

	r	389 Individuals				105 Pairs of Brothers[b]	
		Ratings Entered Separately		All Significant Ratings Entered[c]		Ratings Entered Separately	
	r	(1)	(2)	(3)	(4)	(5)	(6)
Cooperativeness	.286	.155	[.017]			.215	[.082]
Dependability	.322	.182	[.039]	.153		.253	[.154]
Executive ability	.276	.157	[.046]	.132		.188	.195
Emotional control	.252	.125	[.001]			[.118]	[.099]
Industriousness	.337	.207	[.066]	.182	.125	.305	.175
Initiative	.237	[.080]	[.006]	[−.103]		[.026]	[.088]
Integrity	.216	[.080]	[−.043]	−.138	−.109	[−.023]	[−.134]
Perseverance	.308	.191	[.039]			.388	.206
Appearance	.229	.090	[−.014]			[−.024]	[−.062]
Controls:							
Measured family background		X	X	X	X		
All background common to brothers						X	X
Test score		X	X	X	X	X	X
Education			X		X		X
$\bar{R}^2$ with controls only				.271	.552		
$\bar{R}^2$ with controls plus significant traits				.324	.561		

Coefficients in brackets are not significant at the 0.05 level, two-tailed.

[a] Kalamazoo respondents aged 35 to 59 with complete data on father's education, father's occupation, siblings, test score, education, initial occupation, earnings, and the nine teacher ratings.

[b] Pairs of brothers must both have data on test score, education, initial occupation, occupation, earnings, and the nine teacher ratings, and at least one brother must report father's education, father's occupation, and siblings. Regressions based on differences between brothers. Coefficients standardized using SDs for sample, not SDs of differences between brothers.

[c] Traits entered in order of contribution to explained variance until no unentered trait had a statistically significant effect. A rating could, and did, become insignificant once other ratings entered the equation.

Controlling for years of schooling reduces the effects of all traits appreciably. Considered separately, no teacher rating has a statistically significant impact on early occupation after controlling education. If we enter ratings together, "industriousness" appears to have a positive effect and "integrity" a negative effect. Their contribution to the explained variance is minimal, however.

The smaller brothers' sample yields similar results (not shown) when we control only measured background and cognitive ability. Contrary to expectations, however, controlling all characteristics that brothers have in common (through difference equations) *increases* the apparent effects of the ratings (columns 5 and 6). After we controlled all characteristics brothers have in common, as well as cognitive ability and education, three ratings had statistically significant effects on early occupational status, whereas none had significant effects when we controlled measured family characteristics, cognitive ability, and education in this same sample. Chapter 4 found a similar increase in the effect of cognitive skills within Kalamazoo families.

Teacher ratings have less effect in maturity than they had on initial status.° But after controlling education, the ratings' effects on mature status are at least as great as on initial status. Furthermore, regressions of mature occupational status in the smaller sample of brothers are very much like those predicting early occupation. After controlling for differences in ability and schooling, personality differences between brothers appear more important than personality differences between individuals from similar demographic background.

The increase in the apparent effect of most personality traits when we look at differences between brothers suggests that the unmeasured background characteristics that affect personality traits must be *negatively* correlated with those that affect occupational status. This is rather puzzling, since the measured family characteristics that affect teacher ratings are much like those that affect adult success. In any event, these findings suggest that the modest effects of teacher character ratings on occupational achievement would not disappear if family environment had been measured more carefully.

Since the effects of teacher ratings on initial occupational status are similar to their effects on later status after ability and schooling are controlled, these traits must have a continuing influence on status. The sample is too small—especially in analyses that consider brothers—to determine the relative importance of these traits, but it is clear that they have some impact.

Effects on Earnings. Teacher ratings also have positive effects on earnings after we control measured family background and ability.† But once we control education, "executive ability" is the only statistically significant rating, with a coefficient of 0.126. Controlling for occupation decreases the standardized coefficient of executive ability to 0.108. Regressions with the smaller sample of brothers reveal little of interest. No

° The relevant regressions appear in table A5.3 of the Appendix.
† The relevant regressions appear in table A5.4 of the Appendix.

teacher rating has a statistically significant effect on earnings in any regression in this small sample. The regressions of ln earnings on teacher ratings do not differ appreciably from those of earnings.

Conclusions about Teacher Ratings. Given the circumstances under which teachers rated students and the crude scale they used, all coefficients obtained from the Kalamazoo sample are likely to be biased downward. Nonetheless, the effects of the traits teachers rated clearly persist into middle age. Analyses using brothers indicate that these effects would persist even if family environment were measured in more detail.

Negative coefficients for initiative, integrity, and cooperativeness in regressions predicting occupational status suggest that the advantages we normally associate with these traits may be spurious. Apparently, the characteristics that lead to success are not captured in a simple way by the traits teachers rated.

It appears likely, however, that teachers did recognize an important aspect of personal competence or motivation when they rated students on executive ability. Not only does this measure influence occupational status, but it also affects earnings independent of status from 20 to 40 years later.

CONCLUSIONS

Our findings support the notion that individuals possess stable personality characteristics that influence their economic success. Measures of personality based on high school students' self-assessments, personal behavior, attitudes, and ratings by others are related to subsequent occupational status and earnings, even after we control for family background and cognitive ability.

Since the personality measures we used almost certainly capture overlapping concepts, their coefficients cannot be taken to show the importance of single, discrete traits. Our regressions are thus not rigorous causal models. The regressions are useful, however, in that they allow us to eliminate some models that might otherwise appear plausible. They help us to refine our intuitions about the nature and role of personality traits critical to success.

Talent data suggest that the social skills or motivations which make a student see himself as a leader and hold positions of leadership in high school are critical to later achievement. They are particularly salient in helping 28-year-olds get jobs with high wages.

Kalamazoo teacher ratings of executive ability may partially capture these same characteristics. This trait influences earnings throughout an individual's working life.

Student interest in high culture, as measured by self-concept and actual attendance at cultural events, has an appreciable influence on education and hence on occupational status, but it has little effect on earnings, at least at age 28. Intellectual reading habits in high school also raise educational attainment, but they do not raise occupational status and they actually depress earnings, at least at 28. Since such reading habits are associated with high family status, this pattern reduces the benefits ordinarily associated with coming from a privileged background.

Dating experience in eleventh grade is negatively related to family status and appears to reduce both educational attainment and occupational status. Nonetheless, dating experience *increases* hourly earnings at age 28. These findings suggest that the social skills or preferences associated with dating help an individual get a well-paid job *within* most occupations, even though they do not help him acquire the credentials needed to enter a high-status occupation. These data are the first to support the widely held view that success prior to entering the job market requires different personal characteristics than success after labor market entry.

We found little support for the idea that any single personality trait is of critical importance in determining individual success. Rather, each trait that influences success seems to have a small and for the most part separable effect. Only when the effects of numerous measures of personality are considered together do they explain even a moderate portion of the observed variation in individual achievement. In general, the personality characteristics that predict success are not closely tied to family status or to cognitive ability.

The data on brothers indicate that living in the same family and sharing the same parents make men's personalities far more alike than merely growing up in the same socioeconomic stratum of society. But personality traits are not merely proxies for unmeasured family characteristics. They have an independent causal role in determining individual success.

Contrary to expectations, we failed to find any consistent or important interaction effects involving personality traits. In the absence of any compelling theory, all our conclusions about the influence of noncognitive traits have been general and tentative. These analyses suggest, however, that noncognitive traits contribute more to individual achievement than previous research had indicated.

CHAPTER 6

The Effects of
Education

INTRODUCTION

Men with a lot of schooling tend both to work in much higher status
occupations and to earn more money than men with less schooling. Com-
monplaces such as, "If you want to get ahead, get an education," reflect
popular faith that schooling is not only associated with economic success
but actually causes it. Public policy also reflects this view, emphasizing
education as a strategy both for promoting community- or nation-wide
economic growth and for helping the poor improve their economic position relative to other Americans.[1]

American economists have also emphasized the economic benefits of
education, especially in the last twenty years. Theodore Schultz (1960)
and Edward Denison (1962) have argued, for example, that the spread
of formal education played a major role in boosting the aggregate productivity of American workers.[2] Jacob Mincer (1958), Gary Becker (1964),
and others took the argument a step further, asserting that decisions about
whether or not to attend school could be seen as decisions about whether
or not to invest in one's stock of skills, which they, like other economists,
call "human capital." All these economists have also argued that dispar-

Michael Olneck wrote this chapter.

159

ities in individual earnings are at least partly due to the fact that different individuals invest different amounts in their human capital.[3]

In order either to calculate how much education has contributed to economic growth or to assess the efficiency of public or private spending on education, one must know the actual rate of return on "investment" in schooling.[4] If individuals who stayed in school were initially just like those who dropped out, this calculation would be relatively easy, since any observed difference between those with more schooling and those with less would be attributable to the difference in school experience. In practice, however, those who stay in school are likely to have more of the skills that employers value even before they gain their educational advantage. They are also likely to come from family backgrounds and have aspirations that would give them a certain economic advantage even if they dropped out. All this means that only part of the observed economic differential between those with more schooling and those with less is due to school per se. Putting the point slightly differently, if public policy induces individuals who would ordinarily have dropped out to stay in school an extra year, these potential dropouts are not likely to be as successful economically as the average individual who completes the same year of school.

This chapter is concerned principally with estimating the extent to which the apparent economic benefits of lengthier schooling are due to the fact that better-educated men start out with characteristics that affect both their educational attainment and their economic success.[5] It is also concerned with whether the advantages associated with additional schooling vary by level of schooling. If public policy seeks to enhance economic opportunity by extending educational opportunity, it is important to know if all increments in schooling promise the same benefits or if there are levels of schooling whose effects are unusually large or robust. Policies based on relationships estimated over the general population may also be misguided if they are directed toward atypical populations. The chapter therefore devotes considerable attention to whether the benefits of education vary by race, socioeconomic background, or initial ability.

Measuring Education. Our primary measure of school experience is the highest grade of school or college the respondent had completed. Economic estimates of "returns" to schooling should in theory use the number of years men *attended,* not the highest grade they *completed.* Years of attendance will exceed the highest grade completed if the respondent repeated one or more grades. Years of attendance will be lower than the highest grade completed if the respondent skipped one or more grades. Since repeaters are more common than skippers, our data slightly overstate the benefit of the average year of attendance. Since we were concerned with the possibility that different levels of schooling confer different economic benefits, we explored the nonlinear effects of education on occupational status and earnings in some detail. As expected, different levels of schooling had significantly different effects in all our large samples. But the pattern of nonlinearities was not the same for occupational status as for earnings. Nor was the pattern for dollar earnings the same as for ln earnings. Furthermore, the nonlinearities in the Census sample, which gave single years of schooling, were not the same as in OCG, where educational attainment had been grouped. Nor were they the same as in the two SRC samples, where educational attainment beyond high school was initially measured in terms of credentials rather than in terms of the highest grade completed.

Instead of selecting a different "ideal" specification for every sample and every dependent variable, we decided to distinguish those levels of education that seemed most likely to interest policy makers. To accomplish this, we used three education measures: years of education, years of higher education, and college graduation (BA).[6]

Years of education represents the total number of years of schooling the respondent completed. With years of higher education and BA controlled, the regression coefficient of years of education measures the average effect of an extra year of elementary or secondary school. The coefficient of years of higher education measures the *difference* between the effect of a year of college or graduate school and the effect of a year of elementary or secondary school. Its standard error is the standard error of this difference. The coefficient of BA measures the difference between the actual earnings of men with four or more years of higher education and the earnings predicted on the assumption that each year of higher education has the same effect. (The BA variable does *not* measure the difference between the effect of the last year of college and the effect of the next to last year of college. It may either underestimate or overestimate that difference, depending on the effects of other years of college and other years of graduate school and on the proportions of respondents with and without graduate training.)

We can illustrate the implications of our specification by considering 1970 Census data on differences in occupational status between 25- to 64-year-old college graduates (those with exactly 16 years of schooling), high school graduates (those with exactly 12 years of schooling), and elementary school graduates (those with exactly 8 years of schooling). Table A6.7 shows that high school graduates outrank elementary school graduates by 13.9 points, whereas college graduates outrank high school graduates by 28.1 points.*

Our table 6.2, which appears on page 168, implies that the typical year of elementary or secondary education raises status by 2.934 points, and hence that high school graduates outrank elementary school graduates by $(4)(2.934) = 11.6$ points. It implies that a typical year of higher education is worth 2.465 points more than a typical year of elementary or secondary education, and that college graduation is worth an extra 4.013 points, so that college graduates outrank high school graduates by a total of $(4)(2.934 + 2.465) + 4.013 = 25.6$ points. Table 6.2 thus underestimates the actual payoff from four years of high school by $13.9 - 11.7 = 2.2$ points. It underestimates the actual payoff from four years of college by $28.1 - 25.6 = 2.5$ points. These discrepancies are due partly to the simplifying assumptions required to capture effects of education with only three variables and partly to the fact that table 6.2 estimates the effects of education on status from a sample of men with complete data on other variables, whereas table A6.7 covers all men in our target population who reported their education and occupation. Fortunately, the discrepancies between estimates that are derived using our three variable specifications and estimates that are based on more complete information are quite small, so we will not discuss them further.†

It is tempting to interpret the coefficient of BA in these equations as a measure of "credentialism," but this interpretation is only legitimate under rather stringent conditions. If we measure years of higher education accurately, and if the effect of higher education on productivity is linear, the BA dummy will measure the discrepancy between productivity and status or earnings for those with credentials. But our measures of educational attainment are by no means perfect, and the association between higher education and productivity may be truly nonlinear. Both issues deserve comment.

The OCG, PA, PSID, and Veterans surveys group together all men with "some college." The PA and PSID also group men with a BA together with men who have some graduate education but no degree. OCG groups together all men with a year or more of graduate education, regardless of whether they have degrees. If we misestimated the

---

* All tables preceded by the letter A appear in the Appendix.
† A linear equation yields considerably worse estimates than our nonlinear alternative. Table A6.1 shows that when we treat the association between schooling and status as if it were linear, a typical year of schooling is associated with a 4.377 point increase in status. This implies that four years of either high school or college increase a man's status by 17.3 points. This estimate is 3.4 points too high for high school and 10.8 points too low for college.

mean number of years of schooling for any of these groups, as we easily could have, the association between years of higher education and economic success would *appear* nonlinear, even though it was in fact perfectly linear. The Census and NLS, which measure education in single years, therefore provide more reliable evidence than OCG, PA, and PSID on the degree of linearity in the effects of higher education. The Census and NLS show about the same "BA effect" on occupational status as OCG, PA, and PSID, though they show a markedly smaller "BA effect" on ln earnings. This suggests that the apparent nonlinearities in OCG, PA, and PSID are genuine, but we cannot be sure about this.

Even if all the apparent nonlinearities are genuine, we cannot be sure that the BA coefficient measures the effects of "credentialism." Credentialism implies that employers reward men known to have BAs more than they reward similar men who are not known to have BAs. If completing the last year of college is associated with a larger increase in status or earnings than completing the previous three years, and if it is also associated with a larger increase than completing an extra year of graduate school, it is tempting to argue that this is because the last year of college provides a diploma. But the association between years of higher education and actual productivity may follow the same pattern, and credentials per se may be of no economic consequence. It is hard to believe that students *learn* more in their last year of college than in other undergraduate or graduate years. But if the obstacles to completing college eliminate more undesirable employees than the obstacles to entering college and continuing for a few years, future BAs may enter college with traits that make them markedly more attractive employees than men who end up with only three years of college. Likewise, if men who go on to graduate school are short on the characteristics that employers value, and if they do not ordinarily acquire such characteristics in graduate school, they may enjoy less of an economic advantage over men with a BA than BAs enjoy over college dropouts. We have not measured most of the traits that make employers eager to hire men with a lot of education. Thus we cannot rule out the possibility that those traits, whatever they are, account for the apparent "BA effect."

Our suspicion that the apparent effects of holding a BA may not measure credentialism per se is strengthened by the fact that in the Census sample, completing the first year of college, like completing the last, is associated with larger effects than completing either of the two intervening years. While employers may systematically favor individuals who merely enter but do not complete more than one year of college, it seems more likely that college entrants differ in relevant ways from nonentrants. The same may well be true for college graduates and non-graduates. Since none of our large data sets with background and ability also measured education in single years, we cannot explore this reasoning directly. The coefficient of BA must, therefore, remain only a suggestive indicator of the possible size of the "credential effect," not a strong test.

The following discussion considers the effects of years of education on initial occupational status, current occupational status, and ln earnings. We then turn briefly to the effects of school and college "quality" on these outcomes.

1. INITIAL OCCUPATIONAL STATUS

The OCG, PSID, and Kalamazoo surveys include information about the occupations that respondents entered directly after finishing school. The OCG item is flawed, however, and we ignore it here.[7] Table 6.1 shows the effects of education on initial occupational status in the PSID and Kalamazoo samples. Since initial occupation is grouped in PSID but not in Kalamazoo, the coefficients for the two samples are not comparable. Years of higher education and BA have positive coefficients in both samples. This means that a year of higher education raises initial status more than a year of elementary or secondary education. Four years of high school are associated with a 5-point advantage in initial status in PSID, whereas four years of college are associated with a 23-point advantage. The analogous figures in Kalamazoo are 13 vs. 33 points. The "BA effect" is equal to about two years of higher education in the PSID and four years in Kalamazoo. While the differences between the two samples are partly due to the way in which they measure occupational status, they are also partly due to peculiarities in the distribution of the Kalamazoo respondents' occupations.

In order to assess the extent to which education per se affects initial occupational status, we ought to control family background, cognitive skills prior to school completion, personality traits prior to school completion, and age at the time of taking one's first job.*

* Controlling age is far more important when analyzing the determinants of men's *initial* occupational status than when analyzing the determinants of their *current* status. This is because age exerts a substantial impact on status only among very young men. Poorly educated men start their working lives in low status occupations

TABLE 6.1

Regressions of Initial Occupational Status on Education

Sample	Years of Education	Years Higher Education	BA	$\bar{R}^2$	Other Variables Controlled
1971 PSID	1.363 (.212)	2.669 (.614)	6.986 (2.405)	.302	none
	.897 (.227)	2.457 (.620)	8.164 (2.396)	.318	measured background
	1.014 (.224)	2.719 (.610)	7.211 (2.391)	.310	test score
	.690 (.234)	2.493 (.618)	8.222 (2.388)	.322	measured background, test score
1973 Kalamazoo Brothers	3.166 (.701)	[1.295] (1.016)	15.137 (3.264)	.540	none
	2.389 (.718)	[1.710] (1.011)	14.274 (3.215)	.555	measured background
	2.827 (.730)	[1.436] (1.019)	14.868 (3.264)	.542	test score
	2.146 (.740)	[1.804] (1.013)	14.075 (3.217)	.556	measured background, test score
	[1.661] (1.210)	[2.614] (1.543)	13.787 (4.496)	.601	family background
	[1.580] (1.232)	[2.644] (1.547)	13.744 (4.503)	.600	family background, test score difference

Coefficients in brackets are less than twice their standard error. Standard errors appear in parentheses. For the list of demographic background measures controlled in these analyses see the note to Table 2.2. "Family Background" is controlled by regressing the occupational difference between brothers on education and test-score differences between brothers. $\bar{R}^2$ in the equations that include "family background" is estimated using the model in figure 3.1.

The PSID measures only a limited number of demographic background characteristics, but the Kalamazoo sample has data on brothers which allow us to control all aspects of background shared by brothers. The PSID also measures test performance after school completion, so controlling test scores may control some of the effects of schooling itself. The Kalamazoo test was administered when all respondents had six years of school. The PSID has no personality measures prior to school

---

partly because they are poorly educated and partly because they are young. They often experience substantial upward mobility as they get older. Highly educated men, in contrast, have already realized most of the benefits of aging by the time they take their first regular job. They therefore experience less upward occupational mobility in their first few years out of school. As a result, ignoring age makes the effects of education on status appear larger among inexperienced than experienced workers. With age controlled, the effects of education on initial and later status are very similar.

completion, and the Kalamazoo measures explain virtually none of the effects of education on economic success, so we will ignore them. Neither survey provides data on how old men were when they entered their first occupation.

Controlling background and test performance lowers the estimated effect of elementary and secondary education more than it lowers the estimated effect of higher education. In the Kalamazoo sample, controlling all aspects of background and sixth-grade test scores lowers the estimated effect of finishing twelfth rather than eighth grade from 13 to 6 points, whereas it only lowers the estimated effect of four years of college from 33 to 31 points. The pattern in the PSID is almost identical.

These results mean that 25- to 64-year-old men who completed high school got better first jobs than men who dropped out largely because they came from more advantaged homes and had higher initial ability. If the same results were to hold for young men today, discouraging male high school students from dropping out of school would not greatly improve their occupational prospects unless they also went to college. The large and persistent effect of completing college suggests that college augments initial status for reasons unrelated to family background or cognitive skill. This could be because colleges actually help students acquire characteristics employers value. Alternatively, employers may be concerned with the background and skill differences between college and noncollege men, but not with differences within the two groups. Or employers may simply need some arbitrary device for distributing high-status jobs and may feel that giving such jobs to men with higher education causes less trouble than most other alternatives.

2. CURRENT OCCUPATIONAL STATUS

Even though men's initial occupational status depends heavily on whether they have higher education, it does not follow that the same pattern persists later in their careers. While education is positively correlated with age among men seeking their first job, this is not true for experienced workers. Furthermore, the longer men's work histories, the more relevant information employers have about them. This means that, if they wish, employers can base decisions about promotions, transfers, and dismissals on job performance, rather than on education. Thus, if education were merely a "signal" that employers used in lieu of better information, we would expect it to have its maximum effect on initial status. Its effect on later occupational status would be smaller and would be more likely to disappear when we controlled characteristics like test scores and motivation. On the other hand, if workers with more schooling are designated early for training and promotion, if they are more active and successful in searching for better jobs, if they are more productive on the job, or if later jobs depend primarily on initial jobs, we would expect education to have relatively large and robust effects on occupational status throughout life. Our data suggest that the effects of elementary and secondary education on occupational status in maturity are small and mostly spurious, while the effects of higher education are both large and robust.

Effects of Controlling Family Background. High-status families ensure that their sons will have greater than average chances for economic success mainly by ensuring that their sons get a lot of schooling. However, measured family background is associated with occupational status even among men with the same amount of education. Consequently, we somewhat overestimate the effect of schooling on status if we ignore the effects of measured background on both.

Our best information about the effects of education among men with similar socioeconomic background comes from OCG.* Table 6.2 shows the nonlinear regressions.[8] Among men with similar backgrounds in the OCG samples, an extra year of elementary or secondary education is associated with an advantage of 2.0 points on the Duncan scale. This is 74 percent of the apparent effects without background controls. Four years of college are associated with an increment of 25.4 points in occupational status among men from similar backgrounds, which is 90 percent of the increment without background controls. The apparent effects of higher education on occupational status are thus only modestly inflated by the dependence of both educational attainment and occupational status on socioeconomic background.

But socioeconomic variables do not measure family advantages very precisely. If the unmeasured aspects of family background which affect education are related to those which affect occupational status, the OCG results may well overestimate the effects of education per se. To control background more fully, we analyzed the relationship between sibling

* The OCG sample is large and the measures of background are good. The uncontrolled effects of education in the OCG are quite close to the effects in the Census. NLS gives results quite comparable to OCG, but the sample is restricted in age, so we have relied on the OCG here. In the PA and PSID, occupation is grouped.

TABLE 6.2

Regressions of Current Occupational Status on Education

Sample	Years of Education	Years Higher Education	BA	$\bar{R}^2$	Estimated Effect of 4 Years of College	Other Variables Controlled
1970 Census	2.934 (.055)	2.465 (.164)	4.013 (.770)	.411	25.6	none
1962 OCG	2.701 (.073)	3.079 (.287)	5.163 (1.275)	.408	28.3	none
	1.988 (.079)	2.928 (.284)	5.710 (1.234)	.447	25.4	measured background
1962 OCG Brothers (N = 5,780)	2.541 (.098)	3.040 (.430)	7.340 (1.942)	.385	29.7	none
	1.980 (.104)	2.571 (.421)	9.324 (1.892)	.420	27.5	measured background
	1.699 (NA)	2.074 (NA)	9.973 (NA)	NA	25.1	family background
1971 PSID	2.134 (.195)	2.951 (.564)	5.546 (2.210)	.429	25.9	none
	1.684 (.209)	3.103 (.570)	6.001 (2.203)	.442	25.1	measured background
	1.807 (.206)	2.997 (.560)	5.757 (2.197)	.436	25.0	test score
	1.501 (.215)	3.136 (.569)	6.051 (2.197)	.445	24.6	measured background, test score
	1.377 (.211)	2.685 (.560)	4.565 (2.162)	.466	20.8	measured background, test score, initial occupation
1964 Veterans	1.889 (.439)	4.816 (.933)	[4.843] (3.580)	.410	31.7	none
	1.641 (.446)	4.472 (.929)	[5.438] (3.532)	.429	29.9	measured background
	1.046 (.464)	4.851 (.919)	[5.511] (3.530)	.428	29.1	test score
	.979 (.468)	4.466 (.919)	[6.069] (3.497)	.441	27.8	measured background, test score

TABLE 6.2 *(continued)*

Sample	Years of Education	Years Higher Education	BA	$\bar{R}^2$	Estimated Effect of 4 Years of College	Other Variables Controlled
1973-74 Kalamazoo Brothers	5.722 (.809)	−2.709 (1.172)	10.876 (3.766)	.355	22.9	none
	5.654 (.843)	−2.576 (1.187)	10.866 (3.775)	.353	23.2	measured background
	3.035 (1.426)	[−.982] (1.818)	13.700 (5.297)	.416	21.9	family background
	4.693 (.832)	[−2.283] (1.161)	10.058 (3.721)	.371	19.7	test score
	4.739 (.859)	[−2.228] (1.174)	10.133 (3.730)	.370	20.2	measured background, test score
	[2.389] (1.439)	[−.689] (1.807)	13.338 (5.260)	.424	20.1	family background, test score difference
	[2.038] (1.418)	[−1.276] (1.784)	10.287 (5.241)	.443	13.3	family background, test score difference, initial occupation difference

Family background is controlled by regressing the occupational difference between brothers on the education and test-score differences between brothers for Kalamazoo and by using the procedure described in the footnote on page 170 for OCG.

The measured background characteristics controlled in this and subsequent tables in this chapter are as follows:

```
OCG = 1, 1 X 4, 3, 4, 5, 7, 8, 9, 10
OCG Brothers = 1, 3, 4, 5, 7, 8, 9, 10
PSID = 1, 2, 3, 4, 5, 7, 8, 9
PA = 1, 2, 3, 7, 8, 9
Veterans = 1, 3, 4, 7, 8, 10
Talent = 1, 3, 4, 9, 10
Talent Brothers = 3, 4, 9
Kalamazoo = 3, 4, 9
```

where 1 = race, 2 = father native born, 3 = father's education, 4 = father's occupation, 5 = father white collar, 7 = non-Southern birth, 8 = nonfarm upbringing, 9 = siblings, 10 = father absent when son 15 or 16.

Where a demographic background variable is available in a survey (see table 1.1) but not included in these analyses, it is generally insignificant. The inclusion of a variable does not, however, always mean it is significant (see tables A3.1 and A3.2 in the Appendix).

differences on education and occupation in our three samples of brothers and in OCG.* The apparent effect of elementary and secondary education is appreciably smaller than when we control only measured background characteristics. The apparent benefits of four years of college are not appreciably reduced.

In the OCG subsample for which information on brother's education is available, controlling measured background reduces the effect of four years of high school by 23 percent. This is quite close to the reduction in the full OCG sample. Controlling brothers' common background instead of just measured background reduces the coefficient by 33 instead of 23 percent. In the Kalamazoo sample, controlling socioeconomic background does not reduce the effect of four years of high school at all, while controlling brothers' common background cuts it almost in half.

In the OCG subsample, controlling socioeconomic background reduces the effect of four years of college by 7 percent, while controlling all common family background factors reduces it by 16 percent. In the Talent and Kalamazoo samples of brothers, controlling measured background has virtually no effect on the estimated effect of four years of college, while controlling brothers' common background reduces the estimate by only 4 to 10 percent.† It seems safe to conclude that the apparent effects of four years of college are not only larger but less likely to be spurious than the effects of four years of high school.

* The OCG survey asked each respondent to report his eldest brother's educational attainment. If brothers' characteristics do not directly affect one another and if respondents' reports of their brother's education are nearly as reliable as self-reports, we can use this information to calculate the effects of education within families. These assumptions appear tenable (see chapter 3, and also Olneck, 1976).

Letting U denote respondent's education, U′ denote brother's education, and Y denote respondent's occupation, the standardized coefficient (b) with shared background controlled is:

$$b = (r_{YU} - r_{YU'}) / (1 - r_{UU'})$$

Assuming $S_U = S_{U'}$, the unstandardized coefficient is $B = S_Y(r_{YU} - r_{YU'}) / S_U(1 - r_{UU'})$. For exposition of the model underlying this result, see chapters 2 and 3 of this volume and Olneck (1976, p. 160). The logic of the solution is easily extended to a model incorporating our spline variables.

† Virtually all members of the Talent sample completed high school, so the linear coefficient of schooling estimates the benefits of higher education. The linear coefficients for the Talent sample appear in table A6.1. Controlling measured background reduces the linear effect of education on occupation by 16 percent in the OCG subsample and 12 percent in the NORC Brothers sample and raises it by a negligible amount in the Kalamazoo sample. Controlling brothers' shared background reduces the linear effect by 21 percent in OCG, 31 percent in NORC Brothers, and 20 percent in Kalamazoo.

In an OCG-II sample of respondents aged 35 to 59 who reported their eldest brother's education, controlling measured background reduces the effect of education on occupational status by 15 percent, while controlling shared background reduces it by 23 percent. These results agree with those from our OCG-I subsample.

Effects of Controlling Measured Ability. Men from advantaged backgrounds get more schooling and enter higher-status occupations in part because they possess cognitive skills that are useful both at school and at work. When we control family background, we are, to some extent, controlling the effects of such ability. But men from the same socioeconomic stratum and, indeed, from the same families vary substantially in their cognitive skills. We must hold these skills constant if we want an unbiased estimate of the effects of schooling. But our data show that such controls have very modest effects on the estimated effects of education on occupational status. In the two samples with adolescent test scores, the estimated linear effect of an extra year of education on the status of men with the same scores is five-sixths of the estimated effect among men in general.* The reduction is even less in the two samples tested after school completion, suggesting that the effects of education on occupational status do not depend on improving the general cognitive skills measured by our tests.

Effects of Controlling Both Measured Ability and Family Background. Since background and cognitive ability both affect schooling and occupational status, we need to ask what the effects of schooling are among men who come from similar backgrounds and who also have the same test scores. Because background and test scores are correlated, the answer is not a simple combination of the results based on controlling each separately.

We can estimate the effects of elementary and secondary education with both test scores and background controlled from the Kalamazoo, Veterans, and PSID samples, though the Veterans and PSID use tests administered after school completion, so they may slightly underestimate the overall effects of schooling. The estimated effects of elementary and secondary schooling with no controls are appreciably larger in Kalamazoo, and appreciably smaller in PSID and Veterans, than in the more satisfactory Census and OCG samples. The PSID coefficient is low because occupations are grouped. The Veterans coefficient could be low because of random sampling error, sample bias, or both. The Kalamazoo coefficient exceeds the Census and OCG values by almost four times its sampling error, so there must be some systematic reason for the difference. Controlling background and test score reduces the large coefficients more than the small ones. Under these circumstances, we get more con-

---

* Controlling test scores in the 1964 Wisconsin follow-up reduces the schooling coefficient from 8.501 to 7.750, which is consistent with our results. See Sewell and Hauser (1975).

sistent results if we look at the percentage bias in the coefficients from different samples, rather than the absolute bias. Using this approach, we can say that controlling background and test performance lowers the coefficient of elementary and secondary education (primarily the latter) by about half in the Kalamazoo and Veterans samples and by about a third in the PSID. Since the PSID test is less reliable than the others, the best estimate of the bias is about 50 percent.

We can estimate the coefficient of higher education from the linear coefficients for Talent and Talent Brothers (see table A6.1) and from the nonlinear coefficients for Kalamazoo, Veterans, and PSID. Because there is such a high correlation between years of higher education and BA, the coefficients of these two variables have large sampling errors and differ substantially from one sample to another. The two coefficients also seem to vary reciprocally, so that the Kalamazoo sample has a very large coefficient for BA and a negative coefficient for years of higher education, while other samples have small positive coefficients for both. As a result, we get more stable estimates when we combine the coefficients of higher education and BA to estimate the effect of four years of college. These estimates appear in the next to last column of table 6.2. The data suggest that college graduates outrank high school graduates by 22 to 32 points. Once again, controlling background and test score reduces the coefficient more when the initial value is largest, so it seems best to estimate the percentage change rather than the absolute change. The percentage change ranges from a low of 5 percent in the PSID to a high of 24 percent among Talent Brothers. If we discount the PSID on the ground that the test is unreliable and the Talent Brothers on the ground that the sample is small and unrepresentative, the estimated bias is between 12 and 15 percent for the Kalamazoo, Veterans, and representative Talent samples.

Applying these percentages to Census data, the most plausible conclusion seems to be that an extra year of elementary or secondary school is associated with an increase of about 3 points in a man's occupational status, and that about half this advantage is really due to the fact that highly educated men come from advantaged families and have high initial test scores. Among men who do not get BAs, each year of college is associated with a 5 or 6 point increase in occupational status, only 1 point of which is explained by family advantages and test scores. The "BA bonus" is about 5 points, so the average value of each year of college is increased by about 1 point among those who finish college.

Since the effects of higher education on occupational status cannot be explained by differences in cognitive skills and family background among men with different amounts of education, it is tempting to conclude that employers favor men with higher education because of their noncognitive skills. Men with more drive, perseverance, initiative, and other characteristics generally thought to promote job performance may well get more schooling than those whose personalities are less attractive to employers. Brothers are certainly not identical on such characteristics, so controlling family background will not adequately control their effects. We can do somewhat better by controlling the direct measures of personality obtained in the Talent and Kalamazoo surveys. Controlling the nine Kalamazoo teacher ratings leaves the estimated effect of education virtually unchanged. Controlling all the Talent measures, including both self-assessments and behavioral indices, has an equally trivial effect (see chapter 5). This could mean that the specific characteristics rated in these surveys are not the ones that make employers value workers with higher education, that the connection between personality traits and educational attainment is not as strong as conventional wisdom assumes, or that this connection only develops *after* men have had different amounts of schooling, i.e., that schooling affects the traits employers value but it does not depend on them.

If the jobs men hold in their later careers depend upon the jobs they hold at the start of their careers, the occupational advantages of mature men with higher education could be explained simply by their advantage when they first entered the labor force. But even after controlling initial occupational status as well as family background and test scores, the unexplained difference in current status between college graduates and high school graduates is at least two-thirds of the observed difference. This means that even among men from the same homes, with identical test scores, and with similar initial occupations, college graduates end up in substantially higher-status occupations than high school graduates. Our data do not tell us why this is so.[*]

Racial Differences in the Effects of Education on Occupational Status. One common assumption about the "cost of being black" in America is that whites get greater rewards from a given amount of education than

[*] Part of the reason is definitional. The Duncan scale is a function of the proportion of workers in an occupation with twelve or more years of schooling and the proportion earning more than $3,500 in 1950. To the extent that college graduates are concentrated in educationally homogeneous occupations, their Duncan scores will be high. But this logic also applies to secondary education, whose effects are far weaker. In any event, occupational status scales that do not include education appear inferior on other grounds (Featherman, Jones, and Hauser, 1975).

nonwhites. Usually, this assertion means only that whites work in higher-status occupations than nonwhites with the same amount of education. This is clearly true. Our concern here, however, is whether an *extra* year of schooling *raises* a white man's occupational status more than it raises a nonwhite's, i.e., with whether the gap between whites and nonwhites is wider among the highly educated. We cannot answer this question simply by comparing linear regression coefficients among whites and nonwhites. As we have seen, the effects of schooling on occupational status are distinctly nonlinear, with higher education providing greater occupational rewards than elementary or secondary education. Since variation in educational attainment is more likely to include variation in higher education among whites than among nonwhites, the linear coefficients for whites are likely to be larger than for nonwhites, even if the rewards for any particular year of schooling are identical for both groups.

We have four samples with appreciable numbers of nonwhites: the Census, OCG, PSID, and NLS. In the Census, OCG, and NLS, the estimated effect of an extra year of elementary or secondary schooling on occupational status is significantly higher for whites than for non-whites. In the PSID, the apparent effect is virtually identical, but this is probably because SRC's grouping of occupations reduces the true effect for whites more than it does for nonwhites.[9] Comparing OCG and OCG–II, Featherman and Hauser (1978:345) show that returns to elementary and secondary school were still twice as great for whites as for blacks, in 1973, though the gap had narrowed appreciably since 1962, especially for men aged 25 to 34.

The pattern is quite different for nonwhites who attend college. The expected status advantage of a college graduate over a high school graduate is larger for nonwhites than for whites in all four of our samples and also in Featherman and Hauser's OCG–II sample. This does not mean that nonwhite BAs work in higher-status occupations than white BAs. It simply means that nonwhites without college degrees are at even more of a disadvantage relative to whites than nonwhites who finish college. As a result, college graduation is more valuable to nonwhites than to whites, even though secondary schooling is less valuable.

Ability Differences in the Occupational Effects of Education. One plausible reason why schooling might affect occupational status even with test scores controlled is that schools impart useful knowledge or skills not measured by our tests. But if this theory were correct, we would expect men with high initial test scores to realize larger occupational benefits from any given amount of schooling than men with low initial scores. This is because our tests measure fairly basic skills, and individuals with these skills should be able to learn more in a given amount of time than individuals who lack these skills. Yet we found no consistent evidence that the occupational benefits of additional schooling were larger for men with high test scores than for men with low test scores. Perhaps low-scoring individuals acquire economically relevant skills and knowledge from schooling as quickly as high-scoring individuals. Or perhaps schools do not impart any economically relevant skills, and employers value credentials for other reasons.[10]

Background Differences in the Effects of Education on Occupational Status. More and better schooling is frequently proposed as a way to improve the life chances of poor children. For that reason, it is important to ask whether the benefits of schooling are as great for men from disadvantaged backgrounds as for the population in general. Unfortunately, none of our data sets includes good information on parental income. As a substitute, we stratified our OCG, PSID, and NLS samples according to whether a respondent's father held a white-collar, blue-collar, or farm job. The effects of elementary and secondary education were consistently higher for men with white-collar fathers than for men with blue-collar fathers, but the difference was never statistically significant, and in the largest sample (OCG) it was trivial in size. The effects of elementary and secondary education on farm sons do, however, differ appreciably from the effects on white-collar sons in all three samples, and the difference is significant in the OCG and NLS.[11] Farm sons in these samples fail to convert elementary and secondary education into occupational advantages, perhaps because farm sons who finish high school are still quite likely to become farmers themselves.*

The benefits of higher education for white-collar sons are close to or exceed the benefits for blue-collar sons. Farm sons gain appreciably more by graduation from college than do white-collar sons. In this respect, they are similar to nonwhites. Apparently, high school graduation pays off primarily for men from advantaged backgrounds. Men from disadvantaged backgrounds must attend college to reap large occupational benefits from their education.

---

* We could test this possibility directly by excluding respondents who are currently farmers, but we only thought of this possibility after our funds were exhausted.

3. EARNINGS

Occupational status is an important measure of economic success. Nonetheless, most people seem to put greater weight on income than on status.[12] Certainly, economists' theories about human capital are devoted almost exclusively to explaining differences in earnings or wage rates. While occupational status is correlated with income, the correlation is less than 0.50. Furthermore, the factors affecting income are often different from those affecting occupational status. This section therefore looks at the effects of schooling on earnings or income.*

If students' earnings approximately equal the direct costs of their schooling, if earnings profiles for those with different amounts of schooling remain parallel as they acquire experience, and if highly educated men work as many years after school completion as less educated men, the regression coefficients in equations predicting ln earnings are equivalent to rates of return.[13] More cautiously, we can simply say that such coefficients measure the monetary benefits of education, and that the costs are unknown.†

Gaining more schooling requires foregoing experience in the labor market. At least initially, labor-force experience, like schooling, has a positive effect on earnings. If men with more schooling worked fewer years than men who quit school earlier, the effects of schooling averaged over the working life would be best estimated with experience excluded. In fact, however, men with more schooling appear to work as many years as men with less schooling. Ignoring experience will therefore understate the average benefit of additional education over a working life.[14] We therefore estimate the effects of education with experience

---

* The OCG survey measured respondents' personal income, rather than their earnings. Chapter 11 shows that this may raise the bivariate regression coefficient of education, but the difference is slight, so we discuss OCG income as if it were interchangeable with earnings.

† We used logarithmic equations for reasons discussed in chapter 2. These equations estimate the ratio of the geometric means for earners with different amounts of schooling. Equations that predict earnings rather than ln earnings can also be converted to percentage terms, but they then estimate the ratio of the arithmetic means for the two schooling groups. The two ratios are not the same. Suppose, for example, that two earners have eight years of school and earn $5,000 and $7,000 respectively. Two others have twelve years of school and earn $5,000 and $10,000. An ordinary earnings equation will imply that high school raises earnings by a factor of $7,500/$6,000 = 1.25. A ln earnings equation will imply an increase of $[(5,000)(10,000)]^{1/2}/[(5,000)(7,000)]^{1/2} = 1.20$. The two equations will yield identical results only when the shape of the distribution of earnings is the same at all levels of education.

controlled whenever the coefficient of experience or experience^2 is significant.[15]

Association between Education and Earnings. Table 6.3 displays the nonlinear regressions of ln earnings on education.[16] While the non-linearities are significant in the four large national samples of men aged 25 to 64, they are not as important when predicting ln earnings as they were when predicting occupational status. The average year of higher education is associated with a slightly smaller percentage increase in earnings than the average year of elementary or secondary education. But a BA boosts earnings appreciably, especially in OCG. The next to last column shows the estimated percentage increases in earnings associated with four years of elementary or secondary schooling (top row) and four years of college (bottom row).

It is tempting to infer trends in returns to schooling from these data, but the temptation should be resisted. The two large national surveys conducted early in the 1960s (OCG and PA), for example, imply higher returns to elementary and secondary schooling than the two surveys conducted around 1970 (Census and PSID). Yet when Smith and Welch (1977) compared the much larger 1/100 samples from the 1960 and 1970 Censuses, they found no change in returns to elementary and secondary education during the 1960s. This means that the apparent trend in table 6.3 is almost certainly due to methodological differences between the surveys. Similarly, comparison of OCG to the Census suggests that returns to higher education were constant during the 1960s, while comparison of PA to PSID suggests that returns to higher education rose. Since Smith and Welch's data also indicate that returns to higher education rose between 1960 and 1970, we infer that the OCG-Census comparison is misleading, perhaps because OCG's use of income rather than earnings increases the apparent returns to higher education (see chapter 11). The only real "conclusion" one can draw from these comparisons is that estimates of returns to schooling are as sensitive to methodological decisions as to secular trends, so one should not draw conclusions about secular trends unless methodological variations have been eliminated.

Controlling demographic background lowers the estimated benefits of a year of elementary or secondary education somewhat more in the early surveys, where the initial coefficient is large, than in the later surveys, where the initial coefficient is smaller. This suggests that it is wise to think of the bias caused by omitting background characteristics as a percentage of the original coefficient rather than as an absolute

TABLE 6.3

Regressions of Ln Earnings on Education

Sample (age)	Years of Education	Years Higher Education	BA	Standard Deviation of Residuals	$\bar{R}^2$	% Gain in Earnings:[a] 4 Yrs. H.S. / 4 Yrs. College	Other Variables Controlled[b]
1961 OCG 25-64	.1128 (.0031)	−.0837 (.0112)	.2857 (.0493)	.740	.184	57.0 / 49.5	none
	.0814 (.0032)	−.0720 (.0109)	.2840 (.0475)	.713	.242	38.5 / 37.9	measured background
	.0575 (.0033)	−.0915 (.0107)	.2292 (.0462)	.692	.286	25.9 / 9.8	measured background, occupation
1961 OCG Brothers 25-64 (N = 5,780)	.1056 (.0039)	−.1108 (.0172)	.3240 (.0775)	.748	.159	52.6 / 35.4	none[c]
	.0804 (.0041)	−.1184 (.0166)	.4093 (.0740)	.719	.224	37.9 / 29.3	measured background
	.0579 (NA)	−.0170 (NA)	.1700 (NA)	NA	NA	26.1 / 39.6	family background[c]
1964 PA 25-64	.1136 (.0085)	[−.0229] (.0295)	[.0419] (.1176)	.616	.241	57.5 / 49.4	none
	.0862 (.0090)	[−.0152] (.0290)	[.0617] (.1144)	.595	.292	41.2 / 41.3	measured background
1969 Census 25-64	.0849 (.0020)	−.0166 (.0057)	.1256 (.0266)	.650	.176	40.4 / 49.0	none
	.0568 (.0021)	−.0380 (.0055)	.0881 (.0257)	.628	.233	25.5 / 17.7	occupation
1971 PSID 25-64	.0836 (.0087)	[−.0110] (.0235)	.1765 (.0909)	.654	.246	39.7 / 59.5	none
	.0624 (.0092)	[−.0094] (.0235)	.2061 (.898)	.641	.275	28.4 / 57.9	measured background
	.0639 (.0090)	[−.0096] (.0231)	.1918 (.0895)	.644	.269	29.1 / 50.5	test score
	.0512 (.0093)	[−.0086] (.0233)	.2113 (.0891)	.636	.287	22.7 / 46.5	measured background, test score
	.0406 (.0093)	[−.0308] (.0231)	.1685 (.0879)	.626	.309	17.6 / 23.1	measured background, test score, occupation
1964 Veterans 30-34	.0952 (.0177)	[−.0055] (.0245)	.0466 (.0940)	.471	.105	46.3 / 50.0	none
	.0740 (.0175)	[−.0047] (.0239)	.0532 (.0907)	.454	.169	34.5 / 39.2	measured background
	.0610 (.0181)	[−.0037] (.0239)	.0682 (.0918)	.460	.147	27.6 / 34.6	test score
	.0509 (.0179)	[−.0045] (.0236)	.0714 (.0895)	.447	.194	22.6 / 29.3	measured background, test score
	.0437 (.0175)	[−.0287] (.0234)	.0380 (.0876)	.437	.230	19.1 / 10.3	measured background, test score, occupation

TABLE 6.3 *(continued)*

Sample	Years of Education	Years Higher Education	BA	Standard Deviation of Residuals	$\bar{R}^2$	% Gain in Earnings:[a] 4 Yrs. H.S. 4 Yrs. College	Other Variables Controlled[b]
1972 Talent 28-29	.0567[c] (.0077)			.384	.060	25.4[d]	none
	.0508[c] (.0080)			.382	.070	22.5[d]	measured background
	.0464[c] (.0084)			.382	.070	20.3[d]	test score
	.0429[c] (.0085)			.381	.074	18.7[d]	measured background, test score
	.0287[c] (.0093)			.378	.090	12.2[d]	measured background, test score, occupation
1973 Kalamazoo Brothers 35-59	.0792 (.0177)	[−.0265] (.0257)	[.0645] (.0825)	.407	.167	37.3 / 31.7	none
	.0742 (.0185)	[−.0224] (.0260)	[.0582] (.0826)	.408	.163	34.6 / 30.4	measured background
	.0558 (.0182)	[−.0167] (.0254)	[.0459] (.0814)	.402	.188	25.0 / 22.4	test score
	.0535 (.0188)	[−.0144] (.0257)	[.0413] (.0816)	.403	.188	23.9 / 21.9	measured background, test score
	[.0474] (.0310)	[−.0237] (.0395)	[.1772] (.1150)	.384	.259	20.9 / 31.3	family background
	[.0229] (.0306)	[.0148] (.0385)	[.1635] (.1120)	.374	.297	9.6 / 21.6	family background, test score difference
	[.0084] (.0295)	[−.0107] (.0370)	[.0828] (.1086)	.359	.352	3.4 / 7.6	family background, test score difference, occupation difference

[a]Top line = $100 \, (e^{(4)(\text{col } 1)} - 1)$

Bottom line = $100 \, (e^{(4)(\text{col } 1 + \text{col } 2) + (\text{col } 3)} - 1)$

[b]Experience and experience^2 controlled when statistically significant. The measured background variables controlled in each sample appear in the note to table 6.2. "Family background" controlled by regressing earnings difference between brothers on differences in education and other traits, except for OCG, for which see the footnote on page 170. Experience not controlled in Kalamazoo regressions, because it was statistically insignificant.

[c]Since virtually all Talent respondents finished high school, and since the effects of higher education were not significantly non-linear at this age, we report only linear coefficients.

[d]Estimated effect of four years of college.

amount. Controlling demographic background reduces the estimated returns to elementary and secondary schooling by 28 percent in OCG, 24 percent in PA, and 25 percent in PSID.

When we control all aspects of family background, instead of just socioeconomic variables, the apparent effect of elementary or secondary education on ln earnings is further reduced. Among OCG brothers, for example, controlling measured background reduces the estimated monetary benefits of four years of high school by about a quarter, while controlling all aspects of shared background reduces it by almost half. The percentage reduction when we control all aspects of background is almost as great in the Kalamazoo sample as in OCG, despite the fact that measured background has less effect in Kalamazoo.

When we estimate the benefits of higher education, background controls have less consistent effects. Controlling demographic background lowers the estimated benefits of a year of higher education that does not lead to a BA by 0.02 to 0.03 in our major samples of 25- to 64-year-olds, regardless of the initial value, and has no consistent effect on the estimated value of a BA per se. The percentage reduction ranges from a quarter of the uncontrolled effect in OCG to an eighth in PSID. Controlling all aspects of family background should further reduce the estimated returns to higher education, but our results do not follow this pattern in any consistent way. The "within family" effects of higher education are actually stronger than the effects with only demographic background controlled in the OCG and Kalamazoo samples of brothers. The smaller Talent and NORC samples conform more closely to the expected pattern, but the confidence intervals are so large that we cannot draw any firm conclusions. It certainly seems premature to conclude that ignoring unmeasured background inflates the apparent returns to higher education.*

Effects of Controlling Measured Ability. Economists have devoted considerable attention to the possibility that the apparent returns to schooling are inflated by a correlation between educational attainment and initial ability. Unless one is able to identify and measure ability, empirical research can never satisfactorily resolve this issue. Cognitive tests measure only a subset of abilities. Getting through school and

---

* With the exception of the NORC Brothers sample, all our samples with data on brothers suggest that controlling common family background reduces the linear effect of education on ln earnings by one-quarter to one-third. The samples vary in the extent to which the within-family coefficient differs from the coefficient controlling only measured background. See Taubman (1976) and Brittain (1977) for analyses of other brothers' samples that yield similar results.

succeeding at work may require many abilities which are not measured by such tests. But controlling the test scores available in our data should eliminate at least part of the "ability bias" from our estimates.

In estimating the degree to which education is merely a proxy for initial ability, we cannot legitimately control performance on a test administered to students who have had different amounts of schooling, since, if schooling affects performance on the test, controlling scores on the test will underestimate the overall returns to schooling. This means that we must treat the Veterans and PSID results with test score controlled as overestimates of the effect of controlling initial ability, at least as it would be measured by the Veterans and PSID tests. Talent and Kalamazoo are our only samples with a test administered to students who had had the same amount of schooling. The Talent results are for very young men and are not likely to apply to older men.* The Kalamazoo sample should therefore provide our most reliable evidence on the consequences of ignoring ability when estimating returns to education among mature men.

Looking first at the estimated benefits of elementary and secondary education, we see that controlling test scores lowers the Kalamazoo co-efficient from 0.079 to 0.056—a 30 percent reduction. Both the absolute and relative reduction are somewhat greater than in the Veterans sample, which was tested after the respondents had had different amounts of schooling. The reduction is slightly smaller in the PSID, which was also tested after respondents had had different amounts of schooling, but with an unreliable test. Talent tells us virtually nothing about returns to secondary schools. Our evidence thus suggests that controlling initial ability reduces the estimated returns to elementary and secondary education by a quarter to a third, i.e., between two and three percentage points.

Turning to higher education, the estimated advantage of college graduates over high school graduates varies dramatically among the four samples with test scores. The reduction in estimated benefits when we control test score also varies substantially, and not in direct proportion to the observed differentials. One can conjure up all sorts of plausible explanations for these discrepancies, but the fact remains that they leave

---

* Hauser and Daymont (1977) show that bias in estimating the effects of higher education without controlling test performance diminished from 20 percent when their Wisconsin sample was aged 28 to 14 percent when it was aged 32. Taubman and Wales (1974) found that the bias due to omitting test performance from estimates of the benefits of four years of college in the NBER-TH sample fell from 20 percent to 14 percent between 1955 and 1969. Their findings mean that the effects of education on earnings independent of ability increase more with age than the effects of ability.

considerable room for disagreement about the likely degree to which earnings differences between college graduates and high school graduates reflect differences in initial ability. All we can say with confidence is that controlling initial ability is not likely to lower the estimated benefits of a college education by more than a third (the value in the Veterans sample). Nor is the reduction likely to be much less than a sixth. On the whole, the lower value appears more plausible.* The earnings differential between college graduates and high school graduates seems to have fallen since most of these data were collected. It is not clear how much returns to ability have changed, so it is not clear how the effects of higher education with ability controlled are likely to have changed.

Effects of Controlling Both Measured Ability and Family Background. Because variations in both family background and cognitive ability can affect earnings among men with the same amount of schooling, it is necessary to ask what the returns to education are with both background and test score controlled. (In theory we should also control adolescent personality traits, but chapter 5 shows that this would have virtually no effect on the estimated returns to education in our samples.) Our results suggest that the apparent effects of elementary and secondary schooling arise in large measure because men with more schooling are already advantaged, but that this is not true for higher education.

Controlling background and test score reduces the coefficients of elementary and secondary education from 0.08 to 0.05 in PSID, from 0.10 to 0.06 in the Veterans sample, and from 0.08 to 0.02 among Kalamazoo Brothers, for whom we can control all aspects of background. Unreliability in the PSID test probably reduces the bias more than the timing of the test inflates it. The ability bias in the Veterans sample could be either overestimated or underestimated as a result of sample restrictions. But the bias due to family background is probably underestimated because of the exclusion of unmeasured family factors. The Kalamazoo sample may simply be atypical. But it still seems unlikely that if we had data comparable to Kalamazoo for a large national sample, returns to elementary and secondary schooling would exceed 5 percent, and 4 percent seems more likely. This implies a proportionate bias of 40 to 60 percent.

---

* The Talent sample, like the Wisconsin sample, shows a bias of about 20 percent for men aged 28. As noted above, this had fallen to 14 percent by the time Wisconsin men reached 32. The PSID shows a bias of 15 percent. The PSID test is administered after school completion, but it is not very reliable, so the two biases should offset one another.

TABLE 6.4

*Earnings Differences Between College Graduates
and High School Graduates with Various Controls*

Sample	Experience Controlled	Background, Test Score, and Experience Controlled	Difference	Proportionate Bias
PSID	59.5	46.5	13.0	0.22
Veterans	50.0	29.3	20.7	0.41
Talent	25.4	18.7	6.7	0.26
Talent Brothers	27.3	18.3	9.0	0.33
Kalamazoo	31.7	21.6	10.1	0.32

Source: Estimated from equations in table 6.3.

The estimated returns to four years of college education do not fall as much as the estimated returns to secondary school when we control family background and test score. Table 6.4 summarizes the relevant data. The absolute reductions in the Talent samples may be low because the respondents are still young. The reduction in the PSID test is probably low because the PSID test is unreliable. The estimated effect of four years of college in the Kalamazoo sample has a large sampling error, but the estimated bias is in line with our other estimates. The apparent bias in the Veterans sample is higher than in the other samples, but since there is no obvious reason other than the timing of the test for discounting the Veterans results, we take them as an upper limit. Taken together, these results suggest a reduction in the returns to a college education of 7 to 21 percentage points when the effects of family background and cognitive ability are taken into account. The bias seems to be between one-fifth and two-fifths of the observed value.*

On the basis of our findings, we would expect completing four years of high school to raise earnings by no more than 15 to 25 percent, while

* Denison (1964) reports a one-third bias in the returns to four years of college in the Wolfe-Smith data, controlling father's occupation, class rank, and IQ. Taubman and Wales (1974) also report a one-third bias in the effects of finishing college on 1969 earnings in the NBER-TH sample. These results are consistent with our own. They are not consistent with Becker's (1964) conclusion based on data for Bell Telephone employees that the returns to college are biased by only 12 percent.

Our results suggest an absolute bias in the linear returns to education on the order of 3 or 4 percentage points. This would imply a proportionate bias of 35 to 46 percent in the Census data. Correcting for measurement error would reduce the estimate of downward bias somewhat, but controlling for as yet unmeasured differences between brothers with identical test scores could increase it. Taubman (1977) reports a proportionate bias of close to 60 percent in the linear effects of education among MZ twins whose military test scores are controlled. None of our results suggests that Griliches and Mason's (1972) estimate of a 12 percent bias in the linear effects of postmilitary schooling among 21- to 34-year-old veterans is generalizable.

completing four years of college might raise earnings by as much as 40 percent, at least in labor markets like those that prevailed up to 1970.[17] There are at least three possible explanations for this discrepancy between the effects of high school and the effects of college:

1.   College completion could be associated with larger unmeasured differences in initial ability or motivation than high school completion. Our data do not support this view. In the Kalamazoo, Veterans, and PSID samples, the difference in test performance between high school and elementary school graduates is quite similar to the difference between college and high school graduates. The standard deviations of test scores are also similar for college graduates and high school graduates.[18] If the same pattern holds for other personal characteristics, the association between schooling and productivity should be linear. Of course, colleges may select more strongly on personality traits and motivation than high schools do. But since this is not the case with respect to test scores, there is no obvious reason why it should hold for personality traits.

2.   Colleges may enhance productivity more than high schools do. If this were the case, we would expect the effect of an average year of higher education to be larger than the effect of an average year of secondary education. Yet once we control for holding a BA, the percentage effect of an extra year of college is consistently smaller than the percentage effect of an extra year of high school.[19]

3.   Employers may "overreward" men with BAs for reasons unrelated to individual productivity. Taubman and Wales (1974) calculate that almost half of the earnings difference between college graduates and high school graduates can be explained by the exclusion of capable high school graduates from higher-paying jobs.[20] Their estimates are crude, but their conclusion appears consistent with our evidence. Since it is hard to believe that the last year of college enhances individual productivity more than the previous three, it seems likely that employers favor college graduates even when they are quite similar to nongraduates. Employers seem to do this principally by excluding nongraduates from high-status occupations. Controlling occupational status reduces the returns to four years of college by one-half to three-quarters in the PSID, Census, and OCG samples. It reduces returns to elementary and secondary schooling by only one-quarter to one-third.

A Caveat on Measurement Error. We have emphasized omitted variables as a source of upward bias in the observed effects of schooling. We have ignored a well-known source of downward bias, namely measurement error. If education measures include random errors, the effects of education will be underestimated. Controlling measured ability and family background to eliminate spurious effects can worsen the impact of measurement error (Griliches, 1977). The remaining bias depends upon the degree of measurement error, the relationship of errors in measuring schooling to errors in other variables, the relationships among errors and the true values of variables, and the effects of omitted variables that affect both schooling and economic success.

We have ignored the effects of measurement errors because we did not have the data needed to correct for such errors in most samples. The evidence we do have suggests that ignoring measurement errors does not seriously bias estimates of the effects of education. Bielby et al. (1977) indicate that correcting for measurement errors in both parental socioeconomic status and schooling in the 1973 OCG–II data raises the estimated effect of education on occupational status by only 0.52 points, from 4.39 to 4.91. Bielby and Hauser (1978) obtain equally modest effects for earnings.

Bishop (1976) has noted that the use of sibling data can exacerbate the problem of measurement error and has argued that the within-family effect of schooling on earnings is at a maximum only 83 percent of the true effect. However, the accuracy of educational reports in the Kalamazoo data appears somewhat higher than in the CPS data Bishop analyzed.[21] The Kalamazoo results suggest the observed within-family coefficient of education could be close to 90 percent of the true coefficient.[22] If these calculations are reasonable, our conclusions regarding the effects of education would not be substantially altered by corrections for measurement error.

Ability Differences in the Effects of Education on Ln Earnings. If abler men learn more from a given educational experience than less able men, and if the economic benefits of educational attainment depend on learning, the benefits of schooling should be greater for men with high initial test scores than for men with low scores. Certainly, economists have traditionally assumed that this was the case and have used this "fact" to explain the greater likelihood of abler men remaining in school (Renshaw, 1960; Becker and Chiswick, 1966; Weisbrod and Karpoff, 1968; Hause, 1972). Our data do not, however, support this expectation. There are few significant differences between schooling coefficients across ability groups in our samples.[23] Nor are the patterns of observed differences consistent across samples. We also looked at ability effects within educational levels in the Veterans, Talent, and Kalamazoo samples, respectively. We found no consistent and few significant differences.[24]

This finding suggests that abler students do not remain in school longer because they expect to reap proportionately greater economic benefits from their education than less able students do. But abler students presumably find schoolwork less onerous, so their persistence in school is easy to explain in terms of lower psychological costs.

Differences in the Effects of Education on Ln Earnings by Father's Occupational Group. Our evidence on the differential effects of schooling for men from varying social backgrounds is also in accord with previous work. We found no consistent differences among men from white-collar, blue-collar, or farm backgrounds.[25] If white-collar children go to better schools than blue-collar or farm children, this result suggests that the returns to educational attainment do not depend upon educational quality.[26]

Effects of Educational Quality. Individuals often try to attend a "good" college because they believe that going to such a college will help them get a better job and higher earnings. But individuals who go to good colleges are usually also the "right kind of material." Sorting out the effects of school resources, characteristics of classmates, and individual characteristics is difficult. Research on the effects of educational quality is plagued by the confounding of these factors, and our data offer little that is useful with which to unravel the problem.

The Productive Americans Survey rated the college that each respondent had attended as unaccredited, nonselective, selective, highly selective, or very highly selective. The index is based on the ratio of acceptances to applicants, the high school rank of entering freshmen, and similar data.[27]

For men with similar backgrounds, differences in college selectivity bear no significant relationship to occupational status. College selectivity is, however, associated with earnings. Respondents who attended one of the "selective" colleges earned 28 percent more than men who graduated from a "nonselective" college. This advantage persists with both occupational status and weeks worked controlled. The earnings differences between men from colleges classified as "selective," "highly selective," and "very highly selective" were statistically insignificant. Were we able to control individual academic ability in the PA, the apparent disadvantage of attending a "selective" college would presumably fall.[28]

The most important differences in the quality of educational experiences may not be due to qualitative differences between schools or colleges but rather to differences in the way a given school treats different students. The most obvious differences derive from the curriculum. The Talent and Veterans surveys asked respondents to classify their high school curriculum as either college preparatory or of some other type. While completing a college preparatory curriculum was associated with higher educational attainment, it had no continuing effect on economic success among men with the same amount of schooling. This suggests either that men who eventually get the same amount of education learn the same amount in high school regardless of program differences or that learning more in high school does not pay off economically unless it leads to still more education.

Curriculum differences at the college level are likely to have larger effects, but we have not analyzed them.

CONCLUSIONS

The economic benefits of schooling depend on the level of schooling, the measure of economic success, and the population studied. The *estimated* benefits of schooling also depend on the range of causally prior variables a researcher can control and on the amount of measurement error.

Completing high school rather than elementary school is associated with an occupational advantage of close to half a standard deviation among men 25- to 64-years-old. Among men from the same homes and with the same test scores, the expected advantage is only a quarter of a standard deviation. The occupational benefits of secondary education do not appear to vary systematically by cohort or test score. The benefits are larger for whites than for nonwhites and larger for nonfarm sons than for farm sons.

Completing college rather than high school is associated with an occupational advantage of more than one standard deviation among 25- to 64-year-olds. The advantage is almost the same when family background and test score are controlled. Nonwhites and farmers' sons appear to benefit more than others if they complete college. The occupational advantage of completing college does not vary systematically with test scores. The advantage is larger among younger men in our samples.

Four years of high school are associated with a 40 percent increase in earnings among men with the same amount of experience in our most representative recent national samples, namely the Census and PSID. If we could control both family background and test score, we would expect this advantage to fall to between 15 and 25 percent. Four years of college are associated with a 49 percent earnings advantage among Census respondents with the same amount of experience. We would expect controlling family background and test scores to reduce this advantage to between 30 and 40 percent. The earnings advantage of college graduates derives largely from the fact that they enter higher-status occupations than other men. This is not so true of secondary schooling. Unless employers are concerned only with average differences in ability and personality between men with different amounts of schooling, our measures of these characteristics cannot explain the occupational advantages of college graduates.*

The economic benefits of education may, of course, change in the years ahead. Freeman (1976) argues, for example, that because of the dramatic increase in college attendance during the 1960s, a substantial BA "surplus" developed during the 1970s, which sharply reduced the economic

---

* There is a large overlap in test scores between men with high school diplomas and men with college degrees. However, few college graduates have very low scores and few high school graduates have very high scores. Employers who wish to bypass low-scoring individuals and maximize their chances of hiring high-scoring individuals would, in the absence of direct information, hire college graduates. For test-score distributions by educational levels in the Talent and Kalamazoo samples, see Olneck and Crouse (1978). The Kalamazoo personality data also suggest that employers seeking to maximize their chances of hiring men who are above average in dependability, executive ability, or industriousness, or seeking not to hire men below average on these characteristics, would hire college graduates.

According to the "screening hypothesis," employers do in fact use educational credentials as a cheap and unobtrusive way of gathering information about job applicants' cognitive skills and personality traits. Because productivity is difficult to measure directly, employers cannot adequately reward individuals whose productivity exceeds the norms for their educational group, nor can they withhold benefits from individuals whose productivity falls below the norm for their educational group. As a result, education per se affects an individual's economic success, even though employers value such education exclusively as a proxy for other unmeasured traits.

The plausibility of this hypothesis depends on the claim that employers are unwilling or unable to measure the traits they really value, and that they therefore rely on education as a proxy for these traits. If employers really valued the cognitive skills measured by IQ tests, it is difficult to see why they would not administer such tests to job applicants and use the results in lieu of educational credentials. Likewise, if employers were really interested in personality traits of the kind that Kalamazoo teachers rated, it is difficult to see why they would not ask schools and colleges to provide such ratings. Indeed, some employers do precisely this. To keep the "screening hypothesis" plausible, one must assume that employers really value traits too elusive to measure. If this is the case, social scientists are also likely to experience difficulty measuring these traits. This suggests that the screening hypothesis may be untestable in principle.

value of a degree. Freeman's research shows dramatic declines in returns to higher education among young men just entering the labor force. The declines are much more modest if one looks at all men aged 25 to 64, as we have tried to do. CPS surveys indicate, for example, that among men aged 25 and over in 1967, those with BA's enjoyed incomes 47 percent higher than high school graduates. By 1968 the differential was 52 percent. If one adjusts for the fact that CPS underestimated the incomes of highly educated nonrespondents during these years, the differentials were probably 53 percent in 1967 and 58 percent in 1968.[29] By 1975, when CPS was using an improved methodology to estimate missing data, college graduates' advantage had fallen to 43 percent. It was only marginally higher (44 percent) in 1976—the most recent year for which CPS data are currently available.

We cannot be sure how the BA "surplus" will affect returns to education in the future. Young BAs are now entering lower status occupations than in the past where earnings have not traditionally grown very fast as men got older. Thus, one might plausibly expect the earnings differential between college graduates and high school graduates aged 25 to 64 to keep falling as older college graduates retire and younger, more numerous cohorts of BAs compete for their jobs. At the same time, however, high school graduates in lower status occupations are likely to find themselves competing for promotions with college graduates to a greater extent than in the past. If college graduation leads to promotion in these occupations, returns to higher education may rise again as time goes on. In light of all this, we cannot be sure whether today's college graduates will get substantially lower lifetime returns to their education than earlier generations of graduates did. But even if college graduates' relative earnings do decline, the value of the characteristics *created* by college attendance is not likely to change much relative to the value of the personal characteristics that *lead to* college attendance. Thus, the proportion of the apparent returns to college attendance that persists after controlling background, initial ability, and motivation is not likely to change much.

Our findings place a number of widespread presumptions in doubt. The most significant of these is that high school dropouts are economically disadvantaged largely because they fail to finish school. Our results suggest that the apparent advantages enjoyed by high school graduates derive to a significant extent from their prior characteristics, not from their schooling. Unless high school attendance is followed by a college education, its economic value appears quite modest.

Our findings imply that higher education is worth more than secondary education, particularly for those whose primary concern is with occupational status rather than earnings. This finding may help explain why the equalization of men's educational attainment during the twentieth century has not been accompanied by much, if any, equalization in earnings. Schooling as a whole has come to be more equally distributed because almost everyone now finishes high school. The variance of elementary and secondary schooling is therefore very small. But since elementary and secondary education do not have much impact on earnings once we control family background and initial test scores, equalizing the distribution of such education cannot be expected to have much effect on the distribution of earnings. Furthermore, while the distribution of elementary and secondary education has become considerably more equal, the distribution of higher education has become somewhat less equal. Since higher education has more impact on earnings than elementary or secondary education, at least for those who complete college, the increasingly unequal distribution of higher education may more than offset the effects of equalizing the distribution of elementary and secondary education.[30]

By diversifying opportunities for higher education through programs of unequal duration and by increasing the number of BAs without making degrees universal, we may unwittingly have increased rather than decreased the amount of economic inequality. Since our findings indicate that individuals without the traditional attributes of college students (e.g., higher test scores) still receive the traditional benefits from such schooling (or did up to 1972), policies encouraging greater equality in higher education could probably be pursued with no harm to economic efficiency and with the possibility of reducing income inequality.

CHAPTER 7

The Effects of Race
on Earnings

This chapter will examine differences between whites and nonwhites, focusing on differences in the way background characteristics and education affect each group's earnings. We will concentrate on the 1962 OCG, 1970 Census, and 1972 PSID surveys, since these are our only surveys of 25- to 64-year-olds with substantial numbers of nonwhite respondents. These three surveys differ in several potentially important respects.* The reader who wants precise trend data should therefore con-

Joseph Schwartz and Jill Williams wrote this chapter.
* OCG includes students and men without earnings who had current occupations and income from other sources. The Census and PSID exclude such men. The OCG and Census include men who are not household heads, while the PSID excludes them. OCG uses a *grouped income* measure, whereas the other surveys use *ungrouped earnings*. PSID uses broad occupational groups, whereas OCG and the Census use detailed groups. OCG groups years of education, while the Census does not (except at the top). PSID does not distinguish men with graduate education but no degree from men with BAs and assigns nonrespondents to one of the two lowest education categories on the basis of literacy. OCG assigns missing education values using the respondent's other characteristics, while the Census does not assign missing education values. A more complete discussion of these differences appears in the *Final Report*, volume 1, pp. 398–406. Note that to maintain comparability, the PSID analyses reported here treat Hispanic respondents as "white," while those elsewhere combine Hispanic respondents with nonwhites.

One further difference deserves comment. To test for the possibility of spurious trends, we compared the distributions of education and income (earnings) in OCG, Census, and PSID to the published CPS distributions for the same year. While there is no strong evidence that any of our surveys find more highly educated or poorly

sult other sources as well. Winsborough (1975) has analyzed CPS data on the effects of education and race on earnings during the 1960s. Smith and Welch (1977) have performed a more detailed analysis using the 1960 and 1970 1/100 Census samples. Featherman and Hauser (1978) have compared the 1962 OCG to the 1973 replication (OCG-II). Our analyses focus on different questions from theirs, but where we ask similar questions we obtain much the same answers. This increases our confidence that the apparent changes in the effects of race between 1961 and 1971 in our samples are not just methodological artifacts.

1. RACE DIFFERENCES IN RETURNS TO EDUCATION

On the average, nonwhites acquire less schooling than whites. This is a frequently cited, if only partial, explanation of why whites earn more than nonwhites. Others have suggested that the return to additional years of schooling is less for nonwhites than for whites and that nonwhites may therefore be making an economically rational decision when they acquire less education than whites. While we have no data on the costs of education and therefore cannot calculate net returns to education, we can compare gross returns for whites and nonwhites.

In this section we consider three ways of estimating such gross returns. Each method uses the same independent variables: years of schooling (Ed), completion of four years of college (BA), years of experience (Exp), and years of experience squared (Exp^2). The three methods differ only with respect to the dependent variable, i.e., the measure of "returns." Our first model uses dollar earnings to measure returns, our second model uses the log of earnings, and our third uses the cube root of earnings. All three models examine earnings differentials between those with different amounts of education and experience. They ignore questions such as "How do some people come to acquire more education?" and "Why do men with more education have higher

---

educated men than CPS, PSID men reported earnings $1,100 above the corresponding CPS income mean. Part of this difference is attributable to different sample restrictions and variable definitions, but chapters 10 and 11 show that PSID respondents report higher 1969 earnings than Census respondents even when sample restrictions are identical. Chapter 10 shows that more PSID than Census respondents hold white-collar jobs. This means that one should not treat the entire change in earnings between the 1969 Census and 1971 PSID as genuine.

earnings?" Chapter 6 shows that ignoring these questions leads to overestimates of the monetary returns to schooling. With luck, however, ignoring this bias will inflate estimated returns for whites and nonwhites by roughly equal amounts.

Our simplest model assumes that actual earnings (Y) is an additive function of the four independent variables:

$$Y = B_0 + B_1 Ed + B_2 BA + B_3 Exp + B_4 Exp^2 \qquad (1)$$

The earnings equations in table 7.1 estimate this model for the white and nonwhite subsamples of the OCG, Census, and PSID. In the regressions presented in this chapter, we subtracted the total sample mean from each independent variable. This has no effect on the coefficients or their standard errors, but means that the regression constant is equal to the expected value of the dependent variable for an individual who is at the total sample mean on all the independent variables. The difference between the white and nonwhite constants is thus the expected difference between a white and a nonwhite who are both at the sample mean on all the independent variables. Although the earnings data for different years have been converted to 1967 dollars (to control for inflation), it is risky to compare coefficients for different years unless one also takes account of changes in real income. There is, however, no problem comparing whites to nonwhites in any given year.

Table 7.1 shows that whites receive considerably higher dollar returns to education than nonwhites in all three survey years. In the Census, whites also receive more for a BA than nonwhites, but this is not true in OCG or PSID. While the race difference in returns to a BA is significant by conventional standards in the Census sample ($p < 0.001$), we nonetheless believe that it is due to sampling error. The mean earnings of the 149 nonwhites with graduate education in our 1/1,000 Census sample are considerably lower than the published mean for all such men in the full 1/20 Census sample, and this discrepancy is sufficient to explain the apparent difference between the white and nonwhite BA coefficient in our 1/1,000 sample.

Our second variant of the human capital model assumes that earnings change by a constant *proportion* for each unit change in an independent variable. This implies that we should treat ln earnings as the dependent variable in an additive model. Most economists prefer this semilog model. It has the advantage that if pay increases are distributed in proportion to initial earnings, the expected regression coefficients for different years will be the same. The white coefficients for years of education are similar in the three samples and indicate that each year

TABLE 7.1
Regressions of Earnings, LN Earnings, and Earnings$^{1/3}$ on Education and Experience, by Race[a]

		OCC (1961 Income)		Census (1969 Earnings)		PSID (1971 Earnings)	
		White (N = 10,395)	Nonwhite (N = 1,110)	White (N = 23,615)	Nonwhite (N = 2,082)	White (N = 1,307)	Nonwhite (N = 467)
Earnings							
Years of	B	482**	249**	653**	400**	659**	336**
education	(SE)	(18)	(22)	(19)	(30)	(74)	(50)
BA	B	1,879	1,751	2,968**	1,609**	3,026	3,279
	(SE)	(166)	(356)	(162)	(373)	(560)	(602)
Experience[b]	B	57*	34*	462**	114**	39	[−0]
	(SE)	(4)	(7)	(15)	(30)	(15)	(14)
Experience^2	B	−4.61**	−1.32**	−7.61**	−1.47**	−7.55	−5.67
	(SE)	(.30)	(.49)	(.29)	(.57)	(1.08)	(.96)
Constant		6,894	4,278	9,105	6,707	9,672	7,294
R^2		.181	.191	.183	.163	.235	.380
SD of residuals		4,400	2,278	6,442	3,837	5,860	2,881
Earnings[c]	mean	7,031	3,545	9,227	5,895	9,809	6,322
	SD	4,862	2,527	7,125	4,188	6,486	3,644
Percentage of gap eliminated if equalization occurs at level of:							
Nonwhite means		40.7		45.2		47.5	
White means		23.3		26.5		30.4	
Ln earnings							
Years of	B	.085	.102	.075	.082	.076	.045
education	(SE)	(.003)	(.008)	(.002)	(.006)	(.008)	(.014)
BA	B	[.028]	[.071]	.090	[−.034]	.149*	.521*
	(SE)	(.027)	(.134)	(.016)	(.073)	(.062)	(.166)
Experience[b]	B	.005	.010	.044**	.016**	[−.002]*	−.012*
	(SE)	(.001)	(.003)	(.002)	(.006)	(.002)	(.004)
Experience^2	B	−.0006	−.0004	−.0008**	−.0002**	−.0011	−.0017
	(SE)	(.0000)	(.0002)	(.0000)	(.0001)	(.0001)	(.0003)
Constant		8.607	8.094	8.914	8.583	8.977	8.646
R^2		.150	.164	.171	.128	.236	.264
SD of residuals		.708	.859	.633	.750	.632	.794
Ln earnings[c]	mean	8.629	7.851	8.927	8.446	8.992	8.492
	SD	.769	.937	.695	.802	.722	.921
Percentage of gap eliminated if equalization occurs at level of:							
Nonwhite means		28.7		31.7		36.3	
White means		34.6		31.0		33.6	
Earnings$^{1/3}$							
Years of	B	.472	.428	.476	.434	.493*	.311*
education	(SE)	(.015)	(.033)	(.011)	(.028)	(.048)	(.060)
BA	B	.723	[1.050]	1.126*	[.364]*	1.404	2.833
	(SE)	(.140)	(.545)	(.095)	(.347)	(.359)	(.716)
Experience[b]	B	.037	.048	.298**	.096**	[.002]	[−.030]
	(SE)	(.004)	(.010)	(.009)	(.028)	(.010)	(.016)
Experience^2	B	−.0038*	−.0017*	−.0052**	−.0012**	−.0066	−.0073
	(SE)	(.0003)	(.0008)	(.0002)	(.0005)	(.0007)	(.0011)
Constant		18.153	15.392	19.973	17.999	20.442	18.530
R^2		.185	.185	.209	.169	.277	.326
SD of residuals		3.711	3.487	3.775	3.574	3.648	3.428
Earnings$^{1/3c}$	mean	18.277	14.306	20.955	17.226	20.540	17.609
	SD	4.109	3.855	4.249	3.916	4.284	4.159
Percentage of gap eliminated if equalization occurs at level of:							
Nonwhite means		32.4		35.7		40.7	
White means		30.3		29.7		34.2	

Coefficients in brackets are less than twice their standard error.

   *Difference between white and nonwhite coefficients significant at 0.05 level.
   **Difference between white and nonwhite coefficients significant at 0.01 level.
   [a] All samples restricted to men aged 25 to 64 with complete data who were not in institutions or in the military at the time of the survey. Census and PSID samples also exclude students and men with zero or negative earnings. OCG sample includes men with zero income.
   [b] Note that experience^2 is orthogonalized in the OCG and PSID equations but not in the Census equations. This does not affect the coefficient of experience^2, but it does alter the coefficient of experience. Without orthogonalization the experience coefficients in the OCG ln income equations would be 0.035 for whites and 0.030 for nonwhites. The PSID coefficients would be 0.052 for whites and 0.072 for nonwhites. We did not calculate the change in the standard errors, however.
   [c] OCG results cover income from all sources.

of schooling increases earnings by about 8 percent. The nonwhite co-efficients for years of education declined significantly between 1961 (OCG) and 1971 (PSID), indicating lower percentage returns to the first fifteen years of schooling in 1971 than in 1961. Nonetheless, the difference between the white and nonwhite coefficients for years of education is not quite significant in either year, so we cannot be certain that nonwhites had higher returns to the first fifteen years of school in 1961 or lower returns in 1971.

In stating that the proportional "returns" to education are not significantly different for whites and nonwhites we do not wish to imply that a year of education is worth the same for each group. Rather, the *ratio* of nonwhite to white earnings is approximately the same at each level of education. Since nonwhites generally earn less than whites, equal percentage returns imply greater absolute returns for whites. Showing that whites and nonwhites receive similar proportional returns to education does not demonstrate that nonwhites have an equal incentive to pursue additional education. This depends on how incentives actually work.

The coefficient of BA represents the percentage increase in earnings (over and above the average return to a year of education) for completing the fourth year of college. White OCG college graduates earned about what one would expect if percentage returns to schooling were uniform at all levels.* In the Census and PSID, the last year of college is worth two to three times as much for whites as other years of schooling. We are inclined to attribute this difference to a real increase in the value of a BA during the sixties. Nonwhites' percentage returns to a BA do not differ significantly from whites' in the OCG or Census but appear to be very much higher in PSID.†

Our third variant of the human capital model assumes that education and experience have additive effects on "utility" rather than on earnings. We do not, of course, have any direct measure of the subjective utility of money to our respondents. Some argue that the marginal utility of money declines in direct proportion to the amount of money one already

---

* Actually, returns are somewhat higher for BAs, but this is offset by low returns for college dropouts and those with graduate education (see chapter 6).

† One should not place too much emphasis on the PSID nonwhite BA coefficient, since there were only nineteen nonwhites with a BA in the PSID sample. The weight for nonwhites with a BA is also more than twice the nonwhite average. This means that the standard error of the BA coefficient is really greater (after correcting for the design effect) than that reported in table 7.1. A modest increase in the standard error would be sufficient to render the white/nonwhite difference in returns to a BA statistically insignificant. But as we show later in the chapter, CPS data also indicate that black college graduates have improved their position relative to both white college graduates and black nongraduates, so we doubt that the PSID results are misleading.

has, i.e., that a 1 percent increase in income has the same utility regardless of the base. If this were the case, utility would be a linear function of the logarithm of earnings, and our semilog equations would embody our "utility" model. But subjective scaling experiments suggest that this assumption is too extreme, i.e., that a $1,000 increase in income is worth more to a man with $10,000 than a $200 increase is worth to a man with $2,000. The $1,000 increase is not, however, worth five times as much to the first man as the $200 increase is to the second.[1] Experimentation suggests that one can get a reasonable approximation of the subjective value of money by assuming that utility is typically a linear function of the cube root of income. If utility (or subjective well-being) is substantively more important than actual earnings, then this cube-root model may be the most relevant. The earnings$^{1/3}$ equations in table 7.1 show that if utility is a linear function of earnings$^{1/3}$, then the utility of a year of education for whites remained virtually constant from 1961 to 1971, while the utility of a BA increased.[*]

The marginal utility of years of education for nonwhites is not significantly lower than for whites in the OCG and Census samples, but it is significantly lower in the PSID sample. If we assume that utility is a linear transformation of earnings$^{1/3}$, and if we ignore the social and economic *costs* of acquiring education and deferring earnings, we can conclude that nonwhites had almost as much incentive as whites to obtain additional education if they expected to confront economic conditions like those of 1961 or 1969, but less incentive if they expected to confront conditions like those of 1971.[†] Race differences in the utility of a BA are also inconsistent in the three samples. The coefficients are about the same in the OCG, much higher for nonwhites in the PSID, and somewhat lower for nonwhites in the Census. Because of the peculiarities of our 1/1,000 Census sample alluded to above, we believe that the apparent increase in the utility of a BA for nonwhites between the time of the OCG and PSID surveys represents the real trend over this decade.

Our main conclusions about the relationship between education and earnings, based on three versions of a human capital model, are as follows:

---

[*] Increases in productivity (mean constant dollar earnings) over time have considerably less impact on earnings$^{1/3}$ than on earnings. The above conclusions would prevail after any reasonable adjustment for changes in productivity; e.g., changing utility by either a constant or proportionate amount.

[†] We present evidence later in the chapter that the low returns to years of education and high returns to a BA for nonwhites may reflect the great impact of business cycles on nonwhites.

1. Whites receive higher dollar returns to years of education than nonwhites. The proportional returns and marginal utility of years of education are similar for both groups and remained approximately constant from 1961 to 1971.
2. The returns to a BA (absolute, proportional, and utility) were similar for whites and nonwhites in the OCG and probably also the Census (after accounting for the sampling bias for nonwhites with graduate education). These returns increased for both groups from 1961 to 1971.
3. The PSID nonwhite sample is somewhat inconsistent in that, for all three models, the return to years of education is lower than we would expect, while the marginal utility of and proportional return to a BA are higher.

How does one choose the "best" model? There are at least three possible criteria. The first is to opt for interpretability. This criterion is partially imposed a priori because one rarely estimates equations before thinking about how to interpret the likely results. We have discussed the three human capital models in decreasing order of interpretability. The second criterion is parsimony, primarily as it relates to invariant parameters and the absence of significant interactions. Models which show constant returns across time or between whites and nonwhites are preferable by this standard.[2] By this criterion, the semilog and utility models perform better than the untransformed earnings model. The third criterion relates to the "fit" of the model to the data and, in the present situation, involves comparisons of explained variance. If we simply compare values of R^2, the utility model looks somewhat better than the untransformed model which is, in turn, better than the semilog model.[*] While it is difficult to weight the different criteria, we think

---

[*] There is a problem in comparing values of R^2 from models with different dependent variables: the variances being explained are not the same. One solution to this problem is to estimate the expected values of individuals from one model, transform these expected values into the scale (units) of the dependent variable from a second model, compute residuals from the second dependent variable, and compare their standard deviations. This technique is always biased in favor of the second model, because the transformed expected values of the first model are not least-squares estimates of the second dependent variable. Therefore, if the residuals from the transformed expected values have a smaller standard deviation than the residuals of the second model, the first model is clearly superior. Another technique, which is much more difficult and costly, employs nonlinear least-squares regression to estimate the first linear model after it has been translated into a nonlinear model with the same dependent variable as the second model (Goldfeld and Quandt, 1972). We did not try to compare our three models using any of these methods.

Heckman and Polachek (1974) have used maximum likelihood methods to investigate the functional form of the education–earnings relationship. They conclude that an additive model with ln earnings as the dependent variable and years of education as the independent variable constitutes the best "simple" functional form. These results show, however, that a model with earnings$^{1/3}$ as the dependent variable would fit the data better. We understand their reluctance to consider the earnings$^{1/3}$ model "simple" but suggest that when interpreted as a utility model, it should not be dismissed too quickly.

that within the limits of its assumptions, the utility model probably performs the best. However, since the semilog model is more common and yields much the same conclusions as the utility model, we will confine our discussion for the most part to the semilog results.

2. CHANGES IN RETURNS TO EDUCATION FOR NONWHITES SINCE 1967

In an attempt to clarify the causes of apparent changes in nonwhite returns to education between the 1969 Census and the 1971 PSID, we took advantage of the longitudinal aspect of the PSID data. We computed white and nonwhite PSID equations analogous to those in table 7.1 for each year from 1967 through 1971 for all nonstudent, nonmilitary heads of households who were between the ages of 25 and 64 throughout the interval. There are no significant differences among the white equations for the five years, nor are there significant differences between the Census and the PSID equations for whites. This generalization holds for all three transformations of earnings, indicating a high degree of stability in returns to education for whites who were in the labor force throughout this five-year period.[3]

In contrast, the nonwhite PSID equations show a marked change from 1967 to 1971. The coefficient of years of education in the nonwhite ln earnings equations decreases steadily from 0.084 to 0.040. The percentage returns to years of education were thus halved over a five-year period for the same nonwhite men. This result is also consistent with the time trend in table 7.1. Partially offsetting the decline in percentage returns to years of education was an equally remarkable increase in the percentage returns to a BA—from 0.208 to 0.744 in 1971. In the equation predicting nonwhites' 1969 ln earnings, the 95 percent confidence interval of the BA coefficient (not correcting for design effects) runs from 0.168 to 0.616. In a tidy empirical world, the Census nonwhite returns to a BA would fall in this interval. In fact, the analogous Census confidence interval runs from −0.180 to 0.112. The significant difference between these two surveys is largely attributable to the previously noted bias in the mean earnings of nonwhites with graduate education in the 1/1,000 Census sample.[4]

The PSID results suggest that returns to a BA increased dramatically over the short span of five years, while returns to other years of schooling decreased for nonwhites. The implication is clear: by 1971, a nonwhite needed to have completed college in order to realize a substantial return on his investment in education. The implied ratio of nonwhite to white earnings fell as education increased from zero to fifteen years. But nonwhite returns to a BA were so much higher than white returns that the earnings of those with BAs were almost equal for the two groups. Featherman and Hauser (1978) have reached similar conclusions about the relationship between education and both occupational status and earnings; returns to education are lower for members of their black sample until they acquire a BA, at which point they almost catch up with comparable nonblacks. These results support the view that the 1960s helped create a new black elite (see e.g., Moynihan, 1972). The social, political, and public policy implications of such a development, as well as the role of past policies (including university recruitment of minority students) in promoting it, deserve more attention than they have gotten.

Since the PSID longitudinal sample is quite small and could be un-representative due to sample attrition, we also looked at cross-sectional CPS data for the years 1967 through 1976. The comparison poses three problems. First, CPS did not publish data on earnings by educational level until 1977. Earlier CPS tabulations cover total personal income. Second, CPS does not publish income data by race for men aged 25 to 64, but only for all men 25 and over. Neither of these discrepancies would be serious in isolation, since most earners are 25 to 64 and most income of 25- to 64-year-olds comes from earnings. But the two discrepancies together lead to the inclusion of a significant number of men over 64 without earnings. A third source of difficulty is that since 1967, CPS has published income data for blacks, but not for all nonwhites.

The effects of these changes in coverage and definition can be summarized as follows: [5]

a. The shift from a nonwhite to a black subsample has little effect, except that the ninety-one blacks with graduate education in the 1/1,000 sample earn more than the other fifty-eight nonwhites.
b. Since whites report more income from sources other than earnings than blacks do, the change from earnings to total personal income reduces the black/white ratio. This effect increases somewhat with increasing levels of education. When one looks at earnings, the proportional return to the first sixteen years of education is approximately equal for whites and blacks. When one looks at total income, returns appear lower for blacks than whites.[6]
c. The inclusion of men 65 and over increases the black/white income ratio at lower levels of education. This accentuates the apparent difference between black and white returns to the first sixteen years of education.

TABLE 7.2

Mean Income, by Race, Education, and Year[a]

Years of Education		1967	1968	1969	1970	1971	1972	1973	1974	1975	1976
less than 8	White	3,758	4,204	4,455	4,651	4,984	5,591	5,874	5,885	6,096	6,642
	Black	3,004	3,129	3,465	3,671	3,912	3,939	4,378	4,524	4,978	5,294
	ratio	.799	.744	.778	.789	.785	.703	.745	.769	.817	.797
8	White	5,278	5,557	5,920	6,143	6,378	6,847	7,688	7,643	7,890	8,543
	Black	3,976	4,275	4,534	4,633	4,877	5,759	5,640	5,758	6,457	6,850
	ratio	.753	.769	.766	.754	.765	.841	.734	.753	.818	.802
9-11	White	6,558	6,973	7,539	7,902	8,277	8,763	9,461	9,787	9,881	10,740
	Black	4,523	5,078	5,260	5,704	5,909	6,238	6,712	7,151	7,170	7,887
	ratio	.690	.728	.698	.722	.714	.712	.709	.731	.726	.734
12	White	7,787	8,319	9,032	9,389	9,772	10,694	11,452	12,113	12,648	13,393
	Black	5,328	5,737	6,122	6,523	6,748	7,319	8,370	9,090	9,014	9,298
	ratio	.684	.690	.678	.695	.691	.684	.731	.750	.713	.694
13-15	White	8,994	9,559	10,598	11,081	11,248	12,125	12,836	13,768	14,287	14,957
	Black	6,054	6,615	7,069	7,579	7,483	8,284	8,690	10,082	10,429	10,499
	ratio	.673	.692	.667	.684	.665	.683	.677	.732	.730	.702
16 or more	White	12,089	13,126	14,318	14,640	15,355	16,531	17,339	18,512	19,389	20,874
	Black	7,856	8,448	9,030	10,155	10,684	11,402	12,035	12,556	13,399	15,374
	ratio	.650	.644	.631	.694	.696	.690	.694	.678	.691	.737

[a] Males aged 25 and over with nonzero income, not in the military and not in institutions.

Source: Current Population Reports, Series P-60, for 1967 to 1973. Data for 1974 to 1976 are from unpublished tables kindly provided by the Bureau of the Census. The 1975 and 1976 data are not strictly comparable to earlier years (see note 29, chapter 6, p. 369).

This summary suggests that one should be cautious in generalizing from black/white income ratios to nonwhite/white earnings ratios. Nonetheless, if earnings returns to a BA rose substantially for 25- to 64-year-old nonwhites between 1967 and 1971, as the PSID data suggest, this trend should also be apparent in the CPS income data on whites and blacks 25 and over. Table 7.2 shows that the black/white income ratio for those with a BA did indeed increase from about 0.64 to about 0.69 around 1970, which is consistent with our PSID results.[7] While there is some evidence that the black/white income ratio increased slightly at other educational levels during the mid-1970s, the trends are far less clear. The CPS results are consistent with our analysis of Census data in suggesting that the first sixteen years of education raise blacks' incomes (as distinct from earnings) by a smaller percentage than they raise whites' incomes.

3. COMPARABILITY WITH PREVIOUS FINDINGS

It is not as easy as it should be to compare these results to earlier research on returns to education for whites and nonwhites. Thurow (1969), Link (1975), and Weiss and Williamson (1975) all regressed ln earnings on ln education rather than education. Their coefficients represent elasticities, while our semilog coefficients represent the percentage increase associated with an extra year of schooling. While percentage returns to education seem to decline at higher levels of education, they do not decline nearly so quickly as the double-log model implies. As a result, R^2 is consistently lower in their double-log models than in our semilog models. Because of this we have more confidence in our conclusions than in theirs.[8]

The recent study by Smith and Welch (1977) is by far the most thorough contribution to the literature on black/white differences in the returns to education. They use the 1960 and 1970 Censuses to estimate the benefits of education for blacks and whites. Their approach is similar to ours in many respects, but there are several important differences. First, they exclude the self-employed. Second, they also control geographic region, metropolitan or central city residence, and whether an individual is employed by federal, state, or local government or an industry which is somehow dependent on the federal government. Since education is causally prior to these variables, these controls are not appropriate when estimating individual returns to schooling. Third, they analyze men with zero to forty years of imputed work experience, while we analyze men aged 25 to 64. Men with less than ten years of experience are often under 25. Fortunately, Smith and Welch present separate results for men with varying amounts of experience. Men with less than ten years of experience have unusually large educational coefficients in both 1959 and 1969. This is probably because age per se is important for men under 25 and is not controlled.[9] Fourth, their dependent variable is the log of weekly rather than annual earnings. Weekly earnings should be less affected by the fact that the 1959 and 1969 surveys were conducted at different points in the business cycle. But since one benefit of education is to reduce the likelihood of involuntary unemployment, this procedure again lowers estimated returns to schooling.

Smith and Welch found that the percentage return to a year of elementary or secondary schooling was higher for whites than blacks in 1959. There was no change for either race between 1959 and 1969. Percentage returns to years of college were the same for both groups in 1959 and increased equally for both groups during the 1960s.

Smith and Welch thus confirm our finding that returns to elementary and secondary schooling were constant (or decreased by an insignificant amount) during the 1960s for whites, while returns to higher education increased. They also confirm our finding that minority returns to college were roughly equal for whites and nonwhites during the sixties, although our PSID and CPS data suggest that returns to a BA per se may have been greater for nonwhites than for whites after 1969. The primary difference between their results and ours is that they find that blacks receive lower returns to elementary and secondary schooling than whites and that the gap between these returns was the same in 1969 as it had been in 1959. In our 1961 OCG and 1969 Census samples, percentage returns to the first fifteen years of education were at least as large for nonwhites as for whites. This was also true for nonwhites in the first two years of the PSID (1967 and 1968).

This difference could have several explanations. First, we analyzed nonwhites, while Smith and Welch analyzed blacks. Second, by controlling for place of residence, type of employment, and weeks worked, Smith and Welch eliminate several potential sources of disparity between black and white returns to schooling. It is quite possible that more of the total effect of education on wages or earnings is mediated through these variables for blacks than for whites, leaving a smaller direct effect.* Third, they estimated returns to the first twelve years of schooling, while we estimated returns to the first fifteen years.

4. EFFECTS OF EQUALIZING EDUCATION AND EXPERIENCE

One popular proposal for reducing the racial gap in earnings is to eliminate racial differences in educational attainment. Accomplishing this quickly requires increasing the education of nonwhite adults. Past experiences with adult education and job training programs suggest that this type of policy can be quite expensive and, while benefitting certain individuals, is unlikely to have a large effect on the mean earnings of nonwhites. If society is willing to proceed at a more leisurely pace, it can concentrate on encouraging young nonwhites to obtain more education. If the nonwhite educational distribution were eventually to approximate the white distribution and if pay differentials between whites and nonwhites with the same education remained unaltered, table 7.1 shows that between 25 and 30 percent of the present earnings difference between whites and nonwhites would disappear. This estimate must obviously be treated cautiously. First, a large increase in the supply of educated nonwhite workers might lead to a decline in their relative wages. Then, too, unless the entire effect of education on earnings is due to the fact that extra education raises productivity, increasing mean nonwhite education will not increase GNP enough to cover the expected increase in earnings. The only way to finance the increase in earnings for highly educated nonwhites would be to reduce the real wages of whites. (This could be done by wage cuts or through general inflation.) Finally, part of the apparent effect of schooling is really due to causally prior traits like parental status and ability. Unless the means for these traits increased along with education, the benefits of education would be less than our equations imply. The estimates in table 7.1 therefore constitute an upper limit on the likely effects of reducing the education gap between whites and nonwhites.† Even if we ignore (as we have)

---

* To the extent that current location is correlated with where one was raised, the causal order of education and location is ambiguous.

† Differences in experience explain less than 1 percent of the white/nonwhite earnings differential.

the possible development of new or alternative forms of discrimination, changing nonwhite educational attainment is likely to have less effect than table 7.1 indicates.

An alternative policy is to ensure that whites and nonwhites with equal levels of education and experience receive equal pay. We can estimate the effect of this change by substituting the nonwhite means on education and experience into the white equations. The result would be a 55 to 70 percent reduction in the gap between white and nonwhite earnings.* Public policies which ensure that nonwhites earn as much as whites with similar education have several advantages over policies that increase nonwhite educational attainment, though both are clearly desirable. First, the benefits are likely to be felt sooner, since changing mean education is a gradual process and would be of little value to older workers. Second, the estimated effect of equalizing white and nonwhite earnings within educational levels is generally greater than the estimated effect of equalizing the distribution of education. Furthermore, our analysis probably overestimates the actual effect of equalizing the distribution of education. This implies that we probably underestimate the effect of equalizing earnings for equally educated whites and nonwhites.[10]

During the ten years between the OCG and PSID surveys, the average earnings of both whites and nonwhites rose considerably, even after controlling for inflation. Since the earnings of both groups increased by about the same absolute amount, the ratio of nonwhite to white earnings also increased. It seems useful to ask to what extent these increases reflect changes in the average education and experience of the two groups.

Let us begin with whites. The average (geometric mean) earnings of PSID whites were 43.8 percent greater than the average earnings of

---

* Let f_w and f_n denote the regression equations for whites and nonwhites respectively. Let x_w and x_n denote the vectors of means for whites and nonwhites respectively. Let $f_w(x_w)$ denote the value obtained by substituting the white means in the white equations, and so forth. Assuming equal pay for equal credentials, the expected income of nonwhites is $f_w(x_n)$. This is the same as the hypothetical white average income, assuming that white means on the independent variables equal nonwhite means. However, in the first case we are asking how much this change moves nonwhites toward whites, i.e., $[f_w(x_n) - f_n(x_n)]/[f_w(x_w) - f_n(x_n)] = 55$ to 70 percent, and we therefore compare the hypothetical nonwhite average to the observed nonwhite average. In the latter situation, we ask how different (as a percentage of the total white/nonwhite gap) the hypothetical white average income is from the observed white average income $[f_w(x_w) - f_w(x_n)]/[f_w(x_w) - f_n(x_n)] = 30$ to 45 percent. These two cases split the total white/nonwhite gap into two pieces. It follows that the sum of the two pieces will always equal 100 percent of the gap:

$$\frac{f_w(x_w) - f_w(x_n)}{f_w(x_w) - f_n(x_n)} + \frac{f_w(x_n) - f_n(x_n)}{f_w(x_w) - f_n(x_n)} = \frac{f_w(x_w) - f_n(x_n)}{f_w(x_w) - f_n(x_n)}$$

OCG whites. If we insert the 1971 white means on education and experience in the 1961 ln earnings equation, we find that changes in these characteristics account for 20.7 percent of the ten-year increase in real ln earnings. (As we pointed out previously, this figure should be interpreted as a maximum.) This implies that almost 80 percent of the white increase was due to other factors. Changes in the regression coefficients were small. Most of the increase in the white mean is thus due to an increase in the constant. This means that most of the increase in white earnings was an across-the-board increase for everyone in the labor force. If we reverse the process by substituting 1961 white means in the 1971 ln earnings equation, the picture is almost identical. This is also true when we look at earnings and earnings$^{1/3}$. Results for non-whites are similar to those for whites, with education and experience gains accounting for 18 percent of the income gain between 1961 and 1971.

5. DEMOGRAPHIC BACKGROUND AND EARNINGS

Background characteristics influence earnings in much the same way among nonwhites as among whites. In table 7.3 we regress ln earnings on demographic background among whites and among nonwhites. Of the twenty pairs of comparable coefficients, only five differ significantly by race.[11] Growing up on a farm is a greater disadvantage for nonwhites than for whites in the OCG, while growing up in the South constitutes a greater disadvantage for nonwhites than for whites in the PSID. This may reflect nonwhite migration during the sixties from southern farms to cities in both the South and North.

Controlling for other background variables, father's occupation has a significant positive effect for OCG whites, but not for nonwhites. Successful white parents were able to pass on more of their advantages to their children than were nonwhite parents. The negative coefficient of father's occupation among nonwhites more than compensates for the fact that father's education has a larger coefficient among nonwhites. In the PSID, father's occupation does not have a large net effect for either whites or nonwhites. However, nonwhites with fathers at both extremes of the Duncan scale had higher-than-expected earnings, thus making the coefficient of father's occupation^2 significant.

TABLE 7.3

Regressions of Ln Earnings on LN Income on Background Characteristics, by Race[a]

		OCG (1961 Income)		PSID (1971 Earnings)	
		White (N = 10,395)	Nonwhite (N = 1,110)	White (N = 1,307)	Nonwhite (N = 467)
Father's education	B	.014**	.042**	.025	[.016]
	(SE)	(.002)	(.009)	(.007)	(.017)
Father's occupation	B	.005**	−.008**	[−.002]	−.013
	(SE)	(.001)	(.004)	(.002)	(.006)
Father white collar	B	[.040]	[.192]	[.165]	.738
	(SE)	(.027)	(.163)	(.095)	(.280)
Father absent	B	−.119	[−.079]	[−.043]	[.001]
	(SE)	(.021)	(.065)	(.242)	(.253)
Non-South upbringing	B	.172	.146	.102*	.440*
	(SE)	(.017)	(.061)	(.045)	(.118)
Nonfarm upbringing	B	.203*	3.706*	.178	[.147]
	(SE)	(.019)	(.068)	(.049)	(.090)
Siblings	B	−.018	[−.014]	−.029	[−.015]
	(SE)	(.002)	(.009)	(.008)	(.017)
Father's education²	B	[−.0000]	[.0011]	[−.0018]	[.0004]
	(SE)	(.0004)	(.0014)	(.0014)	(.0027)
Father's occupation²	B	[−.0000]	−.0002	[−.0001]**	.0005**
	(SE)	(.0000)	(.0001)	(.0001)	(.0001)
Siblings²	B	[.0008]	[.0002]	[.0017]	[.0081]
	(SE)	(.0006)	(.0017)	(.0027)	(.0063)
Constant[b]		8.609	7.977	8.977	8.687
R²		.099	.083	.080	.128
SD of residuals		.730	.902	.695	.870
Percentage of gap eliminated if equalization occurs at level of:					
Nonwhite means		26.5		36.6	
White means		17.9		42.1	

Coefficients in brackets are less than twice their standard error.

*Difference between white and nonwhite coefficients significant at 0.05 level.

**Difference between white and nonwhite coefficients significant at 0.01 level.

[a] Both samples restricted to men aged 25 to 64 with complete data who were not in institutions or in the military. PSID sample restricted to nonstudents with positive earnings. OCG samples restricted to men with nonzero income.

[b] Estimated in 1967 dollars.

For men at the nonwhite mean on the background variables in 1961, the earnings gap between whites and nonwhites was 27 percent less than the gap between whites and nonwhites generally. For men at the white mean on the background variables, the gap was only 18 percent less than that between whites and nonwhites generally. This implies that the earnings gap between whites and nonwhites widens among those from more advantaged backgrounds.[12] The more recent PSID equations tell a somewhat different story, indicating that by 1971 the gap between whites and nonwhites was marginally *smaller* among men from advantaged backgrounds.[13]

Table 7.3 also shows that background accounted for more of the gap in 1971 than in 1961. Since the overall gap decreased during this period (the ratio of nonwhite to white earnings increased from 0.504 to 0.645), the gap between those from similar backgrounds decreased dramatically.

OCG and PSID equations not shown here indicate that between 35 and 65 percent of the white/nonwhite difference in earnings is associated with differences in background, education, and occupation. This leaves 65 to 35 percent of the gap due to differences in earnings between whites and nonwhites with equivalent background, education, and occupations. The portion of the gap attributable to differences between "equivalent" whites and nonwhites decreased more between 1961 and 1971 than did the portion attributable to white/nonwhite differences in background, education, and occupation. In other words, the determinants of economic attainment among nonwhites became more like those for whites during the 1960s.[14]

CONCLUSIONS

Much of the debate about white/nonwhite (or black/white) differences in earnings (or wages or income) has centered around two principal issues:

1. How much of the earnings differential is attributable to white/nonwhite differences in personal characteristics that affect earnings regardless of race ("human capital")?
2. How much of the earnings differential is due to white/nonwhite differences in returns to personal characteristics, i.e., to differences between white and nonwhite regression coefficients?

The answer to the first question depends on one's answer to a counterfactual question: how large would the earnings gap be if whites did not differ from nonwhites on traits such as education and experience? This is a legitimate question. Those who ask the question sometimes seem, however, to make the implicit assumption that each individual can control or change (and is therefore responsible for) the traits he possesses. This is obviously false in relation to demographic background characteristics. It is also questionable with respect to education. While it is true that once individuals pass the age of compulsory schooling they choose for themselves whether to stay in school or drop out, not all individuals face the same constraints when making these choices. Most sociologists agree, for example, that the economic and psychological costs of remaining in school tend to bear more heavily on nonwhites than on whites. Thus even if the benefits of schooling were equal for whites and nonwhites, we would expect whites to end up with more schooling than nonwhites.

Furthermore, while we cannot blame discrimination by *current employers* for the portion of the earnings gap attributable to white/nonwhite differences in personal characteristics, neither can we simply dismiss the possibility that this portion of the gap is due to discrimination. To the extent that discrimination in education causes white/nonwhite differences in educational attainment, or past discrimination by employers causes white/nonwhite differences in social background, discrimination is an indirect cause of the entire earnings differential.

Whether whites receive higher returns to schooling than nonwhites is a very different question. We concluded that there is not much difference in their percentage (or utility) returns. Since nonwhites start from a lower base than whites, this implied significant differences in actual dollar returns. Others have claimed that whites also have higher percentage returns. This is an important issue, but not because higher returns to whites would explain a substantial portion of the earnings gap. Rather, it is important because the desire for higher earnings has been a major reason for seeking education in modern societies. We cannot measure the nonmonetary costs or benefits of continuing education for either whites or nonwhites. In the absence of such information, we must assume that lower monetary benefits mean lower overall returns and, hence, lower incentives to continue one's education. The issue of differential returns to education is also important because different returns can violate our notions of justice and equity.

Our findings suggest, however, that the main difference between the white and nonwhite earnings equations is the difference between the constants. There is a tendency in regression analyses not to interpret the constants, which usually seem arbitrary. A regression constant represents the expected value of the dependent variable for a (hypothetical) individual with a value of zero on every independent variable. This is usually a person with zero education, zero experience (or age), zero occupational status, and so forth. Such a person's expected earnings are not of much interest. But if, as in this chapter, we redefine the independent variables relative to the average individual, the constants are not only interpretable but very informative.*

The fact that the nonwhite regression constants in our equations are always much lower than those of whites tells us that when whites and nonwhites have identical values on each of the independent variables and these values are equal to the population means, nonwhites have much lower earnings than whites. The similarity of the regression coefficients of the independent variables for whites and nonwhites tells us that if we compare the earnings of "equivalent" whites and nonwhites throughout the distributions of the independent variables, this gap will not change much.

How should we interpret the differences in constants (the equivalent of a race coefficient)? In particular, what does it tell us about discrimination? There are two extreme interpretations, both of which can be misleading. The first is that this difference measures the effect of earnings discrimination, i.e., the effect on earnings of nonwhite skin. But if discrimination is defined as the difference between the expected earnings of whites and nonwhites who are alike on selected measures, errors in specification and measurement will tend to create evidence of discrimination. This is not a satisfactory method for estimating the actual importance of discrimination.

The second alternative is to assume that the difference between the constants embodies the effects of white/nonwhite differences on other determinants of earnings, such as ability and ambition, that have not been included in the model. If these traits were all incorporated into the earnings model, the argument goes, no differences would remain between the white and nonwhite constants. This interpretation is, in principle, testable. Its implication is that we should spend our time collecting better data and generating better earnings models, instead of worrying about white/nonwhite differences in earnings. Some carry

* While our hypothetical reference person is "statistically" representative, he would not in fact exist since he simultaneously has a fraction of a BA and fewer than twelve years of education. The constant might be slightly more interpretable if our reference person were in the modal category of each independent variable.

this argument one step further by assuming that if the constants are equal, there is no discrimination. We discussed this fallacy earlier. While equal constants show that employers are not discriminating on the basis of skin color, they do not prove that discrimination plays no part in creating the other differences between whites and nonwhites that result in unequal earnings.

Nonetheless, there is surely an element of truth in both interpretations. Direct earnings discrimination does occur in our society. Our models also omit many variables, the inclusion of which would probably help explain part of the earnings gap between whites and nonwhites. When the difference between constants changes over time, however, the change is likely to reflect a change in the amount of discrimination. Our regressions of earnings on social background, education, experience, and occupation indicate that 60 percent of the income gap in the 1961 OCG was due to different constants. In the 1971 PSID this was 35 to 45 percent, depending on the earnings measure. We believe that this change reflects a sharp decrease in direct earnings discrimination, but that a significant portion of the remaining difference in constants is still due to such discrimination.

We conclude this chapter with a conjecture evolved from the "missing variables" interpretation. This interpretation assumes that our models have not considered enough of the traits that affect a worker's productivity and, hence, his potential value to his employer. This omission reflects the difficulty of obtaining data on other traits. OCG, Census, and PSID do not, for example, have reliable data on IQ or ability. But how much information does an employer have about a prospective employee? He knows what is contained in a job application—the employee's name, address, sex, education, age, marital status, and previous two or three jobs—and perhaps something about his ability based on oral or written recommendations. The employer does not often know or wish to know the employee's father's education or occupation, or how many siblings the employee has (the sociologist's cherished background variables); nor does he usually test the employee's IQ. In assessing the qualifications of a candidate, the employer also uses his own expectations concerning the relationship between known characteristics and unknown abilities and characteristics, such as initiative or punctuality.[15] If an employer believes that race is associated with these unmeasured traits, he will use race as a source of easily and cheaply gathered information about an applicant's abilities. He will be reluctant to hire nonwhites if there are whites available with the same measured characteristics unless he can pay the nonwhites a lower wage.

Arrow (1972a, 1972b) outlines a model based on these assumptions and shows that the result may be consistently lower wages for non-whites. Furthermore, if individuals incur costs in acquiring skills, qualifications, and/or good work habits, then lower nonwhite wages imply lower incentives for nonwhites to acquire such skills. The result—fewer skilled nonwhites—may cause employers to readjust their expectations, pushing nonwhite wages even lower. In such a situation, nonwhites would be better off if employers had access to more reliable and objective information on which to base their judgments.

Spence (1975) has developed a related model which suggests that the difference between white and nonwhite wages could be completely arbitrary, bearing no relation to differences in productivity. His assumptions include the following:

1. The monetary and psychic cost of acquiring education and other skills is negatively correlated with an individual's "native" ability or productivity.
2. Individuals know both the costs and expected benefits of acquiring different amounts of education and will attempt to maximize their net return.
3. The costs of hiring, training, and firing a potential employee make it desirable for the employer to estimate the job applicant's productivity (not initially observable) from other information about the applicant.
4. The employer can and does measure the productivity of his labor force. If necessary, employers adjust their expectations about the relationship between productivity and the measurable characteristics of job applicants. They also adjust the wages they offer job applicants so that these wages correspond to applicants' expected productivity.

Based on these assumptions, Spence shows that if employers initially assume that the relationship between education and productivity is different for whites and nonwhites, an equilibrium can result in which whites and nonwhites with the same amount of education are offered different wages.° The average wage of each group (but not the distribution of wages within a group) will be arbitrary. An average difference between groups can thus arise even if whites and nonwhites have the same abilities. If it is true that earnings differentials are arbitrary or are caused by employers' mistaken beliefs about the relationship between race and unobserved traits, it should be relatively easy to reduce them. The resulting situation is a nonoptimal equilibrium from the perspective of both employers and employees. Both groups would benefit if the artificial pressures holding down wages and productivity could be broken, yet an external force, such as government or public pressure against discrimination, may be needed in order to initiate such a change.

° This initial assumption may be attributable to prejudice, historical differences, or anything else. Its source need not be rational and is irrelevant to the model.

WHO GETS AHEAD?

As nonwhites' education—and presumably their skills—approach those of whites, it is not clear how quickly employers will respond. If employers' expectations lag behind reality, the closing of the gap between white and nonwhite earnings will be unnecessarily retarded. Thus, models which suggest that discrimination on the part of employers is a rational response to imperfect information should not, in any sense, be seen as a justification of discriminatory practices.

CHAPTER 8

Who Gets Ahead:
A Summary

To what extent do the most desirable jobs go to the brightest, to the most educated, to the most ambitious, or to the sons and daughters of the rich? Previous chapters have looked at the effects of each of these factors separately. This chapter summarizes and synthesizes our findings. It begins by discussing the effects of family background, then takes up cognitive skills and personality traits, and concludes by discussing the effects of education.

1. FAMILY BACKGROUND

Association of Background with Status. We found no convincing evidence that brothers influenced one another's life chances, so we used the degree of resemblance between brothers to assess the overall impact of family background. After correcting first for the fact that pairs of brothers are concentrated in large families and then for the effects of random measurement error, we concluded that all aspects of family background

Mary Corcoran wrote this chapter.

explained about 48 percent of the variance in mature men's occupational statuses. The reader can interpret this statistic in either of two equally correct ways. The first interpretation uses it to explain observed differences in status among sons. If, for example, we pick a sample of doctors—whose Duncan scores are about 53 points above the national average—our data imply that their brothers' scores will typically be about $(0.48)(53) = 25$ points above the national average. The typical doctor thus owes about 48 percent of his occupational advantage to family background and 52 percent to factors that operate independent of background, differentiating him from his brothers. The second interpretation asks how much parents can influence their sons. If we could measure all aspects of family background and construct a properly weighted composite index of family advantages, our data imply that this index would correlate $0.48^{1/2} = 0.69$ with a son's occupational status. Thus if parents were two standard deviations above the mean on our composite index of advantages, they could expect their sons to be 1.4 standard deviations above the mean. This is a strong association—almost as strong as the association between education and occupational status.

The most important single measured background characteristic affecting a son's occupational status is his father's occupational status, but father's ocupation accounts for only a third of the resemblance between brothers. If we also consider other demographic characteristics, such as father's and mother's education, parental income, family size, race, ethnicity, religion, and region of birth, we can account for at least another third of the resemblance between brothers. The remaining third is presumably due to unmeasured social, psychological, or genetic factors that vary within demographic groups.

The influence of most measured background characteristics on occupational status declined slightly between the early 1960s and the early 1970s. The effects of race fell quite markedly. Unfortunately, we do not have trend data on occupational resemblance between brothers, so we cannot say whether the effects of unmeasured background changed during those years.

Mechanisms by Which Background Affects Status. Men from advantaged backgrounds have higher test scores than men from disadvantaged backgrounds, but this does not explain most of their occupational advantage. This is partly because the background characteristics that affect test scores are somewhat different from those that affect status ($\bar{r} = 0.80$). Test performance accounts for 40 to 60 percent of demographic background's effect in three samples with reliable scores. But when we also take account of all the unmeasured background characteristics that make brothers alike, controlling test scores only accounts for a quarter of these shared background characteristics' eventual impact on occupational status.

Controlling education as well as test scores accounts for 65 to 92 percent of the effect of measured background on status and 56 to 77 percent of family background's overall effect. Five background characteristics consistently influenced occupational status independent of educational attainment: race, ethnicity, religion, father's occupational status, and farm background.

The effects of race persist no matter what we control, at least among men over 30. This could mean that there are unmeasured behavioral differences between blacks and whites with similar backgrounds, test scores, and education; that employers hire or promote on the basis of racial identity per se; or both.

Ethnicity also appears to have modest effects on occupational status even after one controls educational attainment. Jews work in occupations that rank about a third of a standard deviation above the level one would expect on the basis of their schooling and place of residence. White Anglo-Saxon Protestants and German Catholics enjoy a more modest advantage. Italian and French Catholics and Irish Protestants are about a sixth of a standard deviation below the expected level.

A father's occupational status exerts a modest effect on his son's occupational status in OCG and OCG-II, even after we control the son's educational attainment. This could be due to unmeasured behavioral differences between men from different backgrounds with the same amount of education. Speech patterns differ by background, for example, even among men with the same amount of schooling, and employers may prefer to hire or promote men who talk as if they were brought up in middle-class homes. But if this were the explanation, father's education, mother's education, and family income should capture these effects about as well as father's occupation. The peculiar potency of father's occupational status relative to other measures of a family's position suggests that we are not dealing with the general effects of privileged upbringing but with something specific to occupations. Direct transmission of specific jobs may be part of the story, but even after we eliminate sons in the same detailed occupational category as their father, the father's occupational status has a small direct effect on his son's status in OCG. Perhaps this is because the father's status affects his son's willingness to accept a job in a low-status occupation.

The negative effects of farm upbringing are hard to distinguish from the negative effects of having a father who was a farmer. Insofar as the two *are* distinguishable, the effects of farm upbringing seem to disappear once we control the size of the community in which the respondent lives as an adult. This suggests that men reared on farms work in low-status occupations partly because they often remain in small towns where job opportunities are limited.

Since brothers end up more alike in terms of occupational status than we would expect on the basis of their common demographic background and educational and cognitive resemblance, there must also be other background characteristics that have a direct influence on a son's occupational status. Parental attitudes and values may be important, but we have little direct evidence for this. We know, for example, that brothers end up more alike on Talent's noncognitive measures than we would expect on the basis of the fact that they come from the same demographic background. If these noncognitive measures also explained a substantial fraction of the variance in occupational status with test scores and education controlled, we could infer that noncognitive traits explained the remaining occupational resemblance between brothers. This would strongly imply that parental noncognitive traits were also involved. In fact, however, Talent's noncognitive measures explain only 1.5 percent of the variance in occupational status after test scores and education have been controlled. Thus, even if brothers were completely alike on these noncognitive measures, which they are not, such resemblance could not account for much of their occupational resemblance.

The fact that brothers share roughly half their genes could also help explain part of their occupational resemblance, but our data certainly do not prove this. Still less do our data explain *how* genes might exert such effects. We know, for example, that genes affect test performance. But if test performance were the only source of occupational resemblance between brothers, the correlation between brothers' statuses would be less than 0.15. For genes to explain the rest of the resemblance between brothers, they would have to affect status independent of test scores. This is quite possible. Physical and mental health, physical stamina, and appearance (including skin color) all depend partly on genotype and probably all affect occupational status. Unfortunately, we cannot assess their quantitative importance with our data. We would, however, be astonished if such traits accounted for most of the unexplained occupational resemblance between brothers.

Given the difficulty of identifying background characteristics that explain the full resemblance between brothers, we cannot reject the hypothesis that brothers affect one another. If they do, we have overestimated the impact of shared background.

Association of Background with Earnings. After correcting for the unrepresentativeness of our samples of brothers and random measurement error, we concluded that family background might explain anywhere from 15 to 35 percent of the variance in 25- to 64-year-old men's earnings. This means that 15 to 35 percent of a mature man's advantage or disadvantage in earnings typically derives from characteristics he shares with his brothers. The best paid fifth of all male earners aged 25 to 64 in the Census, for example, earned 2.01 times the mean for such men. Even if the correlation between brothers were as high as 0.35, the brothers of men earning twice the cohort average could only be expected to earn 1.35 times the cohort average. If the correlation were as low as 0.15, the brothers of the best paid fifth could be expected to earn only 1.15 times the cohort average.

Another interpretation of these results, which makes family background sound considerably more important, involves ranking parents according to their ability to enhance their sons' earnings, ignoring all their other advantages and disadvantages. When we rank parents in this way, their rank correlates 0.39 to 0.59 with specific sons' earnings. This correlation is somewhat stronger than that between education and earnings. If the correlation were as high as 0.59, and if families' only objective were to increase their sons' earnings, the most "successful" fifth of all families could expect their sons to earn nearly 80 percent more than the national average. If the correlation were as low as 0.39, the most "successful" fifth of all families could still expect their sons to earn at least 45 percent more than the average man.[*]

Parental income only seems to account for about 4 percent of the variance in incomes. If one also takes account of race, ethnicity, father's occupation, father's and mother's education, region of birth, whether the family remained intact while the sons were growing up, errors in measuring these traits, and errors in measuring income, one can explain 13 to 19 percent of the variance. This leaves much of the resemblance between brothers unexplained.

The effects of demographic background on earnings, like their effects on occupational status, declined between the early 1960s and early 1970s. The decline was particularly marked for race. Again, we have no trend data on the effects of unmeasured background characteristics.

---

[*] These estimates assume that the distribution of predicted values is normal, and that parents in the top fifth of the distribution therefore average 1.4 standard deviations above the mean. If the standard deviation of ln earnings for sons is 0.70, and the correlation between parents and sons is between 0.39 and 0.59, the expected ratio of sons in the top fifth to all sons will be between $e^{(1.4)(0.39)(0.70)}$ and $e^{(1.4)(0.59)(0.70)}$, i.e., between 1.47 and 1.78.

Mechanisms by Which Background Affects Earnings. Background affects earnings partly by affecting the cognitive skills measured on standard tests, but this is not the primary mechanism involved. The fact that demographic background affects test performance accounts for between 25 and 50 percent of demographic background's impact on earnings in the four samples with test scores. Test scores account for 15 to 21 percent of the overall effect of common background characteristics on earnings in the two samples of brothers with relevant data.

Education and test scores together explain somewhat more of the effect of demographic background, reducing the demographic measures' coefficients by 36 to 107 percent in the four samples with test-score data. But when we include the unmeasured background characteristics that make brothers alike, education and test scores explain only a quarter of background's effect.

Thus, while family background has less overall impact on ln earnings than on occupational status, its "direct" effects on earnings, once we control test scores and educational attainment, are at least as large as its direct effects on status. This holds true both when we look at the overall effects of background in our small samples of brothers and when we look at the effects of measured background in larger and more representative samples.

We were not able to identify most of the background characteristics that affect earnings independent of cognitive skills and education. The only demographic characteristics with such effects are race, religion, region of birth, father's occupation, and whether the respondent grew up on a farm. Farm origins and southern birth affect earnings only insofar as they affect where the respondent is likely to live as an adult. Father's occupation affects earnings primarily by affecting occupational status, though this is not quite the whole story. Race has large effects with everything controlled. This could be because nonwhites do not seek jobs that pay as well as the jobs whites seek, because employers are less inclined to hire nonwhites than whites with similar qualifications, or because nonwhites are less likely to get raises once they have been hired. If nonwhites earn less because they get fewer raises, this could either imply that the two groups perform differently on the job or that employers discriminate. Catholics and Jews also seem to enjoy higher incomes than Protestants with similar demographic backgrounds and schooling, but again we cannot say why.

2. EFFECTS OF COGNITIVE SKILLS

Association between Cognitive Skills and Adult Occupational Status. The Talent, Kalamazoo, Wisconsin, and EEO surveys include a cognitive test score obtained before students finished school, while the Veterans and PSID surveys include scores obtained after school completion. The association between test scores and occupational status in our samples does not depend on the age at which an individual is tested. Nor does it depend on the age at which we ascertain occupation. These six surveys imply that men whose test scores differ by fifteen points (one standard deviation) can expect to work in occupations whose status differs by one-third to one-half a standard deviation.

Effects of Cognitive Skills on Adult Status with Background Controlled. Part of the association between test performance and occupational status derives from the fact that they both depend on family background. In the Kalamazoo Brothers sample, controlling demographic background reduces the estimated effect of test performance on adult occupational status by one-eighth, while controlling all aspects of family background reduces the estimated effect by three-eighths. The same pattern holds among Talent Brothers. With all aspects of family background controlled, a one standard-deviation difference in adolescent test performance is associated with an occupational difference of one-quarter to one-third of a standard deviation in all our samples. These results do not support Bowles and Gintis's (1973) argument that IQ tests are merely proxies for family background. The skills that these tests measure vary substantially even within families, and these variations have appreciable effects on economic success.

Mechanisms by Which Adolescent Cognitive Skills Affect Adult Status. From 60 to 80 percent of the effect of adolescent cognitive skills on adult occupational status derives from the fact that adolescent cognitive skills affect educational attainment. Among men with the same amount of schooling, a one standard-deviation difference in adolescent test performance is associated with a difference of only 0.16 standard deviations in occupational status in the Talent and Kalamazoo samples. The difference is even smaller in the Wisconsin and EEO samples.

Test scores have virtually no effect on first occupation in the Kalamazoo or PSID samples once we control education. This suggests that adolescent cognitive skills affect adult occupational status in two distinct ways. First, they affect how much education men get, which then influences their initial occupation. Later, cognitive skills seem to exert a modest influence on occupational mobility, so that men with high test scores have a slightly greater chance of improving their initial position than men with low scores. Most of this improvement seems to take place fairly soon after men enter the labor force, since there is no evidence that the effect of test performance increases appreciably after the age of 25 or 30. Contrary to what one might expect, high test scores do not increase the percentage value of an extra year of high school or college.

Association of Cognitive Skills with Earnings.   A fifteen-point increase in adolescent test scores was associated with a 17 percent increase in earnings for Kalamazoo men aged 35 to 59 and with a 9 percent increase in earnings for Talent 28-year-olds. This discrepancy is likely to be caused by the age difference between the two samples. The effects of adolescent cognitive skills would probably look even larger if we had data on representative national samples, since earnings would be more varied in such samples.

The correlation of adult test scores with earnings does not increase consistently as PSID men get older, but since the variance of earnings increases, the earnings differential between men with different scores grows wider. On average, a fifteen-point difference in test performance is associated with a 30 percent difference in earnings among PSID 25- to 64-year-olds. The difference would probably be close to 40 percent if the PSID test were more reliable.

Effects of Cognitive Skills on Earnings with Background Controlled. Less than a quarter of the relationship between test scores and earnings arises because men with high test scores come from families with demographic advantages. Controlling all aspects of background by looking at brothers does not alter the estimated effect in Kalamazoo and reduces it only trivially in Talent.

The effects of test scores did not vary consistently with background, age, education, or experience. This suggests that one cannot account for the modest size of the correlation between test scores and earnings by saying that high scores are a necessary but not sufficient condition for high earnings. High scores are neither necessary nor sufficient. They are merely helpful.

Mechanisms by Which Adolescent Cognitive Skills Affect Earnings. Cognitive skills affect earnings partly because men with high adolescent scores tend to get more schooling and enter higher-status occupations than men with low scores, but that is not the whole story. In Kalamazoo, a fifteen-point difference in Kalamazoo brothers' test scores is associated with a 17 percent difference in earnings. The expected difference is still 14 percent if the brothers have the same amount of schooling. Indeed, it is an 11 percent difference if they have the same occupational status as well as the same amount of schooling. Results for Talent brothers are similar. The full Talent sample shows much weaker test-score effects, but schooling and occupational status play a comparable role as intervening variables. This means that while test scores are not as strongly correlated with earnings as with occupational status, their standardized direct effect with education controlled is equally large. The PSID and Veterans samples show roughly comparable effects for adult test scores with education controlled.

Adult Scores. The Veterans and PSID surveys measure test scores after school completion. If cognitive skills affect job performance directly, adult scores should predict performance more accurately than adolescent scores do. Fagerlind's Swedish study, which is the only one that has test scores both before and after school completion for the same individuals, yields this result. Our samples do not. This may be because the PSID test is unreliable and the Veterans sample underrepresents high and low-scoring men. Yet even after correcting for unreliability, the PSID correlations are no higher than those obtained using tests administered before school completion. This suggests that both adolescent and adult tests may predict economic success largely because they are proxies for stable underlying aptitudes, not because they measure skills that are themselves directly useful. If so, school-induced changes in test performance may not have much effect on economic success. Better data on this problem are badly needed.

3. ADOLESCENT PERSONALITY TRAITS

We used four different kinds of measures of adolescent personality: teacher ratings, self-assessments, attitude measures, and reports of actual behavior. Most previous research in this area had relied primarily on attitude measures and had obtained largely negative results. We found that teacher ratings and actual behavior predicted later success somewhat better than either attitudes or self-assessments. This suggests that adolescent personality traits play a larger role than previous research had indicated. While no single, well-defined trait emerged as a decisive determinant of economic success, the combined effects of many different measures were typically as strong as the combined effects of the different items that we used to measure cognitive skills.

Adolescent Personality and Occupational Status. Of the nine teacher ratings collected in Kalamazoo, ratings of "industriousness" proved to be the best predictors of occupational status in maturity ($r = 0.30$). About a third of this association is traceable to the fact that both "industriousness" and adult status depend on family background and sixth-grade test scores. Another third is explained by the fact that "industriousness" affects educational attainment. None of the other ratings had significant effects with background controlled. The label "industriousness" may not prove much, however, since teacher ratings of students' "cooperativeness," "dependability," and "emotional control" correlated 0.6 to 0.7 with their ratings of "industriousness."

Among the Talent measures, no one stands out as crucial. Nonetheless, even if we ignore occupational aspirations and focus on high school self-assessments and behavior, these measures have as much impact on occupational status as the Talent test-score battery. With background and test performance controlled, a one standard-deviation advantage on our combined measure of personality traits is associated with one-third of a standard-deviation advantage in occupational status twelve years later. About half this advantage is attributable to the fact that personality traits affect educational attainment.

Adolescent Personality and Earnings. The personality traits that affect earnings do not appear to be the same as those that affect occupational status. In Kalamazoo, for example, teacher ratings of tenth graders' executive ability predicted adult earnings more accurately ($r = 0.26$) than did teacher ratings of industriousness ($r = 0.18$). About a third of this association derives from the fact that both executive ability and earnings depend on background and sixth-grade test scores. A third of the remainder is explained by the fact that executive ability affects educational attainment.

The personality measures that affect Talent 28-year-olds' earnings are also quite different from those that affect their occupational status. Again, no one trait is decisive, but measures of "leadership" are more important than any other single self-assessment or behavioral measure. All personality traits together have a combined standardized coefficient of 0.29 with background characteristics controlled. Less than a sixth of this effect works through test scores, education, or occupation.

4. EDUCATIONAL ATTAINMENT

Association of Education with Occupational Status. When an individual first enters the labor market, the highest grade of school or college he has completed is the best single predictor of his eventual occupational status. Four years of secondary schooling are associated with an increase in status of almost half a standard deviation. Four years of college are associated with an increase of more than one standard deviation. If one allows for measurement error, education explains about half the variance in occupational status.

The last year of high school, the first year of college, and the last year of college have larger effects on occupational status than other years of high school or college. The first and last years of college also have larger effects on status than the first year of graduate school. The "bumpiness" of the relationship could mean that initial ability, personality, or family background characteristics have more effect on decisions to complete high school, enter college, or complete college than on decisions to continue in school or college for one more year. Alternatively, the bumpiness of the relationship could reflect certification effects. Employers may see workers as high school dropouts, high school graduates, college dropouts, or college graduates without knowing exactly how much schooling either high school or college dropouts got. This would yield the observed result. The peculiar potency of the first year of college could also mean that students change more during their first year of college than later, perhaps by acquiring a stronger preference for white-collar rather than blue-collar or farm work.

Effects of Education on Status with Background, Test Scores, and Personality Controlled. Both education and status depend on family background, adolescent ability, and adolescent personality traits, so it is essential that we control these factors when estimating the actual effect of an extra year of schooling on an individual's occupational status. Past research has generally concluded that schooling has almost as much impact on occupational status among men from similar demographic backgrounds as among men in general (Griffin, 1976). Our analyses confirm this. If we take a weighted average of the OCG, NLS, PA, and PSID results, the estimated occupational difference between men with twelve rather than eight years of school is 11 points on the Duncan scale. This difference drops to 8 points when we control demographic background. The expected difference between college graduates and high school graduates falls from 28 to 25 points once we control demographic background. This pattern does not change much when we control all aspects of background that brothers share.

When we also control test scores prior to school completion, the difference between elementary and secondary schooling and higher education is even more apparent. Controlling both family background and adolescent test scores reduces the apparent effects of high school by nearly 60 percent for Kalamazoo men. These controls only reduce the estimated benefits of four years of college by 12 percent in Kalamazoo and 22 percent among Talent Brothers.

An extra year of elementary or secondary schooling still raises whites' occupational status twice as much as nonwhites'. But a BA is worth more to nonwhites than to whites. This reflects the low status of nonwhites who do not finish college, not the high status of nonwhite BAs. Racial differences in returns to the first fifteen years of schooling could conceivably result from differences in the average quality of such schooling (Welch, 1974; Freeman, 1973), though this does not seem likely. Alternatively, there may have been more discrimination against nonwhites seeking middle-level jobs than against nonwhite BAs who sought to enter the professions. Whatever the reason, nonwhites have less incentive to complete high school than do whites. But among those who complete high school, the occupational incentives to get a BA are higher for nonwhites than for whites.

Men with white-collar fathers also obtain a greater occupational advantage from elementary and secondary schooling than men with blue-collar fathers, though the difference is not significant in any one sample. Men from farm backgrounds gain significantly more by graduating from college than other men do.

Mechanisms by Which Education Affects Occupational Status. Schooling could affect occupational status by teaching cognitive skills that employers value. But controlling adult test scores in the PSID and Veterans surveys reduced the apparent occupational value of education by 7 percent or less. This suggests that schooling does not enhance men's chances of entering a high-status occupation primarily by improving their general cognitive skills. Of course, schools may impart specific skills or knowledge which enable men to enter and remain in high-status occupations. For example, those who hire attorneys want applicants to know something about law, and such knowledge presumably depends to some extent on attending law school. Schools that teach such specific skills usually assume, however, that an applicant with high scores on general tests of the kind we used will learn more than applicants with low scores. It follows that men with high test scores should get greater occupational benefits from a year of schooling than men with low test scores. They do not. Furthermore, if grades measure how well one has acquired economically useful specific skills, the "cognitive" theory implies that high school grades should influence occupational status independent of years of schooling. Again, they do not. Moreover, a number of studies suggest that college and graduate school grades are minimally related to worker performance within specific occupations (Jencks et al., 1972, p. 187). Also, if schooling increases work-related cognitive skills, one would expect that within a given occupation, educational attainment would be positively related to measures of worker performance. Berg (1970) reports a number of studies which imply that this is not the case. Of course, less-educated men may have to have other compensating skills to get into a given occupation.

Building on evidence of this kind, Bowles and Gintis (1976) argue that spending time in school must impart attitudes, values, and behavior patterns that employers value. If this were true, controlling measures of adult attitudes and behavior should considerably reduce the apparent impact of educational attainment on occupation. So far as we know, no investigator has ever found a set of attitude measures that explained a significant fraction of the relationship between education and occupational status. But since attitudes are seldom a good proxy for behavior, negative evidence of this kind is not sufficient to refute Bowles and Gintis's argument. Our behavioral measures from high school also explain a negligible fraction of the association between education and status, but the measures are not well suited to testing Bowles and Gintis's theory, and they tell us nothing about the effects of subsequent education on attitudes or behavior.

Indirect evidence suggests that schooling may affect aspirations. Both Sewell and Hauser's Wisconsin sample and the Talent sample provide data on the status of occupations to which students aspired in high school and on their actual status seven or eleven years after high school. Those who finished college tend to be working in occupations of slightly higher status than the occupations to which they aspired in high school. Those who did not attend college tend to be working in occupations of appreciably lower status than the ones to which they aspired in high school. Leaving school could, of course, be a result of declining aspirations. But we cannot dismiss the possibility that education actually *affects* aspirations, increasing workers' aversion to low-status occupations and thereby increasing their willingness to do whatever an employer demands in order to get and keep a job in a high-status occupation.

Another possibility is that schooling simply serves as an arbitrary occupational rationing system. Berg argues, for instance, that educational attainment is virtually unrelated to job performance and that school attendance is valuable only because it leads to formal credentials. Yet, if schooling were valuable only because it led to formal credentials, attending high school, college, or graduate school would be of no economic value unless one finished. Census data suggest that the last year of high school has twice as much effect on occupational status as previous years have. The first and last years of college also have twice as much effect as other years of college or graduate school.[1] But the "extra" effects of the last year of school and the first and last years of college account for only a quarter of the overall difference in status between men with eight and eighteen years of education. Thus even if these "extra" effects were entirely due to credentialism rather than selectivity, such credentialism would only account for a quarter of the overall association between schooling and status. Of course, one could argue that an extra year of school constitutes a "credential" even if it does not result in a diploma, and that this credential provides access to high-status occupations even with background, test scores, and personality traits controlled. Our data are consistent with this view in the limited sense that they provide no solid alternative explanation for the effect of education on occupational status. But we have not measured behavior at work or aspirations after school completion, so we can hardly claim to have tested the importance of credentials rigorously.

College Quality. The PA ranked colleges according to selectivity. Differences in college quality had no impact on occupational status once schooling was controlled.

Association of Schooling with Earnings. Years of education correlated 0.38 to 0.49 with ln earnings in our four large national surveys of 25- to 64-year-olds. The variation is probably caused by sampling and measurement differences. The percentage increase in earnings associated with an extra year of schooling does not vary much by level of education, at least up through college graduation. In the 1970 Census, for example, the geometric mean of 25- to 64-year-old male college graduates' earnings was 1.43 times that for high school graduates. The geometric mean for high school graduates was, in turn, 1.38 times that for elementary school graduates (i.e., those with eight years of school).

Effects of Education on Earnings with Background, Test Scores, and Personality Controlled. Controlling demographic background reduces the 11 percent income advantage associated with an extra year of elementary or secondary schooling to 8 percent.[2] Data on brothers' educational attainments suggest that controlling all aspects of background reduces the returns still further. When we control not only the background characteristics shared by brothers but also sixth-grade test scores, the apparent payoff to a year of secondary schooling falls from 6.8 to 2.3 percent in Kalamazoo.

The apparent returns to higher education are more robust. Controlling demographic background lowers the apparent benefits of four years of college from 51 to 41 percent in our four large national samples. OCG data on brothers suggest a slightly larger reduction when one controls all aspects of background. Controlling both test scores and all aspects of family background reduces the estimated benefits of four years of college from 32 to 22 percent for Kalamazoo Brothers and from 27 to 18 percent for Talent Brothers. This suggests that if we had test-score and sibling data for a representative national sample, we would still find that at least two-thirds of the apparent effect of college persisted with everything controlled.

The first and last years of both high school and college raise earnings twice as much as the intervening years. The unusual potency of the last year of high school and college suggests that employers reward credentials per se. But the almost equal potency of the first year of high school or college raises questions about this interpretation. Employers may, of course, favor individuals who have attended high school or college, even if they have not completed it, and they may do this regardless of whether an individual stayed one, two, or three years. Those who decide to enter high school or college may also differ in important ways from those who do not enter, and employers may be paying premium wages for these traits. The Kalamazoo Survey provides some modest support for this view, since it shows that the apparent effects of college entrance disappear once one controls sixth-grade IQ scores. The effects of college graduation, in contrast, persist with all available controls. Nonetheless, our data do not suggest that the economic benefits of education depend *primarily* on certification effects. *Any* year of schooling raises earnings to some extent.

Controlling noncognitive measures obtained in tenth or eleventh grade does not appreciably alter the monetary benefits of subsequent education. If we calculate the benefits of education solely in terms of earnings, our data suggest that an extra year of elementary or secondary education raises earnings by only 4 or 5 percent, while an extra year of college raises earnings by 7 to 9 percent. The reader should bear in mind, however, that these estimates are for the 1960s and early 1970s. Returns to higher education may have fallen since, especially for younger men (Freeman, 1976).

Annual percentage returns to formal education did not vary in any consistent way between whites and nonwhites; men with white-collar, blue-collar, and farm fathers; men with high, medium, and low test scores; or men aged 25 to 34, 35 to 44, 45 to 54 and 55 to 64. This implies, of course, that absolute dollar benefits were higher for whites, for men with white-collar fathers, for men with high test scores, and for men over 35.*

Mechanisms by Which Education Affects Earnings. Many people assume that education influences men's earnings because it provides intellectual skills that employers value. Fagerlind's Swedish data support this hypothesis only to a limited extent. Our American data are less satisfactory. In our samples, controlling test scores after school completion does not lower the estimated benefits of education any more than controlling test scores before school completion. This suggests that the economic benefits of extra education do not derive from increases in test scores, but this inference might not hold up if we had better data.

If schools increase men's earnings by improving skills, and if school grades measure the acquisition of these skills, then men who perform well in school should also have a better chance of doing well economically. Even if grades do not measure the acquisition of economically useful skills, they might measure how hard an individual works or how

---

* We also tested for interactions between education and other variables by creating multiplicative interaction terms. No interaction involving education was significant with the same sign in more than one survey. This is not surprising, since samples other than the OCG and the Census are fairly small, and the different interaction terms are highly correlated with one another.

A more useful test of consistency across samples is to ask whether an interaction that was significant in one survey would be significant (or at least have the right sign) if it were the first interaction added to the additive equation in other surveys. We asked this question for each of the six interactions involving education or experience that was significant in at least one survey other than the Census. None of these interactions had the same sign in OCG, PA, NLS, PSID, and Census.

well he adapts to institutional norms. Yet high school grades have no significant effects on earnings once education is controlled in the Talent or Wisconsin samples. Good grades are associated with high earnings only because they are associated with staying in school rather than dropping out. Contrary to Bowles and Gintis's (1976) argument, they are not proxies for traits that employers find valuable independent of schooling.

Higher education increases earnings primarily by helping men enter high status occupations. In PSID, half the estimated benefits of four years of college derive from the fact that college graduates work in higher status occupations. In OCG, which uses a more detailed occupational classification, nearly three-quarters of the payoff from college graduation derive from this fact. Our other samples of mature men fall between these two extremes. The reason why elementary and secondary education raises earnings less than higher education, at least after we control background and initial ability, is that additional elementary or secondary education does not provide men with anything like as large an occupational advantage as additional higher education. Indeed, once we control detailed occupational category, returns to elementary and secondary schooling *exceed* returns to higher education in both the Census and OCG. The robust effects of higher education on earnings may, then, derive in large part from occupational licensing requirements or other exclusionary devices.

College Quality. PA respondents who attended any sort of selective college earned 28 percent more than those from similar background who had attended unselective colleges. The differences between graduates of selective, highly selective, and very highly selective colleges were not significant. Controlling years of graduate school did not alter this. Neither did controlling broad occupational categories or weeks worked. We cannot say to what extent the apparent effects of college selectivity are really effects of initial ability.

CONCLUSIONS

We initially asked "Who gets the most desirable jobs?" Our first answer was that background exerts a larger influence on economic outcomes than past research had suggested, accounting for something like 48 percent of the variance in occupational status and 15 to 35 percent of the variance in annual earnings. This is as strong an association as that between education and economic success. If our aim is to reduce the impact of being born to one set of parents rather than another, we still have a long way to go.

A man's test scores also influence his job prospects, and test scores are not simply proxies for family background. Two brothers whose test scores differ by one standard deviation can expect to have occupational statuses which differ by 0.3 to 0.4 standard deviations and earnings which differ by 17 percent. While high test scores increase both expected status and expected earnings, high scores were neither necessary nor sufficient to obtain these goals. If one makes the dubious assumption that test performance measures "ability," and if one defines "meritocracy" as a situation in which ability determines success, America is not very "meritocratic."

Unlike most past researchers, we found a moderately strong relationship between adolescents' noncognitive traits and their later economic success. Taken together, noncognitive measures explained at least as much of the variance in men's status and earnings as test scores did. While we could not isolate any single personality characteristic that was critical to success, we can say that the relevant traits are largely independent of both cognitive skills and parental status.

The best readily observable predictor of a young man's eventual status or earnings is the amount of schooling he has had. This could be because schooling is an arbitrary rationing device for allocating scarce jobs; or because schooling imparts skills, knowledge, or attitudes that employers value; or because schooling alters men's aspirations. Our data do not allow us to choose between these alternate explanations. We did find, however, that the first and last years of high school and college are usually worth more than intervening years. This fact, along with the substantial reduction in the apparent effect of schooling when we control causally prior traits, suggests that only part of the association between schooling and success can be due to what students actually learn from year to year in school.

CHAPTER 9

Individual Earnings and Family Income

This chapter will examine the relationship of individual earnings to a family's total income, using data from the PSID. It will try to answer three questions:

1. What is the relationship between male earnings (the factor examined in depth in previous chapters) and total family income?
2. What is the relationship of family members' demographic and social background, test scores, education, and attitudes to the family's income?
3. How do a man's earnings affect his wife's earnings and vice versa?

We will define families as having a principal male adult and/or a principal female adult plus their dependent children, and we will ignore other adults in the household. Where possible, we will also ignore the distinction between the "head" and the second adult family member. However, PSID sampled households, not individuals, and asked for detailed information only on the "household head," whom it defined as the principal male adult whenever a male adult was present. Among married couples, then, far more data are available on the principal male adult than on the principal female adult. We eliminated all families in which the "head" was under 25, over 64, a student, or in the military in 1971.* In contrast to previous analysis in this book, we retained earners with zero or negative income and households with no principal

Joseph Schwartz wrote this chapter.
* If the head changed between 1971 and 1972, we had no way of knowing whether the head had been a student or in the military in 1971, and so we eliminated those who were students or in the military in 1972.

male. These restrictions left 3,495 families, 3,160 of whom had complete data. Many of the analyses were further restricted to the 2,245 families with two principal adults and complete data. We call these "husband-wife" families. Some analyses were still further restricted to the 1,134 two-adult families with complete data in which both adults worked during 1971.

We define family income as the sum of five separate components:

1. *Male earnings:* the principal male's income from wages, salary, and self-employment. If no male was present, or if the male present did not work, this component is zero.
2. *Female earnings:* the principal female's income from wages, salary, and self-employment. If no female was present, or if the female present did not work, this component is zero.
3. *Asset income:* the combined income of all family members from interest, dividends, and rent.
4. *Welfare:* the family's income from Aid to Families with Dependent Children, Aid to Dependent Children, and payments by a welfare department for items such as clothing, furniture, or rent.
5. *Other transfers:* the family's income from Unemployment Insurance, Social Security, pensions, alimony, and money received from relatives or friends.

We will call the sum of the first three components the family's "taxable income," although this does not correspond exactly to the Internal Revenue Service's definition of taxable income. "Total transfer income" is the sum of welfare and other transfers.* We will ignore other sources of family income, such as earnings of other family members.

We divided all 1971 income figures by 1.213, converting them to 1967 dollars. (Standardization to constant dollars was necessary for certain longitudinal analyses, though in retrospect it would have been preferable to inflate earlier income figures to 1971 levels.) This transformation has no substantive effect on any conclusion.

1. COMPONENTS OF FAMILY INCOME

Table 9.1 gives the mean and standard deviation of family income and its components for all families in the sample. It shows that 73 percent of these families' income comes from male earnings, 18 percent from female

---

* Asset income is operationally defined as the difference between taxable income and the sum of male and female earnings. Similarly, other transfer income is the difference between total transfer income and welfare. In those cases in which SRC assigned values to male earnings, female earnings, taxable income, total transfer income, or total family income, we treated the data as missing.

earnings, 4 percent from assets, and 5 percent from transfers. Few if any families receive their income in exactly these proportions, however. Most families receive no transfer income, for example. Among those families that receive *any* transfer income, such income averages 24 percent of total family income.

Table 9.1 also shows the correlations between components of family income. Three points are notable:

1. There is a positive relationship ($r = 0.21$) between male earnings and asset income. This finding at least partially contradicts the naive view that American society is divided into workers who derive most of their income from earnings and capitalists who rely on asset income and do not work. It suggests that even in families with substantial asset income men not only work but are paid (or pay themselves) a relatively high salary.
2. There is a negative relationship ($r = -0.14$) between male earnings and female earnings. This may seem somewhat surprising. The correlation is positive among husband-wife families where both adults worked ($r = 0.12$; see table 9.2). But if male earnings are high, the female is slightly less likely to work. Thus if one considers all two-adult families, the correlation between male and female earnings falls to -0.02 (see table A9.1). If one also considers one-adult families, as table 9.1 does, the correlation falls even further. This is because most one-adult families are headed by a female. These females are more likely to work and have higher earnings than the average female, but their households have no male earnings whatever. Including such households, therefore, makes the covariance between male and female earnings negative. It is important to remember that the apparent correlation between spouses' earnings depends on the treatment of one-adult families and of nonworking adults.
3. Both types of transfer income are negatively related to both sources of earnings. This relationship is strongest between total transfer income and male earnings ($r = -0.33$), suggesting that transfer income partially compensates for low earnings.

Other things being equal, a one-dollar increase in any component of income always leads to a one-dollar increase in total income. Thus, if we regress family income on all its components simultaneously, the regression coefficient of each component is necessarily 1.000. But other things are rarely equal, so the bivariate regression coefficients are seldom 1.000. An advantage in earnings, for example, is usually associated with a disadvantage in transfers. The net increase in family income associated with a one-dollar increase in earnings is thus less than a dollar. The bivariate regression coefficient of family income (Y) on one of its components (C) is the covariance of Y and C divided by the variance of C. The lower part of table 9.1 gives the relevant variances and covariances and the regression coefficients. An increase of $1.00 in asset income is associated with an increase of $2.15 in total family income.

TABLE 9.1

Components of 1971 Family Income for PSID Households[a]

A. Means, Standard Deviations, and Correlations

	Male Earnings	Female Earnings	Asset Income	Welfare	Other Transfers	Total Taxable Income	Total Transfers	Total Family Income
Male earnings	1.000							
Female earnings	-.141	1.000						
Asset income	.211	.023	1.000					
Welfare	-.198	-.110	-.045	1.000				
Other transfers	-.264	-.061	.050	-.009	1.000			
Taxable income	.921	.227	.346	-.232	-.260	1.000		
Total transfers	-.326	-.104	.025	.436	.896	-.337	1.000	
Total family income	.908	.220	.365	-.170	-.124	.988	-.187	1.000
Mean[b]	7,074	1,807	362	106	411	9,233	516	9,749
SD[b]	6,892	2,606	1,195	516	1,046	7,353	1,162	7,047
Percent of total income	72.6	18.5	3.7	1.1	4.2	94.7	5.3	100.0

B. Variances, Covariances, and Unstandardized Bivariate Regression Coefficients (B) When Predicting Family Income from Its Components[b,c]

	Male Earnings	Female Earnings	Asset Income	Welfare	Other Transfers	Total Taxable Income	Total Transfers	Total Family Income
Male earnings	47.49							
Female earnings	-2.53	6.79						
Asset income	1.74	.07	1.43					
Welfare	-.71	-.15	-.03	.27				
Other transfers	-1.90	-.17	.06	-.00	1.09			
Taxable income	46.68	4.36	3.04	-.88	-2.00	54.07		
Total transfers	-2.61	-.31	.03	.26	1.09	-2.88	1.35	
Total family income	44.07	4.04	3.07	3.07	-.91	51.19	-1.53	49.66
B	.928	.595	2.151	-2.324	-.834	.947	-1.134	1.000

[a] All households with a nonstudent, nonmilitary head aged 25 to 64 in 1971 and with complete data on basic variables in table A9.2 (N = 3,160).
[b] All values in 1967 dollars.
[c] All figures divided by 1,000,000. Numbers in the diagonal are variances. The variance of male earnings is thus ($6,892)^2 = 47.49 millions. Numbers off the diagonal are covariances, where $Cov(X,Y) = s_X s_Y r_{XY}$.

An increase of $1.00 in transfer income, in contrast, is associated with a *decrease* of $1.13 in total family income, implying a decrease of $2.13 in taxable income.

Table 9.1 includes families with male and female heads and with zero, one, or two employed adults. Restricting the sample to husband-wife families does not alter the variance–covariance matrix in any important way, except to make the correlation between male and female earnings virtually zero.[*]

One can decompose the variance of family income into the variances of income from each separate source and the covariances between incomes from different sources. Suppose, for example, that we separate family income (Y) into taxable income (I) and transfer income (T). Then:

$$\text{Var}(Y) = \text{Var}(I) + \text{Var}(T) + 2\text{Cov}(I,T)$$

or

$$s_Y{}^2 = s_I{}^2 + s_T{}^2 + 2s_I s_T r_{IT}$$

Part B of table 9.1 shows that the variance of taxable income is 54.1 million, the variance of transfer income is 1.4 million, and the covariance is –2.9 million. The total variance of family income is thus 54.1 + 1.4 + (2)(–2.9) = 49.7. This implies that transfers make the variance of family income 49.7 million instead of 54.1 million. The standard deviation of family income is thus $49.7^{1/2}$ instead of $54.1^{1/2}$: a 4.4 percent reduction. Since transfers must be paid for out of taxable income, they do not really change the mean. They therefore lower the coefficient of variation— the ratio of the standard deviation to the mean—a common, if flawed, measure of inequality—by 4.4 percent.

We can also use the decomposition of variance to explore the relationships among components of taxable income. Given that male earnings are the largest source of income, we can determine how female earnings and asset income affect inequality. The variance of female plus male earnings is 47.5 + 6.8 + 2(–2.5) = 49.3. The standard deviation of male plus female earnings is thus 1.8 percent greater than the standard deviation of male earnings. The mean of the sum is 25.5 percent greater, making the coefficient of variation 100 – (101.8/125.5) = 18.9 percent

[*] The matrix for husband-wife families appears in table A9.1 of the Appendix. Further restricting the sample to husband-wife families where both adults worked makes the correlations among the components of taxable income positive. For this reason, each of these components has a bivariate regression coefficient greater than 1.000 when predicting family income. The analysis in the text could therefore yield different results if applied to these restricted samples.

smaller. Analogous calculations show that the coefficient of variation of male earnings plus asset income is 0.1 percent less than that of male earnings alone. These results suggest that female earnings reduce overall inequality substantially, relative to what it would be if male earnings were the only source of family income. Asset income has a negligible effect on inequality. The net result is that family income is more equally distributed than any of its major components, including male earnings. The evidence for this conclusion is even stronger if one uses a measure of inequality like the standard deviation of ln income, which is more sensitive than the coefficient of variation to changes in the lower range of the income scale.

Since most income attainment models examine male earnings rather than family income, the relationship between the two is of considerable interest. Almost 90 percent of the men in our target population live in husband-wife families. Table A9.1 in the Appendix shows that male earnings are not only the largest component of family income in such families but also the largest source of variance. Furthermore, while husbands with above average earnings tend to have above average asset income, their wives earn no more than average, and they receive less from transfers. Thus it happens that a personal characteristic that raises male earnings by $1.00 can be expected to raise family income by about the same amount; $B = \$0.99$ for male earnings in table A9.1. This suggests that the effects of exogenous variables on family income are probably quite similar to their effects on male earnings. However, since family income for husband-wife families is greater than their male earnings, each extra dollar increases male earnings by a greater percentage than it increases family income. An equation predicting ln male earnings should therefore have larger coefficients than an equation predicting ln family income.

2. ASSOCIATION OF FAMILY CHARACTERISTICS
WITH FAMILY INCOME

Earlier chapters explore the relationship between men's characteristics when they enter the labor force and their later earnings. This section of this chapter examines the bivariate relationship between men's characteristics and *all* components of their family income, as well as the relationship of other family characteristics to family income. In an equation predicting family income, the unstandardized regression coefficient of a single trait (such as husband's education) is the sum of the coefficients obtained from regressing each of the five components of family income on this same trait. This means that the bivariate relationship between husband's education and family income can be decomposed into five other bivariate relationships. We can then see whether the relationship is entirely due to the effect of a husband's education on his own earnings, or whether his education is also related to other components of his family's income, such as his wife's earnings. Since we are interested here in the effects of each spouse's characteristics on family income, the analysis is confined to the 2,245 husband-wife families.[1] For this sample of families, the questions the PSID asked of the "household head" always refer to a male.

The male characteristics examined in earlier chapters—demographic background, test scores, personality traits, and schooling—are never strongly related to sources of family income other than male earnings. Having had economically advantaged parents, for example, adds thirteen times as much to a man's earnings as to his family's asset income. The same holds for being white. A married man with an extra year of school has, on average, $882 more earnings, $39 more asset income, $13 less welfare, and a wife who earns $95 more. In general, then, a man's traits have minimal effects on sources of family income other than the man's own earnings.

Children have an insignificant effect on the husband's earnings but are related to other components of income: the greater the number of children and the younger they are, the lower the wife's earnings, presumably because she is less likely to work. There is also a negative relationship between the number of children and asset income. Finally, those families with more children receive more welfare and less other transfer income. The last relationship reflects the fact that despite our having excluded family "heads" over 64, a large fraction of other transfer income is social security and private pensions.

If a male is self-employed, his earnings and the family's asset income are above average, but his wife's earnings are below average. Not surprisingly, those husbands who are handicapped or have other physical limitations earn considerably less and receive more other transfer income. However, the increase in transfer income covers only about 20 percent of the loss in earnings.

Each extra year of wife's education is associated with an increase of $894 in husband's earnings, compared to an increase of only $233 in wife's earnings. This suggests that a woman's education affects her expected family income less by increasing her earnings than by increasing the probability that she will marry a man with high earnings. This latter effect is largely attributable to prospective spouses' tendency to marry someone of similar education ($r = 0.60$). As we shall see, however, highly educated women may also contribute directly to their husband's earnings.

3. SPOUSES' EFFECTS ON ONE ANOTHER

Since the second most important component of family income (after husband's earnings) is wife's earnings, it is natural to ask how a husband's economic behavior affects his wife's behavior, and vice versa. Part A of table 9.2 shows the correlations among spouses' hours and

TABLE 9.2

Correlations among PSID Husbands' and Wives' 1971 Wages, Hours, and Earnings

A. All Husband-Wife Families (N = 2,245)[a]

	Husband's Hours	Husband's Earnings	Wife's Hours	Wife's Earnings
Husband's hours	1.000			
Husband's earnings	.322	1.000		
Wife's hours	−.027	−.128	1.000	
Wife's earnings	−.016	−.020	.830	1.000
Mean	2,131	9,224	656	1,599
SD	773	6,667	837	2,357

B. Husband-Wife Families in Which Both Work (N = 1,134)

	Husband's Hours	Husband's Wages	Husband's Earnings	Wife's Hours	Wife's Wages	Wife's Earnings
Husband's hours	1.000					
Husband's wages	−.204	1.000				
Husband's earnings	.216	.581	1.000			
Wife's hours	.016	−.067	−.118	1.000		
Wife's wages	−.048	.175	.273	−.036	1.000	
Wife's earnings	−.023	.080	.118	.689	.488	1.000
Mean	2,174	4.253	8,777	1,255	2.504	3,093
SD	619	3.724	4,904	751	1.815	2,493

[a]All husband-wife households with a nonstudent, nonmilitary husband aged 25 to 64 in 1971 and with complete data on the basic variables listed in Table A9.2. Because this sample includes husbands and wives who did not work, some respondents' wages are unknown, and wages are omitted from the matrix.

earnings. These correlations can be interpreted as fitting into a model in which hours are the individual's input and earnings are the output, with wages defining the relationship between the two. Since individuals have very little short-term control over their wages, they can usually vary their earnings only by varying the hours they work (including the possibility of not working). Examination of the interspouse correlations in table 9.2 shows that husband's hours worked are unrelated to wife's hours worked or earnings. The most significant correlation (−0.128) is between wife's hours worked and husband's earnings, which suggests that the husband's output (earnings) causally influences the wife's input (hours). This result is consistent with the image of the traditional American family in which the husband is employed full time (subject to the constraints of the labor market), while the wife may or may not be employed but is more likely to seek employment when the family's income from other sources is low. When we examine the same relationship for families with two working adults (part B of table 9.2) we observe a moderate positive correlation between spouses' wages. This is presumably due to the similarity between spouses with respect to social background and human capital. Within this subsample, wife's earnings are also positively correlated with husband's earnings.

4. A CLOSER LOOK AT WAGES AND HOURS

In order to analyze these relationships in more detail, multivariate analysis is helpful. We will look at a model with eight exogenous variables, which we can separate into three groups:

1. *Own characteristics:* age, age^2, and education.
2. *Spouse's characteristics:* same as above.
3. *Other family characteristics:* number of children and age of youngest child.

A major advantage of such a simple model is that it can be made symmetric, since the PSID has age and education data for both spouses. Since the PSID does not contain other background data on wives, it is difficult to examine a more complicated symmetric model.

In order to study the interplay between wages and hours worked, we restricted the sample to those who worked. (A person's wage is not defined if he or she did not work.) [2] Because the product of hours worked and wages equals earnings, it is conventional to treat the logs of these variables as the endogenous variables in an additive model.*

Table 9.3 shows regressions predicting ln hourly wages of the husband and wife. Table 9.4 shows regressions predicting ln hours worked. In both tables, the first equation regresses the dependent variable on an individual's own personal characteristics. We see that the effect of age on wages (table 9.3) is similar for both husbands and wives; wages increase with age, but at a decreasing rate. Controlling for age, an extra year of education increases a husband's wage by about 7.5 percent. If the wife has an extra year of education, her wage typically increases by about 10 percent, assuming she works at all.† However, it must be recognized that a 10 percent increase in the average wife's wage is less in absolute terms than a 7.5 percent increase in the average husband's wage.

The second equation regresses each spouse's wage on all eight exogenous variables—personal characteristics, spouse's characteristics, and other family characteristics. Not surprisingly, the coefficients of number of children and age of youngest child are insignificant in predicting both husbands' and wives' wages; we expect these variables to affect a wife's decision on how much to work (if at all), but not to affect how much she is paid if she works. The coefficients of husband's age and age² are also insignificant in predicting wife's wages. Husband's education is significant in the wife's wage equation, but this is because it picks up some of the nonlinear effect of wife's education. (When we added wife's education² to the equation, the coefficient of husband's education approached zero.) More surprisingly, the coefficients for each of the wife's characteristics are significant in the husband's wage equation. A husband's wage proves to be even more strongly related to his wife's age than to his own age. A wife's education also seems to have a direct "effect" on her husband's wages. Among men at a given educational level, well-paid men are more likely than poorly paid men to be married to well-educated women. Since it is hard to believe that many employers are directly interested in a spouse's traits, these results suggest that among men at any given educational level, those with high "potential earnings" are more likely to

---

* The multiplicative relationship between wages and hours is not perfect for females in the following analyses because six women had positive hours worked but had no earnings. These women were inadvertently assigned a value of 0 for ln wages. While the discussion is restricted to regression equations predicting ln wages, ln hours, and ln earnings, we examined analogous regressions for the untransformed variables and found that they support the conclusions of this section.

† Equations not shown here indicate that this relationship is essentially linear for husbands but not for wives. Wife's wages increase at rates ranging from 4.2 percent per year of primary school to over 15 percent for each year of college. This nonlinearity may reflect a significant correlation between wives' education and their commitment to the labor force.

TABLE 9.3

Regressions of Husbands' and Wives' Ln Wages on Characteristics of PSID Households in Which Both Spouses Worked[a]

		Male Ln Wages[b]			Female Ln Wages[c]		
		(M1)	(M2)	(M3)	(F1)	(F2)	(F3)
Own education	B	.07485	.6393	.06009	.10032	.07720	.07346
	(SE)	(.00482)	(.C0582)	(.00580)	(.00680)	(.00823)	(.00817)
Own age	B	.06767	[.C0189]	[.C0712]	.03834	.07236	.06007
	(SE)	(.01130)	(.C1923)	(.C1904)	(.01200)	(.02021)	(.02012)
Own age^2	B	-.00072	[-.C0006]	[-.00011]	-.00039	-.00081	-.00068
	(SE)	(.00013)	(.C0021)	(.C0021)	(.00015)	(.00025)	(.00024)
Number of children	B		[.C0976]	[.01138]		[-.01210]	[-.01380]
	(SE)		(.C1441)	(.01425)		(.01645)	(.01626)
Age of youngest child	B		[.C0274]	[.00183]		[.00678]	[.00630]
	(SE)		(.C0409)	(.00405)		(.00467)	(.00462)
Spouse's education	B		.02146	[.01111]		.02862	.01745
	(SE)		(.00721)	(.00741)		(.00664)	(.00691)
Spouse's age	B		.07037	.06067		[-.03903]	[-.03936]
	(SE)		(.01770)	(.01760)		(.02195)	(.02170)
Spouse's age^2	B		-.00077	-.00066		[.00042]	[.00043]
	(SE)		(.00021)	(.00021)		(.00024)	(.00024)
Spouse's ln wages	B			.13413			.17472
	(SE)			(.02583)			(.03364)
Constant		-1.09329	-1.23625	-1.07000	-1.33867	-1.23944	-1.02344
R^2		.19092	.21086	.22936	.16901	.19155	.21050
SD of Residuals		.51447	.50922	.50344	.58793	.58119	.57460

Coefficients in brackets are less than twice their standard error.

[a] All husband-wife households with a nonstudent, nonmilitary husband aged 25 to 64 in 1971 and complete data on basic variables in table A9.2, in which both spouses worked (N = 1,134).

[b] Mean = 1.286; SD = .571.

[c] Mean = .729; SD = .644.

marry well-educated women.* This result probably tells us more about the marriage market than the labor market.[3]

Equations M3 and F3 in table 9.3 add spouse's wages to equations M2 and F2. The coefficient of spouse's wage is highly significant in both cases. Since the dependent variable in each equation is an independent variable in the other, and since the other independent variables are the same, we can also express the relationship between spouses' wages with other characteristics controlled in terms of a partial correlation. In this case the value is 0.153. This correlation could arise in three ways. First, and least likely, one spouse's wage could have a direct effect on the other spouse's wage. Second, and considerably more likely, wives with highly paid husbands could decide to work only if they found a job that paid somewhat more than the norm for women of their age and educational attainment, whereas wives with poorly paid husbands might feel more obliged to take jobs that paid less than the norm for their age and education. Then even if there were no partial correlation between husbands' and wives' potential wages in the population as a whole, the partial correlation between spouses who both decided to work would be positive. Third, husbands' and wives' wages are undoubtedly subject to common influences that are not captured in our equations. We know, for example, that even after controlling age and education, wages of both males and females vary somewhat from place to place. The fact that husbands and wives seek jobs in the same labor market will therefore create a modest partial correlation between their wages. Likewise, we know that race affects wages, so the fact that husbands and wives are usually of the same race will add to the partial correlation between their wages. Controlling the available community characteristics plus race lowers the partial correlation between spouses' wages to 0.115. If we could also control all the other characteristics on which spouses resemble each other, such as cognitive skills and personality traits, we might be able to reduce the partial correlations still further.†

Table 9.4 shows equations predicting ln hours worked for couples who both worked in 1971. Own education has a small positive effect on annual hours for both husbands and wives. Age has a significant curvilinear effect on husbands' hours. (One percent of the husbands in this

---

* In equations predicting husband's dollar wages, the effects of wife's characteristics are much smaller. This suggests that the relationship between wife's education and husband's wages is stronger at the lower end of the male wage distribution.

† PSID only collected test score and attitude data for the "head" of the household, so we cannot estimate the effect of these attributes on wives' wages. Nor can we estimate the degree of resemblance between husbands and wives on these traits. Given their modest effects on husbands' wages, we doubt that controlling such traits would suffice to explain the entire partial correlation between husbands' and wives' wages.

TABLE 9.4

Regressions of Husbands' and Wives' Ln Hours on Characteristics of PSID Households in Which Both Spouses Worked[a]

		Male Ln Hours[b]				Female Ln Hours[c]			
		(M1)	(M2)	(M3)	(M4)	(F1)	(F2)	(F3)	(F4)
Own education	B	.00876	[.00463]	.01278	.01427	[.00774]	.03047	.02164]	[.01897]
	(SE)	(.00402)	(.00488)	(.00508)	(.00509)	(.01222)	(.01458)	(.01512)	(.01508)
Own age	B	.04241	.04489	.04513	.04743	[.03855]	.10469	.09641	.09415
	(SE)	(.00942)	(.01615)	(.01597)	(.01593)	(.02157)	(.03579)	(.03593)	(.03580)
Own age²	B	−.00057	−.00059	−.00060	−.00063	[−.00032]	−.00142	−.00132	−.00130
	(SE)	(.00011)	(.00018)	(.00018)	(.00018)	(.00027)	(.00043)	(.00044)	(.00043)
Number of children	B		[−.01966]	[−.01841]	[−.01544]		−.08224	−.08086	−.07634
	(SE)		(.01210)	(.01197)	(.01197)		(.02913)	(.02909)	(.02901)
Age of youngest child	B		−.00983	−.00948	−.01037		.02432	.02355	.02572
	(SE)		(.00343)	(.00340)	(.00340)		(.00827)	(.00826)	(.00826)
Spouse's education	B		[.00965]	.01238	[.01124]		−.04426	−.04754	−.04877
	(SE)		(.00606)	(.00601)	(.00600)		(.01176)	(.01184)	(.01179)
Spouse's age	B		[.00794]	[.01691]	[.01298]		[−.06334]	[−.05888]	[−.06876]
	(SE)		(.01487)	(.01480)	(.01481)		(.03887)	(.03886)	(.03884)
Spouse's age²	B		[−.00007]	[−.00016]	[.00011]		[.00083]	[.00078]	.00091
	(SE)		(.00018)	(.00018)	(.00018)		(.00043)	(.00043)	(.00043)
Own ln wages	B			−.12749	−.12569			.11435	.12081
	(SE)			(.02476)	(.02468)			(.05272)	(.05255)
Spouse's ln hours	B				.03633				.22573
	(SE)				(.01221)				(.07143)
Constant		6.80255	6.61474	6.45714	6.23631	5.71685	6.13935	6.28108	4.79592
R²		.05369	.06318	.08478	.09194	.01851	.07294	.07680	.08494
SD of residuals		.42879	.42758	.42281	.42134	1.05679	1.02935	1.02766	1.02358

Coefficients in brackets are less than twice their standard error.

[a]Sample identical to table 9.3 (N = 1,134).
[b]Mean = 7.625; SD = 0.440.
[c]Mean = 6.785; SD = 1.065.

sample reported that they were in semiretirement, and a number of others had probably reduced their hours as they neared retirement, either for health or for other reasons.) Age has a similar curvilinear effect on wives' hours, but because wives' hours are more variable than husbands', the coefficients of age and age^2 have larger standard errors and are not statistically significant for wives.

When we add variables describing other family members in equation 2, the only additional variable related to husband's hours is the age of the youngest child; men in families with young children work more hours. One might argue that husbands compensate for wives' tendency to work less when there are young children. However, instead of reducing the magnitude of the coefficient for age of the youngest child, as this hypothesis predicts, the inclusion of wife's hours in equation M4 (in table 9.4) raises it. Perhaps men with young children feel a greater need for earnings for their families, possibly in order to save for the purchase of a house. Accordingly, they would probably work longer hours or take a second job, since hours are more subject to individual control than wages.

The second equation for wives' hours is more interesting. As expected, children, especially young children, have a negative effect on wives' hours. In addition, wives' hours exhibit a stronger curvilinear relationship with age than husbands' hours. Finally, the coefficients of wives' and husbands' education have opposite signs; equations 2, 3, and 4 for wife's hours all indicate that the more education her husband has, the fewer hours she works. This could be because highly educated men earn more, but when we add husband's earnings to the equation, its coefficient is insignificant, while husband's education retains its effect. In a sample that included all households, this finding would suggest that men with more education had prejudices against their wives' working, or that women who did not want to go to work tended to marry highly educated men. However, neither of these explanations is very plausible in an analysis restricted to women who did work. We have no explanation for this observed relationship.

Equation 3 in table 9.4 adds own wages to the equation predicting own hours. Equation 4 then adds spouse's hours to the equation predicting own hours. (Spouse's wages were not significantly related to own hours after controlling own wages.) The coefficients of the eight exogenous variables in equations 3 and 4 are very similar to those in equation 2, except that own education becomes somewhat more important for men's hours and less important for wives' hours after controlling own wages. Surprisingly, there is a *positive* relationship between spouse's and own hours for both husbands and wives, even after controlling own wages and the eight exogenous variables. This directly contradicts conventional wisdom, which would predict a pattern of substitution between spouses' hours. Perhaps women whose husbands work long hours prefer to work longer hours rather than spend time alone at home. The reader should remember, however, that this sample is restricted to spouses who both worked some hours. As we shall see, the relationship disappears when we include spouses who did not work at all in the sample.

Perhaps the most interesting result in table 9.4 is that a husband's wages are negatively related to his hours, while a wife's wages are positively related to her hours; men with higher wages work shorter hours than other men, while women with higher wages work longer hours. Classical utility theory can explain both results as a function of the difference in average wage rates for men and women ($4.25 vs. $2.50 per hour). For any given individual, there exist a series of alternative combinations of income and leisure that all seem equally desirable. These combinations define an "indifference curve" that represents a specific level of well-being ("utility"). Figure 9.1 shows several such curves. Every point on a particular indifference curve represents a combination of income and leisure that is just as desirable as the other combinations represented by other points on the curve. The curves are numbered in ascending order of desirability; all points on curve 2 are more desirable than those on curve 1, and so on. For any particular individual, though, the possible trade-off between income and leisure is likely to be a straight line, not a curve. The slope of this line depends on the individual's hourly wage rate, since for each hour less of work, income decreases by an amount equal to one's hourly wage. These lines are called wage constraints because they represent the possible combinations of leisure and income that are available to an individual with a given wage. All wage-constraint lines must intersect at the leisure axis, because those who use all their time for leisure have zero earnings. Figure 9.1 shows two "low-wage" lines, labeled A and B, and two "high-wage" lines, C and D. Utility theory predicts that each individual will choose that combination of leisure and income where his or her wage-constraint line intersects the highest utility curve. These points are indicated in figure 9.1 as a_1, b_2, c_3, and d_4. The arrows between them show how income and hours of leisure would change if an individual moved from wage A to wage B or from wage C to wage D. The arrow from a_1 to b_2 has a negative slope, indicating that those with low wages (in this case, women) will respond to an increase in wages by working more (consuming less leisure). For them, leisure is an "inferior good" because they choose less of it when their wage constraint increases. Men work more hours and

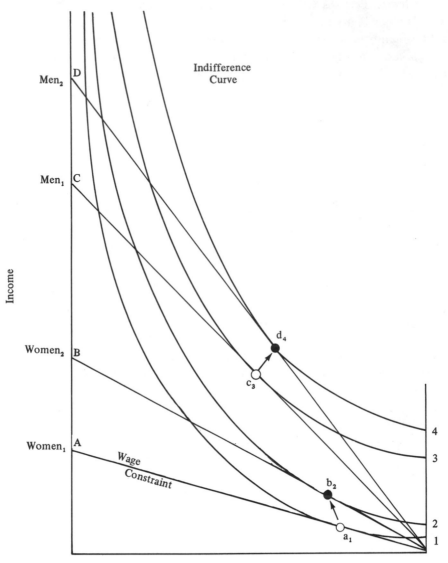

FIGURE 9.1

Hypothetical Relationship of Utility to Wages, Income, and Leisure for Men and Women

Indifference
Curve

Men₂ D

Men₁ C

Income

Women₂ B

d₄

c₃

Women₁ A

Wage
Constraint

b₂

a₁

4

3

2

1

Hours of Leisure

receive higher wages than women. For them, an increase in wages is associated with both an increase in income and a decrease in hours worked (increase in leisure). This is the typical pattern of substitution among "superior" commodities discussed in the economic literature.[*]

An alternative explanation of the positive relationship between women's hours and wages is that many women have part-time jobs, and these tend to pay less per hour. This reasoning does not apply to men because most of them have full-time jobs. The negative relationship between men's hours and wages could be due to a tendency for better-paying jobs to be associated with shorter work weeks. Also, men who work overtime or have a second job are likely to do so because they are paid low wages and need the money. If this view that part-time workers and second-job holders receive lower wages than other full-time workers were true, one would expect to observe a curvilinear relationship between hours worked and wages received. However, there is no such relationship between female hours and wages in the PSID data. Male wages and hours exhibit a significant negative relationship, with no significant deviation from linearity.

Some personal characteristics not entered in table 9.4 also deserve attention. First, race has opposite effects on husband's and wife's hours. An obvious explanation is that black men face a much higher unemployment rate than whites, thus decreasing their hours. Because of this and also because of the fact that employed black men earn lower wages, there is more pressure on black wives to work. Controlling husband's hours and wages does not, however, appreciably reduce the effect of race on wife's hours. Black women are thus working more hours than white women even when their husbands are equally well off. Perhaps black women are more reluctant than white women to quit work because black women more often suspect that they will have to support themselves and their children without help from their husbands in the future. Self-employed husbands also work more hours and earn less per hour than wage recipients. As a result, their total earnings do not differ significantly from those of salaried men of similar age and education.

The results from tables 9.3 and 9.4 can be summarized as follows:

1. Own age has a curvilinear effect on both wages and hours. Both curves peak in middle age.
2. A wife's age is, perversely, a better predictor of her husband's wage than is his own age.

[*] See Becker (1965). The indifference curves in figure 9.1 are hypothetical. They have been drawn to demonstrate the *logical possibility* of men and women reacting differently to an increase in wages. One can, of course, also draw curves that imply similar reactions for men and women.

3. Education affects earnings predominantly through its influence on wages, not hours.
4. The age of the youngest child and the number of children have major effects on a wife's hours and slight effects on a husband's hours, but they are unrelated to either husband's or wife's wages.
5. Spouses' wages are positively related, as are their hours worked.

The above analysis of husbands' and wives' wages and hours is based on families with two working adults. Such families represent only about half of all husband-wife families and slightly more than a third of all families. We therefore estimated comparable regressions (not presented here) predicting ln hours and ln earnings for all two-adult families. In this sample, 51 percent of the wives and 96 percent of the husbands worked during at least part of 1971. The variance of ln hours and ln earnings in this expanded sample is largely associated with the dichotomy between those who work and those who do not.[*]

The regressions predicting ln hours for this larger sample are quite similar to those in table 9.4. One exception is that the number of children has a significant negative effect on a husband's as well as a wife's hours in this sample. Another and more interesting exception from an economic perspective is the absence of any correlation between spouses' hours after controlling their age, education, and number of children. In particular, these additional regressions exhibit neither the positive association between spouses' hours found in the sample of families with two working adults nor the pattern of substitution predicted by conventional economics. This result suggests that when husbands work long hours their wives tend either not to work at all or else to work long hours.

The regressions predicting ln earnings in the sample of all spouses conform more closely to traditional economic theory. After controlling the eight exogenous variables and one's own hours, spouse's hours have a significant negative coefficient, while spouse's earnings have a positive coefficient. This holds for both husbands and wives. Presumably each spouse reduces his or her hours when the other spouse brings in additional income. In economic theory this is called the "substitution" effect. The positive relationship between spouses' earnings after controlling hours worked reflects the positive association between working spouses' wages discussed already.

---

[*] We did not try to predict wages, since it is not possible to determine what wage a nonworker would command if he or she worked. There is also a problem in predicting ln hours for those who do not work, since the log of 0 is undefined. We therefore treated those who did not work as if they had worked one hour. This greatly increased the estimated variance of ln hours and ln earnings for both husbands and wives.

The longitudinal character of the PSID also permitted us to investigate the effects of *changes* in spouses' wages and hours. Much of the year-to-year variation in hours is associated with national and local fluctuations in economic conditions that are beyond the scope of this chapter. Nonetheless, if we think of the family as a production unit wishing to attain a specific level of income, we would expect that when income from one source declines, family members would try to increase their income from other sources by adjusting their hours. To test this hypothesis, we regressed the change in own earnings on the change in spouse's earnings, controlling own and spouse's earnings last year. Examining such regressions for five different years and for several transformations of earnings revealed no relationship approaching significance. Since there is not even a consistent sign pattern, the predicted negative relationship between changes in earnings receives no support from the PSID data. To allow for possible delays in the predicted effect, we also tested this hypothesis using two-year rather than one-year intervals. Again, there was no significant relationship. This raises serious questions about standard economic interpretations of the cross-sectional relationships between husbands' and wives' hours and earnings.*

CONCLUSION

Male earnings and female earnings are the two largest components of family income, comprising more than 90 percent of total income for families with heads aged 25 to 64. The relationship between these two components is positive if the sample is restricted to families with two working adults. It is zero if one looks at all husband-wife families. Spouses' hours are uncorrelated, although a small positive correlation emerges with other traits controlled. Longitudinal data on stable families show that changes in the earnings of one spouse are unrelated to changes in the earnings of the other. Taken together, these data suggest very weak effects of each spouse's economic success on the other. The one causal

---

* It could be that an annual accounting period is too long and that the hypothesized effects operate over a shorter period. It could also be that by looking for relationships between spouses' earnings we unnecessarily inflated the standard errors of our estimates. We are currently investigating whether a stronger relationship emerges when we correlate changes in one spouse's earnings with later changes in the other spouse's hours.

relationship of substantive significance seems to be the negative effect of a husband's earnings on his wife's hours.* Taken together, this evidence suggests that it is fairly safe to ignore a wife's wages and hours when analyzing the determinants of economic success among men. It is not safe, however, to ignore a husband's economic situation when analyzing the determinants of economic success among women.

---

* This statement assumes that the substantial positive relationship between working husbands' and wives' wages is attributable to causally prior factors, including social background and education as well as unmeasured factors. If this is so, it might prove useful to treat spouse's wage as a proxy for unmeasured variables when predicting either husband's or wife's wage.

CHAPTER 10

Do Different Surveys Yield Similar Results?

Chapter 1 described our overall target population: nonstudent, nonmilitary, noninstitutional males aged 25 to 64 with positive earnings. Our OCG, PA, Census, PSID, and NORC Brothers samples purport to represent this target population, except that the PA and PSID samples exclude men who lived in a household with a male head other than themselves. Nonetheless, there are differences in the way different survey organizations drew these samples, in the survey instruments, in the definitions of certain concepts, and in the way variables are recorded on data tapes sold to the public. We can eliminate many of these differences, but in order to do this we must reduce the data to relatively crude form, wasting much of their potential value. To extract maximum information from each survey, we based our substantive analyses on samples and coding procedures we knew to be somewhat dissimilar.

The purpose of this chapter is to see whether supposedly similar surveys yield similar results when we eliminate known differences. This involves making both the target populations and the variable definitions and coding as similar as possible. Of course, even when this is done, we cannot escape the fact that each of our surveys covers a different year. Nonetheless, if the differences between samples are small, it seems safe to assume that the surveys represent a common population.

Gregory Jackson wrote this chapter.

251

If the differences are large, we must be cautious when combining results from different surveys.

In theory, we have five national surveys conducted by three survey organizations (the Census Bureau, the Survey Research Center at Michigan, and NORC) that cover men aged 25 to 64. But the NORC Brothers sample is so small that even large differences between it and national norms can be due to sampling error. We will therefore ignore it, focusing on the two Census Bureau surveys (OCG and the 1970 Census) and the two SRC surveys (PA and PSID).

PA and PSID surveyed only heads of households, and our OCG tape provided data only on income, not earnings. To maximize comparability between the four samples we therefore restricted them all to household heads with nonzero incomes in the year prior to the survey. Unlike the samples discussed in previous chapters, the samples discussed in this chapter do not try to exclude students or military personnel living off bases.

We next restricted all four samples to respondents with complete data on all the variables discussed in this chapter.* Unfortunately, this restriction has somewhat different effects in different samples, because certain surveys allocated values to men who failed to report certain items, and we were not always able to eliminate these men. OCG respondents who failed to report education or income were allocated values using standard CPS procedures. There were no flags on our OCG tape for identifying allocated values, so OCG respondents who had complete data on other items but failed to report education or income remain in the sample. Census respondents who failed to report an item also received allocated values. The flag identifying allocated income values was defective on the tape used for the analyses in this chapter, so men who failed to report one or more components of their income remain in the Census sample. When men failed to report their education, but said they were illiterate, SRC allocated them to the lowest education category. Again, there were no flags for such allocations, so these men remain in the PA and PSID samples.

The resulting samples thus consist of male household heads, aged 25 to 64, with nonzero income and complete data on the relevant variables. This leaves 10,770 men in the OCG sample, 1,223 men in the PA, 33,738 in the Census, and 2,301 in the PSID.

---

* The one exception to this rule was that we retained OCG men who reported that their father had not been living at home when they were 16, and who failed to report both his education and his occupation.

1. VARIABLES

We used nineteen variables for these sample comparisons. Father absent, father white collar, father foreign, race, age, non-South upbringing, and nonfarm upbringing required no modification. All other variables were modified in some way to make the surveys as comparable as possible.

The PA and PSID coded father's occupation and respondents' occupation into only nine categories. We therefore coded occupational data from all four surveys into nine broad categories. We then assigned each category its estimated mean Duncan score (see table 10.1). If an OCG respondent had no father at home when he was 15 or 16 years old and failed to report father's occupation, we assigned him the sample mean.

The PA and PSID also coded father's education and respondent's education into different categories from the Census and OCG. We collapsed categories to make all four surveys relatively alike (see table 10.1). Unfortunately, PSID and PA respondents were coded 18 only if they had advanced degrees, while OCG and Census respondents were coded 18 if they had any schooling beyond a BA. This inflates the estimated effect of college graduation and of graduate schooling on occupational status and income in the PSID and PA surveys. If an OCG respondent who had no father at home at age 15 or 16 failed to report father's education, we assigned him the mean.

Our OCG tape did not provide data on earnings as distinct from total personal income, so we used total personal income in all four surveys. Income was available in dollars in the PSID and PA surveys, in hundred-dollar intervals in the Census, and in seventeen broad categories in the OCG. Moreover, the mean income of Americans almost doubled from 1961 to 1973. We therefore deflated income in all surveys to 1961 levels, using CPS estimates of the ratio of mean income for 25- to 64-year-old men in the year under study to mean income in 1961 as a divisor.[1] If the respondent's deflated income was less than $10,000, we assigned him the midpoint, in dollars, of the OCG category into which his deflated income fell. If his income exceeded $10,000, we assigned him the estimated mean of his OCG category (see table 10.1).

TABLE 10.1

TABLE 10.1

*Frequencies, Means, and Standard Deviations of "Comparable" Variables in
Four National Surveys with Similar Target Populations[a]*

Variable Description	Coding	Frequencies			
		OCG	PA	Census	PSID
N		10,770	1,223	33,738	2,301
White	0	8.7	9.5	8.4	11.0
	1	91.3	90.5	91.6	89.0
	Mean	.913	.905	.916	.890
	SD	.282	.293	.277	.313
Father absent at age 15-16[b]	0	84.8	NA	NA	98.9
	1	15.2			1.1
	Mean	.152			.011
	SD	.359			.104
Father's occupation					
Laborer or service	12	13.0	NA	NA	9.7
Farmer	14	26.3			26.9
Operative	18	14.1			16.2
Craftsman or foreman	31	17.7			22.2
Clerical or sales	47	7.5			5.2
Self-employed business	48	7.5			7.3
Manager	58	3.8			4.9
Professional	75	4.7			6.6
Father absent & NA[b]	27.1/25[b]	5.5			1.1
	Mean	27.590			28.739
	SD	17.172			18.245
Father's education					
No high school	6.5	66.3	75.6	NA	68.2
Some high school	10	9.5	6.2		7.2
Finished high school	12	12.7	10.2		13.6
Some college	14	4.2	3.7		4.4
Finished college	16	2.7	3.4		3.7
Some graduate education	18	1.7	0.8		1.8
Father absent & NA[b]	8.4/8[b]	3.0	—		1.1
	Mean	8.351	7.976		8.411
	SD	2.951	2.816		3.103
Father foreign	0	75.7	80.9	NA[c]	84.2
	1	24.3	19.1		15.5
	Mean	.243	.191		.155
	SD	.429	.394		.362
Siblings	0	5.8	7.4	NA	6.2
	1	12.2	14.8		16.2
	2	15.0	17.3		15.8
	3	13.8	12.4		15.3
	4	11.1	10.3		12.2
	5	9.5	10.1		8.6
	6	7.8	7.8		7.0
	7	6.6	5.6		6.0
	10	18.4	14.2		12.7
	Mean	4.515	4.065		3.967
	SD	3.179	3.062		2.955

TABLE 10.1 *(continued)*

Variable Description	Coding	Frequencies			
		OCG	PA	Census	PSID
Non-South upbringing	0	29.4	31.9	NA[c]	31.0
	1	70.7	68.1		69.0
	Mean	.707	.681		.690
	SD	.455	.466		.462
Nonfarm upbringing	0	21.4	37.9	NA	31.7
	1	78.6	62.1		68.3
	Mean	.786	.621		.683
	SD	.410	.485		.465
Age	25-29	12.0	12.3	13.2	16.7
	30-34	14.2	12.1	12.5	12.7
	35-39	15.6	13.2	12.7	12.2
	40-44	14.9	14.6	13.7	15.5
	45-49	13.4	14.6	14.1	13.7
	50-54	12.6	12.4	12.8	11.8
	55-59	10.0	11.0	11.5	9.2
	60-64	7.5	9.6	9.4	8.2
	Mean[d]	42.899	43.769	43.697	42.481
	SD[d]	10.619	11.057	11.114	11.137
Education					
No high school	6.5	27.8	24.2	21.4	18.0
Some high school	10	19.1	19.1	19.4	16.2
Finished high school	12	28.6	29.9	31.3	30.9
Some college	14	10.4	11.5	11.9	16.5
Finished college	16	8.2	11.7	7.9	11.9
Some graduate education	18	6.0	3.6	8.1	6.4
	Mean	10.988	11.202	11.375	11.878
	SD	3.470	3.329	3.571	3.312
Experience	0	0.1		0.2	0.1
	1-5	2.7	3.4	3.4	5.1
	6-10	9.9	10.4	11.1	13.1
	11-15	13.3	10.9	12.1	13.2
	16-20	14.1	13.1	11.9	11.4
	21-25	14.1	13.6	12.2	13.6
	26-30	12.7	13.1	13.3	13.5
	31-35	11.4	11.6	11.9	10.6
	36-40	9.9	9.9	10.6	8.6
	41-45	7.5	8.3	8.4	7.0
	46-50	4.3	5.8	4.8	3.9
	Mean[d]	24.772	25.446	25.108	23.513
	SD[d]	11.859	12.354	12.340	12.221
Occupation					
Laborer or service	12	12.4	9.4	12.3	8.9
Farmer	14	5.9	5.8	2.9	3.8
Operative	18	18.9	15.5	18.8	16.4
Miscellaneous	29		3.5		
Craftsman or foreman	31	21.2	21.9	23.6	21.5
Clerical or sales	47	11.6	11.1	13.7	11.5
Self-employed business	48	7.5	9.5	3.5	7.3
Manager	58	9.2	9.4	9.4	13.7
Professional	75	13.5	13.8	15.7	16.9
	Mean	36.745	38.147	37.937	40.752
	SD	20.986	20.453	21.310	21.298

TABLE 10.1 *(continued)*

Variable Description	Coding	Frequencies			
		OCG	PA	Census	PSID
Income					
<0 or 1-499	250	2.6	0.8	1.4	0.5
500-999	750	2.0	1.7	1.8	0.9
1,000-1,499	1,250	2.4	2.0	2.3	1.9
1,500-1,999	1,750	2.4	2.5	3.0	2.0
2,000-2,499	2,250	3.7	2.4	2.4	3.2
2,500-2,999	2,750	3.7	3.9	4.1	4.2
3,000-3,499	3,250	5.7	3.4	5.5	3.8
3,500-3,999	3,750	5.1	4.8	6.4	4.5
4,000-4,499	4,250	6.5	7.5	4.7	6.1
4,500-4,999	4,750	6.7	5.9	8.9	6.6
5,000-5,999	5,500	16.2	13.4	16.6	13.2
6,000-6,999	6,500	13.0	13.1	12.4	12.6
7,000-7,999	7,500	10.3	11.4	9.4	11.0
8,000-8,999	9,000	8.8	13.0	9.3	14.4
10,000-14,999	12,000	7.4	8.8	7.5	10.2
15,000-24,999	18,000	2.8	3.3	2.9	3.7
25,000 or more	33,000	1.0	2.0	1.3	1.2
	Mean	6,250	7,049	6,436	7,066
	SD	4,397	5,082	4,626	4,601
Ln income	Mean	8.499	8.646	8.549	8.678
	SD	.792	.702	.726	.646
Income$^{1/3}$	Mean	17.535	18.312	17.752	18.435
	SD	4.047	4.010	3.935	3.753

[a]Samples include males heads of households aged 25 to 64 in the survey year who reported all items in this table or were allocated a value on these items that could not be distinguished from an actual report (see text), and who had nonzero incomes for the year prior to the survey. Note that these samples are not strictly comparable to samples covered by other tables in this volume (see text).

[b]Only OCG asked this question. When an OCG respondent failed to report his father's education or occupation, and when it appeared plausible that this was because he had no father living at home at the relevant time, we allocated him the first value shown in the "Coding" column. When a PSID respondent failed to report both his father's education and his father's occupation, we assumed that this was because his father was not living at home when he was growing up and allocated him the second value shown in the "Coding" column. When PA respondents failed to report their fathers' education we treated them as nonrespondents.

[c]The Census asked this question, but we inadvertently failed to include it on the extract tape used in these analyses.

[d]Calculated from data grouped into one-year rather than five-year intervals.

2. WHEN ARE SAMPLES "SIMILAR"?

Our basic criterion for sample similarity is that it must be reasonable to assert that the samples are drawn from the same population. This is impossible to determine directly, since the characteristics of the population are unknown. The usual procedure is to use data from different samples to infer a set of population parameters and then to see whether the distribution of sample estimates accords with statistical predictions. However, even when deviations from such ideal distributions are significant, as they almost always are for the two largest samples in this analysis, they are often too small to deserve serious attention. Therefore, rather than rely on statistical tests of significance, we will present the actual estimates, along with enough statistics for the reader to make such tests as he or she may desire.

The bulk of the analysis in this volume involves multiple regression equations. Regression results depend on sample means, standard deviations, and correlations. The next section of this chapter discusses frequency distributions, which determine means and standard deviations. After that we examine bivariate relationships, both by comparing regression coefficients and by considering changes in the mean and standard deviation of the outcome variables—education, occupation, and income—across categories or specified ranges of the background variables.

This set of analyses will permit us to evaluate the general hypothesis that these four samples represent the same population and to identify differences in some detail. Since we have chosen not to use formal statistical tests to examine the differences, we must specify some alternative criteria for similarity. For frequency distributions, three characteristics are important: general shape, the presence of outliers, and central tendency. (We consider dispersion to be part of shape.) We will assess variation in the general shape and in outliers from a simple frequency table. Variation in central tendency can be assessed from the mean, median, or mode of the distribution. We will also look at three characteristics of bivariate relationships: whether the relationship is linear, the slope of the regression line, and the amount of variation around the regression line. We will assess these characteristics from tables which give the mean and standard deviation of a dependent variable for everyone with a given value or range of values on an independent variable. The tables include enough information to perform standard statistical tests.

3. FREQUENCY DISTRIBUTIONS

Table 10.1 presents frequencies, means, and standard deviations for each variable by sample. In examining these statistics it is important to remember that the data span ten years, and that only income is adjusted for changes over this period. With that warning in mind, we will consider each variable in turn.

The PSID sample has the highest proportion of nonwhite respondents, 11 percent, while the Census has the lowest, 8.4 percent. The difference between PSID and the other surveys derives from the inclusion of Spanish Americans as nonwhites—a regrettable error, which we corrected in the analyses of racial differences in chapter 7. The other differences are too small to deserve analysis.

The mean Duncan scores for father's occupation in the OCG and the PSID differ by 1.1 points. An examination of the frequencies suggests that this difference arises in the extremes of the distribution: there are 3.3 percent fewer laborers and service workers (Duncan score 12), 1.1 percent more managers (58), and 1.9 percent more professionals (75) in the PSID than there are in the OCG. Again, given the ten-year interval between surveys, the differences appear reasonable and minor.

The distributions of father's education are remarkably similar for the OCG, PA, and PSID samples. The PA mean is half a year lower than the others, primarily because about 8 percent more respondents in this survey had fathers with eight or fewer years of schooling. Since two-thirds or more of the responses are grouped in this lower category, it is difficult to say whether the differences across the four samples on this variable are consistent with any particular explanation.

The proportion of respondents whose fathers were born outside the U.S. varies widely, from 24.9 percent in the OCG to 15.5 percent in the PSID. This presumably reflects the decline in immigration after 1914.

The data for siblings reflect the uneven long-term American trend toward smaller families. The mean declines from 4.5 in OCG to 4.0 in PSID. The incidence of small families increases, while that of large families declines.

The proportion of respondents born or raised in the South does not vary much from survey to survey. This is not true for farm upbringing: 10 percent fewer respondents appear to have been raised on a farm in OCG than in PA, and 16 percent fewer in OCG than in PSID. This is surprising, since there is no difference in the percentage of OCG and PSID men reporting that their fathers were farmers. The difference on this question is probably due to the way in which the Census Bureau asked the OCG question. SRC asked all PSID and PA respondents whether they had grown up on a farm. The Census Bureau asked OCG respondents whether they were still living in the same community as when they were sixteen. Only if they had moved were they specifically asked if they had lived on a farm at sixteen. If they had not changed communities, they were only assumed to have lived on a farm at sixteen if they lived on a farm at the time of the survey. Those who had moved from a farm to a town in the same "community," or whose farm had ceased to be a farm, were thus misclassified as having not grown up on a farm.

The age distributions do not vary markedly from survey to survey. The education distributions show a continuing increase in average educational attainment, though as we shall see, this may not be the whole story. Among college graduates, more Census than PSID men were coded as having graduate education. The same holds when we compare OCG to PA. This is due to the fact that Census and OCG asked about graduate education, while PA and PSID only asked about graduate degrees. The experience variable in each survey is constructed from age and education, and we will not analyze it in any detail.

The occupational distributions vary from survey to survey, with recent surveys showing more professionals and managers, and fewer laborers, operatives, and farmers. Since the growing occupations have a higher status in Duncan's scheme than the declining occupations, the average Duncan score has risen. However, the four surveys also display some systematic variations that are not attributable to this trend. Specifically, the PA and PSID respondents, who were selected and interviewed by the University of Michigan's Survey Research Center, have a higher average Duncan score than the OCG and Census respondents, who were selected and interviewed by the Census Bureau. The source of these differences is apparent in the distributions themselves: SRC seems to interview fewer laborers and operatives and more self-employed businessmen than the Census Bureau does. This may be related to the fact that SRC has more refusals than the Census Bureau.

The differences between SRC and Census Bureau samples reappear in the income statistics, which are adjusted to 1961 levels. There are fewer poor and more well-off respondents in the PA and PSID samples than there are in the Census and OCG samples. The PA and PSID means are virtually identical. They are $600 to $800 higher than the OCG and Census means.

It is clear from this review that the four samples do not describe the same population. Instead, they describe populations that differ in two systematic ways, over time and by survey organization. The first of these differences is to be expected and need cause no worry. The second is more troubling.

The basic difference between the populations sampled by the Survey Research Center and the Census Bureau is in their current socioeconomic status, as measured by their mean Duncan score, the size of different occupational categories, and their mean income. SRC interviews fewer poor, low-status respondents and more well-off, high-status respondents than it should to get a representative sample. SRC might, of course, argue that its sampling frame is better than that used by the Census Bureau, or that it gets more realistic data from the same respondents. But the Census Bureau's evaluations of its own surveys suggest that they under-enumerate low-status respondents, not that they overenumerate them. And while respondents may systematically understate their income to official agencies like the Census Bureau, it is hard to believe that they also understate their occupational status.

If SRC oversamples economically successful respondents, this should also affect the SRC means on traits that correlate with economic success. Education, for example, correlates about 0.6 with occupational status and 0.4 with income in these samples. Other things being equal, we would therefore expect PSID respondents to rank about 0.3 years above Census respondents on education.* But other things are not equal. CPS data show that the mean education of 25- to 64-year-old men in 1972 exceeded the mean in 1970 by about 0.2 years. The overall difference between PSID and Census respondents should therefore be about 0.5 years. The observed difference is in fact 0.5 years. Analogous comparisons between PA and OCG lead one to expect a difference of 0.4 years. The observed difference is 0.2 years.

The expected bias in the SRC means for other traits, such as father's education, father's occupation, and siblings, is much smaller than the expected bias in education, because demographic background is not very strongly correlated with occupation and income. Given the real changes that took place between 1962 and 1972, the coding differences between SRC and Census, and the likelihood of random sampling errors, it is

---

* This estimate is based on regressing education on occupation and income in the Census sample and then inserting the PSID means in the Census equation.

hard to say whether the SRC means on these traits exhibit the expected bias or not.

4. BIVARIATE RELATIONSHIPS

Only a two-way joint frequency distribution fully describes the relationship between two variables. Unfortunately, displaying these distributions takes a great deal of space, and they contain so much detail that they are very difficult to interpret, let alone compare. In this analysis we will examine summary tables giving the mean and standard deviation of education, occupation, and income for each category of each causally prior variable. Such tables can be used to construct regression equations and assess their explanatory power, but we will not emphasize this application. Our interest is whether the relationship of these three outcomes to background variables varies from survey to survey. These tables provide a clearer answer than regression coefficients do. The progression of means reflects the linearity or nonlinearity of the relationship, while the pattern of standard deviations indicates how tight the relationship is, i.e., how dispersed individuals are around the trend line. From this information it is possible to infer how accurately the bivariate linear correlation and regression coefficients summarize the relationships. Tables 10.2 through 10.6 give means and standard deviations of each outcome variable by categories of five background variables. They also give the corresponding correlation and regression coefficients. We will start by looking at the association of a respondent's traits with education. Then we will look at these same traits' association with occupation. Finally, we will look at their association with income.

Associations with Father's Occupation. Table 10.2 displays the education, occupation, and income means for OCG and PSID respondents whose fathers were in different occupations. The PSID means are generally higher, particularly for laborers, service workers, farmers, and operatives. Since almost half of each survey's respondents fall in this lower range, the best-fitting regression lines have different slopes: a ten-point difference in father's Duncan score is associated with an 0.85-year increase in education in OCG and an 0.67-year increase in PSID. There are also differences in the amount of variation around this line: the

TABLE 10.2

*Means and Standard Deviations of Education, Occupational Status,
and Income, by Father's Occupation*[a]

Father's Occupation (Duncan Score)	Education		Occupation		Income (1961 equivalent)	
	OCG Mean (SD)	PSID Mean (SD)	OCG Mean (SD)	PSID Mean (SD)	OCG Mean (SD)	PSID Mean (SD)
Laborer or service (12)	10.09 (3.07)	10.28 (3.18)	30.5 (18.8)	32.4 (19.7)	5,368 (3,284)	6,105 (3,938)
Farmer (14)	9.45 (3.17)	10.67 (3.18)	28.6 (18.0)	34.2 (20.3)	4,755 (3,144)	6,248 (4,582)
Operative (18)	10.72 (3.08)	11.81 (3.09)	34.9 (20.1)	40.6 (21.6)	6,124 (3,444)	6,949 (4,155)
Craftsman or foreman (31)	11.21 (3.11)	11.90 (2.82)	38.7 (19.7)	42.0 (20.0)	6,590 (3,616)	7,189 (4,078)
Clerical or sales (47)	13.15 (2.94)	13.30 (2.73)	48.4 (20.5)	48.1 (19.4)	7,932 (5,689)	7,709 (5,708)
Self-employed business (48)	12.85 (3.43)	13.84 (3.20)	48.01 (19.3)	51.4 (19.2)	8,026 (5,589)	9,290 (6,073)
Manager or official (58)	13.86 (2.80)	14.27 (1.99)	51.5 (19.4)	54.5 (17.8)	9,320 (6,268)	8,976 (4,527)
Professional (75)	14.50 3.17	14.38 2.63	55.10 (21.2)	49.2 (22.1)	8,900 (6,237)	7,622 (4,394)
Father absent	9.91 (3.10)	10.81[b] (3.14)	31.6 (19.1)	34.5[b] (19.7)	5,610 (5,073)	5,325[b] (2,671)
Total	10.99 (3.47)	11.88 (3.31)	36.7 (21.0)	40.8 (21.3)	6,251 (4,397)	7,066 (4,601)
r	.419	.375	.381	.276	.186	.157
B	.0847	.0676	.456	.323	47.6	39.7

[a]Male heads of households aged 25 to 64 with nonzero incomes and complete data. For cell sizes see table 10.1.

[b]Question not asked in PSID. Category includes men who failed to answer questions on both father's education and father's occupation.

PSID men with low-status fathers have more varied education than their OCG counterparts, while PSID men with high-status fathers report less varied education than their OCG counterparts.

Since men with low-status fathers got more education in the PSID than in the OCG, one might expect these better-educated men to have entered higher-status occupations. The data mostly fulfill this expectation. But while the 152 men in the PSID sample whose fathers' occupations were professional or technical got about the same education as their OCG counterparts, their occupational status was 6 Duncan points—or about two-sevenths of a standard deviation—lower. Thus, while the PSID regression line lies above the OCG line through most of its range, the PSID line flattens out and falls below the OCG line at the top.

This pattern is repeated for income and accounts for the difference in the correlation and regression coefficients. The variance of income for both OCG and PSID respondents with high-status fathers is larger than the average variance.

Associations with Father's Education.   The apparent effects of father's education in table 10.3 resemble one another more than those of father's occupation. There appears to be a rather uniform, linear relationship between father's education and education. In each survey, however, about three-quarters of the respondents' fathers completed eight or fewer years of schooling. This weights the lower end of the distribution, where the surveys differ most, very heavily in least-squares calculations. The regression coefficients in table 10.3 reflect this. The PSID, where the increase in education associated with having a father who at least entered high school is smallest, also yields the smallest regression coefficient.*

The sample-to-sample differences in the effect of father's education on education also carry forward into occupation. Again the regression and correlation coefficients are heavily influenced by the mean for respondents with less-educated fathers, but in general the regression lines are parallel. The ten PA respondents whose fathers got seventeen or more years of schooling had a mean occupation strikingly lower than their OCG and PSID counterparts, but since there are only ten of them, their statistical impact is small.

These similarities do not recur for income. The association of income with father's education is linear in the PA, except for the top two categories. The same pattern recurs in OCG, despite the fact that the association of occupational status with father's education in OCG is virtually linear. In the PSID sample, mean income rises less rapidly with father's education than in OCG or PA, except that the forty-two PSID men whose fathers got graduate degrees had a mean income of $10,758, which was $2,600 more than the mean for respondents whose fathers got only a BA.

One possible reason for these differences among samples is that the top category of father's education includes all those with seventeen or more

---

* Differences among less-educated fathers may have a smaller impact on education in the PSID than they do in other surveys. An alternative explanation, however, is that 6.5 years reasonably characterizes the 0–8 category in the OCG and PA samples but is too low for the PSID.

TABLE 10.3

Means and Standard Deviations of Education, Occupational Status, and Income, by Father's Education[a]

Father's Education (Coding)	Education			Occupation			Income (1961 equivalent)		
	OCG Mean (SD)	PA Mean (SD)	PSID Mean (SD)	OCG Mean (SD)	PA Mean (SD)	PSID Mean (SD)	OCG Mean (SD)	PA Mean (SD)	PSID Mean (SD)
0-8 (6.5)	10.19 (3.27)	10.42 (3.15)	11.10 (3.25)	33.1 (19.5)	34.7 (19.3)	37.3 (20.6)	5,699 (3,823)	6,403 (4,467)	6,700 (4,494)
9-11 (10)	12.01 (3.05)	12.79 (2.46)	12.89 (2.88)	40.1 (21.5)	45.0 (20.4)	44.4 (22.3)	6,534 (4,100)	8,164 (5,996)	7,367 (4,373)
12	12.66 (3.05)	13.30 (2.70)	13.33 (2.69)	44.3 (21.8)	47.5 (20.0)	47.9 (20.4)	7,479 (4,785)	9,030 (5,950)	7,884 (4,339)
13-15 (14)	13.39 (2.93)	14.41 (2.51)	14.18 (2.38)	48.3 (20.5)	52.3 (21.1)	50.8 (20.4)	8,070 (5,864)	10,028 (6,349)	7,711 (3,792)
16	14.45 (2.89)	14.90 (2.13)	14.41 (2.52)	54.0 (20.5)	56.1 (17.1)	52.8 (18.4)	9,485 (7,315)	9,732 (7,470)	8,150 (5,233)
17 or more (18)	15.67 (2.59)	15.60 (1.84)	15.98 (1.90)	57.2 (19.4)	46.9 (23.5)	55.7 (21.4)	9,024 (5,920)	8,875 (5,508)	10,757 (8,289)
Father absent	9.37 (3.01)	NA	10.80[b] (3.14)	31.4 (18.4)	NA	34.5[b] (19.7)	5,370 (4,922)	NA	5,325[b] (2,671)
Total	10.99 (3.47)	11.20 (3.33)	11.88 (3.31)	36.8 (21.0)	38.1 (20.5)	40.8 (21.3)	6,251 (4,398)	7,049 (5,082)	7,066 (4,600)
r	.387	.431	.373	.293	.302	.255	.134	.226	.142
B	.456	.509	.398	2.08	2.19	1.75	200	407	210

[a]Male heads of households aged 25 to 64 with nonzero incomes and complete data. For cell sizes see table 10.1.
[b]Question not asked in PSID. Category includes men who failed to answer questions on both father's education and father's occupation.

years of schooling in the OCG but includes only those with a graduate degree in the PA and PSID. One test of this explanation is to calculate a combined mean income for everyone whose father finished college. This procedure yields a mean of about $9,300 for OCG, $9,560 for PA, and $9,000 for PSID. Thus, the incomes of all men with well-educated fathers in the three samples are not so different after all. But even after collapsing the education categories, PA men whose fathers had "some college" make more than PA men whose fathers finished college, and PSID men whose fathers had "some college" make less than PSID men whose fathers merely finished high school.

These uneven effects of father's education are not apparent in the regression coefficients, which suggest that the average impact of a year of father's education on income in the PA is about twice what it is in the OCG and the PSID. This is due to the preponderance in all three samples of respondents whose fathers had only elementary education. It is compounded by the tendency of income variances to increase as the mean increases, particularly in PSID.

Associations with Siblings. The correlations between education and siblings in table 10.4 cluster around −0.32. The regression coefficients are also similar.

The relationship between siblings and occupation is also quite similar in the different samples, except that the 152 PA respondents who had three siblings seem to have had a higher mean than their counterparts in the other surveys. This discrepancy is not due to differences in education.

The association of income with siblings is also very similar in all three samples.

Associations with Education. Duncan's status scores for occupations depend on the education and income that men in each occupational category reported to the 1950 Census. The data in table 10.5 indicate that the distribution of Duncan scores within education categories remained virtually stable from 1962 to 1972. This in turn suggests that recalibrating Duncan's scale would have little impact on the relative standing of broad occupational groups. This conclusion may not hold, however, for the income component of the scale, which we discuss later. PA and PSID respondents are in higher-status occupations than OCG and Census respondents at the same educational level.

The association of income with education is remarkably similar in all four surveys, except that the PA and PSID means are again higher than

TABLE 10.4

Means and Standard Deviations of Education, Occupational Status, and Income, by Number of Siblings[a]

Siblings	Education			Occupation			Income (1961 equivalent)		
	OCG Mean (SD)	PA Mean (SD)	PSID Mean (SD)	OCG Mean (SD)	PA Mean (SD)	PSID Mean (SD)	OCG Mean (SD)	PA Mean (SD)	PSID Mean (SD)
0	12.58 (3.30)	12.56 (3.27)	13.34 (2.99)	43.6 (22.2)	42.8 (22.2)	44.8 (23.8)	7,266 (5,116)	8,316 (6,660)	8,150 (5,279)
1	12.87 (3.27)	12.68 (3.20)	13.19 (2.98)	45.2 (22.1)	43.5 (21.2)	47.9 (20.6)	7,577 (5,262)	7,711 (5,316)	8,203 (5,532)
2	12.11 (3.26)	12.01 (3.22)	12.87 (3.19)	41.2 (21.5)	42.0 (21.1)	46.0 (21.5)	7,116 (4,740)	7,588 (4,935)	7,279 (4,037)
3	11.19 (3.39)	11.64 (2.92)	12.37 (3.06)	37.4 (20.8)	42.5 (20.3)	40.8 (21.5)	6,397 (4,349)	8,189 (5,819)	7,406 (5,068)
4	10.87 (3.27)	10.91 (2.99)	11.48 (3.08)	36.5 (20.0)	36.1 (18.4)	38.1 (19.8)	6,157 (4,344)	6,960 (5,181)	6,684 (4,105)
5	10.34 (3.29)	10.46 (2.90)	11.24 (3.07)	33.6 (19.8)	33.3 (18.8)	37.8 (20.0)	5,777 (3,833)	6,454 (4,720)	7,155 (5,029)
6	9.84 (3.06)	9.90 (3.28)	10.45 (2.97)	31.6 (18.6)	33.3 (18.9)	36.6 (20.1)	5,528 (3,704)	6,032 (4,212)	5,972 (3,049)
7	9.66 (3.19)	9.60 (3.24)	10.16 (2.88)	31.7 (19.2)	32.4 (18.4)	33.0 (19.3)	5,378 (3,134)	6,386 (4,870)	5,865 (3,573)
8+ (10)	9.55 (3.24)	9.67 (3.3)	10.09 (3.4)	30.7 (18.9)	31.5 (18.5)	33.6 (19.6)	5,159 (3,741)	5,348 (3,153)	5,893 (3,694)
Total	10.99 (3.47)	11.20 (3.33)	11.88 (3.31)	36.7 (21.0)	38.1 (20.5)	40.8 (21.3)	6,251 (4,397)	7,049 (5,082)	7,066 (4,601)
r	-.326	-.319	-.339	-.228	-.216	-.221	-.116	-.179	-.162
B	-.355	-.372	-.380	-1.51	-1.44	-1.59	-18	-297	-252

[a] Male heads of households aged 25 to 64 with nonzero incomes and complete data. For cell sizes see table 10.1.

TABLE 10.5

Means and Standard Deviations of Occupational Status and Income, by Education[a]

	Occupation				Income (1961 equivalent)			
(Education Coding)	OCG Mean (SD)	PA Mean (SD)	Census Mean (SD)	PSID Mean (SD)	OCG Mean (SD)	PA Mean (SD)	Census Mean (SD)	PSID Mean (SD)
-8 (6.5)	24.3 (13.8)	24.4 (12.7)	24.2 (12.9)	25.5 (14.4)	4,280 (2,695)	4,414 (3,097)	4,359 (3,147)	4,559 (2,892)
-11 (10)	29.3 (15.8)	30.5 (14.5)	29.1 (15.5)	30.2 (15.8)	5,538 (3,576)	6,293 (4,246)	5,391 (3,171)	5,709 (2,571)
	36.2 (18.2)	37.7 (18.1)	35.7 (18.5)	37.1 (17.9)	6,375 (3,430)	7,115 (3,768)	6,317 (3,660)	6,863 (3,562)
-15 (14)	46.4 (19.3)	48.9 (19.7)	47.3 (20.1)	46.9 (18.6)	7,582 (5,155)	8,223 (4,923)	7,326 (4,798)	7,354 (4,376)
	61.7 (15.4)	59.5 (16.5)	60.0 (16.6)	61.8 (15.7)	9,488 (5,837)	10,435 (6,943)	9,491 (5,991)	10,017 (5,949)
and over (18)	69.9 (10.7)	70.5 (10.4)	68.4 (12.7)	72.6 (6.9)	10,310 (6,770)	13,148 (8,938)	10,503 (7,235)	12,282 (6,935)
total	36.7 (21.0)	38.1 (20.5)	37.9 (21.3)	40.8 (21.3)	6,251 (4,397)	7,049 (5,082)	6,432 (4,629)	7,066 (4,601)
	.605	.597	.601	.608	.399	.413	.381	.423
	3.66	3.67	3.59	3.91	505	631	493	587

[a] Male heads of households aged 25 to 64 with nonzero incomes and complete data. For cell sizes see table 10.1.

the OCG and Census means. The impact of years of schooling beyond "some college" is also larger in the PA and PSID than it is in the OCG and Census, partly because PA and PSID respondents with graduate training but no graduate degree are grouped with BAs.[*]

Association of Occupation with Income. The association of occupation with income in table 10.6 is not entirely consistent from sample to sample. The regression slopes are quite linear—and indeed almost coincident—for blue-collar and clerical/sales occupations (Duncan scores 12, 14, 31, and 47). Moreover, the variances around the line are small and consistent in this range. But self-employed businessmen (48) have un-

---

[*] If we combine incomes for all men with sixteen or more years of school, using the frequencies in table 10.1, the means are $9,835 in OCG, $11,073 in PA, $10,102 in Census, and $10,809 in PSID. If we divide these means by the mean for men with twelve years of school, we find that the ratios are 1.54 in OCG, 1.56 in PA, 1.60 in Census, and 1.57 in PSID. These ratios are quite close, and they do not imply consistent "survey organization effects." If we estimate dollar differences between men with sixteen-plus versus twelve years of schooling, the SRC values are larger, because SRC high school graduates earn more.

systematically different mean incomes in the four samples, and the corresponding variances are twice what they were for lower-status respondents. This may be due to inconsistencies in the definition of "self-employed" in the four surveys. In the Census, managerial and professional respondents had about the same mean income as self-employed businessmen. In the other samples, mean income was highest for managers. These inconsistent relationships combine with different occupation distributions to yield different regression coefficients in the four samples.

TABLE 10.6

Means and Standard Deviations of Income (1961 Equivalent), by Occupation[a]

Occupation (Duncan Score)	OCG Mean (SD)	PA Mean (SD)	Census Mean (SD)	PSID Mean (SD)
Laborer or service (12)	3,886 (2,206)	3,291 (2,041)	4,082 (2,548)	3,931 (2,199)
Farmer (14)	3,197 (3,255)	5,729 (5,716)	4,640 (4,633)	4,793 (4,180)
Operative (18)	5,028 (2,148)	5,636 (2,996)	4,940 (2,593)	5,129 (2,095)
Miscellaneous (29)	–	5,983 (2,522)	–	–
Craftsmen or Foremen (31)	5,964 (2,620)	6,320 (2,595)	5,825 (2,927)	6,260 (2,600)
Clerical or sales (47)	6,233 (3,420)	6,835 (3,997)	6,681 (4,327)	6,481 (3,015)
Self-Employed Business (48)	7,374 (6,395)	9,772 (7,760)	9,190 (7,746)	8,439 (6,574)
Manager (58)	9,774 (6,199)	10,459 (6,922)	9,163 (5,967)	9,973 (5,726)
Professional (75)	8,898 (5,534)	9,161 (5,575)	8,853 (5,920)	9,583 (5,462)
Total	6,251 (4,397)	7,049 (5,082)	6,433 (4,628)	7,066 (4,601)
r	.229	.351	.364	.419
B	48	87	79	90

[a] Male heads of households aged 25 to 64 with nonzero incomes and complete data. For cell sizes see table 10.1.

5. CAN DIFFERENT SAMPLES BE MADE TO
YIELD SIMILAR RESULTS?

It is obviously possible to make different samples yield similar distributions and relationships. This is what "weighting for nonresponse" tries to do. But if one does not already "know the answer," weighting may not assure comparability. If one merely follows uniform procedures, our data suggest that survey results will be similar but not identical. Nor are the differences random. Nonetheless, the four surveys analyzed in this chapter provide a quite consistent view of the relationships between background and economic success. The major differences are as follows:

1. There is a systematic difference in the surveys over time: the average respondent's education, occupational status, and income rise, and the size of his family declines.
2. Survey Research Center respondents are somewhat better off, in both income and occupational status, than Census Bureau respondents.
3. The average PA respondent whose father had a graduate degree got less education, entered a lower-status occupation, and earned less than predicted either by simple extrapolation or from the corresponding OCG and PSID data.
4. The average PA respondent with three siblings entered a higher-status occupation and earned more than his OCG or PSID counterparts, although he got no more schooling.
5. The average income of managers, officials, and self-employed businessmen varies unsystematically from survey to survey.

None of these differences seriously challenges the view that these samples are drawn from roughly the same population. But neither do they permit us to blindly combine multiple-regression results from different surveys. The statistics relevant to least-squares calculations—in particular, correlation coefficients—do vary from survey to survey, influenced by small differences in large categories, different clusterings of sample respondents, and the five sample differences just listed.

The influence of large categories and the concentration of a sample's respondents in a particular region of a nonlinear plot are general problems in regression analysis. The nonlinear relationship of, say, occupation to siblings in the OCG requires attention even if no other samples are involved. Moreover, such attention is likely to reduce findings' dependence on single coefficients. In doing so, it will reduce the effect of sample-to-sample differences. The analyses we conduct in the rest of this study pay attention to nonlinearities, so the effect of the differences in frequency distributions should diminish.

The analyses in previous chapters made far less effort to ensure comparability between samples than we made here. They are thus able to capitalize on the strengths of each sample. But they also produce results that differ from sample to sample. Most of these differences disappear when we define variables and samples similarly, but a few do not.

CHAPTER 11

The Effects of
Research Style

The research reported in this chapter was motivated by an intellectual puzzle and a problem in group dynamics. One of the original aims of our research project was to discover why researchers asking similar questions and often using identical data sources had come to such sharply differing conclusions about what determines economic success.[1] In any comparison of published findings, it was easy to evade the issue by attributing differences to the years of the survey or the age groups covered or definitions and coding of the variables. But we began to worry about whether purely methodological considerations were responsible for apparent substantive differences.

At about the same time, the group dynamics problem was developing. The first step in our joint research effort was to produce a set of comparable tables describing the relationship between economic success and family background factors in different samples. Giving each member of the research team responsibility for one of the surveys at our disposal, we discussed our objectives, communed with the computer for some weeks, and then reassembled to compare our results. What we found was a distressing lack of uniformity of opinion about procedural details. Confronted with the necessity of making apparently arbitrary and inconsequential decisions, some had made one choice, some another. Even

Kent McClelland wrote this chapter.

when we had supposedly explicit instructions, we had interpreted them in different ways. Manipulations that seemed self-evidently correct to some baffled others. To combat the drift toward entropy, we held more meetings and issued ever more detailed instructions to ourselves. This process culminated in a set of memos (called the Mueser Memos in honor of their principal author) containing truly exhaustive answers to the minutest of procedural questions. Yet even these memos failed to produce perfect uniformity, partly because they did not cover "everything" and partly because we did not all read and follow them as carefully as we should have.

Both in dealing with the published research and in our internal group process, we thus found ourselves having to cope with the fact that individual researchers, following their own instincts, resolve procedural questions in quite disparate ways. Major survey organizations have research "styles" in the same way that individual researchers do. Over the years the U.S. Bureau of the Census, the Survey Research Center in Ann Arbor, and the National Opinion Research Center in Chicago have all developed routine answers to the many procedural questions that arise in conducting social surveys. Although the broad outlines of these answers are quite similar, they differ on nearly every detail of sampling method, question construction, coding, data handling, and documentation.

From one perspective, this is all to the good: individual innovations in procedure and a wide variety of methodological approaches are surely necessary to the healthy growth of any science. On the other hand, if certain procedures seriously distort the underlying substantive truth being conveyed, or if anarchy in approach threatens the possibility of replication and cumulation of results, science will suffer. Chapter 10 imposed a uniform scheme of analysis on four national surveys from different organizations and found a "survey organization effect"—apparently due to "minor" differences in survey method. Our purpose here is to impose even greater uniformity, in order to ferret out the sources of the discrepancies between results from different surveys, and then to consider the effects of various alternative procedures on results obtained from these surveys.

Because of the complexities involved in our multivariate analyses and the complications that arise in trying to compare surveys covering different populations in different years, we attempted to simplify the exploration by restricting it to two major surveys from the same year and by concentrating on a single statistical relationship—that between earnings and education. We chose to focus on education and earnings partly because of the important policy questions surrounding the relationship and partly because of preliminary indications that these variables were especially sensitive to methodological manipulations.

This chapter begins by asking whether the procedural choices made by two major survey organizations (SRC and the U.S. Bureau of the Census) lead to irreconcilable differences in results. For this purpose we will use results from the 1970 Census and the 1970 wave of the Panel Study of Income Dynamics (PSID). Section 1 contains a list of the methodological differences between the two surveys. Section 2 discusses sampling error and how it may affect our analyses. Section 3 describes the sample restrictions and the coding manipulations needed to eliminate some of the apparent differences between the surveys and shows that major differences persist even after making every effort to achieve comparability. Section 4 describes some blind alleys we followed in trying to explain these differences. Section 5 summarizes our conclusions about differences between the two survey organizations. Sections 1 to 5 as a whole address the question of whether applying identical methods to different surveys will yield the same results. The underlying question is whether different survey organizations can replicate one another's work, as theory leads us to believe they can.

We then turn to the effects of individual research styles, comparing the effects of different procedural choices on both the Census and the PSID data. Section 6 deals with the logarithmic transformation of earnings, section 7 with definitions and coding of earnings.

The conclusions focus on the policy implications of this research and on recommendations for future research practices.

1. DIFFERENCES BETWEEN THE CENSUS AND THE PSID

Two of the nation's leading survey organizations, the United States Bureau of the Census and the Survey Research Center of the Institute for Social Research at the University of Michigan, conducted major surveys of educational attainment and economic success in 1970. Table 11.1 summarizes the main differences between the Census and PSID with respect to sampling and weighting, missing data routines, question wording, and the coding of the education and earnings variables. There are, of course, a number of other ways in which the two surveys may differ, e.g., inter-

TABLE 11.1

Principal Differences Between the 1970 Census and the 1970 PSID[a]

	Census	PSID
Sampling		
Population	All individuals in all 50 states.	Household "heads" in the 48 contiguous states.
Interviewing	Mail-back questionnaire with follow-up interview.	Personal interview.
Type of sample	Cross-sectional sample (1/1,000 Public Use Sample). Drawn as a stratified, systematic subsample of the 5 percent of the population who received a long form of the Census population and housing questionnaire.	Longitudinal sample drawn from these sources: a) Subsample of low-income respondents from 1967 Survey of Economic Opportunity. b) Multistage, stratified, cluster sample of dwelling units first contacted in 1968. c) Children and separated spouses from original sample who formed "split-off" households after 1968.
Stratification of sample	Stratified by local area, sex of household head, household size, number of children under 18, and race.	Stratified geographically by region and locality.
Sample weights	a) Original (5 percent) sample weighted by sex of household head, household size, children under 18, race, and age. b) Double weighting of some units to compensate for nonresponse of nearby units with similar characteristics.	a) Weighted in 1968 to compensate for nonresponse and oversampling of low-income respondents. b) Reweighted in 1972 to compensate for sample attrition by regional and demographic characteristics.
Response rate	95 to 97 percent for white males; about 90 percent for black males.[b]	76 percent in 1968; 66 percent of original cases interviewed in 1970.
Questions asked		
Education questions	a) Highest grade of school or college attended. b) Completion of highest grade attended.	a) School grades finished. b) Reading difficulty. c) Other schooling. d) College degrees.

274

TABLE 11.1 *(continued)*

	Census	PSID
Earnings questions	a) Net farm earnings (includes tenant farming and sharecropping). b) Net nonfarm business earnings (includes professional practice or partnership). c) Wages and salaries (includes commissions, bonuses, and tips).	a) Net farm income (includes soil bank payments and commodity credit loans). b) Net unincorporated business income. c) Wages and salaries (includes bonuses, overtime, and commissions). d) Income from professional practice or trade. e) Income from farming or market gardening, roomers, and boarders.
Coding		
Education coding	Single years of schooling up to six or more years of college.	Eight categories: 0-5 grades, reading difficulty; 0-5 grades, no difficulty; 6-8 grades; 9-11 grades; 12 grades; 12 grades plus non-academic training; college, no degree; B.A. degree; advanced degree.
Earnings coding	Components a, b, and c (see "Earnings Questions") categorized in $100 intervals up to $50,000. Values over $50,000 grouped together.	"Labor income" includes all of components c and d and portions of a, b, and e (see "Earnings Questions"). Labor income and component c are coded in exact dollars to $99,999. Other components are coded in nine categories.
Missing Data		
Missing data rate	Education: 2.0 percent. Earnings: 12.0 percent.	Education: 0.9 percent. Earnings: 0.9 percent.
Missing data allocations	Education: a) Assume completion of highest grade attended for those not reporting whether it was completed. b) Substitute response of last previous case with same sex, race, household relationship, age, and employment status for those providing no data. Earnings: Identical to routine b for education.	Education: No allocations.[c] Earnings: a) Substitute response from previous year of survey. b) If previous data unavailable, allocate from tables based on education, age, marital status, distance to city center, race, sex, population density of county, and hours worked.

[a]For a more detailed explanation of the differences described in this table, see *Final Report*, pp. 712-17. The original sources for the technical information presented here are the U.S. Bureau of the Census (1973) and the Survey Research Center (1972: 9-22).

[b]The estimates of Census response rates come from the U.S. Bureau of the Census (1973: 4-7, 28-29).

[c]Although the documentation is not entirely clear, it is probable that the PSID coders did make some education allocations on the basis of answers to the "reading difficulty" question from the education question sequence.

viewer and staff recruitment and training procedures, data cleaning and management techniques, computer software employed. But these other differences are not well documented, and we have assumed that the differences listed in table 11.1 are the most important ones for the purposes of this comparison.

2. SAMPLING ERROR

Conventional methods for estimating the probability of getting a given difference between two samples assume simple random sampling. Neither the Census nor the PSID sample was drawn in that way. Since the PSID sample is only 1/15 as large as the Census, the sampling error of differences between the two samples depends almost exclusively on the sampling error of the PSID value. Morgan et al. (1974, Appendix B) estimate that the sampling errors of multiple regression coefficients from the PSID are 1.2 to 1.8 times larger than one would expect in a simple random sample of the same size. These multipliers would probably be slightly smaller for bivariate coefficients. Since the exact multiplier is uncertain, we will report sampling errors that assume simple random sampling. We then inflate these values by 50 percent for significance testing. This means that our significance tests are at best approximate.

3. THE PSID–CENSUS COMPARISON

This section investigates whether two researchers who tried to conduct identical analyses of the Census and PSID would come to the same conclusions about earnings and education. In order to conduct identical analyses, the researchers would have to transform the basic data on their tapes so as to make the definitions and coding of the education and earnings variables comparable. Then they would have to eliminate certain individuals from each sample so as to make the target populations the same. We will discuss these steps in turn.

In order to make the two education variables as comparable as possible, we reduced them both to six categories: o to 5 years of schooling completed, 6 to 8 years, 9 to 11 years, 12 years, 13 to 15 years, and 16 or more years. We assigned these categories means of 3 years, 7.5 years, 10 years, 12 years, 14 years, and 17.25 years. This sacrifices some of the information supplied by each of the surveys. The information loss from the PSID has to do with literacy, nonacademic schooling, and advanced degrees. The information loss from the Census has to do with the exact number of years of school completed by men in each category.

In order to make the earnings variables alike, we converted PSID labor income to approximate the Census definition for earnings.[2] The PSID also records income in exact dollars, while the Census does not (see table 11.1). We therefore converted PSID responses to Census categories, i.e., hundred-dollar intervals from $1 to $50,000 (and, for self-employment losses, intervals down to –$9,899). We assigned all respondents in the closed categories the midpoint of that category and assigned those in the $50,000-and-up category a value of $70,000.

Having imposed identical metrics, we tried to make the target populations identical. We restricted both samples to men aged 25 to 64 in order to maintain comparability with other analyses in this volume. We also eliminated respondents with missing data regarding sex, age, or whether they were the "head" of their household. Then we eliminated men who were not heads of households from the Census sample. Table 11.2 shows the effects of this restriction.

Men who are not heads of households make up almost 10 percent of Census sample A. They are more likely than household heads to be non-white, under 35, attending school, or without education past elementary school. About 15 percent of the Census nonheads are disabled. Nonheads are disproportionately likely to have zero earnings, work less than full-time, and have Duncan scores under 30.

The two samples labeled B in table 11.2 are restricted to heads of households. PSID sample B has more education than its Census counterpart, but the difference in means (about 0.2 years) is of only border-line statistical significance. The PSID earnings mean is significantly higher than the Census mean. The standard deviation of earnings is significantly larger in the Census than in the PSID, while the correlation between education and earnings is significantly higher in the PSID than in the Census. Education explains nearly half again as much variance in PSID earnings as in Census earnings.

Sample B includes men with allocated values on education and earnings. These men constitute only 1.8 percent of all PSID respondents, compared to 12.6 percent of Census respondents. Most allocated values

TABLE 11.2

Comparison of Census and PSID Means, Standard Deviations,
and Bivariate Regressions Using Similar Samples and Metrics

Sample A: All male respondents aged 25 to 64 years in 1970
Sample B: Male heads of households, aged 25 to 64 in 1970
Sample C: Male heads of households, aged 25 to 64 in 1970, with complete data on education and earnings
Sample D: Male heads of households, aged 25 to 64 in 1970, with complete data and earnings > 0

	Sample A		Sample B		Sample C		Sample D	
	Census	PSID	Census	PSID	Census	PSID	Census	PSID
N	41,251		37,237	2,393	32,549	2,349	30,969	2,255
Education Mean	11.4		11.5	11.7	11.5	11.7	11.6	11.8
Education SD	3.6		3.6	3.6	3.6	3.6	3.5	3.6
Earnings Mean	8,840		9,320	9,900	9,330	9,840	9,810	10,150
Earnings SD	7,480		7,580	6,890	7,480	6,810	7,350	6,680
Correlation	.36		.36	.43	.37	.44	.36	.43
Regression coefficient	740		760	830	770	830	750	800
R^2	.13		.13	.19	.14	.19	.13	.18
SD of Residuals	6,980		7,080	6,210	6,950	6,110	6,870	6,030

Standard errors for Census samples in this table: Education Mean, 0.02; Earnings Mean, $40; Regression Coefficient, $10. Standard errors for PSID samples: Education Mean, 0.10; Earnings Mean, $210; Regression Coefficient, $50. All these are approximate, and PSID standard errors have been inflated by 50 percent (see page 276). Earnings is the dependent variable in the regression calculations. Respondents with missing data on age, sex, or household relationship have been eliminated from all samples.

are for earnings. Presumably, the disparity between the PSID and Census allocation rates is partly due to the fact that the PSID made more effort than the Census to get data directly from respondents, rather than from their spouses. PSID also used face-to-face interviews, which may make it harder for respondents to omit the question. In addition, PSID respondents who did not want to report their incomes were likely to have dropped out of the survey entirely by 1970, lowering the PSID allocation rate. Sample C eliminates men with allocated values on education or earnings from both samples. This reduces the disparity in mean earnings from $580 to $510, but it does not appreciably reduce the disparity between the standard deviations or correlations in the two samples.[3] Missing data allocation routines do not seem to explain much of the difference between Census and PSID results.

In the Census, 4.9 percent of respondents reported zero earnings in 1969. In PSID, 3.0 percent did so. Sample D eliminates these men, cutting the earnings gap from $510 to $340. This gap is not quite statistically significant. Deletion of zero earners has very little impact on the other differences between the Census and the PSID.

All in all, eliminating groups that the two surveys cover differentially reduces disparities between the sample means but does not reduce disparities between the sample standard deviations for earnings. Nor does it make the sample correlations more alike.

4. SOME UNFRUITFUL HYPOTHESES

We explored several possible explanations for the difference between the Census and PSID standard deviations and correlations. These were:

1. Different levels of measurement error.
2. Different treatment of earnings from self-employment.
3. Different response rates.
4. Different respondents.

None of these explanations proved adequate.

The larger correlation between education and earnings in the PSID and the smaller standard deviation of PSID earnings could mean that the PSID earnings measure contained less random error than the Census measure. This would not be surprising, since the PSID used trained interviewers who returned to the same households year after year, whereas the Census relied on a mail-back questionnaire in most cases. But there is no direct evidence on the reliability of variables from either survey. Indirect methods of estimating reliability are open to a variety of interpretations.

We found, however, that even choosing PSID education and earnings reliabilities from the top of their plausible ranges and Census reliabilities from the bottom of their plausible ranges was insufficient to account for the difference in correlations. Nor did such choices of reliabilities make the standard deviations of earnings identical.

The differences between the PSID and Census are apparently not just a matter of random measurement error.[4]

Another possible source of the differences between the Census and PSID is in coverage of self-employment income. Miller (1966) reports that wages and salaries were more fully and reliably reported in the 1960 Census than self-employment earnings. If the PSID personal interviews and detailed questions resulted in a fuller accounting of self-employment earnings, this could explain some of the discrepancy in mean earnings. Moreover, if self-employment earnings are more highly correlated with education than wages and salaries, better coverage of self-employment earnings could strengthen the education–earnings relationship in the PSID. To pursue this hypothesis, we divided the Census and PSID samples into subgroups with wage and salary income only, both kinds of income, and neither kind of income. In the PSID, 17.5 percent of the respondents reported some self-employment income; in the Census, 13.7 percent did so. PSID respondents were almost twice as likely as Census respondents to report both kinds of income. But the discrepancies between the Census and PSID in wage and salary means were just as large as the discrepancies in self-employment means. Since wage and salary income make up about 90 percent of total earnings, reporting of wage and salary income is clearly the more important source of non-comparability between the two surveys. Furthermore, while Census respondents who reported only self-employment earnings had a higher education–earnings correlation than the rest of the sample, this was not true of the PSID.[5] The figures suggest that some Census respondents with small amounts of one kind of income and larger amounts of the other failed to report the smaller source of income. They do not suggest that such omissions account for the differences between the Census and PSID standard deviations or correlations.

Our next hypothesis was that differing response rates accounted for the difference in the education–earnings relationship. The 1970 PSID sample retained only about two-thirds of the respondents in the original sample. Moreover, we had to use 1972 PSID weights, so the samples we examined were subject to attrition over at least five interviewing years.[6] Respondents who remained in the sample are likely to be less mobile than average. This means they are more likely to work throughout the year, since moving often involves a loss of work time. This could increase their mean earnings, reduce the standard deviation, and increase the correlation between earnings and other personal characteristics, such as education.

To test this hypothesis, we compared the PSID to the NLS. The NLS is also a longitudinal survey, but it is conducted by the Census Bureau. The NLS had two drawbacks for our purposes, however. First, it has income data for 1968 and 1970 but not 1969. Second, it is restricted to men who were between the ages of 45 and 59 in 1966. Imposing similar limitations on the PSID left fewer than 700 respondents. The differences between the PSID and the NLS were similar in direction and magnitude to those between the PSID and Census. The standard deviation of PSID earnings was significantly smaller than the NLS figure, which had also been the case for the Census–PSID comparison. The other differences were not significant, because the PSID sample was so small.[7]

Finally, we investigated the effect of the survey informant on earnings responses. PSID interviewers succeeded in talking to the respondent himself about nine times out of ten. In one case out of ten they had to accept information from his wife or from some other member of the household.

A wife who answers questions about her husband's income is not likely to be as well informed about his financial affairs as he is. But it is not clear how a wife's errors will affect the overall distribution of responses or the relationship of income to other variables. We examined PSID data from 1968 to 1972 on men who were between 25 and 64 in 1970, were "heads" of their household all five years, and had complete earnings data each year. Wives were less likely to give complete income responses, so eliminating men with missing earnings data eliminated a large proportion of those whose wives provided the data. In a small number of cases, the wife was the informant all five years. These wives reported that their husbands were older on the average, worked longer hours on the average, and made more money than the rest of the sample. Their husbands' earnings correlated very highly with their education. The most interesting cases, however, are those in which the respondent reported on himself in some years while his spouse reported on him in others. The intercorrelations between husbands' and wives' re-

sponses in succeeding years suggest that wives' reports on their husbands' earnings may be a little less reliable than husbands' reports on
themselves, but the difference is not large. We found no evidence that
using wives' reports of earnings leads to any serious bias.[8] Certainly,
this cannot account for much of the difference between the Census and
PSID standard deviations or correlations.

5. CAN RESEARCHERS USING DIFFERENT SURVEYS COME TO THE SAME CONCLUSIONS?

The answer to our first major question is a much-qualified yes. Education and earnings results for the 1970 Census and the 1970 wave of the
PSID are certainly in the same ballpark. The degree of similarity in
results depends in part on what the researcher is looking at. If we compare PSID and Census sample B, mean education differs by 2 percent,
mean earnings by 6 percent, the standard deviation of earnings by 10
percent, the coefficients of variation by 16 percent (0.813 in the Census
vs. 0.696 in the PSID), the correlations by 18 percent, and the unstandardized regression coefficients by 9 percent. The difference in mean
education is "small" by almost any standard. The difference in the coefficient of variation is "large" by almost any standard, with the PSID
implying a more equal distribution of earnings than the Census. A researcher using ln earnings would find less impressive differences in
the measure of inequality but an equally large gap in r^2 (see table 11.5).

Our explorations of measurement reliability, components of earnings,
and sex of informants lead us to suspect that the major source of the
discrepancies between the Census and the PSID is less a matter of how
questions were asked, answered, and coded, than a matter of sample
design, attrition, and weights in the PSID. This does not seem to
be a peculiarity of the PSID's longitudinal design. The NLS looks more
like the Census than like the PSID. Conversely, chapter 10 shows that
SRC's cross-sectional 1964 PA sample differs from its Census counterparts in many of the same ways as the PSID. Researchers should be
warned that even the most professionally executed surveys can have
sampling problems. Policy-oriented readers can conclude that surveys
agree well on the broad, general picture, but detailed interpretations
must still be treated with some caution.

6. RESEARCH STYLE: ZERO AND NEGATIVE EARNERS

In this and the following sections, we ask to what extent researchers using the same survey but different methods will reach different conclusions. This section focuses on whether retaining men with zero or negative earnings will alter the estimated effect of education on earnings. Comparing samples C and D in table 11.2 shows that eliminating these men has little effect on correlation and regression statistics when one predicts dollar earnings. But if one tries to predict ln earnings, the retention of zero earners can have large effects. The log of zero is $-\infty$. The log of a negative number is undefined. Using $-\infty$ for zero earners in a regression equation will yield nonsense. The usual alternative is to substitute zero for $-\infty$. This is equivalent to assuming that respondents with no earnings actually earned $1.00. One could just as well assume that the respondents who report zero earnings actually had earnings of $0.01 or $100.00. The decision is entirely arbitrary, but table 11.3 shows that it can have drastic effects on one's results.

The first column of table 11.3 assigns $0.01 to zero and negative earners. The second column assigns them $1.00. The third column assigns them $100. The fourth column shows a sample from which zero and negative earners have been deleted. Since the logarithmic transforma-

TABLE 11.3

*Effects of Nonearners on Means, Standard Deviations,
and Bivariate Regressions of Ln Earnings on Years of Education*[a]

| | Nonearners Included and Assigned: | | | Nonearners Excluded |
	$.01	$1.00	$100	
N	32,549	32,549	32,549	30,969
Mean	8.320	8.544	8.768	8.977
SD	3.001	2.051	1.166	.713
Standard error of mean	.017	.011	.007	.004
Correlation coefficient	.23	.26	.34	.37
Unstandardized regression coefficient	.194	.151	.109	.076
Standard error of regression coefficient	.004	.003	.002	.001
R^2	.05	.07	.11	.14
SD of residuals	2.920	1.978	1.098	.661

[a]Male heads of households aged 25 to 64 with complete data on age, sex, household relationship, education, and income (census samples C and D in table 11.2).

tion compresses the upper end of the income scale and inflates the differences at the lower end of the scale, the zero and negative earners are extreme outliers under any assignment scheme. Thus, the value assigned to them dominates the results. The more extreme the value assigned, the larger the variance. Since having zero earnings is not strongly related to education, the correlations are depressed. The regression coefficients are inflated but meaningless.

7. RESEARCH STYLE: INCOME DEFINITIONS AND CODING

Duncan, Featherman, and Duncan (1972), Jencks et al. (1972), and the OCG analyses in this volume all rely on data from a tape that did not record exact earnings. Instead, it recorded total personal income, grouped in rather broad categories. This section compares Census and PSID results for grouped income to results for the finer-grained measure of earnings described previously.*

Substituting income for earnings ordinarily means dropping respondents who fail to answer questions about unearned income. It ordinarily means adding respondents who had zero or negative earnings but whose total income was positive because they received income from other sources. Comparing samples D and E in table 11.4 shows that the net change in sample size is very small. But most respondents without earnings have relatively low incomes. As a result, the mean income of all respondents with positive income is not much higher than the mean earnings of all respondents with positive earnings.† The standard deviation of income is, however, 6 to 7 percent higher than the standard deviation of earnings. Since the correlation between education and income is almost identical to the correlation between education and earnings, the regression coefficient of education is slightly higher when predicting income than when predicting earnings. Overall, it seems safe to

---

* The Census and PSID define personal income somewhat differently. Both surveys ask about Social Security payments, welfare, interest, dividends, and pensions. The PSID also asks about unemployment compensation, money from relatives, alimony, and child support. The Census asks about veterans benefits.

† After taking logarithms, the mean income of Census respondents with positive income is actually lower than the mean earnings of respondents with positive earnings (see table 11.5).

say that choosing income rather than earnings as a dependent variable will not in itself make much difference.

OCG income is also grouped into seventeen categories, using $500 intervals up to $4,999, $1,000 intervals from $5,000 to $7,999, and then intervals of $8,000 to $9,999, $10,000 to $14,999, $15,000 to $24,999, and $25,000 and over. Mean income has risen since 1961. This increases the effect of grouping, since it puts more people in the broad categories at the top. To avoid this bias, we used the 1970 CPS income categories, rather than the 1961 categories, when grouping the Census and PSID data. These categories are broader at the bottom and narrower at the top.

TABLE 11.4

Means, Standard Deviations, and Bivariate Regressions of Earnings and of Grouped and Ungrouped Income on Years of Education[a]

| | Sample D (Earnings > 0) | | Sample E (Income > 0) | | | |
| | 1969 Earnings | | 1969 Income | | 1969 Income (Broad Categories) | |
	Census	PSID	Census	PSID	Census	PSID
an	30,969	2,255	30,909	2,310	30,909	2,310
	9,810	10,150	9,920	10,450	10,170	10,620
ndard deviation	7,350	6,680	7,770	7,150	7,760	7,220
relation coefficient	.36	.43	.37	.42	.37	.43
standardized regression						
coefficient	750	800	810	830	810	860
	.13	.18	.14	.18	.14	.19
of residuals	6,870	6,030	7,220	6,480	7,200	6,520

cation Mean: Census sample D, 11.6; PSID sample D, 11.8; Census sample E, 11.5; PSID sample E, 11.6.
cation Standard Deviation: 3.6 for all samples.
roximate Standard Error of Income Means: Census samples, $40; PSID samples, $220.
roximate Standard Error of Regressions: Census samples, $10; PSID samples, $50.
[a]Male heads of households aged 25 to 64 with complete data on age, sex, household relationship, educa-, and income, and with positive earnings or income.

The effects of grouping depend on the values assigned to each category. Ideally, one wants to assign everyone in a group the mean for that group. The standard practice, however, is to assign category midpoints on the assumption that responses are uniformly distributed within categories. In fact, however, as many as 30 or 40 percent of income responses are rounded off to the nearest thousand dollars, either for the convenience of the respondent or because salaries are actually set that way. Thus, if categories use multiples of $1,000 as their lower limits, the

TABLE 11.5

Means, Standard Deviations, and Bivariate Regressions of Ln Earnings and of Grouped and Ungrouped Ln Income on Years of Education[a]

| | Sample D (Earnings > 0) | | Sample E (Income > 0) | | | |
| | Ln Earnings | | Ln Income | | Ln Income (Broad Categories) | |
	Census	PSID	Census	PSID	Census	PSID
N	30,969	2,255	30,909	2,310	30,909	2,310
Mean	8.977	9.032	8.965	9.060	9.004	9.084
Standard deviation	.713	.692	.797	.719	.717	.642
Correlation coefficient	.37	.45	.38	.44	.41	.48
Unstandardized regression coefficient	.076	.087	.085	.087	.083	.085
R^2	.14	.20	.14	.19	.17	.23
SD of residuals	.661	.618	.738	.648	.654	.562

Approximate Standard Errors of Means: Census samples, 0.005; PSID Samples, 0.022.
Approximate Standard Errors of Regressions: Census samples, 0.001; PSID samples, 0.005.
[a]Samples identical to those in table 11.4.

category mean is usually several hundred dollars below the midpoint. Means calculated in this way from broad categories are therefore biased upward by about $200. Table 11.4 illustrates this phenomenon.[9]

Categorization also biases standard deviations, because of the loss of variance from within categories. This shows up most clearly in the results for ln income (table 11.5). Using broad categories changes the lower limit of the income distribution from $50 to $500. In logs, this is equivalent to reducing the upper limit from, say, $250,000 to $25,000. As a result, the standard deviation of ln income drops by about 10 percent. But because the variance lost at the extremes of the scale is not very closely related to education, categorization of ln income biases the correlation coefficients upward, again by almost 10 percent. The net result is that unstandardized regression coefficients are hardly affected by the categorization of income.

Comparing the first columns to the last columns in table 11.4 suggests that using grouped income rather than detailed earnings raises both the mean and the standard deviation by about 5 percent. It raises the regression coefficient of education by about 8 percent, but it hardly alters the correlation. The results using logs (table 11.5) are less consistent. The mean rises slightly when one substitutes grouped ln income for ln earnings, but the standard deviations show no consistent trend. The correlation with education also rises, but the regression coefficient shows no consistent trend. All in all, this exercise suggests that individual income and earnings are relatively interchangeable, but that categorization of income should be avoided when possible.*

8. CONCLUSIONS

We have tried to show that even when survey organizations and individual researchers try to follow established professional precedents, they must make seemingly arbitrary decisions about sampling and coding that can have an important effect on their findings. We have illustrated this argument by looking at education and earnings, but we could have done the same thing with other variables.

* The demographic background characteristics available for both OCG and OCG–II (see table A3.2, columns 1 and 2) explain 9.6 percent of the variance in ln grouped income, 7.8 percent of the variance in ln ungrouped income, and 6.8 percent of the variance in ln ungrouped earnings, in OCG-II samples with unallocated positive income and earnings respectively.

Differences between research organizations are more troubling than differences between individual researchers, since they are less obvious and harder to explain. We have shown that either the sampling frame or measurement procedures of the Survey Research Center at the University of Michigan and the U.S. Bureau of the Census differ in some important way that affected not only the mean and standard deviation of earnings but the strength of the association between earnings and education in their major 1970 surveys. We have not been able to identify all the reasons for these differences.

Differences between individual researchers are relatively easy to identify and analyze. We have shown, for example, that if a researcher wants to emphasize the strength of the association between education and earnings, and if he uses R^2 as his measure of association, he should group earnings in relatively broad categories, eliminate men with no earnings whatever, eliminate men with assigned values, and then use the logarithm of earnings as the dependent variable.* He should also use data collected by SRC. If he wants to emphasize how much earnings vary independent of education, he should leave earnings ungrouped, retain men with assigned values, assign men without earnings $0.01 or less, take the logarithm of earnings as the dependent variable, and use data collected by the Census Bureau. We do not, however, wish to exaggerate the importance of these decisions. Grouping, eliminating men with assigned values, taking logarithms, and using SRC rather than Census data have relatively modest effects so long as one restricts the sample to men with positive earnings. Only the combination of retaining nonearners and taking logarithms seriously affects R^2.

These comments may suggest that we think researchers habitually massage their data to achieve results consistent with their a priori prejudices. Yet while many of us fiddle with our data until we get results that seem "right," deliberate manipulation of results appears to be relatively rare. Furthermore, a researcher who wants to maximize or minimize the apparent association between measures like education and earnings can do far better by selecting a suitable target population than by fiddling with details of coding. Chapter 2 shows, for example, that the association between education and earnings is weakest for very young men and strongest for middle-aged men. An investigator anxious to alter the association can also achieve dramatic results by altering the length of the accounting period over which he measures earnings. Lifetime earnings, for example, will correlate far better with education than

---

* He could do even better taking the cube root of earnings as the dependent variable (see chapter 7).

annual earnings do. And annual earnings are more predictable than earnings in an arbitrarily selected week or hour. But few quantitative researchers engage in this sort of chicanery. Indeed, we might be better off if they did, since this would eventually make everyone more sensitive to the way in which seemingly innocuous "procedural" or "methodological" decisions affect outcomes. As it is, most people make such decisions with virtually no attention to their consequences, on the basis of tradition, convenience, or intuition. Our findings should serve as a warning that some of these decisions have a significant effect on one's conclusions. They should also reassure skeptics that most such decisions are inconsequential.

Our analysis also suggests that survey research has reached the point at which some standardization of method would be desirable. Questionnaire language would be an easy place to begin. Major survey organizations have an understandable stake in preserving continuity with their past surveys, but individual researchers designing surveys should not feel obliged to exercise their originality in inventing new questions for measuring standard demographic variables. Adequate, well-tested versions already exist. The "best" questions are those that encourage the greatest precision and detail in answers. Modern computer programs make it easy to eliminate unwanted detail, but nothing can replace information that was never recorded. Since the public seems to be growing more resistant to survey research, designers of new surveys should keep the needs of secondary users in mind.

CHAPTER 12

Who Gets Ahead? *and* Inequality: *A Comparison*

This chapter returns to one of the questions that originally stimulated our work, namely, whether *Inequality* presented an accurate picture of the determinants of economic success. We will begin by contrasting *Inequality*'s objectives with those of the present volume. Then we will assess the quantitative estimates presented in *Inequality* in light of the evidence presented here. Finally, we will discuss the way *Inequality* interpreted the data it presented.

1. PREDICTING VARIANCES VS. PREDICTING MEANS

This book analyzes the determinants of individual success by asking to what extent individuals who differ with respect to one set of traits can be expected to differ with respect to other, causally subsequent, traits. We have answered this question by comparing means. When we wanted to know the effect of four years of college, for example, we com-

Christopher Jencks wrote this chapter.

pared the mean earnings of college graduates to the mean earnings of high school graduates. Then we asked how much of this difference was due to differences between the kinds of people who entered college and the kinds who did not. We imputed the rest to college attendance per se. Comparisons of this kind are quite useful if we want to estimate the effects of additional schooling on individual success. If, as some economists believe, individual earnings are proportionate to productivity, such data also tell us something about the likely effect of college attendance on gross national product.

Inequality had a different purpose. Rather than assessing strategies for increasing either national income or the income of specific individuals, *Inequality* sought to assess the likely effectiveness of various strategies for reducing economic inequality. In assessing the relationship of education to income, for example, *Inequality* was not primarily concerned with estimating the value of extra schooling but, rather, with estimating the impact of giving everyone the same amount of schooling. This meant that while *Inequality* looked briefly at the mean income of individuals with different amounts of schooling, it was primarily concerned with the standard deviation of income among individuals with the same amount of schooling.*

The question asked in *Inequality* was relatively novel, and the analytic strategy used to answer it had a number of flaws, to which we will return at the end of this chapter. For present purposes, however, the crucial point is that most of the statistics presented in *Inequality* were quite different from those presented in earlier chapters of the present volume. This chapter therefore presents statistics from our eleven surveys analogous to those in *Inequality*.

2. FAMILY BACKGROUND

Inequality estimated the impact of family background on economic success from the correlations between brothers, just as we did in this volume. It concluded that shared background characteristics explained

---

* The standard deviation of income among individuals with the same amount of schooling has the same weighted mean as the standard deviation of the residuals from a properly specified regression of income on schooling. The ratio of the standard deviation of the residuals to the standard deviation for all men is $(1 - R^2)^{1/2}/1$. Thus, if the nonlinear correlation of schooling with income is 0.40, the standard deviation of the residuals will be $(1 - 0.16)^{1/2} = 92$ percent of the overall standard deviation.

32 percent of the true variance in occupational status, whereas we concluded that the proportion was more like 48 percent.[*] *Inequality* also concluded that unmeasured aspects of family background affected men's occupational statuses entirely by affecting their test scores and education.[†] Our findings suggest that unmeasured background characteristics have substantial effects on occupational status even with test scores and education controlled.

Inequality concluded that family background probably explained about 15 percent of the variance in incomes but suggested that the value could be as high as 20 percent.[‡] Our "best" estimate is that family background explains 22 percent of the variance in annual earnings. The true value could, however, be anywhere between 15 and 35 percent. Since the value for income is likely to be similar, this finding suggests that *Inequality* may have underestimated the impact of family background on income as well as occupational status. To assess the maximum impact of equalizing everyone's family background characteristics, *Inequality* estimated the degree of economic inequality among brothers. To make

[*] *Inequality* relied primarily on unpublished data supplied by Robert W. Hodge, who reported a correlation of 0.29 between men's reports of their own occupation and their reports of their brother's occupation when both were ranked on the NORC occupational prestige scale. Using a prestige scale rather than the Duncan scale depresses the correlation between a respondent's current occupational status and his father's status. It also depresses the correlation between his current occupational status and his own status when he first entered the labor market (Featherman, Jones, and Hauser, 1975). It is therefore likely to depress the correlation between brothers' statuses as well (Hauser and Dickinson, 1974).

In addition, *Inequality* assumed that brothers were representative of all men, ignoring the effect of restricting the variance in family size.

Finally, *Inequality* assumed that a respondent's report of his own occupation and his brother's occupation both had reliabilities of 0.91. The present volume uses data obtained independently from each brother and assumes a reliability of 0.86. Thus while *Inequality* estimated the true correlation between "representative" 25- to 64-year-old brothers' Duncan scores at 0.29/0.91 = 0.32, we estimate it at (0.37 + 0.04)/0.86 = 0.48.

[†] *Inequality*'s model implied that if unmeasured background had no direct effect on occupational status, the correlation between Duncan scores of 25- to 64-year-old white nonfarm brothers born into the same ten-year cohort would be between 0.304 and 0.315. Since *Inequality* estimated the true correlation at only 0.32, it concluded that unmeasured background characteristics did not have appreciable effects on brothers' adult statuses.

[‡] *Inequality* had no data on brothers' incomes. The correlations between brothers' test scores and educational attainments, plus the fact that they had fathers with the same education and occupation, implied that white nonfarm brothers aged 25 to 64 would have incomes that correlated at least 0.119 to 0.130. Since Morgan et al. (1962) had found that direct inheritance of assets had little impact on most people's income, since the Wisconsin sample showed quite modest direct effects of parental income on earnings, and since unmeasured background characteristics did not appear to increase occupational resemblance between brothers, *Inequality* assumed that unmeasured background characteristics had very modest direct effects on incomes. *Inequality*'s estimates were derived primarily from data on ten-year cohorts of nonblack, nonfarm males, but they were discussed as if they applied to the entire male labor force.

such a calculation intuitively understandable, it compared the expected difference between pairs of brothers to the expected difference between random pairs of unrelated individuals. *Inequality* assumed that this ratio (R) was a simple transformation of the correlation between brothers (r_{SIB}), namely:[*]

$$R = \sqrt{1 - r_{SIB}}$$

Using this formula, *Inequality* claimed that the expected difference between brothers' "true" occupational statuses was about 82 percent of the expected difference between pairs of unrelated individuals. Our data suggest that the difference between brothers' occupational statuses averages only 72 percent of the difference between unrelated individuals. *Inequality* estimated the true difference between brothers' incomes as at least 90 percent of the difference between random pairs of unrelated individuals. Our estimates range from 80 to 92 percent.

3. EDUCATIONAL ATTAINMENT

Inequality concluded that after controlling family background and adolescent test scores, an extra year of secondary schooling raised income about 4 percent and that a year of college raised it by 7 percent.

---

[*] If we draw random pairs of individuals from a population, the expected absolute difference (D) between them depends on the shape of the distribution and on its standard deviation (s). If the distribution is normal, D = 1.13s. If the distribution is dichotomous and symmetrical, D = s. If the distribution is dichotomous and asymmetrical, D < s.

Most of the mechanisms responsible for the shape of the occupational or income distribution in the population as a whole are also likely to operate within large families. Thus, if we had distributional data for large sibships, we would expect the occupational or income distribution within such sibships to have much the same shape as in the population as a whole. If this were the case, the ratio of D to s within families would be roughly the same as for the population as a whole.

If we do not correct variances for degrees of freedom, the total variance within sibships is the sum of the variance of individual values around the family mean plus the variance of the family means around the population mean. If sibships were infinitely large, the ratio of the between-family variance to the total variance (s^2_T) would equal the correlation between siblings. The within-family variance would therefore be $(1 - r_{SIB})s^2_T$, and the within-family standard deviation would be $(1 - r_{SIB})^{1/2}s_T$. In the real world, of course, families are not infinitely large, but this has no effect on the correlation between brothers, the expected difference between pairs of brothers, or the expected difference between random pairs of individuals. It merely reduces the observed within-family variance to less than $(1 - r_{SIB})s^2_T$. If "families" consist of *random* pairs, for example, $r_{SIB} = 0$, but the expected variance within pairs is $s^2_T/2$.

Brittain (1977) takes a different approach to such data, but we believe his analysis is flawed.

Our estimates are very similar.* *Inequality*'s main concern, however, was not with individual returns to schooling but with the potential effects of equalizing the distribution of schooling. *Inequality*'s OCG data implied that schooling explained 42 percent of the true variance in occupational status and 12 percent of the variance in income in ten-year cohorts of nonblack males aged 25 to 64 whose fathers were not farmers. In our sample of all economically active OCG men aged 25 to 64, we estimate that education explains about 55 percent of the true variance in occupational status and 20 percent of the true variance in income.†

Inequality thus implied that the standard deviation of occupational status among men with the same amount of education averaged 76 percent of the standard deviation among men generally. Our results imply that the ratio is 68 percent. For income, *Inequality* implied that inequality among men with the same amount of schooling averaged 94 percent of inequality among men in general, whereas our data imply

---

* Our estimates of returns to schooling differ from those presented in *Inequality* in several important respects. First, we estimated returns to schooling using semilog equations, which place more emphasis on variations near the bottom of the distribution. This lowers the apparent benefits of higher education, which increases a man's chances of getting rich more than it reduces his chances of ending up poor. Second, we estimated the discrepancy between real and apparent returns to schooling separately for different levels of schooling. This raises returns to higher education and lowers returns to secondary education. Third, we controlled unmeasured background characteristics and adolescent personality traits in some of our samples.

† Using Duncan, Featherman, and Duncan's (1972) matrices for ten-year cohorts of nonblack OCG men whose fathers were not farmers, *Inequality* estimated the mean correlation between education and occupational status at 0.61. The analogous correlation for grouped income data was 0.33. If we expand the OCG sample to include blacks and men whose fathers are farmers and drop those with no 1961 income, the correlations for ten-year cohorts average 0.61 for occupational status and 0.40 for income. If we pool the four ten-year cohorts, the correlations are 0.60 and 0.40. If we use 1970 Census data instead of 1962 OCG data, the correlations are 0.62 and 0.42. If we use ungrouped rather than grouped income data, the correlation drops from 0.42 to 0.39. If we substitute ungrouped ln earnings for ungrouped ln income, the correlation becomes 0.38. If we allow for nonlinearities, the Census correlations are 0.65 for occupational status and 0.39 for ln earnings. (The nonlinear correlations for ln earnings in the two SRC samples are higher than in Census Bureau samples: 0.49 in the PA and 0.45 in the PSID.) The only change that appreciably increases the education–occupation correlation is thus allowing for nonlinearities (0.65 vs. 0.62). The only changes that appreciably alter the education–income relationship are including blacks and men born on farms (0.40 vs. 0.33) and using ungrouped data (0.39 vs. 0.42).

Inequality assumed that the reliabilities of education, occupational status, and income were 0.98, 0.91, and 0.90 respectively, and therefore concluded that schooling explained $0.61^2/(0.98)(0.91) = 42$ percent of the variance in occupational status and $0.33^2/(0.98)(0.90) = 12$ percent of the variance in income. We estimate the reliabilities of these three measures in Census Bureau samples at about 0.90, 0.86, and 0.84 respectively. After expanding the sample to include blacks and men with farm fathers and allowing for nonlinear effects, we calculate that education explains about $0.65^2/(0.90)(0.86) = 55$ percent of the variance in occupational status and $0.39^2/(0.90)(0.84) = 20$ percent of the variance in ln income.

a ratio of 89 percent. These differences reflect the fact that *Inequality* started with a more homogeneous sample, plus the fact that it underestimated the amount of measurement error.

Inequality also ignored the fact that the degree of economic inequality among men with the same schooling depends to some extent on the actual amount of schooling the men have had. The standard deviations of occupational status and ln earnings for men aged 25 to 64 with eight, twelve, sixteen, and eighteen or more years of schooling were as follows in the 1970 Census:

Years of Schooling	Occupational SD	Ln Earnings SD
8	15.7	.764
12	21.1	.603
16	17.3	.688
18 or more	15.4	.829
Total Sample	24.5	.743

These data suggest that occupational inequality is greater among high school graduates than among either elementary school graduates or college graduates but that this pattern is reversed for earnings.*

Inequality argued that qualitative differences among elementary and secondary schools were unlikely to explain much of the variance in status or earnings among their graduates. More recent research supports this judgment. Some investigators have found evidence that school quality exerts a statistically significant effect on later economic success while others have not, but none has found that school quality explains an appreciable fraction of the total variance in status or earnings once prior influences are controlled.[1]

Inequality suggested that college quality might have a larger impact than high school quality, at least on earnings. Our PA results indicate that without controlling initial ability, a crude measure of college selectivity explains something like 5 percent of the variance in graduates' earnings. Since relatively few individuals receive BAs, college selectivity

---

* These data, from table A6.7 of the Appendix, cover all Census respondents reporting the relevant pairs of variables.

It is not necessarily legitimate to treat these standard deviations as direct measures of inequality, independent of the group mean. The difference in status between men with scores of 70 and 85 may not have the same subjective meaning as the difference between men with scores of 10 and 25. Likewise, the 60 percent income difference between men earning $10,000 and $16,000 respectively may "feel" larger than the 60 percent difference between men earning $5,000 and $8,000. Nonetheless, the ordinal statements in the text probably hold, even though the magnitude of the differences is problematic.

explains less than 1 percent of the variance in earnings among men in general.

Inequality did not devote much attention to the effects of studying one subject rather than another. Nor have we given this issue the attention it deserves. We found that a man's high school curriculum had no consistent effect on his later status or earnings, except insofar as it affected the amount of schooling he eventually got. We assume that the same generalization holds for college dropouts, since most dropouts quit college before they specialize. However, a substantial fraction of those who complete high school but not college enroll in some kind of vocational training program. The subjects these men study appear to explain a modest fraction of the variance in their subsequent status and earnings, although we cannot say how much because our surveys do not tell us whether our respondents received their training before or after taking their present job. Among those who finish college, Reed and Miller (1970) report that ten broad curriculum categories explained 4 percent of the income variance. Among those with graduate training, the figure was 7 percent. Reed and Miller do not present analogous figures for occupational status, but we would expect them to be even higher, since the link between training and occupation is generally stronger than that between training and income.

Something like a third of the labor force has completed some sort of formal professional or vocational training. If the field in which an individual is trained explains 4 to 7 percent of the variance in earnings among all those who receive training, it presumably explains about 1 to 2 percent for the labor force as a whole. If institutional quality has a comparable effect, and if—as seems to be the case—there is a relatively weak relationship between institutional quality and field of study, both these qualitative aspects of education could explain 2 to 4 percent of the variance in earnings.

4. COGNITIVE SKILLS

Inequality relied on test-score data from a wide variety of sources, none of which covered a sample identical to the OCG sample with which they were synthesized. Chapter 4 suggests that the correlation between adolescent test performance and adult economic success is probably somewhat higher than *Inequality* implied.* Chapter 4 does not, however, suggest that adult test scores are more closely related to adult economic success than *Inequality* claimed. The differences between our results and those in *Inequality* are not large enough to be of much substantive interest.

5. ECONOMIC DIFFERENCES AMONG BROTHERS WITH THE SAME TEST SCORES AND SCHOOLING

To estimate the degree of economic inequality among brothers who grew up in the same homes, had the same test scores, and had the same number of years of schooling, *Inequality* synthesized test-score and sibling data from various sources with OCG data on the demographic background, schooling, and economic success of ten-year cohorts of economically active nonblack males aged 25 to 64 whose fathers were not farmers. *Inequality's* synthetic model implied that if we were to compare pairs of brothers with the same test scores and schooling, the observed status difference between such brothers would average 78 percent of that between random pairs of men from the same population.† The three samples of brothers analyzed in this volume suggest that observed status differentials between brothers with the same test scores and schooling average 70 to 76 percent of status differentials between random pairs of men from the same population.‡

* *Inequality* (p. 325) also noted the possibility that its models might understate this relationship.

† The estimate in the text was derived from the model in figure B–7 of *Inequality*. The parameter estimates in figure B–7 are, however, corrected for measurement error. Uncorrected parameters were estimated using the data in table B–1 of *Inequality*. These yield an R^2 of 0.395 for occupational status and a standardized residual of 0.778. (The footnote on page 293 discusses the logic of assuming that the mean within-pair difference is proportional to the standardized residual.)

‡ Schooling plus measured and unmeasured family background explain 45 percent of the variance in occupational status in the NORC Brothers sample, 42 percent in the Kalamazoo sample, and 51 percent in the tiny Talent sample (see tables 6.2 and A6.1). Only Kalamazoo and Talent have test-score data on brothers, but since adding test scores to the model raises R^2 by less than 1 percent in these two samples, we assume it would have an equally modest effect in the NORC sample.

Taking account of measurement error does not seem to alter this picture much. We

Unfortunately, none of our samples of brothers appears to be fully representative of all men 25 to 64. Demographic background and education, for example, explain 45 percent of the variance in occupational status in OCG, and 44 percent in PSID, but only 38 percent for NORC brothers and 35 percent for Kalamazoo brothers.° If unmeasured background increased R^2 by as much as in the PSID and OCG samples as it does in the NORC or Kalamazoo samples, measuring these traits would allow us to explain 51 to 53 percent of the variance in status in OCG and 50 to 52 percent in PSID.† If test scores also raised R^2 with family background and education controlled by as much in OCG and PSID as in Kalamazoo, we could explain 52 to 54 percent of the OCG variance and 51 to 53 percent of the PSID variance, compared to 40 percent of the variance in *Inequality*.‡ Status differentials between brothers with the same test scores and schooling would then average 68 to 70 percent of those between random pairs of men from the same population, rather than 70 to 76 percent, as our samples of brothers imply or 78 percent as *Inequality* implied. Correcting for measurement

---

assume that measurement error in the NORC sample is roughly comparable to that in Census Bureau samples, i.e., that education (U) has a reliability of about 0.90 and occupation (D) a reliability of 0.86. Figure 3.1, which we used to estimate the explanatory power of family background and education, implies that $R^2 = r_{DD'} + (r_{DU} - r_{DU'})^2/(1 - r_{UU'})$. If we correct the NORC correlations in tables A2.6 and A3.4 for attenuation and reestimate R^2, the value is 0.55 instead of 0.45. The true occupational difference between brothers with the same amount of schooling would then average 67 percent of the true difference between random NORC respondents, instead of 74 percent.

Inequality used higher reliabilities for education (0.98) and occupation (0.91), so correcting for measurement error only raises R^2 from 0.40 to 0.44 and only lowers the estimated status differential between brothers with the same test scores and schooling from 78 to 75 percent of that between random men from the same population.

The Talent and Kalamazoo samples are more advantaged than the NORC, Census, or *Inequality* samples, which presumably reduces the absolute amount of reporting error. But for precisely this reason, education also has less true variance in these two samples than in the NORC, Census, and *Inequality* samples. This means that for any given amount of reporting error, the reliability of education will be lower in Talent and Kalamazoo than in more heterogeneous samples. Olneck's (1976) estimates imply that these two factors roughly cancel out, making the reliability of education about the same in Kalamazoo as in the Census samples. This implies that correcting for measurement error would have about the same effect on the Kalamazoo results as on the NORC results, assuming the same level of error in occupational status.

° R^2 is 0.51 in the Talent sample of brothers, but this sample is very small, and education has far more effect on status in it than in the full Talent sample. We therefore have even less faith in the Talent Brothers sample than in our other samples of brothers.

† The increments in R^2 are estimated from table 6.2 and A6.1. The 8 percent maximum is based on the NORC results. The 6 percent minimum is based on Kalamazoo results. The increment in Talent is nil, but we do not think this proves much, for reasons discussed in the preceding footnote.

‡ Test scores also raise R^2 by 1 percent in the Veterans sample and in the full Talent sample (see tables 6.2 and A6.1).

error would further accentuate the difference between our results and *Inequality*'s.*

Turning to income, *Inequality* implied that if one looked at nonblack males aged 25 to 64 who were born within ten years of each other and did not have fathers who were farmers, the observed income difference between two brothers with the same test scores and the same amount of schooling would average 93 percent of the difference between random men from the same population.† Our three samples of brothers imply that the ratio is 84 to 89 percent.‡ If unmeasured background characteristics and test scores explained as much additional variance in OCG and PSID as they do in our samples of brothers, the implied earnings differential between OCG or PSID brothers with the same test scores, schooling, and experience would be only 76 to 80 percent of that between random men aged 25 to 64.§ Correcting for measurement error would somewhat reduce all these percentages.**

---

* We have not attempted an exact correction for attenuation, since there is no formal justification for adding increments in R^2 in the first place. But the calculations in the footnote on page 298 show that the magnitude of the reliability correction is likely to be appreciably greater using our estimates than using *Inequality*'s.

† Having previously indicated that *Inequality* estimated the income difference between brothers in general as "at least 90 percent" of the income difference between random men from the same population, it may seem contradictory for us now to say that *Inequality* implied income differences between brothers *with the same test scores and schooling* averaging 93 percent of those between random men. The 90 percent figure comes from the text of *Inequality*, is corrected for measurement error, and allows for the possibility that unmeasured background characteristics make brothers' incomes appreciably more alike than the model in *Inequality*'s Appendix implied. The 93 percent figure is not corrected for measurement error and comes from the use of uncorrected data in a model such as the one in figure B–7 of *Inequality*. This model assumes that father's occupation is the only background characteristic exerting a direct effect on income with test scores and education controlled.

‡ Tables 6.3 and A6.5 show that measured and unmeasured background, schooling, and experience explain 20 percent of the variance in ln earnings in NORC, 26 percent in Kalamazoo, and 25 percent in Talent. Test scores raise R^2 by 4 percent in Kalamazoo, though by less than 1 percent in the small and youthful Talent sample. If adding test scores to the NORC equations also raised R^2 by 4 percent, the expected earnings difference between brothers with the same test scores, schooling, and experience would be 87 rather than 89 percent of the expected difference between random pairs of men from the same population.

§ Demographic background, schooling, and experience explain 24 percent of the variance in ln income in OCG and 28 percent of the variance in PSID. (They explain 12 percent in NORC, 16 percent in Kalamazoo, and 15 percent in Talent.) Once demographic background and education are controlled, unmeasured background raises R^2 by 8 percent in the Talent and NORC samples and by 10 percent in the Kalamazoo sample (see tables 6.3 and A6.5). Test scores then raise R^2 by another 4 percent in Kalamazoo. If these increments also held in PSID and OCG, R^2 would be 36 to 38 percent in OCG and 40 to 42 percent in PSID.

** If we assume reliabilities of 0.93 for ln earnings (the OCG-II value) and 0.90 for schooling, the implied NORC value of R^2 (without test scores in the equation) rises from 0.20 to 0.24. If we assume that the ln earnings variable has a reliability of 0.86 (the minimum PSID estimate), the NORC R^2 rises to 0.26. If we included test

These comparisons seem to suggest that *Inequality* overestimated the degree of economic inequality between brothers with the same test scores, schooling, and experience. In fact, matters are not quite that simple. The previous paragraph compared brothers to random men from the same population. This means that the *absolute* amount of inequality between brothers depends on the absolute amount of inequality in the sample from which the brothers are drawn—a statistic that varies appreciably from one sample to another. The standard deviation of ln income is 0.82 in our OCG sample, for example, compared to 0.68 in the OCG sample on which *Inequality* based its analyses. The difference derives from the fact that our sample includes blacks and men whose fathers were farmers, whereas *Inequality*'s sample excluded them. In addition, we pooled all men aged 25 to 64, whereas *Inequality* averaged results for men aged 25 to 34, 35 to 44, 45 to 54, and 55 to 64. Since the extra variance in our sample is due to race, farm origins, and experience, our models explain it. The unexplained variance is virtually identical.[2] Thus, if we could compare brothers from our OCG sample who had the same test scores, schooling, and experience, we would expect the more affluent brother to report about twice as much income as the less affluent brother.* If we made a similar comparison using the restricted sample covered by *Inequality*'s surveys, we would expect to obtain almost exactly the same result.†

---

scores, R^2 could reach 0.30. Estimated inequality between brothers with the same test scores, schooling, and experience would then be 84 percent of that between random NORC respondents.

We have no strong basis for estimating the reliability of ln earnings in either the Kalamazoo or Talent samples. The range of earnings is severely restricted in comparison to the range in PSID, OCG, or Census samples, so the reliability of earnings *could* be much lower. If this were the case, the difference between Kalamazoo and Talent brothers with the same test scores, schooling, and experience might average only 75 to 80 percent of the difference between random men from these samples.

The reliability estimates in *Inequality* raise R^2 from 0.14 to 0.16. Thus, *Inequality*'s data and model imply that true income inequality between brothers with the same test scores and schooling is 92 rather than 93 percent of that between random men from the same population.

* This estimate assumes that R^2 would be 0.36 to 0.38 (see the footnote on page 299) and, hence, that the standard deviation of the residuals would be between $(1 - 0.36)^{1/2}(0.82) = 0.66$ and $(1 - 0.38)^{1/2}(0.82) = 0.65$. It further assumes that the residuals from the logarithmic equation are approximately normally distributed, so that the expected difference between pairs is approximately 1.13 times the standard deviation. The expected ratio of earnings is therefore between $e^{(1.13)(0.66)} = 2.11$ and $e^{(1.13)(0.65)} = 2.08$. Given the large number of outliers, the expected difference between pairs is probably a bit less than 1.13 times the standard deviation. If so, the earnings ratio is also a bit less than 2.08:1.

† This estimate assumes that $R^2 = 0.14$ for ln income, just as it does for income, and that the absolute difference between brothers averages $(1 - 0.14)^{1/2}(0.68)(1.13) = 0.71$. The estimated ratio of the better-paid brother's income to the worse-paid brother's income is thus $e^{0.71} = 2.04:1$.

But while our "synthetic" analyses and *Inequality*'s seem to imply much the same degree of income inequality between brothers with similar traits, the same cannot be said for our actual surveys of brothers. Talent and Kalamazoo imply that if two brothers have the same test scores, schooling, and experience, the better-paid brother is likely to report earning only 50 to 53 percent more than the worse-paid brother. In Taubman's sample, the expected earnings differential between fraternal twins with the same schooling is about 58 percent. The NORC Survey implies an average difference of 141 percent between brothers with the same schooling.[3] Correcting for measurement error would reduce all these expected differences, but there is no reason to suppose that it would help us to reconcile the NORC results with those from Talent or Kalamazoo. The difference between these samples reflects the fact that earnings are more unequal in the NORC sample than in more representative samples, while the bias is reversed in the Talent, Kalamazoo, and Taubman samples. We therefore believe that our "synthetic" OCG estimate conveys a more accurate picture of the absolute level of earnings inequality between brothers in the population as a whole than do our surveys of brothers. Thus, we believe that in a representative sample of brothers aged 25 to 64 with the same adolescent test scores, the same amount of schooling, and the same amount of labor-force experience, the better-paid brother would earn almost twice as much as the worse-paid brother.

6. EXPLANATORY POWER OF TRAITS AT THE TIME OF LABOR MARKET ENTRY

The previous section suggested that family background, test scores, and years of schooling might explain 51 to 54 percent of the observed variance in adult occupational status. The adolescent personality traits and aspirations measured in Project Talent raise R^2 by about 2 percent with demographic background, test scores, and schooling controlled. The field an individual studied in school (or in a vocational training program) should raise R^2 a bit more. This suggests that men's traits at the time they enter the labor force could well explain 55 to 60 percent of the observed variance in their later occupational status.

Fortunately, there is a way to check this estimate. The traits just listed are by definition stable once a man enters the labor force—at least if we define labor-force "entry" as occurring only after formal schooling is complete. Furthermore, these traits seem to have roughly stable effects on men's occupational statuses throughout their working lives.[4] Moreover, while a man's occupational status usually rises somewhat during his first years in the labor force, the variance of men's statuses does not change appreciably once they all finish school. It follows that men's traits when they enter the labor force explain about the same percentage of the variance in their occupational status throughout their working lives. Furthermore, this percentage cannot exceed the correlation between men's occupational statuses at different points in their working lives. The correlation between statuses at any two times therefore sets an upper limit on the explanatory power of stable traits, both measured and unmeasured.

To estimate this upper limit, we correlated OCG-II men's 1973 status with the status of their first occupation after they finished their formal education. After standardizing for year of birth, the correlation for men aged 25 to 64 averaged 0.62.* It follows that men's attributes at the time they enter the labor force cannot explain more than 62 percent of the observed variance in their status at later times.

In fact, stable traits must explain less than 62 percent of the variance in status, since a man's occupation when he first enters the labor force must exert some direct effect on his subsequent status. When a worker gets a job, for example, he usually acquires certain proprietary "rights" to that job. Workers are seldom fired, even when better-qualified applicants are available. Thus, if a worker's first job gives him a higher status than most workers with his characteristics, he may be able to retain his advantage simply by retaining his job. In addition, many jobs provide training that is useful if one looks for another job in the same occupation. This means that those whose first job gives them a status advantage may be able to retain it even if they change employ-

---

* To standardize for age, we simply averaged correlations for five-year age cohorts. The correlation fluctuated in the 0.65 to 0.67 range for cohorts between 25 and 44 in 1973, i.e., those who entered the labor market after World War II. It declined steadily from 0.63 to 0.56 for cohorts aged 45 to 49, 50 to 54, 55 to 59, and 60 to 64 in 1973.

The correlation between status in 1973 and 1962 among OCG-II respondents who reported on both years and had finished school by 1962 was 0.74. This reflects the fact that fewer men had changed occupations since 1962 than since entering the labor force. Among those who *had* changed, the correlation of initial with 1973 occupation was 0.51. The correlation of 1962 with 1973 occupation for changers was 0.55.

In principle, it would have been more appropriate to use OCG than OCG-II data, but the OCG question about initial occupation was defective in certain respects.

ers.[5] Under these circumstances, the correlation between initial status and later status is likely to exceed the percentage of variance explained by men's traits when they enter the labor market.* The 0.62 correlation between initial and current status is thus consistent with our argument that pre-labor-market traits explain 55 to 60 percent of the observed variance in men's status at any given moment after entering the labor market. About 14 percent is due to measurement error.[6] The remaining 26 to 31 percent is presumably due to traits that fluctuate from year to year, such as health, motivation, values, and job-specific skills.

Traits at the time of labor-market entry explain less of the variance in earnings than in occupational status. Demographic background, schooling, and experience explain 24 to 28 percent of the variance in annual earnings in our best national samples of 25- to 64-year-olds. Unmeasured background characteristics explain another 8 to 11 percent of the variance in our three samples of brothers. Test scores explain another 1 to 2 percent. Since these increments in R^2 are quite robust across samples with different variances and different amounts of experience, we expect all aspects of family background plus test scores, schooling, and experience to explain 33 to 41 percent of the variance in 25- to 64-year-old men's annual earnings. We argued earlier that qualitative aspects of schooling might explain another 2 to 4 percent of the variance in earnings. Kalamazoo teachers' ratings of tenth graders' personality traits raise R^2 by 1 percent among men aged 35 to 54, while Talent's more diverse measures of eleventh graders' noncognitive traits raise R^2 by 0.06 among 28 year olds. The Talent results could change in either direction as the respondents get older. Thus, men's traits at the time they enter the labor force almost certainly explain at least a third of the variance in their annual earnings between the ages of 25 and 64, and the fraction could be as large as half.

Once again we can check this estimate by looking at the degree to which men's earnings remain stable throughout their working lives. The analysis is somewhat more problematic for earnings than for occupational status, however, because the personal characteristics that interest us exert

---

* Let us denote the weighted sum of the prework characteristics that affect later occupational status as D^*, and let us denote status at any two points in time as D_1 and D_2. We assume on the basis of the evidence in the note on pages 372–73 that $r_{D*,D1} = r_{D*,D2}$. Let us denote this value as a. If D_1 has a direct effect on D_2, we can write $D_2 = bD^* + cD_1 + e$, where b and c are standardized regression coefficients. The recursive structure of this system ensures that $r_{D2,D*} = b + ac$. But since $r_{D2,D*} = a$, $b = a - ac$. In addition, the recursive structure means that $r_{D1,D2} = c + ab$. Substitution then yields $r_{D1,D2} = c + a^2(1-c)$. Rearranging, we find that the percentage of variance in D_1 and D_2 explained by D^* is $a^2 = (r_{D1,D2} - c)/(1-c)$. Thus, if $c > 0$, $a^2 < r_{D1,D2}$.

somewhat more effect at some ages than at others. Featherman and Hauser (1978) show, for example, that demographic background and schooling together explain an increasing fraction of the variance in annual earnings until men reach about 45. After that the percentage declines again. This pattern holds not only in cross-sectional analyses of OCG and OCG–II but also when one follows specific OCG cohorts from 1961 to 1972. Featherman and Hauser's data also suggest, however, that demographic background and schooling explain at least as much variance among men aged 30 to 34 and 55 to 59 as among all men aged 25 to 64. This suggests that earnings stability from 30 to 60 sets at least a rough upper limit on the overall explanatory power of stable personal characteristics among men aged 25 to 64.

Unfortunately our eleven surveys provide no data on the stability of earnings over intervals this long. We therefore turned to Social Security data, which are available from 1937 on. These data have three important limitations:

1. Social Security records do not provide information on a man's demographic background, except for his race. Nor do they provide information on schooling, test performance, or personality traits.

2. Social Security records do not provide information on earnings above the maximum amount subject to Social Security tax in a given year. Since 1946 the Social Security Administration has used the number of months it took an individual to reach the maximum in a given year to estimate his total earnings for that year, but the estimation procedure was very crude until 1956. The imprecision of the pre-1956 data lowers the interannual correlations prior to 1956. It also gives the pre-1956 and post-1956 distributions quite different shapes, further lowering correlations that span the 1956 dividing line.[7]

3. Social Security records also omit earnings from certain sources that are not subject to Social Security tax. Until 1950, earnings from self-employment were exempt. Certain major groups, such as federal employees, are still exempt. These omissions have two contradictory effects. On the one hand, earnings from self-employment fluctuate more from one year to the next than wage and salary earnings do. The omission of those who are fully self-employed, therefore, inflates the apparent stability of earnings prior to 1950.[8] On the other hand, if a man receives earnings from both covered and uncovered employment in the same year, either because he moves from one to the other or because he supplements his wage or salary through self-employment, Social Security records understate his total earnings in that year. If he works in fully covered employment in some other year, the correlation between earnings in the two years will be artificially depressed. Our preliminary estimates suggest that if we confine our attention to earnings, ignoring ln earnings, these two biases roughly cancel out; but our investigation of the problem is not yet complete.[9]

While Social Security data clearly exaggerate changes in earnings between 1955 and 1956, the correlations between earnings in 1940, 1950, 1960, and 1970 are still instructive. The observed correlations for all men aged 30 to 34 in 1940 who had covered earnings in the relevant years are:[*]

Year (Age)	1940	1950	1960	1970
1940 (30–34)	1.000			
1950 (40–44)	.553	1.000		
1960 (50–54)	.430	.626	1.000	
1970 (60–64)	.412	.562	.724	1.000

The correlations between these men's earnings in 1939, 1949, 1959, and 1969 are very similar. The correlations for men born five, ten, and even twenty years later are also quite similar once they reach the same age range. This suggests that correlations of this kind have not been greatly affected either by ups and downs in the business cycle or by long-term changes in the labor market since 1939.

These six correlations have two striking features. First, while earnings at the ages of 30 to 34 predict earnings ten years later better than they predict men's earnings twenty or thirty years later, the decline is not at all linear. The observed correlation is 0.55 after ten years, 0.43 after twenty years, and 0.41 after thirty years. Furthermore, half the decline between ten and twenty years is a byproduct of the fact that the Social Security Administration changed its method of estimating earnings above the maximum during this interval. After eliminating this bias, the implied correlation is 0.55 after ten years, 0.50 after twenty years, and 0.48 after thirty years. If earnings stability over long periods were primarily due to the fact that men simply stayed in the same jobs and thereby maintained their initial economic advantage or disadvantage relative to others, the correlations should continue to decline so long as workers continue to change jobs. Such changes continue after the age of 45 (Miller, 1977). The fact that the correlation approaches an asymptote of around 0.50, and that it does this relatively quickly, suggests that something like half the observed variance in these men's annual earnings is attributable to stable personal characteristics that they carry with them from one job to the next. Expanding the sample to include the self-employed would somewhat reduce this fraction. Taking account of measurement error would increase it.

[*] These correlations are for earnings, not ln earnings.

The second striking feature of the Social Security correlations is that they rise as men get older. Men's earnings at the ages of 40 to 44 predict their earnings twenty years later better than do their earnings at the ages of 30 to 34. Men's earnings at the ages of 50 to 54 also predict their earnings ten years later better than do their earnings at either 40 to 44 or at 30 to 34. As we have seen, this is not because demographic background and schooling explain increasing fractions of the variance in earnings after the age of 45. One alternative possibility is that other personal characteristics, such as cognitive skills and personality traits, are relatively unstable during men's early years in the labor force and become more stable as men get older. The other possibility is that while 30- to 34-year-olds can seldom establish strong proprietary claims to unusually well-paid jobs, older men are often able to do so. As a result, older men may be able to maintain their earnings advantage from one year to the next even when these earnings exceed the market average for men with their personal characteristics.

Be that as it may, these Social Security correlations suggest to us that stable personal characteristics explain something like half the variance in annual earnings after the age of 30. Since many economically valuable skills depend on one's experiences after school completion, it seems reasonable to infer that men's traits when they finish school explain less than half the variance in earnings. Our work with these data is not yet complete, however, so this conclusion must be tentative.

7. "LUCK"

One of *Inequality*'s most controversial claims was that "luck" explained as much of the variation in individuals' annual incomes as "competence." Unfortunately, *Inequality* did not offer a rigorous definition of either luck or competence; it merely offered examples. Using definitions derived from everyday usage, "luck" and "competence" are not mutually exclusive. Most people use the term luck to include everything that an individual cannot personally control. If we define luck in this sweeping way, an individual's genes are a matter of luck. So are his parents' characteristics. It follows that "competence" can often depend on "luck."

But one can use "luck" in a more restricted sense. Imagine a group of workers with the same genes, the same kind of family background, the same personality traits, the same tastes, the same cognitive skills, and the same educational credentials—individuals so similar that all employers regard them as interchangeable. Even an omniscient social scientist would assign these workers the same "expected" status and earnings when they entered the labor force. Nonetheless, some would inevitably end up in higher-status occupations than others, and some would end up earning more in a given year than others. By definition, such variance is not traceable to these economic clones' personal characteristics. Rather, it arises because structural features of the economy make it unlikely that workers will end up in identical jobs even when they enter the labor market with identical tastes, skills, and other personal characteristics. In addition, of course, "luck" ensures that even those who are identical when they enter the labor force will not remain that way.

The list of personal characteristics examined in this volume is not exhaustive, so we cannot estimate the overall variance of earnings among "identical" workers. We have argued that men's personal characteristics when they enter the labor force are unlikely to explain more than two-thirds of the variance in occupational status or half the variance in annual earnings between the ages of 25 and 64. But the remaining variation in both status and earnings could be almost entirely due to labor-market imperfections, or it could be almost entirely due to personal characteristics that change over time. If we could measure changes in personal characteristics and show that they led to changes in earnings, this would reduce our maximum estimate of the importance of labor-market imperfections. But we cannot imagine a research design that would measure the importance of such imperfections directly. An economist who starts by assuming that labor-market imperfections are unimportant can always tell himself that variations in earnings among apparently similar individuals are really due to unmeasured personal traits. With a little ingenuity he can even convince himself that these inequalities derive from workers' own choices at some earlier time.

But suppose we could "prove" that personal characteristics explained only half the variance in men's earnings for any given year, and that the rest was attributable to labor-market imperfections. What would follow from this "finding"? *Inequality* tried to use statistics of this kind to predict the variance of earnings in a society where public policy had given everyone the same demographic, cognitive, and educational advantages. It assumed that the amount of economic inequality in such a society would be at least as great as that presently found among brothers with the same test scores and schooling.

Inequality recognized that if the basic structural features of the economy remained unchanged, there might be *more* inequality in a completely homogeneous labor force than there now is among brothers with the same test scores and schooling. This would happen if the level of economic inequality really depended on "history," "shared values," "exploitation," or other "exogenous" influences.[10] If this were the case, making all workers alike would not reduce economic inequality, or at least not as much as *Inequality*'s estimation procedure implied that it would. Workers with the same personal characteristics would therefore end up more unequal than they are today.

This would happen if wage differentials between various jobs remained fixed even when the number of fully qualified applicants for the better-paid jobs greatly exceeded the number of vacancies. Conventional economic theory predicts that profit-maximizing firms will cut the wages of their better-paid workers if they can hire equally satisfactory workers at a lower price. Firms will only maintain traditional wage differentials if reducing these differentials threatens their profits. If, for example, other firms refused to do business with any firm that cut the wages of its skilled workers and supervisors, perhaps out of "class solidarity," even profit-maximizing firms would be reluctant to economize in this particular way. Likewise, if key managers were permanently demoralized by a more egalitarian pay structure, this might lower output and discourage other firms from changing their traditional wage structure. For the existing level of inequality to persist indefinitely, however, such pressures would not only have to maintain existing wage differentials between jobs, but would also have to maintain the traditional definitions of what constituted a "job" within each firm. The economy would also have to exclude new firms with more economical labor practices from most markets. Some pessimists believe that managerial collusion and union featherbedding have reduced the English economy to this state. Certain sectors of the American economy, where entry costs are extremely high or workers' norms about labor practices are very strong, may also operate this way. But it is hard to believe that the American economy as a whole has become so ossified that reducing the variance of personal characteristics would leave earnings differentials completely unchanged.

Nonetheless, structural rigidities could easily make the effect of equalizing workers' personal characteristics smaller than fully competitive models of the labor market imply it should be. Structural rigidities probably mean that existing wage differentials between workers with different personal characteristics are only partly due to differences in productivity. If a firm has several jobs that demand equally scarce skills, and if one job pays more than the other for structural reasons, the firm must find some acceptable basis for giving the better-paid job to one worker rather than another. If appreciable numbers of firms make such decisions on the basis of educational credentials, test performance, skin color, or the other traits investigated in this volume, wage differentials between groups that differ along these lines will exceed the average difference in productivity. Even if the next generation of job applicants were identical in these respects, structural rigidities might persist, preventing firms from eliminating pay differentials between jobs that required equally scarce skills. Instead, firms might have to invent new criteria for allocating the better-paid jobs. (In the absence of "meritocratic" criteria, managers usually give such jobs to their friends.) As a result, equalizing worker characteristics might have less effect than competitive models of the economy imply it should.

What *Inequality* failed to recognize was the possibility that making all workers alike might lead to changes in the structure of the labor market itself, eliminating many of the rigidities that now generate economic inequality among interchangeable (or at least equally valuable) workers. If both workers and employers *realized* that all workers were interchangeable, the labor-market imperfections that now generate inequality among identical workers might diminish or even disappear. Three examples should suffice to illustrate this point.

1. The business cycle currently creates economic inequality among otherwise indistinguishable workers. By keeping the market in a permanent state of disequilibrium, the business cycle makes it impossible for individual workers to know in advance how many weeks they will be able to work in a given year if they accept a given job. Therefore, some end up earning more in a given year than others with the same "expected" earnings. If all workers were interchangeable, increases in aggregate demand would not generate shortages of any one kind of worker until all other workers were employed. Policies aimed at moving the economy toward full employment would therefore produce less wage inflation than at present and would become more politically acceptable. This would reduce the variance of weeks worked among workers with the same preferences and motivations.

2. Institutionalization of work relationships is another structural source of inequality among identical workers. Large firms do not usually negotiate wages directly with individual workers. Rather, they create jobs with set wages—and often set hours—and then try to recruit the best workers they can for these jobs. Job descriptions are not completely rigid, but neither are they completely responsive to market conditions.

If a firm has difficulty recruiting unskilled workers, for example, it may nonetheless be reluctant to raise their starting wages, because this will set off demands for similar increases from more highly skilled workers. Even if the skilled workers' demands cannot be justified in terms of labor shortages, rejecting them may lower morale and productivity or even lead to a strike. A firm may therefore find it cheaper to put up with high turnover and chronic shortages of unskilled workers than to pay them a more competitive wage. Alternatively, if the firm pays unskilled workers a competitive wage and then increases skilled workers' wages according to some traditional concept of how large skill bonuses "ought" to be, it may have to pay some highly skilled workers and some of those in supervisory roles more than they could get on the open market. If such situations are widespread, large firms with complex internal wage hierarchies may end up paying a substantial fraction of their employees more than the market average for workers with the same personal characteristics.

If the idea that all workers were interchangeable became generally accepted, our ideas about the appropriate wage differential between workers who held different jobs would change. We would be less likely to feel that those in authority "deserved" higher wages than their subordinates, or even that they deserved to stay in authority. We would be more likely to reorganize work so as to make all jobs equally demanding. In situations where this proved impossible, we would be more likely to rotate the most powerful positions. In short, if we believed all workers were equally competent, the norm of equal rewards might end up even more rigidly institutionalized than the norm of unequal rewards now is.

3. Information costs are a third source of labor-market imperfections. Firms do not know how much they must pay to attract workers with specified characteristics, so they sometimes offer more than they would have to offer to get acceptable workers. Workers, in turn, do not know how high a wage they can command, so they sometimes settle for less than they could get if they kept looking. These suboptimal bargains mean that identical workers do not always earn identical amounts. Putting the point slightly differently, they mean that the economy is never in equilibrium. Indeed, if one judges by the number of men who change jobs each year and by the amount that this often changes their wages, equilibrium may be quite remote. Information costs would disappear if all workers were alike. Firms would have no reason to offer more than the going wage in hope of getting better workers, and workers would have no reason to settle for less than the going wage out of fear that other firms would underestimate their capacities.

These three examples suggest that if we could completely eliminate variation in the personal characteristics that employers value and convince them that all workers were really interchangable, variation in both occupational status and wages might fall precipitously. But egalitarian reformers have seldom contemplated policies that would completely eliminate variation in all the personal characteristics that employers value. They have limited their attention to a few such characteristics, notably performance on standardized tests and exposure to formal education, and, even in these areas, they have sought only modest reductions in inequality, not its complete elimination. Such limited goals are certainly realistic, but they mean that even if this kind of egalitarian reform were completely successful, it would not do much to convince employers that all workers were interchangable. As a result, it would not do much to alter the basic character of the labor market or to eliminate those labor market forces that currently generate economic inequality among workers with exactly the same personal characteristics. Thus there is no reason to suppose that *Inequality* was wrong when it minimized the likely effect of such egalitarian reforms on disparities in status and earnings.

Nonetheless, while *Inequality's* approach to estimating such effects was consistent with the approach economists often take to this problem, it now strikes us as fundamentally flawed. Analyzing the distribution of status or income as if it were nothing more than the product of innumerable individual decisions taken in a historical and cultural vacuum is at best risky and at worst absurd. A realistic analysis of economic inequality also requires historical data on the extent to which changes in the distribution of personal characteristics have actually been associated with changes in the distribution of status and earnings in various societies. At present, such data are hard to find.

It does not follow, however, that *Inequality's* major policy conclusion was unjustified. *Inequality* argued that trying to equalize men's personal characteristics was an unpromising way of equalizing their incomes. This argument had two parts. *Inequality* first argued that even if personal characteristics were equalized, this would have very marginal effects on the distribution of income. This conclusion, while still plausible, may have been premature. But *Inequality* also argued that past efforts at equalizing the personal characteristics known to affect income had been relatively ineffective. This assertion, sad to say, remains as true as ever. Thus, if we want to redistribute income, the most effective strategy is probably still to redistribute income.

APPENDIX OF
SUPPLEMENTARY TABLES

TABLE A2.1

Means and Standard Deviations for Men with Complete Data from Eleven Samples[a]

	OCG		PA		Census	
Year	1962		1965		1970	
N: Basic sample	18,094		1,392		36,693	
Complete-data sample	11,504		1,188		25,697	
Age range	25–64		25–64		25–64	
Variables	**Mean**	**SD**	**Mean**	**SD**	**Mean**	**SD**
Race	.904	.295	.907	.290	.919	.273
Father's education	7.728	3.920	7.978	3.165	—	—
Father's occupation	27.485	20.517	—	—	—	—
Father white collar	.241	.416	—	—	—	—
Father foreign	.247	.431	.195	.397	—	—
Father absent	.156	.363	—	—	—	—
Siblings	4.358	3.143	3.939	2.793	—	—
Nonfarm	.790	.408	.614	.487	—	—
Non-South	.707	.455	.678	.468	.700	.458
Test score	—	—	—	—	—	—
Age	42.574	10.713	43.547	10.855	42.935	11.004
Education	10.925	3.690	11.149	3.469	11.598	3.513
Experience	24.331	11.857	25.166	11.996	24.168	12.068
Occupation	38.101	24.873	37.879	20.610	40.795	24.543
Ln weeks worked	—	—	3.864	.268	3.856	.270
Earnings	6,065[g]	4,348[g]	7,632	6,122	9,835	7,397
Ln earnings	8.455[g]	.819[g]	8.723	.707	8.981	.716
Earnings 1/3	17.315[g]	4.113[g]	18.243	3.960	20.482	4.427
Family income	—	—	9,495	8,259	—	—

[a]Except as noted in the text, all samples are restricted to men aged 25 to 64 with positive earnings who were not in school, in t.e military, or in institutions.
[b]Hispanic respondents coded *nonwhite*.
[c]Constructed from indirect evidence.
[d]These statistics describe samples of brothers who *both* have complete data.
[e]Hourly, not annual earnings.
[f]Inferred from father's occupation.
[g]Includes income from all sources, not just earnings.

TABLE A2.1 (continued)

	NLS		Talent		Talent Brothers		Kalamazoo Brothers	
Year	1966		1972		1971-72		1973	
N: Basic sample	4,689		1,369		310		1,243	
Complete-data sample	2,830		839		198[d]		692[d]	
Age range	45-59		28±		28±		35-59	
Variables	**Mean**	**SD**	**Mean**	**SD**	**Mean**	**SD**	**Mean**	**SD**
Race	.911	.284	.951	.216	.985	.123	1.000	.000
Father's education	7.542	3.658	11.342	3.471	11.114	4.051	9.507	3.323
Father's occupation	29.775	20.803	35.551	22.345	34.293	21.815	38.329	22.504
Father white collar	.254	.387	—	—	—	—	.350	.477
Father foreign	.224	.417	—	—	—	—	.206	.405
Father absent	.201	.400	.124	.330	.061	.240	.067	.250
Siblings	—	—	3.678	2.206	4.283	1.846	3.721	2.524
Nonfarm	.646	.478	—	—	—	—	1.000	.000
Non-South	.701	.458	—	—	—	—	1.000	.000
Test score	—	—	102.585	14.602	107.570	13.588	100.893	15.326
Age	51.221	4.212	28.947	.704	—	—	46.135	6.013
Education	10.448	3.681	14.337	2.437	14.439	2.471	13.197	2.730
Experience	33.437	5.490	8.819	2.396	—	—	26.938	7.044
Occupation	37.982	24.794	51.082	23.744	49.601	25.643	49.912	23.157
Ln weeks worked	3.888	0.247	—	—	—	—	—	—
Earnings	8.111	5.858	5.258[e]	2.079[e]	4.745[e]	1.850[e]	16,746	7,631
Ln earnings	8.747	.883	1.586[e]	.396[e]	1.480[e]	.407[e]	9.625	.446
Earnings1/3	19.180	4.451	1.711[e]	.220[e]	—	—	25.048	3.668
Family income	10,392	6,710	—	—	—	—	19,132	8,343

	PSID		NORC Brothers		OCG-II		Veterans	
	1971		1974		1973		1964	
	2,366		454		—		1,021	
	1,744		300[d]		15,817		803	
	25-64		25-64		25-64		30-34	
	Mean	SD	Mean	SD	Mean	SD	Mean	SD
	.895[b]	.307[b]	.933	.250	.910	.287	.940	.238
	8.580	3.185	8.994	3.697	8.310	4.098	8.980	2.531
	28.368	18.104	29.295	20.982	28.919	22.139	28.611	19.705
	.230	.419	.207	.406	.259	.438	—	—
	.160	.367	—	—	—	—	—	—
	.008[c]	.091[c]	.113	.318	.073	.261	.136	.343
	3.869	2.707	4.267	2.697	3.747	2.690	—	—
	.685	.465	.840[f]	.367[f]	.755	.430	.759	.428
	.698	.459	—	—	.674	.469	.727	.446
	100.318	14.825	—	—	—	—	102.671	14.286
	42.484	10.925	43.753	11.032	12.026	3.378	—	—
	11.956	3.330	12.237	3.106	28.097	11.089	12.256	2.746
	23.403	11.912	25.413	12.085	41.740	25.396	11.670	3.087
	41.009	21.067	40.100	24.194	—	—	40.008	23.368
	3.844	.350	—	—	—	—	—	—
	11.549	7.730	12.605	7.621	11,864[g]	8,733[g]	6,824	3,145
	9.144	.753	9.193	.870	9.166[g]	.774[g]	8.722	.498
	21.648	4.637	22.188	5.170	—	—	—	—
	14.941	8.830	14.777	8.014	—	—	—	—

TABLE A2.2

Correlations from OCG Complete Data Sample
(N = 11,504)

	Race	Father's Education	Father's Occupation	Father White Collar	Father Foreign	Father Absent	Siblings
Race	1						
Father's education	.144	1					
Father's occupation	.139	.464	1				
Father white collar	.103	.391	.785	1			
Father foreign	.093	−.151	−.032	−.004	1		
Father absent	−.140	.009	−.032	−.012	−.023	1	
Siblings	−.132	−.273	−.264	−.236	.040	−.058	1
Nonfarm	.016	.151	.288	.246	.125	.048	−.191
Non-South	.291	.152	.140	.100	.318	−.066	−.162
Age	.034	−.139	−.070	−.042	.135	.016	.124
Education	.210	.428	.417	.374	−.003	−.108	−.332
Experience	−.013	−.237	−.178	−.142	.121	.039	.200
Occupation	.234	.321	.402	.356	.040	−.078	−.262
Income	.214	.220	.301	.260	.073	−.063	−.184
Ln income	.280	.219	.253	.211	.080	−.077	−.184
Income$^{1/3}$	.276	.235	.290	.244	.084	−.079	−.199

TABLE A2.3

Correlations from PA Complete Data Sample
(N = 1,188)

	Race	Father's Education	Father Foreign	Siblings	Non-farm	Non-South	Age
Race	1						
Father's education	.118	1					
Father foreign	.099	−.038	1				
Siblings	−.159	−.215	−.039	1			
Nonfarm	.086	.223	.225	−.272	1		
Non-South	.302	.138	.317	−.168	.326	1	
Age	.042	−.102	.054	.109	−.106	.010	1
Education	.211	.414	.040	−.334	.324	.255	−.266
Experience	−.007	−.199	.040	.184	−.175	−.046	.970
Occupation	.213	.306	.061	−.222	.267	.145	−.073
Ln weeks worked	.097	.098	.036	−.062	.079	.049	−.119
Earnings	.170	.234	.071	−.179	.212	.132	.054
Ln earnings	.257	.260	.142	−.207	.306	.232	−.056
Earnings$^{1/3}$	.246	.276	.128	−.219	.303	.222	−.014
Family income	.150	.217	.053	−.147	.177	.115	.105

Non-farm	Non-South	Age	Education	Experience	Occupation	Income	Ln Income	Income$^{1/3}$
1								
.169	1							
−.102	.024	1						
.212	.218	−.243	1					
−.147	−.027	.966	−.475	1				
.209	.160	−.045	.609	−.207	1			
.166	.185	.037	.399	−.072	.481	1		
.191	.216	−.021	.404	−.116	.434	.796	1	
.194	.222	.000	.432	−.108	.488	.912	.970	1

Education	Experience	Occupation	Ln Weeks	Earnings	Ln Earnings	Earnings$^{1/3}$	Family Income
1							
−.484	1						
.591	−.222	1					
.207	−.146	.074	1				
.391	−.051	.336	.186	1			
.488	−.170	.403	.463	.759	1		
.496	−.136	.418	.360	.888	.967	1	
.338	.009	.296	.119	.911	.657	.763	1

TABLE A2.4

Correlations from 1970 Census Complete Data Sample
(N = 25,697)

	Race	Non-South	Age	Education	Experience	Occupation	Ln Weeks	Earnings	Ln Earnings	Earnings[1/
Race	1									
Non-South	.252	1								
Age	.030	.028	1							
Education	.145	.191	−.214	1						
Experience	−.004	−.020	.967	−.451	1					
Occupation	.173	.128	−.056	.621	−.219	1				
Ln weeks worked	.051	.019	−.040	.096	−.060	.110	1			
Earnings	.135	.133	.059	.375	−.047	.420	.203	1		
Ln earnings	.183	.169	.004	.385	−.096	.424	.447	.768	1	
Earnings$^{1/3}$	.182	.173	.026	.420	−.086	.467	.365	.903	.961	1

TABLE A2.5

Correlations from PSID Complete Data Sample
(N = 1,774)

	Race	Father's Education	Father's Occupation	Father White Collar	Father Foreign	Father Absent	Siblings	No far
Race	1							
Father's education	.101	1						
Father's occupation	.080	.461	1					
Father white collar	.052	.396	.877	1				
Father foreign	−.027	−.083	.024	.002	1			
Father absent	−.076	−.000	.000	.000	−.000	1		
Siblings	−.195	−.242	−.265	−.227	−.000	−.029	1	
Nonfarm	.047	.155	.398	.301	.146	.018	−.242	
Non-South	.266	.085	.119	.092	.253	−.053	−.128	.:
Test score	.266	.239	.243	.217	.069	−.023	−.258	.
Age	.027	−.181	−.109	−.082	.145	−.021	.120	−.
Education	.205	.379	.369	.349	.062	−.055	−.337	.:
Experience	−.020	−.262	−.196	−.168	.117	−.009	.198	−.
Occupation	.191	.282	.290	.275	.048	−.021	−.240	.
Ln weeks worked	.088	.067	.034	.052	−.007	.005	−.099	.
Earnings	.148	.174	.185	.192	.107	−.024	−.189	.
Ln earnings	.200	.175	.179	.172	.096	−.019	−.196	.
Earnings$^{1/3}$	.195	.193	.202	.197	.105	−.023	−.214	.
Family income	.139	.165	.185	.198	.137	−.027	−.182	.

on-uth	Test Score	Age	Educa-tion	Expe-rience	Occu-pation	Ln Weeks Worked	Earn-ings	Ln Earn-ings	Earn-ings$^{1/3}$	Family Income
1										
09	1									
04	−.118	1								
16	.473	−.215	1							
52	−.226	.968	−.448	1						
32	.358	−.104	.618	−.259	1					
06	.130	−.120	.140	−.147	.153	1				
52	.337	−.012	.446	−.127	.412	.252	1			
71	.353	−.117	.443	−.221	.408	.578	.776	1		
83	.378	−.082	.489	−.201	.450	.444	.911	.956	1	
53	.313	.086	.432	−.033	.397	.172	.899	.688	.813	1

TABLE A2.6

Correlations from NORC Brothers Complete Data Sample
(N = 300)

	Race	Father's Education	Father's Occupation	Father White Collar	Father Absent	Siblings	Nonfarm	Age	Education	Experience	Occupation	Earnings	Ln Earnings	Earnings$^{1/3}$	Family Income
Race	1														
Father's education	.020	1													
Father's occupation	.077	.518	1												
Father white collar	.070	.437	.782	1											
Father absent	−.073	−.016	.018	−.182	1										
Siblings	−.202	−.250	−.263	−.173	−.043	1									
Nonfarm	.029	.154	.326	.223	.156	−.126	1								
Age	.064	−.332	−.156	−.210	.100	.166	−.056	1							
Education	.120	.398	.339	.296	−.139	−.356	.142	−.254	1						
Experience	.037	−.401	−.226	−.264	.123	.233	−.080	.972	−.471	1					
Occupation	.139	.291	.338	.294	−.055	−.292	−.106	−.066	.595	−.205	1				
Earnings	.099	.133	.110	.053	.089	−.150	.009	.015	.303	−.058	.359	1			
Ln earnings	.066	.163	.124	.085	.073	−.167	.059	−.095	.356	−.170	.318	.816	1		
Earnings$^{1/3}$	.085	.157	.128	.077	.082	−.169	.045	−.051	.356	−.130	.356	.928	.971	1	
Family income	.050	.084	.056	.022	.057	−.119	.004	.056	.278	−.014	.299	.868	.691	.796	1

TABLE A2.7

Correlations from Veterans Complete Data Sample

(N = 803)

	Race	Father's Education	Father's Occupation	Father Absent	Non-farm	Non-South	Test Score	Education	Experience	Occupation	Earnings	Ln Earnings
Race	1											
Father's education	-.049	1										
Father's occupation	.100	.445	1									
Father absent	-.025	.081	-.003	1								
Nonfarm	-.012	.200	.313	.086	1							
Non-South	.213	.145	.166	-.028	.236	1						
Test score	.171	.223	.234	.030	.193	.255	1					
Education	.019	.300	.311	-.043	.204	.185	.554	1				
Experience	.002	-.262	-.275	.038	-.182	-.129	-.474	-.902	1			
Occupation	.092	.260	.297	-.005	.204	.093	.431	.596	-.519	1		
Earnings	.149	.144	.269	-.020	.146	.217	.377	.332	-.253	.382	1	
Ln earnings	.178	.139	.272	-.023	.171	.218	.351	.312	-.236	.381	.886	1

TABLE A2.8

Correlations from NLS Complete Data Sample
(N = 2,830)

	Race	Father's Education	Father's Occupation	Father White Collar	Father Foreign	Father Absent	Nonfarm
Race	1						
Father's education	.107	1					
Father's occupation	.090	.442	1				
Father white collar	.066	.404	.893	1			
Father foreign	.116	−.158	.015	.000	1		
Father absent	−.179	.009	.019	.017	.038	1	
Nonfarm	.090	.174	.428	.366	.202	.094	1
Non-South	.306	.101	.120	.086	.298	−.058	.242
Age	.007	−.047	.051	.048	.042	−.004	−.024
Education	.235	.410	.378	.330	.004	−.180	.304
Experience	−.094	−.270	−.190	−.164	.036	.092	−.183
Occupation	.216	.320	.381	.346	.011	−.081	.323
Ln weeks worked	.056	.068	.061	.062	−.004	−.011	.049
Earnings	.173	.286	.316	.287	.086	−.097	.256
Ln earnings	.196	.230	.244	.221	.078	−.060	.285
Earnings$^{1/3}$	.217	.286	.303	.273	.092	−.089	.308
Family income	.178	.282	.294	.271	.083	−.104	.240

Non-South	Age	Education	Experience	Occupation	Ln Weeks	Earnings	Ln Earnings	Earnings$^{1/3}$	Family Income
1									
.011	1								
.214	−.107	1							
−.083	.825	−.625	1						
.149	−.042	.605	−.388	1					
.036	−	.130	−.096	.126	1				
.150	−.050	.476	−.315	.541	−	1			
.153	−.105	.438	−.320	.462	.271	.726	1		
.181	−.097	.515	−.361	.561	−	.910	.921	1	
.144	−.055	.478	−.318	.528	−	.881	.658	.817	1

TABLE A2.9

Correlations from Project Talent Complete Data Sample
(N = 839)

	Race	Father's Education	Father's Occupation	Father Absent	Siblings	Test Score	Education	Experience	Occupation	Earnings	Ln Earnings	Earnings$^{1/3}$
Race	1											
Father's education	.041	1										
Father's occupation	.088	.488	1									
Father absent	−.116	−.031	−.016	1								
Siblings	−.136	−.108	−.164	.032	1							
Test score	.215	.276	.318	−.174	−.240	1						
Education	.022	.332	.332	−.122	−.204	.561	1					
Experience	.043	−.257	−.274	.127	.172	−.413	−.705	1				
Occupation	.076	.259	.264	−.094	−.157	.474	.643	−.469	1			
Earnings	.005	.144	.121	−.066	−.096	.203	.244	−.099	.261	1		
Ln earnings	.017	.149	.105	−.063	−.090	.203	.224	−.068	.250	.932	1	
Earnings$^{1/3}$	.015	.150	.115	−.065	−.095	.209	.237	−.083	.259	.972	.990	1

Note: Statistics are for hourly rather than annual earnings.

TABLE A2.10

Correlations from Project Talent Brothers Complete Data Sample
(N = 198)

	Race	Father's Education	Father's Occupation	Father Absent	Siblings	Test Score	Education	Occupation	Earnings	Ln Earnings
Race	1									
Father's education	.055	1								
Father's occupation	.026	.626	1							
Father absent	.032	.054	-.083	1						
Siblings	-.183	-.161	-.163	.237	1					
Test score	-.020	.367	.387	-.117	-.141	1				
Education	-.096	.465	.371	-.097	-.196	.632	1			
Occupation	-.057	.309	.356	-.134	-.113	.484	.706	1		
Earnings	.033	.068	.124	.026	-.146	.365	.392	.337	1	
Ln earnings	.036	.035	.096	.013	-.136	.356	.366	.321	.960	1

TABLE A2.11

Correlations from Kalamazoo Brothers Complete Data Sample
(N = 692)

	Father's Education	Father's Occupation	Father White Collar	Father Foreign	Father Absent	Siblings	Test Score	Age	Education	Experience	Occupation	Earnings	Ln Earnings	Earnings$^{1/3}$	Family Income
Race															
Father's education	1														
Father's occupation	.470	1													
Father white collar	.413	.723	1												
Father foreign	-.251	-.171	-.113	1											
Father absent	-.053	-.059	-.016	.021	1										
Siblings	-.250	-.224	-.193	.147	.114	1									
Test score	.261	.260	.200	-.109	-.136	-.276	1								
Age	-.182	-.165	-.113	.203	.013	.066	-.162	1							
Education	.400	.383	.377	-.081	-.164	-.328	.576	-.183	1						
Experience	-.310	-.289	-.243	.205	.075	.183	-.361	.925	-.544	1					
Occupation	.215	.218	.224	-.096	-.093	-.220	.453	-.105	.591	-.318	1				
Earnings	.171	.212	.243	-.042	-.045	-.155	.360	-.071	.432	-.228	.482	1			
Ln earnings	.162	.200	.213	-.045	-.047	-.152	.366	-.070	.409	-.218	.493	.942	1		
Earnings$^{1/3}$	.167	.210	.232	-.045	-.048	-.157	.373	-.073	.430	-.229	.503	.981	.988	1	
Family income	.173	.182	.218	-.032	-.029	-.183	.343	-.020	.413	-.177	.433	.847	.820	.845	1

TABLE A2.12

Correlations from OCG-II Complete Data Sample
(N = 15,817)

	Race	Mother's Education	Parental Income	Father's Education	Father's Occupation	Father White Collar	Father Absent	Siblings	Non-farm	Non-South	Education	Experience	Occupation	Income	Ln Income
Race	1														
Mother's education	.157	1													
Parental income	.148	.352	1												
Father's education	.134	.632	.377	1											
Father's occupation	.159	.392	.436	.522	1										
Father white collar	.108	.309	.356	.425	.790	1									
Father absent	-.119	-.164	-.121	.013	-.051	.014	1								
Siblings	-.157	-.310	-.224	-.327	-.290	-.237	-.046	1							
Nonfarm	.110	.211	.234	.278	.408	.337	.050	-.262	1						
Non-South	.276	.146	.150	.184	.151	.103	-.048	-.171	.190	1					
Education	.156	.466	.368	.473	.422	.361	-.042	-.360	.310	.195	1				
Experience	.023	-.251	-.113	-.239	-.119	-.084	-.000	.141	.173	.022	-.214	1			
Occupation	.174	.318	.307	.336	.385	.332	-.017	-.278	.254	.120	.615	-.044	1		
Income	.140	.180	.231	.182	.228	.194	-.032	-.162	.146	.118	.353	.080	.425	1	
Ln Income	.169	.182	.201	.177	.198	.156	-.041	-.146	.174	.136	.344	.034	.404	.725	1

TABLE A2.13

Reliability Estimates for Selected Measures of Economic Success

Measure of Success	Grouped	Includes Zeros	Data Base	Year	Age Range
1) Total income	Yes	Yes	CPS-Census match[a]	1959	14+
2) Total income	Yes	No	CPS-Census match[b]	1969	14+
3) Self-employment earnings	Yes	No	CPS-Census match[b]	1969	14+
4) Wage & salary earnings	Yes	No	CPS-Census match[b]	1969	14+
5) Husband's & wife's wage & salary earnings	Yes	Yes	CPS-IRS match[b]	1972	14+
6) Husband's & wife's wage & salary earnings	Yes	No	CPS-IRS match[b]	1972	14+
7) Earnings	No	No	OCG-II reinterview[c]	1973	20-64
8) Earnings	No	No	PSID[e]	1971	25-64
9) Duncan score	No	–	OCG-II reinterview[d]	1973	20-64
10) Duncan score	Yes	–	Census-CPS match[a]	1960	14+
11) Duncan score	Yes	–	PSID[e]	1971	25-64

S_{M1} = SD of observations in first survey listed; S_{M2} = SD in second survey.

r^* = correlation between surveys.

$\hat{S}_{E1}$ = SD of errors in first survey if errors are random, i.e..

$\hat{S}_{E2}$ = SD of errors in second survey if errors are random.

[a]Calculated by Siegel and Hodge (1968).
[b]Calculated by McClelland (*Final Report*, chapter 16).

N	Transformation	Approx. Mean	S_{M1}	S_{M2}	r*	$\hat{S}_{E1}$	$\hat{S}_{E2}$
~ 10,000	None	4,800	3,892	4,143	.823	1,370	1,952
6,443	None	7,881	6,579	7,167	.781	2,540	3,813
	Ln	8.581	.988	1.021	.841	.316	.440
343	None	10,010	10,676	11,098	.694	5,639	6,395
	Ln	8.637	1.173	1.182	.652	.687	.702
5,036	None	7,964	5,820	6,257	.842	1,792	2,915
	Ln	8.639	.972	.983	.875	.331	.361
39,273	None	8,034	7,506	7,504	.887	2,523	2,523
33,390	None	9,296	7,285	7,330	.904	2,186	2,341
	Ln	8.793	1.070	1.057	.922	.321	.274
763	None	11,131	8,001	—	.782	3,736	
	Ln	9.077	.741	—	.927	.200	—
2,255	None	11,371	7,224	—	.952	1,583	—
	Ln	9.161	.664	—	.864	.245	—
578	—	41.3	25.2	—	.86	9.43	—
~ 10,000	—	34.5	20.8	21.0	.861	7.53	8.05
1,263	—	41.4	21.3	—	.964	4.04	—

[c]Calculated by Jencks from data supplied by Bielby. The low r* for untransformed earnings derives from five outliers. For an analysis that excludes these outliers, plus all values below $1000, see Bielby and Hauser (1977).

[d]Calculated by Jencks (*Final Report*, chapter 13) from data supplied by Bielby.

[e]Calculated by Jencks (*Final Report*, chapter 13) using simplex model of status determination and 1969-71 panel data.

TABLE A2.14

Reliability Estimates for Measures of Education and Demographic Background

Variable	Data Base	Year	Age	Sex	N	S_{M1}	S_{M2}	r^*	$\hat{S}_E$
1) Education	Census-Post-Enumeration Survey match	1960	25+	M & F	5,000	3.58	3.61	.933	.93
2) Education	Census reinterview[a]	1960	25+	M & F	7,500	NA	NA	.915	NA
3) Education	Census-CPS match[a]	1970	25+	M	10,000	NA	NA	.887	NA
4) Education	Census-CPS match[a]	1970	25+	F	10,000	NA	NA	.875	NA
5) Education	CPS-OCG-II match[b]	1973	20-64	M	25,223	3.07	NA	.854	1.17
6) Education	PSID reinterview[c]	1968-75	25-64	M	767	2.97	2.99	.915	.87
1) Father's education	OCG-II reinterview[d]	1973	20-64	M	~ 549	4.19	4.14	.939	1.03
2) Father's education	Kalamazoo Brothers[e]	1973	35-59	M	391	3.28	3.28	.777	1.55
3) Father's education	Talent Twins[f]	1960	14-18	M & F	468	3.75	3.75	.820	1.59
4) Father's education	NLS father-son match[g]	1966	14-24	M	943	3.97	3.89	.954	.63
5) Father's education	OCG[h]	1962	25-34	M	3,000	3.82	3.87	.78	1.79
6) Father's education	PSID father-son	1976	23-30	M	219	3.59	3.39	.726	1.77

Variable	Source	Year	Age	Sex	N				
	reinterview[d]	19?3	20-64	M	549	24.27	23.73	.869	8.78
2) Father's occupation	Kalamazoo Brothers[e]	1973	35-59	M	409	22.04	22.04	.765	10.68
3) Father's occupation	Kalamazoo Brothers eliminating job changers[j]	1973	35-59	M	409	22.04	22.04 ~	~.85	~8.54
4) Father's occupation	NLS father-son match[g]	1966	14-24	M	661	24.02	NA	.89	~8.0
5) Father's occupation	OCG[h]	1962	25-34	M	2,000-3,000	23.21	24.46	.73	12.06
6) Father's occupation (grouped)	Talent Twins[f]	1960	14-18	M & F	481	23.24	23.24	.856	8.82
7) Father's occupation (grouped)	PSID father-son match[i]	1976	23-30	M	219	20.54	19.39	.772	9.23
1) Siblings	Kalamazoo Brothers[e]	1973	35-59	M	446	3.04	3.04	.942	.73

[a]Calculated by Bishop (1974).
[b]Hauser (in correspondence).
[c]Calculated by Bartlett from data tape.
[d]Bielby et al. (1977).
[e]Olneck (1976).
[f]Calculated by Jencks and Brown from data base described by Schoenfeldt (1968).
[g]Borus and Nestel (1975).
[h]Calculated by Jencks, assuming $r_{ED,OC}$ for men 55-64 should equal $r_{POPED,POPOC}$ for men 25-34 after weighting by the reciprocal of family size. (See Final Report, chapter 13.)
[i]Corcoran (1979).
[j]Estimated by assuming a 0.90 correlation between a father's true occupational status when a respondent reached 15 and when his brother reached 15 —a time interval averaging 4.5 years.

TABLE A3.1

Standardized Regressions of Occupational Status on Demographic Background in Eight Surveys[a]

	1962-73 Trend		1962 OCG (25-64)		1965 PA (25-64)	
	OCG	OCG-II				
1) White	.147	.090	.149	.112	.160	.114
2) Father native	–	–	–.046	–.021	[–.010]	[–.020]
3) Father's education	.127	.140	.140	.022	.275	[.038]
3a) Father's education^2	–	–	.034	[.003]	.057	[–.019]
4) Father's occupation	.190	.171	.188	.103	–	–
4a) Father's occupation^2	–	–	–.034	–.036	–	–
5) Father white collar	.089	.071	.079	.013	–	–
6) Father absent	–.061	[–.011]	–.065	–.019	–	–
7) Non-South	.024	[–.002]	[.009]	–.020	[–.010]	[–.038]
8) Nonfarm	.087	.078	.080	.068	.174	.092
9) Siblings	–.120	–.132	–.123	–.043	–.103	[–.003]
9a) Siblings^2	–	–	.030	[.011]	NS	NS
10) Mother's education	–	–	–	–	–	–
11) Parental income	–	–	–	–	–	–
Significant interactions[c]	–	–	4 × 9 (–)	9 × U (–)	1 × 7 (–)	8 × X (+)
Controls	–	–	–	U, X	–	U, X, CQ
R^2	.242	.208	.247	.460	.178	.435
Approximate SE of coefficients[b]	.009	.008	.009	.009	.029	.029

A = age
CQ = college quality (four dummies)
G = high school grades
Q = test score + test score^2 (where significant)
U = years of education + years of higher education + BA
U* = years of education
X = experience + experience^2 (where significant)
P = friends' educational plans in eleventh grade + own educational plans in eleventh grade + own occupational aspirations in eleventh grade

1972 PSID (25-64)			1973 OCG-II (25-64)		1964 Veterans (30-34)		
.126	.092	.077	.082	.071	.085	[.035]	.062
[−.047]	[−.029]	[.013]	−	−	−	−	−
.180	.145	[.041]	.058	−.019	.164	.113	[.043]
NS	NS	NS	−	−	NS	NS	NS
[.020]	[.013]	[.025]	.137	.102	.178	.141	[.058]
−.067	−.075	−.057	−	−	NS	NS	NS
.131	[.109]	−.007	.066	.032	NS	NS	NS
[−.021]	[−.016]	[.003]	.020	.020	[−.026]	[−.033]	[−.008]
[.022]	[.009]	[−.001]	[−.006]	−.034	[−.007]	−.069	[−.049]
.062	[.039]	.041	.072	.020	.121	.086	.076
−.113	−.078	[.001]	−.113	−.034	−	−	−
[.041]	[.038]	[.002]	−	−	−	−	−
−	−	−	.109	[−.002]	−	−	−
−	−	−	.112	.048	−	−	−
None	None	None	−	−	None	None	None
−	Q	Q, U, X	−	U*	−	Ω	Q, U
.169	.226	.158	.226	.407	.128	.244	.448
.024	.024	.024	.009	.009	.035	.035	.035

[a]All analyses are based on complete data samples. Coefficients in brackets are less than twice their standard error. Variables with a dash rather than a coefficient were not tested. Variables with NS were tested but not included because they were less than twice their standard error.

[b]Approximated using $1/N^{1/2}$. The standard error falls as R^2 rises, but it increases when the variable in question is correlated with others in the equation.

[c]Multiplicative interactions more than twice their standard error. To interpret variable numbers, see table 3.1. Signs of interactions shown in parenthesis.

TABLE A3.1 *(continued)*

	1972 Talent (29-39)			
1) White	[.032]	[−.031]	[.021]	[.027]
2) Father native	−	−	−	−
3) Father's education	.164	.108	[.056]	[.026]
3a) Father's education^2	NS	NS	NS	NS
4) Father's occupation	.162	.078	[.053]	[.019]
4a) Father's occupation^2	NS	NS	NS	NS
5) Father white collar	−	−	−	−
6) Father absent	−.079	[−.016]	[.004]	[.003]
7) Non-South	−	−	−	−
8) Nonfarm	−	−	−	−
9) Siblings	−.106	[−.028]	[−.024]	[.000]
9a) Siblings^2	NS	NS	NS	NS
10) Mother's education	−	−	−	−
11) Parental income	−	−	−	−
Significant interactions[c]	None	1 × Q (−)	1 × Q (−)	1 × Q (−)
Controls	−	Q	Q, G, P	Q, U
R^2	.112	.250	.316	.437
Approximate SE of coefficients	.035	.035	.035	.035

1973 Kalamazoo (35-39)			1966 NLS (45-59)	
−	−	−	.146	.102
[.013]	[.014]	[.041]	[.028]	[.027]
[.067]	[.027]	[−.055]	.177	[.024]
[.008]	[.023]	[−.034]	.059	[.030]
[.002]	[−.041]	[−.036]	.154	[.019]
NS	NS	NS	NS	NS
.118	.118	[.024]	[.043]	−.051
[−.053]	[−.020]	[−.016]	[.055]	.014
−	−	−	[.019]	[−.001]
−	−	−	.200	.131
−.131	−.062	[−.003]	−	−
.078	[.045]	[.039]	−	−
.090	[.068]	[.046]	−	−
−	−	−	−	−
2 × 3 (+)	None	None	3 × 4 (−)	3 × 4 (−)
				1 × U (+)
				8 × U (+)
[A]	[A], Q	[A], Q, U	−	U, X
.125	.244	.384	.242	.464
.038	.038	.038	.020	.020

Standardized Regressions of Ln Earnings on Demographic Background in Eight Surveys

	1961-72 Trend (25-64)		1961 OCG[a] (25-64)		1964 PA (25-64)	
	OCG[a]	OCG-II[a]				
1) White	.207	.122	.205	.172	.177	.125
2) Native father	–	–	–.041	–.034	–.063	–.071
3) Father's education	.082	.073	.091	.026	.174	.063
3a) Father's education²	–	–	NS	NS	NS	NS
4) Father's occupation	.103	.087	.106	.071	–	–
4a) Father's occupation²	–	–	NS	NS	–	–
5) Father white collar	[.023]	[.010]	[.019]	[–.008]	–	–
6) Father absent	–.049	–.031	–.049	–.022	–	–
7) Non-South	.093	.063	.108	.050	.060	[.017]
8) Nonfarm	.113	.087	.079	.090	.192	.136
9) Siblings	–.068	–.065	–.070	–.024	–.073	[–.009]
9a) Siblings²	–	–	[.013]	[.008]	NS	NS
10) Mother's education	–	–	–	–	–	–
11) Family income	–	–	–	–	–	–
Significant Interactions	–	–	1 × 4 (+)	1 × 4 (+)	3 × 7 (–)	3 × 7 (–)
Controls	–	–	–	U, X	–	U, X
R²	.165	.096	.167	.244	.194	.321
Approximate SE of beta[e]	.009	.008	.009	.009	.029	.029

[a]Dependent Variable = Ln Grouped Income.
[b]Dependent Variable = Ln Ungrouped Income.
[c]Dependent Variable = Ln Grouped Earnings.

1971 PSID (25-64)			1972 OCG-II (25-64)[b]		1964 Veterans (30-34)[c]		
.146	.092	.094	.105	.099	.130	.095	.100
−.080	−.062	−.044	−	−	−	−	−
.103	.071	[.033]	[.013]	−.029	[.023]	−.014	[−.032]
[−.034]	[−.010]	[−.010]	−	−	NS	NS	NS
[−.053]	[−.056]	[−.056]	.054	.035	.203	.176	.158
[−.011]	[.010]	[.018]	−	−	NS	NS	NS
.117	.087	[.041]	[.001]	[−.018]	NS	NS	NS
[−.013]	[−.010]	[.005]	[−.007]	[−.007]	[−.023]	[−.028]	[−.019]
.055	[.033]	[.009]	.050	.035	.135	.091	.083
.108	.091	.070	.082	.053	.075	.050	[.047]
−.095	−.055	[−.005]	−.039	[.004]	−	−	−
NS	NS	NS	−	−	−	−	−
−	−	−	.064	[.005]	−	−	−
−	−	−	.098	.064	−	−	−
3 × 4 (−)	3 × 4 (−)	1 × 9 (+)	−	−	None	None	None
3 × 9 (−)	3 × 9 (−)	3 × 9 (−)					
−	Q	Q, U, X	−	U*, X	−	Q	Q, U, X
.117	.178	.298	.089	.142	.124	.185	.203
.024	.024	.024	.008	.008	.035	.035	.035

[d]Dependent Variable = Ln Hourly Earnings.
[e]See note b, table A3.1.

All notes for table A3.1 also apply.

	1972 Talent (27-29)[d]			
1) White	[−.008]	[−.033]	[−.016]	[−.016]
2) Native father	−	−	−	−
3) Father's education	.124	.099	.075	.076
3a) Father's education^2	NS	NS	NS	NS
4) Father's occupation	[.033]	[−.002]	[−.021]	[.012]
4a) Father's occupation^2	NS	NS	NS	NS
5) Father white collar	NS	NS	NS	NS
6) Father absent	[−.057]	[−.033]	[−.027]	[−.024]
7) Non-South	−	−	−	−
8) Nonfarm	−	−	−	−
9) Siblings	−.071	[−.043]	[−.039]	[−.034]
9a) Siblings^2	NS	NS	NS	NS
10) Mother's education	−	−	−	−
11) Family income	−	−	−	−
Significant Interactions	None	None	None	None
Controls	−	Q	Q, G, P	Q, U
R^2	.032	.054	.075	.074
Approximate SE of coefficients	.035	.035	.035	.035

1973 Kalamazoo (35-39)[c]			1966 NLS (45-59)	
–	–	–	.128	.088
[–.012]	[–.012]	[.006]	–.046	–.051
[.075]	[.040]	[–.002]	.152	.048
NS	NS	NS	[–.028]	[–.019]
[.035]	[.003]	[–.004]	[.042]	[–.020]
NS	NS	NS	NS	NS
.131	.131	[.084]	[.040]	[.045]
–.021	[–.006]	[.031]	[–.063]	[–.003]
–	–	–	[.017]	[–.003]
–	–	–	.202	.138
–.102	[–.044]	[–.011]	–	–
[.078]	[.050]	[.048]	–	–
[–.040]	[–.059]	[–.075]	–	–
–	–	–	–	–
2 × 3 (+)	None	None	2 × 3 (+)	2 × 3 (+)
[A]	[A], Q	[A], Q, U	–	U, X
.080	.164	.207	.151	.242
.038	.038	.038	.020	.020

TABLE A3.3

Bivariate Regressions of Respondent Characteristics on Characteristics of Male Head of Family in Which Respondent Grew Up, by Type of Family[a]

Dependent Variable	Male Head's Education		Male Head's Occupation	
	Intact Family	"Other Male" Head	Intact Family	"Other Male" Head
Education				
B	.393	.412	.0726	.0808
(SE)	(.007)	(.042)	(.0014)	(.0085)
R^2	.188	.169	.188	.165
Occupation				
B	2.064	1.682	.4879	.4232
(SE)	(.055)	(.272)	(.0098)	(.0525)
R^2	.108	.077	.175	.123
Ln income				
B	.0450	.0352	.0097	.0078
(SE)	(.0020)	(.0099)	(.0004)	(.0022)
R^2	.049	.036	.067	.035

[a]All regressions are restricted to OCG men aged 25 to 64 with complete demographic background data. Respondents raised in families headed by females or in families not including the mother are excluded.

Education and occupation regressions cover 11,773 men from intact families and 462 men from families headed by an "other male."

Income regressions cover 9,537 men from intact families and 311 men from families headed by an "other male."

TABLE A3.4

Sibling Correlations for NORC, Kalamazoo, Talent, and Taubman Twin Samples

	Q'	U'	D'	Y'
Test Score (Q)				
NORC	NA			
Kalamazoo	.469			
Talent	.580			
Education (U)				
NORC	NA	.528		
Kalamazoo	.400	.549		
Talent	.451	.546		
Taubman-DZ	NA	.545		
Taubman-MZ	NA	.765		
Occupation (D)				
NORC	NA	.401	.371	
Kalamazoo	.300	.378	.309	
Talent	.359	.417	.329	
Ln earnings (Y)				
NORC	NA	.171	.230	.129
Kalamazoo	.169	.269	.218	.220
Talent	.216	.210	.125	.208
Taubman-DZ	NA	.292	–	.295
Taubman-MZ	NA	.406	–	.545

Note: Individual level correlations for NORC, Kalamazoo, and Talent appear in tables A2.6, A2.10, and A2.11. Taubman (1976b) reported $r_{YU} = 0.44$ for both MZ and DZ twins. Here, as in tables A2.6, A2.10, and A2.11, NORC, Kalamazoo, and Talent correlations are based on a file in which all pairs appear twice, with order reversed. Taubman's twin correlations are based on random ordering.

TABLE A4.1

First Principal Components of Talent's Academic Ability, Verbal, Quantitative, and Rote-Memory Tests[a]

| | Factor Loadings | | | | | | | |
| | Observed | | | | Corrected for Unreliability | | | |
	Academic Ability	Verbal Ability	Quantitative Ability	Rote Memory	Academic Ability	Verbal Ability	Quantitative Ability	Rote Memory
English	.821	.850			.853	.877		
Literature	.783	.855			.843	.895		
Social studies	.822	.882			.879	.920		
Mathematics information	.891		.911		.933		.953	
Arithmetic computation[b]	.638		.652		.641		.660	
Arithmetic reasoning	.789		.807		.857		.864	
Introductory mathematics	.870		.903		.910		.943	
Advanced mathematics	.761		.809		.827		.864	
Physical science	.833		.828		.890		.879	
Biological science	.694		.670		.797		.749	
Reading comprehension		.876				.905		
Vocabulary		.906				.942		
Memory for sentences				.805				.659
Memory for words				.805				.846
Percent of variance explained by first principal component[c]	63.0	76.4	64.4	64.9	85.1	95.0	86.5	80.0

[a] Talent complete data sample (N = 839).
[b] Reliability estimates not available.
[c] Principal components of tests listed. These groupings are a priori. Resulting components are neither independent nor orthogonal.

Correlations of Selected Talent Tests, Factors, and Composites with Later Outcomes[a]

	Measures of Success				Factors			
Factor or Composite	Educa-tion	Occu-pation	Hourly Earn-ings	Ln Hourly Earn-ings	Q_{AF}	Q_{VF}	Q_{QF}	Q_{RF}
Factors								
Academic ability (Q_{AF})[b]	.585	.490	.211	.204	1.000			
Verbal ability (Q_{VF})[c]	.560	.487	.200	.202	.924	1.000		
Quantitative ability (Q_{QF})[d]	.564	.460	.205	.194	.980	.841	1.000	
Rote memory (Q_{RF})[e]	.234	.185	.089	.090	.417	.412	.397	1.000
Composites								
Academic ability (Q_{AC})[f]	.561	.474	.203	.203	.953	.928	.925	.423
Verbal ability (Q_{VC})[g]	.531	.470	.182	.188	.905	.959	.826	.442
Quantitative ability (Q_{QC})[h]	.554	.445	.208	.198	.932	.772	.966	.356
Selected Tests								
English (Q_E)	.471	.423	.164	.173	.823	.850	.752	.421
Social studies (Q_{SS})	.499	.436	.176	.172	.821	.882	.730	.353
Introductory mathematics (Q_M)	.516	.421	.191	.189	.870	.711	.903	.338
Table reading (Q_{TR})	.003	.054	.087	.109	.085	.063	.088	.067
Clerical checking (Q_{CC})	.051	.054	.092	.107	.040	.011	.047	.048
Reading comprehension (Q_{RC})	.489	.405	.178	.176	.780	.875	.731	.341
Vocabulary (Q_{VOC})	.482	.428	.184	.191	.831	.906	.779	.370
Memory for sentences (Q_{MS})	.095	.071	.040	.037	.209	.209	.206	.805
All thirty tests[i]	.609	.520	.219	.226	–	–	–	–

[a] Talent complete data sample (N = 839).

[b] First principal component of English, Literature, Social Studies, Mathematics Information, Arithmetic Computation, Arithmetic Reasoning, Introductory Mathematics, Advanced Mathematics, Physical Science, and Biological Science.

[c] First principal component of the English, Literature, Social Studies, Reading Comprehension, and Vocabulary tests.

[d] First principal component of the Mathematics Information, Arithmetic Computation, High School Mathematics, Advanced Mathematics, Physical Science, and Biological Science tests.

[e] First principal component of Memory for Sentences and Memory for Words tests.

Composite			Selected Tests							
Q_{AC}	Q_{VC}	Q_{QC}	Q_E	Q_{SS}	Q_M	Q_{TR}	Q_{CC}	Q_{RC}	Q_{VOC}	Q_{MS}
1.000										
.933	1.000									
.904	.770	1.000								
.893	.949	.715	1.000							
.754	.773	.656	.662	1.000						
.855	.713	.953	.669	.609	1.000					
.085	.084	.071	.095	.070	.080	1.000				
.022	.034	.034	.031	.003	.046	.458	1.000			
.870	.789	.678	.713	.704	.623	.039	−.017	1.000		
.828	.875	.709	.723	.753	.643	.049	−.007	.748	1.000	
.231	.239	.174	.235	.176	.169	.073	.007	.192	.199	1.00
—	—	—	—	—	—	—	—	—	—	—

[f]Talent's Academic Composite, C-002, a weighted sum of Mathematics Information, Vocabulary, English, Reading Comprehension, Creativity, Abstract Reasoning, Arithmetic Reasoning, and High School Mathematics.

[g]Talent's Verbal Composite, C-003, a weighted sum of Literature, Vocabulary, and English.

[h]Talent's Quantitative Aptitude Composite, C-004, a weighted sum of Mathematics Information, Arithmetic Reasoning, High School Mathematics, and Advanced Mathematics.

[i]Multiple correlation of each measure of success with all thirty tests, corrected for degrees of freedom, i.e., $\overline{R}$.

TABLE A4.3

Regressions of Occupational Status on Adult Test Scores Controlling Selected Background and Intervening Variables

Sample (Year of Occupation)	Variables Controlled									Coefficient of Test Score		% Reduction in Test-Score Coefficient	R²
	NONE	MEASURED BKG	TEST SCORE²	ED	EDPASTHS	BA	VOCTRAIN[a]	WORKEXP	JOB TENURE[b]	B	Beta		
PSID (1971) N = 1,774	X									.503	.358	–	.128
		X[c]	X[e]							.334	.238	33.6	.226
		X[c]	X[e]	X	X	X	X			.099	.071	80.3	.458
		X[c]	X[e]	X	X	X	X	X	X	.099	.070	80.4	.458
NORC Veterans (1964) N = 803	X									.705	.431	–	.186
		X[d]	X[e]	X						.603	.369	14.5	.244
		X[d]	X[e]	X	X	X				.230	.140	67.4	.448

All coefficients are larger than twice their standard error.

[a]VOCTRAIN = vocational training.

[b]JOB TENURE = years on current job.

[c]White, father's education, father's occupation, father white collar, father foreign, father absent, siblings, nonfarm upbringing, non-South upbringing, father's occupation², and siblings².

[d]White, father's education, father's occupation, no male head, nonfarm upbringing, and non-South upbringing.

[e]Test score² is orthogonal to test score, so it is not responsible for the change in the coefficient of test score in these equations.

TABLE A4.4

Regressions of Earnings on Adolescent Test Scores Controlling Selected Intervening Variables

Sample (age and type of earnings)	MEASURED BKG	ALL BKG	PERSONALITY	HS CURRICULUM	GRADES	T-INFLUENCE	P-INFLUENCE	F-PLANS	EDPLANS	OCPLANS	EARNPLANS	ED	EDPASTHS	BA	WORKEXP	OCCUPATION	B	Beta	% Reduction in Test-Score Coefficient	R²
Talent representative Age 28 Hourly Earnings/$5.26	X[a]																.0046	.171	—	.057
	X[a]		X														.0025	.092	46.2	.073
	X[a]		X	X	X												.0021	.078	54.5	.080
	X[a]		X	X	X	X	X	X	X	X							[.0017]	.062	64.0	.086
	X[a]		X	X	X	X	X	X	X	X	X	X					[.0016]	.058	66.4	.115
	X[a]		X	X	X	X	X	X	X	X	X	X			X		[.0016]	.060	65.2	.127
	X[a]		X	X	X	X	X	X	X	X	X	X				X	[.0011]	.039	77.1	.127
	X[a]		X	X	X	X	X	X	X	X	X	X			X	X	[.0011]	.041	76.1	.139
Wisconsin Age 27 to 28 Annual Earnings/$7,574	X[a]																.0032	.137	—	.048
	X[a]				X	X	X	X	X								.0020	.085	38.0	.063
	X[a]				X	X	X	X	X	X							.0016	.068	50.2	.067
	X[a]				X	X	X	X	X	X		X					[.0013]	.056	59.2	.069
	X[a]				X	X	X	X	X	X		X				X	[.0012]	.050	63.3	.076
EEO Age 30 to 31 Annual Earnings/$11,303	X[c]																[−.0012]	−.045	—	.092
	X[c]				X	X	X	X	X								−.0026	−.098	−120.7	.106
	X[c]				X	X	X	X	X	X							−.0026	−.099	−121.5	.106
	X[c]				X	X	X	X	X	X		X					[−.0025]	−.095	−113.3	.113
	X[c]				X	X	X	X	X	X		X				X	[−.0027]	−.099	−123.0	.124
Talent Brothers Age 28 to 29 Hourly Earnings/$4.75	X[b]																.0108	.379	—	.150
	X[b]											X	X	X			.0060	.209	44.9	.205
	X[b]											X	X	X		X	.0059	.205	45.8	.209
		X[c]															.0075	.263	—	NA
		X[c]										X	X	X			[.0039]	.135	48.6[d]	NA
		X[c]										X	X	X		X	[.0037]	.130	50.3[d]	NA
Kalamazoo Brothers Age 35 to 59 Annual Earnings/$16,746	X[b]																.0093	.313	—	.142
	X[b]											X	X	X			.0050	.167	46.8	.202
	X[b]											X	X	X		X	.0033	.110	64.7	.270
		X[c]															.0102	.341	—	NA
		X[c]										X	X	X			.0080	.269	21.2[d]	NA
		X[c]										X	X	X		X	.0066	.225	34.1[d]	NA

Coefficients less than twice their standard error are in brackets.

[a] Father's education, father's occupation, mother's education, parental income.

TABLE A4.5

Regressions of Ln Earnings on Adolescent Test Scores Controlling Selected Intervening Variables

Sample (age and type of earnings)	MEASURED BKG	ALL BKG	PERSONALITY	HS CURRICULUM	GRADES	T-INFLUENCE	P-INFLUENCE	F-PLANS	EDPLANS	OCPLANS	EARNPLANS	ED	EDPASTHS	BA	EARLYOC	WORKEXP	OCCUPATION	Coeff. of Test Score B	Coeff. of Test Score Beta	% Reduction in Test-Score Coefficient	R^2
Talent representative Age 28 to 29 Ln hourly earnings	X[a]																	.00477	.176	–	.057
	X[a]		X															.00303	.112	36.5	.068
	X[a]		X	X	X													.00256	.094	46.3	.077
	X[a]		X	X	X	X	X											[.00210]	[.077]	56.0	.102
	X[a]		X	X	X	X	X	X	X	X	X							[.00216]	[.080]	54.7	.119
	X[a]		X	X	X	X	X	X	X	X	X	X						[.00159]	[.058]	66.7	.113
	X[a]		X	X	X	X	X	X	X	X	X	X				X	X	[.00164]	[.061]	65.6	.131
Talent Brothers Age 28 to 29 Ln hourly earnings	X[b]																	.01152	.385	–	.147
	X[b]											X						.00678	.226	41.2	.195
	X[b]											X					X	.00667	.222	42.1	.200
		X[c]																.00996	.333	–	NA
		X[c]										X						[.00667]	[.223]	33.0[d]	NA
		X[c]										X					X	[.00652]	[.218]	34.5[d]	NA
Kalamazoo Brothers Age 35 to 59 Ln earnings	X[b]																	.0094	.320	–	.137
	X[b]											X	X	X				.0056	.191	40.4	.202
	X[b]											X	X	X			X	.0038	.129	59.6	.283
		X[c]																.0105	.357	–	NA
		X[c]										X	X	X				.0086	.293	18.1[d]	NA
		X[c]										X	X	X			X	.0072	.245	31.4[d]	NA

Coefficients less than twice their standard errors are in brackets.

[a] Father's education, father's occupation, mother's education, and family income.
[b] Father's education, father's occupation, siblings.
[c] Controlled using differences between brothers.
[d] Percent reduction in difference between brothers.

TABLE A5.1

Standardized Regressions of Talent's Self-Assessed Personality Traits
When Predicting Hourly Earnings, and Entering Each Trait Separately[a]

	(1)	(2)	(3)	(4)
Sociability	.130	.116	.111	.098
Social sensitivity	.136	.107	.090	.075
Impulsiveness	.028	[.013]	[.014]	[.015]
Vigor	.120	.104	.087	.077
Calmness	.127	.097	.077	.067
Tidiness	.127	.110	.092	.080
Culture	.109	.085	.075	[.059]
Leadership	.215	.202	.191	.181
Self-confidence	.136	.111	.092	.096
Mature personality	.156	.132	.107	.105
Controls				
Background		X	X	X
Test score			X	X
Grades			X	X
Education[b]				X
$\bar{R}^2$ for controls only		.026	.040	.065
$\bar{R}^2$ with leadership[c]		.065	.073	.094

Coefficients in brackets are not significant at the 0.05 level, two-tailed.

[a]Sample includes 875 Talent males with complete data on self-assessed personality measures, background controls, test score, grades, years of education, and hourly earnings.

[b]Years of education, college graduation, and years of graduate school.

[c]The self-assessments other than leadership did not raise $\bar{R}^2$ significantly.

TABLE A5.2

Talent Questions Relating to Student Activities and Attitudes

Social Activities

Age on first date

How old were you when you first went out on a date? A. I have never been on a date. B. 12 or younger. C. 13 or 14. D. 15. E. 16. F. 17 or older.

Coding: A = 19/B = 10/C = 13.5/D = 15/E = 16/F = 17.

Dates per week

On the average, how many dates do you have in a week? A. I never have dates. B. About 1. C. About 2. D. About 3. E. About 4 or 5. F. About 6 or 7.

Coding: A = 0/B = 1/C = 2/D = 3/E = 4.5/F = 6.5.

Times gone steady

How many times have you gone "steady" in the past three years? A. None. B. Once. C. Twice. D. Three times. E. Four times. F. Five times or more.

Coding: A = 0/B = 1/C = 2/D = 3/E = 4/F = 6.

Times out per week

On the average, how many evenings a week during the school year do you usually go out for fun and recreation? A. Less than one. B. One. C. Two. D. Three. E. Four or five. F. Six or seven.

Coding: A = 0.3/B = 1/C = 2/D = 3/E = 4.5/F = 6.5.

Student Employment

During the school year, about how many hours a week do you work for pay? Do not include chores done around your own home. A. None. B. About 1 to 5 hours. C. About 6 to 10 hours. D. About 11 to 15 hours. E. About 16 to 20 hours. F. About 21 hours or more.

Coding: A = 0/B = 3/C = 8/D = 13/E = 18/F = 22.

Intellectual Reading (principal component four questions)[a]

How many books have you read (not including those required for school) in the past 12 months? Don't count magazines or comic books. A. None. B. 1 to 5. C. 6 to 10. D. 11 to 15. E. 15 to 20. F. 21 or more.

Coding: A = 0/B = 3/C = 8/D = 13/E = 18/F = 21.

How many books or magazines have you read in each of the following groups (not including those required for school) in the past 12 months? Mark your answers as follows: A. None. B. 1. C. 2. D. 3. E. 4. F. 5 or more.

—Science, nonfiction.

—Plays, poetry, essays, literary criticism, or classics.

—Politics, world affairs, biography, autobiography, historical novels.

Coding: A = 0/B = 1/C = 2/D = 3/E = 4/F = 6.

Science Fiction Reading

Included in previous question. Response category asks about "science fiction books or magazines (not comic books)."

Cultural Events

How often have you done any one or more of the following in the past three years? Mark your answers as follows: A. Very often. B. Often. C. Occasionally. D. Rarely. E. Only once. F. Never.

—Attending concerts, lectures, plays (not motion pictures), ballet; visiting art galleries or museums.

Coding: A = 5/B = 4/C = 3/D = 2/E = 1/F = 0.

Hobbies (constructed by Project Talent but altered to omit attendance at cultural events)[b]

How often have you done any one or more of the following in the past three years? Include extracurricular activities at school, but do not include things done for school assignments. In each group of activities, answer for one or more in the group.

—Drawing, painting, sculpting, or decorating.

—Acting, singing, or dancing for a public performance.

—Collecting stamps, coins, rocks, insects, etc.

—Building model airplanes, ships, trains, cars, etc.

—Working with photographic equipment (do not include taking occasional snapshots).

—Making jewelry, pottery, or leatherwork.

—Making or repairing electrical or electronic equipment.

Hobbies (continued)

—Cabinet making or woodworking.
—Metal working.
—Mechanical or auto repair.
—Raising or caring for animals or pets.
—Sewing, knitting, crocheting, or embroidering.
—Cooking.
—Gardening, raising flowers, or raising vegetables.

Participation in Sports (constructed by Project Talent)[b]

How often have you done any one or more of the following in the past three years?
—Playing baseball, football, or basketball.
—Play golf or tennis; swimming.
—Play hockey, lacrosse, or handball; boxing, wrestling, track, field events.
—Go bicycling, ice skating, skiing, canoeing, horseback riding.

Insurance Important

For a man who has a wife and children, having a life insurance policy is: A. Extremely
important. B. Very important. C. Important. D. Neither important nor unimportant.
E. Unimportant. F. Not at all important.
Coding: A = 6, B = 5, C = 4, D = 3, E = 2, F = 1, no answer = 4.[c]

Education Necessary

For each of the following statements indicate how much you agree or disagree. Mark one of
the following choices for each statement: A. Agree strongly. B. Agree. C. Neither agree
nor disagree. D. Disagree. E. Disagree strongly.
It is not necessary to have a college education to be a leader in the community.
Coding: A = 1, B = 2, C = 3, D = 4, E = 5, no answer = 6.[c]
(Other agree-disagree statements referred to by the question not used in constructing this
variable.)

Work Orientation

Imagine that you have been working for an employer for several years. How important do
you think each of the following conditions would be in influencing you to quit to go to
work for another employer? Mark your answers as follows: A. Extremely important.
B. Very important. C. Important. D. Neither important nor unimportant. E. Unimpor-
tant. F. Not at all important.
—If I could get better pay at another place.
Coding: A = 6, B = 5, C = 4, D = 3, E = 2, F = 1, no answer = 2.[c]
—If the work was not interesting enough.
—If I do not receive expected promotions or salary increases.
Scores on first question define the variable labelled "materialistic."
Scores on second question define the variable labelled "interest."
Scores on third question define the variable labelled "advancement."

Perception of Ability (principal component six questions)[d]

For the following statements, indicate how often each applied to you. Please answer the
questions sincerely. Your answers will not affect your grades in any way. Mark one of
the following choices for each statement: A. Almost always. B. Most of the time.
C. About half the time. D. Not very often. E. Almost never.
—I seem to accomplish very little compared to the amount of time I spend studying.
—I enjoy writing reports or compositions.
—I have difficulty with the mechanics of English composition.
—My grades on written examinations or reports have been lowered because of careless errors
in spelling, grammar, or punctuation.
—When studying for a test, I am able to pick out important points to learn.
—I have trouble remembering what I read.

Coding for these questions was on an equal-interval scale, with high scores going to those
who perceived themselves as having greater ability.

TABLE A5.2 *(continued)*

Grades

The following questions ask you to report grades in courses you have taken in the ninth grade or later. Please consider only semester grades. If you have not taken any courses in the topic, skip the item. In these questions, choose the one answer that best describes your grades. Mark your answers as follows: A. All A's or equivalent. B. Mostly A's or equivalent. C. Mostly A's and B's or equivalent. D. Mostly B's and C's or equivalent. E. Mostly C's and D's or equivalent. F. Mostly D's or below or equivalent.

If your school does not use letter grades, please use the following equivalents: For a grade of A: excellent, 90-100; for a grade of B: good, 80-90; for a grade of C: average, 70-79; for a grade of D: fair, 60-69; for a grade below D: failing, 59 or lower.

—My grades in mathematics have been:
—My grades in science courses have been:
—My grades in foreign languages have been:
—My grades in history and social studies courses have been:
—My grades in all courses starting with ninth grade have been:
    Coding: A = 6, B = 5, C = 4, D = 3, E = 2, F = 1.[e]

[a]Principal component explained 56.2 percent of the variance in responses to these four questions.

[b]See Project Talent (1972) for detailed coding.

[c]Nonresponse for these questions ranged from 28 to 46 percent. Since the absence of specific plans or ideas about the future is itself a personal characteristic, it did not make sense to omit individuals who did not respond. Instead, we ran regressions of education, occupation, hourly earnings, and ln hourly earnings on each question, assigning nonrespondents a valid value and including a dummy for nonresponse. The coefficient of the dummy indicated that in terms of education, occupational status, and earnings, nonrespondents were like some specific group of respondents. For example, 38 percent did not answer the question on the importance of life insurance. They were similar in all outcomes to men who said life insurance was "important." We therefore coded the two groups in the same way. This was also possible for other questions.

[d]The principal component explains 34.3 percent of the variance in responses to these six questions.

[e]Recoding grades on the usual four-point scale (As = 4.0, Bs = 3.0, etc.) lowered their correlation with all outcomes.

TABLE A5.3

Standardized Regressions of Occupational Status on Kalamazoo Teacher Ratings of Personality Traits[a]

| | r | 389 Individuals | | | | 105 Pairs of Brothers[b] | |
		Ratings Entered Separately		All Significant Ratings Entered[c]		Ratings Entered Separately	
Cooperativeness	.208	.099	[−.009]		−.111	[.025]	[−.064]
Dependability	.242	.121	[.009]			[.072]	[.008]
Executive ability	.240	.135	[.050]			[−.001]	[.003]
Emotional control	.212	.108	[.012]			[.011]	[−.001]
Industriousness	.301	.203	.097	.203	.166	.318	.243
Initiative	.256	.130	[.074]			[−.027]	[.012]
Integrity	.198	[.091]	[−.003]			[.020]	[−.049]
Perseverance	.288	.194	[.081]			.397	.300
Appearance	.237	.123	[.044]			[.032]	[.009]
Controls							
Measured background		X	X	X	X		
All background common to brothers						X	X
Test score		X	X	X	X	X	X
Education			X		X		X
R̄² controls only				.193	.360		
R̄² significant traits				.229	.371		

Coefficients in brackets are not significant at the 0.05 level, two-tailed.

[a]Kalamazoo respondents aged 35 to 59 with complete data on father's education, father's occupation, siblings, test score, education, initial occupation, occupation, earnings, and nine teacher ratings.

[b]Pairs of brothers must both have data on test score, education, initial occupation, occupation, earnings, and the nine teacher ratings. In addition, at least one brother must report father's education, father's occupation, and siblings. Regressions based on differences between brothers.

[c]Traits entered in order of contribution to explained variance, until no unentered measure had a statistically significant effect.

TABLE A5.4

Standardized Regressions of Earnings on Kalamazoo Teacher Ratings of Personality Traits[a]

	r	(1)	(2)
Cooperativeness	.177	[.091]	[.015]
Dependability	.149	[.051]	[−.033]
Executive ability	.262	.184	.126
Emotional control	.147	[.061]	[−.009]
Industriousness	.181	[.096]	[.016]
Initiative	.219	.119	[.080]
Integrity	.135	[.047]	[−.021]
Perseverance	.163	[.085]	[−.001]
Appearance	.200	.115	[.059]
Controls			
Measured background		X	X
Test score		X	X
Education			X
R̄² controls only		.109	.195
R̄² with executive ability[b]		.139	.207

Coefficients in brackets are not significant at the 0.05 level, two-tailed.

[a]For sample definitions see note a, table A5.3.

[b]After executive ability was entered, no other measure had a significant effect on earnings. Controlling occupation decreased the coefficient for executive ability to 0.113, and controlling early occupation as well decreased it to 0.108.

TABLE A6.1

Linear Regressions of Current Occupational Status on Education with Selected Controls

		Variables Controlled					
Sample	None	Measured Back-ground[a]	All Back-ground[c]	Test Score	Measured Back-ground[a] & Test Score	All Back-ground[c] & Test Score	All Back-ground,[c] Test Score, & First Occupation
1970 Census							
B	4.337						
(SE)	(.034)						
$\bar{R}^2$	.385						
1962 OCG							
B	4.105	3.354					
(SE)	(.050)	(.058)					
$\bar{R}^2$	.371	.411					
1962 OCG Brothers[b]							
B	3.883	3.258	3.058				
(SE)	(.071)	(.081)	NA				
$\bar{R}^2$	.320	.358	NA				
1971 PSID							
B	3.910	3.579		3.664	3.438		
(SE)	(.119)	(.139)		(.135)	(.148)		
$\bar{R}^2$	.382	.391		.386	.393		
1964 Veterans							
B	5.070	4.677		4.385	4.131		
(SE)	(.242)	(.258)		(.287)	(.296)		
$\bar{R}^2$	.354	.378		.368	.387		
1974 NORC Brothers							
B	4.634	4.098	3.193				
(SE)	(.363)	(.419)	(.487)				
$\bar{R}^2$	.352	.367	.449				
1972 Talent							
B	6.268	5.992		5.361	5.294		
(SE)	(.258)	(.284)		(.306)	(.321)		
$\bar{R}^2$	.413	.417		.431	.430		
1971-72 Talent Brothers							
B	7.324	7.307	6.613	6.912	7.098	6.506	
(SE)	(.525)	(.595)	(1.091)	(.678)	(.713)	(1.206)	
$\bar{R}^2$	.495	.508	.508	.495	.506	.503	
1973 Kalamazoo Brothers							
B	5.012	5.031	4.002	4.192	4.280	3.499	2.150
(SE)	(.261)	(.302)	(.524)	(.314)	(.342)	(.557)	(.639)
$\bar{R}^2$	.348	.346	.407	.366	.369	.416	.441

[a]The demographic background variables controlled in each sample appear in the notes for table 6.2.
[b]Based on 5,780 men reporting their oldest brother's education and with complete data on other items. For method of computing column 3, see note on p. 170.
[c]Family background controlled by regressing the difference between brothers' occupational statuses on the difference between their educational attainments and other traits indicated.

TABLE A6.2

Regressions of Current Occupational Status on Education, by Race

Sample	Years of Education	Years of Higher Education	BA	$\bar{R}^2$	Estimated Effect of Four Years of College	Other Variables Controlled[a]
1970 Census						
White (N = 23,615)	3.217 (.065)	2.211 (.173)	4.165 (.790)	.407	25.9	experience, experience²
Nonwhite (N = 2,082)	1.481 (.134)	5.015 (.560)	[2.891] (2.910)	.414	28.9	experience, experience²
1962 OCG						
White (N = 10,395)	2.708 (.094)	2.365 (.299)	5.221 (1.283)	.428	25.5	measured background, experience, experience²
Nonwhite (N = 1,110)	.804 (.152)	3.509 (.866)	21.103 (4.012)	.419	38.4	measured background, experience, experience²
1972 PSID						
White (N = 1,260)[b]	1.476 (.297)	3.379 (.703)	5.129 (2.552)	.417	24.6	measured background, test score, vocational training, experience, experience²
Nonwhite (N = 514)[b]	1.473 (.273)	[1.116] (1.085)	25.166 (5.298)	.523	35.5	measured background, test score, vocational training, experience, experience²
1966 NLS 45-49-year-olds						
White (N = 2,580)[b]	2.043 (.194)	3.112 (.643)	5.413 (2.747)	.431	16.0	measured background, vocational training, experience, experience²
Nonwhite (N = 250)[b]	.671 (.322)	7.219 (2.256)	[-.857] (10.921)	.445	30.7	measured background, vocational training, experience, experience²

[a] For a list of the background variables controlled in each sample see table 6.2.
[b] Weighted N. Unweighted N is larger for nonwhites and smaller for whites.

TABLE A6.3

Regressions of Current Occupational Status on Education, by Test Score

Sample & Test Score Group[a]	Years of Education	Years of Higher Education	BA	Standard Deviation of Residuals	$\bar{R}^2$	Other Variables Controlled[b]
Veterans (30-34)						
Below 31st percentile (N = 236)	[.557] (.612)	5.003 (2.219)	[18.451] (11.158)	16.504	.142	measured background, test score
31st to 64th percentile (N = 264)	[.762] (.892)	5.845 (1.648)	[3.914] (6.396)	15.882	.434	measured background, test score
Above 64th percentile (N = 303)	[3.569] (1.868)	[.690] (2.357)	[6.467] (4.830)	19.059	.376	measured background, test score
Talent (28-29)						
Below 90 (N = 173)	5.698 (1.453)			17.212	.214	measured background, test score, education², experience
90 to 110 (N = 395)	5.075 (.602)			18.777	.314	measured background, test score, education², experience
Above 110 (N = 271)	5.220 (.708)			16.677	.396	measured background, test score, education², experience
Kalamazoo Brothers (35-59)						
Below 90 (N = 168)	4.003 (1.401)	[3.057] (3.294)	[−6.157] (13.523)	19.364	.146	measured background, test score
90 to 110 (N = 349)	5.749 (1.482)	[3.269] (2.003)	10.440 (5.854)	19.306	.261	measured background, test score
Above 110 (N = 175)	[−.803] (3.696)	[−2.710] (3.913)	13.011 (4.659)	15.274	.339	measured background, test score

[a] For a description of the tests, see chapter 4.
[b] For a list of the background variables controlled in each sample see table 6.2.

354

Regressions of Current Occupational Status on Education, by Father's Occupation

Sample & Father's Occupation	Years of Education	Years Higher Education	BA	Standard Deviation of Residuals	$\bar{R}^2$	Other Variables Controlled[a]
OCG (25-64)						
Father white collar (N = 2,631)	2.879 (.317)	1.635 (.571)	3.729 (1.871)	19.004	.368	measured background, experience, experience²
Father blue collar (N = 4,915)	2.604 (.136)	2.221 (.466)	10.991 (2.094)	18.647	.373	measured background, experience, experience²
Father farm (N = 3,288)	1.943 (.128)	3.168 (.647)	10.185 (3.089)	17.197	.311	measured background, experience, experience²
PSID (25-64)						
Father white collar (N = 329)	2.966 (.910)	[.397] (1.403)	4.776 (3.811)	14.740	.406	measured background, vocational training, test score, experience, experience²
Father blue collar (N = 962)	1.248 (.339)	3.832 (.878)	[6.573] (3.422)	15.947	.401	measured background, vocational training, test score, experience, experience²
Father farm (N = 583)	1.285 (.339)	4.446 (1.089)	9.090 (4.484)	15.494	.407	measured background, vocational training, test score, experience, experience²
NLS (45-59)						
Father white collar (N = 550)	3.290 (.592)	1.963 (1.183)	[6.417] (4.232)	18.299	.419	measured background, vocational training, experience
Father blue collar (N = 1,438)	2.232 (.246)	4.202 (.893)	[−1.984] (4.179)	18.942	.355	measured background, vocational training, experience
Father farm (N = 825)	.965 (.268)	[1.334] (1.307)	24.201 (6.372)	16.756	.495	measured background, vocational training, experience
Talent (28-29)						
Father white collar (N = 315)	4.532 (.700)	NA[b]	NA[b]	17.917	.397	measured background, test score, education², experience
Father blue collar (N = 448)	5.103 (.557)			17.982	.355	measured background, test score, education², experience

[a]For a list of the background variables controlled in each sample see table 6.2, page 168.
[b]Since virtually all Talent respondents finished high school, and since the effects of higher education were not yet significantly nonlinear, we report only the linear regressions.

TABLE A6.5

Linear Regressions of Ln Earnings on Education with Selected Controls

Sample	None	Measured Background[a]	All Background[b]	Test Score	Measured Background[a] & Test Score	All Background[b] & Test Score	All Background[b] & Occupation	All Background[b] & Test Score & Occupation	Measured Background[a] & Test Score & Occupation
1961 OCG									
B	.1005	.0732							
(SE)	(.0021)	(.0024)							
R̄²	.181	.240							
1969 Census									
B	.0867								
(SE)	(.0013)								
R̄²	.176								
1971 PSID									
B	.0931	.0756		.0756	.0654				
(SE)	(.0053)	(.0059)		(.0057)	(.0062)				
R̄²	.243	.271		.266	.284				
1964 Veterans									
B	.0964	.0765	.0566	.0658	.0557	.0420	.0357	.0219	.0310
(SE)	(.0140)	(.0139)	(.0214)	(.0145)	(.0143)	(.0233)	(.0249)	(.0185)	(.0146)
R̄²	.109	.173	.252	.150	.194	.256	.265	.286	.238
1972 Talent									
B	.0567	.0508		.0464	.0429				.0287
(SE)	(.0077)	(.0080)		(.0084)	(.0085)				(.0095)
R̄²	.060	.070		.070	.074				.090
1972 Talent Brothers									
B	.0604	.0707		.0388	.0494				.0397
(SE)	(.0110)	(.0124)		(.0140)	(.0146)				(.0181)
R̄²	.128	.147		.151	.174				.183
1974 NORC Brothers									
B	.0997	.1002	.1097				.1070		
(SE)	(.0152)	(.0178)	(.0211)				(.0321)		
R̄²	.125	.121	.200				.191		
1973 Kalamazoo Brothers									
B	.0671	.0642	.0499	.0492	.0480	.0310	.0230	.0072*	.0181
(SE)	(.0057)	(.0066)	(.0113)	(.0069)	(.0075)	(.0118)	(.0116)	(.0019)	(.0079)
R̄²	.151	.147	.259	.171	.171	.297	.328	.364	.255

TABLE A6.6

Regressions of Ln Earnings on Education, by Test Scores

Sample & Test-Score Group[a]	Years of Education	Years of Higher Education	BA	Standard Deviation of Residuals	$\bar{R}^2$	Variables Controlled in Addition to Experience[b]
Veterans (30-34)						
Below 31st percentile (N = 236)	.1064 (.0313)	[−.0761] (.0662)	[.2499] (.3335)	.487	.109	measured background, AFQT
31st to 64th percentile (N = 264)	[−.0016] (.0318)	[.0221] (.0431)	[−.0068] (.1670)	.414	.131	measured background, AFQT
Above 64th percentile (N = 303)	[.0497]	[−.9971]	.0534	.427	.135	measured background, AFQT
Talent (28-29)						
Below 90 (N = 173)[b]	[.0151] (.0247)			.380	.010	measured background, test score
90-110 (N = 395)	.0540 (.0109)			.362	.078	measured background, test score
Above 110 (N = 271)	.0484 (.0173)			.405	.034	measured background, test score
Kalamazoo Brothers (35-59)						
Below 90 (N = 168)[c]	.0881 (.0268)	[−.0655] (.0631)	[.2582] (.2590)	.371	.081	measured background, test score
90-110 (N = 349)	[.0370] (.0334)	[.0273] (.0451)	[−.1701] (.1318)	.435	.061	measured background, test score
Above 110 (N = 175)	[.0355] (.0870)	[−.0215] (.0921)	.2155 (.1097)	.360	.126	measured background, test score

Coefficients in brackets are less than twice their standard error.

[a]For a description of the tests, see chapter 4.
[b]For a list of the background variables controlled in each sample see table 6.2, page 168.

TABLE A6.7

Occupational Status and Earnings by Single Years of Education[a]

Years of Education	N	Occupation		Earnings		Ln Earnings		Earnings$^{1/3}$	
		Mean	SD	Mean	SD	Mean	SD	Mean	SD
All	36,693	40.0	24.5	9,608	7,365	8.946	.743	20.28	4.50
0	214	19.1	15.7	5,728	7,456	8.295	.890	16.53	4.67
1	72	18.1	14.3	4,371	3,523	7.905	1.188	14.92	4.95
2	151	15.8	10.5	4,198	2,681	8.034	.982	15.22	3.96
3	280	15.9	10.4	4,675	3,245	8.170	.868	15.81	3.95
4	386	19.0	13.6	4,860	3,105	8.234	.824	16.09	3.84
5	539	20.6	13.7	5,464	3,341	8.347	.880	16.75	3.99
6	983	21.4	14.0	5,971	3,358	8.495	.733	17.43	3.67
7	1,291	23.0	14.7	6,667	4,660	8.595	.738	18.02	3.87
8	3,793	24.8	15.7	7,252	5,217	8.672	.764	18.52	4.03
9	2,226	26.9	16.3	7,750	4,887	8.781	.682	19.10	3.72
10	2,689	29.8	18.0	8,020	4,330	8.840	.640	19.42	3.51
11	2,127	32.5	19.6	8,399	5,110	8.863	.691	19.36	3.79
12	11,511	38.8	21.1	9,339	5,525	8.997	.603	20.42	3.69
13	1,484	48.3	21.4	10,736	7,712	9.103	.650	21.23	4.19
14	1,951	52.8	21.7	11,244	8,308	9.131	.693	21.49	4.46
15	668	58.1	20.1	12,147	8,582	9.221	.645	22.09	4.45
16	2,795	66.9	17.3	14,061	9,665	9.355	.638	23.15	4.81
17	802	70.7	16.0	14,575	9,191	9.416	.637	23.55	4.58
18+	1,942	75.6	15.4	17,076	13,913	9.464	.829	24.27	6.09
NA	789	34.4	22.0	8,513	4,851	8.865	.700	19.67	3.98
eta^{2}[b]		.418		.150		.148		.175	
N reporting dependent variable		34,745		32,020		32,020		32,020	

[a] 1/1,000 Census sample of men aged 25 to 64 in 1970, not in school, institutions, or the military, reporting relevant pair of variables and reporting positive 1969 earnings.
[b] Calculated using single years of education.

TABLE A7.1

Regressions of Earnings/Income on Background Characteristics, by Race[a]

		OCG (1961 Income in 1967 Dollars)		PSID (1971 Earnings in 1967 Dollars)	
		White (N = 10,395)	Nonwhite (N = 1,110)	White (N = 1,307)	Nonwhite (N = 467)
Father's education	B	80	80	214	81
	(SE)	(13)	(23)	(64)	(65)
Father's occupation	B	36**	[−9]**	[−40]	[−12]
	(SE)	(4)	(10)	(22)	(21)
Father white collar	B	585	[239]	2,650	[1,354]
	(SE)	(171)	(435)	(850)	(1,051)
Father absent	B	−487	−486	[−1,424]	[−563]
	(SE)	(132)	(174)	(2,176)	(952)
Non-South upbringing	B	888	843	1,055*	2,576*
	(SE)	(107)	(162)	(406)	(445)
Nonfarm upbringing	B	810	963	1,642	[656]
	(SE)	(119)	(182)	(441)	(339)
Siblings	B	−120*	−47*	−241	[−105]
	(SE)	(16)	(23)	(70)	(64)
Father's education^2	B	9.00	[1.26]	[−1.89]	[−7.70]
	(SE)	(2.21)	(3.72)	(12.28)	(10.09)
Father's occupation^2	B	[.06]*	−.45*	[−.79]*	1.52*
	(SE)	(.10)	(.22)	(.56)	(.53)
Siblings^2	B	8.20	[1.10]	[42.53]	48.12
	(SE)	(3.82)	(4.47)	(24.48)	(23.59)
Constant		6,915	4,146	9,680	7,728
R^2		.111	.100	.081	.213
SD of Residuals		4,587	2,409	6,242	3,269

Percentage of gap eliminated if equalization occurs at level of:

Nonwhite means		34.5	44.9
White means		19.1	44.0

[a]All samples restricted to civilian, noninstitutional males aged 25 to 64 with complete data; PSID sample further restricted to nonstudents with positive earnings. OCG sample restricted to men with nonzero income.

*The difference between white and nonwhite coefficients is significant at the .05 level.

**The difference between white and nonwhite coefficients is significant at the .01 level.

TABLE A7.2
Regressions of Earnings$^{1/3}$/Income$^{1/3}$ on Background Characteristics, by Race^a

		OCG (1961 Income in 1967 Dollars)		PSID (1971 Earnings in 1967 Dollars)	
		White (N = 10,395)	Nonwhite (N = 1,110)	White (N = 1,307)	Nonwhite (N = 467)
Father's education	B	.080*	.165*	.157	[.094]
	(SE)	(.011)	(.036)	(.042)	(.076)
Father's occupation	B	.029**	[−.029]**	[−.014]	[−.044]
	(SE)	(.003)	(.015)	(.014)	(.024)
Father white collar	B	.321	[.742]	1.261	2.804
	(SE)	(.144)	(.666)	(.557)	(1.225)
Father absent	B	−.603	[−.496]	[−.540]	[−.282]
	(SE)	(.111)	(.266)	(1.426)	(1.110)
Non-South upbringing	B	.941	.841	.689*	2.392*
	(SE)	(.090)	(.248)	(.266)	(.519)
Nonfarm upbringing	B	.988*	1.596*	1.197	.824
	(SE)	(.100)	(.278)	(.289)	(.395)
Siblings	B	−.108	[−.062]	−.184	[−.112]
	(SE)	(.013)	(.035)	(.046)	(.074)
Father's education^2	B	[.0030]	[.0041]	[−.0078]	[−.0038]
	(SE)	(.0019)	(.0057)	(.0080)	(.0118)
Father's occupation^2	B	[−.0001]	.0008	[−.0006]**	.0022**
	(SE)	(.0001)	(.0003)	(.0004)	(.0006)
Siblings^2	B	[.0056]	[.0005]	[.0198]	[.0509]
	(SE)	(.0032)	(.0068)	(.0160)	(.0275)
Constant		18.165	14.987	20.445	18.828
R^2		.118	.096	.095	.178
SD of Residuals		3.862	3.683	4.090	3.812

Percentage of gap eliminated if equalization occurs at level of:			
Nonwhite means	29.2		39.6
White means	19.0		45.4

Coefficients in brackets are less than twice their standard error.

^{a}Samples restricted to noninstitutionalized, nonmilitary males aged 25 to 64 with complete data. PSID sample further restricted to nonstudents with positive earnings. OCG sample restricted to men with nonzero income.
*The difference between white and nonwhite coefficients is significant at the .05 level.
**The difference between white and nonwhite coefficients is significant at the .01 level.

Components of 1971 Family Income for PSID Husband-Wife Households[a]

	Male Earnings	Female Earnings	Asset Income	Welfare	Other Transfers	Total Taxable Income	Total Transfers	Total Family Income
A. Means, Standard Deviations, and Correlations								
Male earnings	1.000							
Female earnings	−.020	1.000						
Asset income	.250	.006	1.000					
Welfare	−.138	−.062	−.013	1.000				
Other transfers	−.253	−.059	.083	.021	1.000			
Taxable income	.934	.301	.392	−.146	−.232	1.000		
Total transfers	−.282	−.075	.074	.343	.946	−.266	1.000	
Total family income	.919	.299	.414	−.100	−.099	.990	−.125	1.000
Mean[b]	9,224	1,599	391	41	326	11,214	366	11,581
SD[b]	6,667	2,357	1,220	351	1,001	7,414	1,066	7,205
Percent of total	79.6	13.8	3.4	.4	2.8	96.8	3.2	100.0
B. Variances, Covariances and Unstandardized Bivariate Regression Coefficients (B) when Predicting Family Income from Its Component[b,c]								
Male earnings	44.45							
Female earnings	−.32	5.56						
Asset income	2.04	.02	1.49					
Welfare	−.32	−.05	−.01	.12				
Other transfers	−1.69	−.14	.10	.01	1.00			
Taxable income	46.17	5.26	3.54	−.37	−1.72	54.97		
Total transfers	−2.01	−.19	.10	.13	1.01	−2.10	1.14	
Total family income	44.16	5.07	3.64	−.25	−.71	52.87	−.96	51.91
B	.994	.912	2.444	−2.082	−.713	.962	−.847	1.000

[a]Husband-wife households with a nonstudent, nonmilitary head aged 25 to 64 in 1971 and with complete data on the basic variables in table A9.2 (N = 2,245).

[b]All values in 1967 dollars.

[c]All figures divided by 1,000,000. Numbers in diagonal are variances. Numbers off diagonal are covariances.

TABLE A9.2

Means, Standard Deviations, and Bivariate Regression Coefficients of Components of Family Income on Selected Characteristics of PSID Husband-Wife Households[a]

			Bivariate Regression Coefficients							
	Mean	SD	Male Earnings[b]	Female Earnings[b]	Asset Income[b]	Welfare[b]	Other Transfers[b]	Taxable Income[b]	Total Transfers[b]	Total Income[b]
Head white	.892	.311	2,597	[-38]	194	-143	36	2,753	[-107]	2,646
Husband's father's education (years)	8.643	3.053	445	64	17	-9	[-9]	525	-18	508
Husband's father's occupation (Duncan score)	27.724	17.283	71	10	3	-1	[-1]	84	-3	81
Husband's father white collar	.222	.399	3,161	550	195	-41	-111	3,906	-151	3,755
Husband's father U.S. citizen[b]	.839	.365	-1,642	[-16]	-337	-49	[-2]	-1,995	[-51]	-2,046
Husband's siblings[b]	3.724	2.484	-516	-60	[-2]	12	20	-578	32	-546
Husband's nonfarm origins[b]	.685	.465	2,986	243	112	[-8]	[45]	3,341	[37]	3,378
Husband's city origins[b]	.291	.454	2,934	[116]	219	[-15]	[82]	3,268	[67]	3,335
Husband's non-South origins[b]	.682	.466	2,426	[-1]	141	[-1]	[-63]	2,567	[-64]	2,503
Husband's parents' economic situation[c]	2.294	1.398	619	[14]	46	-16	[-27]	679	-42	637
Husband's nonschool training[b] (0,1)	.235	.424	[-477]	[-30]	[-38]	[-19]	173	[-544]	154	[-390]
Number of children	1.719	1.692	170	-268	-62	35	-41	[-160]	[-6]	[-166]
Age youngest child (no children = 18)	10.560	6.442	[-10]	66	24	-3	21	80	19	99
Husband's low education goals for children (1-5)	1.295	1.249	-320	-237	-75	28	[-23]	-632	[5]	-628
Husband's achievement motivation (0-16)	9.134	2.630	571	54	31	-9	[-8]	656	-17	638
Husband's risk avoidance (0-8)	5.260	1.580	1,373	190	129	-34	[-16]	1,692	-50	1,642
Husband union member[b]	.309	.462	-47	-15	-15	[-1]	[-6]	-77	-7	-84
Husband's job tenure[b] (months)	109.018	100.290	10	[-1]	1	-0	-1	10	-2	8
Husband self-employed[b],[d]	1.288	.665	1,328	-252	200	[-3]	-66	1,276	-69	1,207
Husband physically handicapped	.145	.352	-3,591	[-142]	[64]	125	711	-3,669	836	-2,832
Local shortage of female labor (0-7)	4.374	1.319	[-25]	[-8]	[23]	[9]	[14]	[-9]	[23]	[14]
	1.020	908	[162]	[-19]	[39]	[13]	[-0]	[182]	[12]	[194]

	Mean	SD								
(percent in August 1972)	5.735	2.168	[137]	-51	32	7	20	[118]	27	145
Non-South region	.718	.450	1,891	[55]	164	[22]	[-29]	2,110	[-8]	2,103
Distance to nearest city[b] (0-65 miles)	25.808	22.825	-49	-9	[-2]	[-0]	-2	-60	-3	-63
Typical local male wage (dollars per hour)	2.295	.523	1,730	[52]	162	[6]	[-5]	1,944	[1]	1,945
Typical local female wage (dollars per hour)	2.003	.352	2,840	407	253	[17]	[36]	3,500	-53	3,552
Husband's sentence completion score (0-13)	9.907	1.835	1,197	113	45	-20	-30	1,355	-50	1,305
Husband's age	42.962	11.029	-37	[2]	20	[1]	19	[-15]	20	[4]
Husband's education[b] (years)	11.714	3.413	882	95	39	-13	-23	1,015	-36	979
Husband's occupational status (Duncan score)	39.039	21.728	139	12	7	-2	-9	158	-11	148
Husband's hours > 0[b]	.961	.193	9,462	670	-466	-322	-2,849	9,666	-3,171	6,496
Husband's weeks worked[b]	44.764	11.774	200	[7]	-8	-8	-48	199	-56	143
Husband's hours/week worked[b]	43.200	13.277	146	[-2]	[-2]	-5	-31	142	-36	106
Husband's hours worked[b]	2,131.017	773.495	2.77	[-.05]	[-.06]	-.10	-.57	2.67	-.67	1.99
Husband's hourly wage	4.399	4.355	1,088	[-1]	49	-6	-28	1,136	-34	1,102
Wife's sentence completion score (0-13)	9.878	.623	1,463	[103]	175	[-17]	[-21]	1,741	[-38]	1,703
Wife's age	39.988	11.260	[-17]	[-2]	20	[.1]	18	[1]	19	[19]
Wife's education[b] (years)	11.702	2.648	894	233	51	-18	-35	1,178	-54	1,124
Wife's occupational status (Duncan score)	19.806	24.627	[6]	65	[-0]	-1	-2	71	-3	68
Wife's hours > 0[b]	.519	.500	1,418	3,082	-110	-44	-77	1,553	-121	1,433
Wife's weeks worked[b]	18.855	21.457	-34	86	[-0]	-1	[-2]	52	-3	49
Wife's hours/week worked[b]	17.341	18.915	-47	93	-3	-1	[-2]	43	-3	40
Wife's hours worked[b]	656.448	837.036	-1.02	2.34	[-.02]	-.02	[-.03]	1.29	-.05	1.24
Wife's hourly wage	1.289	1.796	[134]	945	[-2]	-10	-32	1,076	-42	1,034

[a]Sample restricted to households with nonmilitary, noninstitutional, nonstudent husband aged 25 to 64 and with complete data on basic variables (N = 2,245).
[b]A "basic variable."—respondents with missing data on these variables were excluded from the multivariate analyses.
[c]Husband's retrospective report, coded 1 = poor, 3 = average, 5 = pretty well off.
[d]Coded 1 = no, 2 = partially, 3 = yes.

NOTES

CHAPTER 1

1. For a more detailed discussion, see the *Final Report,* chapter 11.
2. See Schwartz (1975) and Coleman, Rainwater, and McClelland (1978), as well as Hamblin (1974).
3. See chapter 7 and tables A2.2–A2.12 in the Appendix.
4. These are the principal background measures available in the OCG sample, which provided the basis for Blau and Duncan's classic study *The American Occupational Structure* (1967).
5. Taubman and Wales (1974) and Griliches (1977) had more than one test, but nothing like the array available in Project Talent.
6. Our work is parallel in this respect to that of Chamberlain and Griliches (1975) and Taubman (1976a). The general approach is taken from Jencks et al. (1972) but is implemented with more suitable data.

CHAPTER 2

1. Some analyses of the PSID in the *Final Report* used the number of correct answers (Mean = 10.0; SD = 2.0), so some tables in the *Final Report* differ from those shown here.
2. Values of eta², R² for quadratic regressions, and B_t for the orthogonal squared terms appear in the appendices of the *Final Report*. For additional discussion of orthogonal terms see, e.g., Gocka (1974) and the sources cited there, as well as Stinchcombe (1976).
3. Details regarding the construction of these terms and some information about their coefficients, signs, and significance levels can be found in the appendices to the *Final Report*.
4. Table A2.13 in the Appendix shows the variances for these three measures in matched samples.
5. See chapter 11 for a comparison of PSID husbands' and wives' reports.
6. Bielby et al. (1976) tested for correlated errors in reports of the respondent's own education and rejected it. They assumed that if errors were uncorrelated for self-reported education they would also be uncorrelated for reports of parental characteristics, but this need not follow if sons simply have fixed but erroneous ideas about their fathers.
7. See chapter 3.
8. See Olneck (1976) and *Final Report,* Appendix I.
9. These comparisons appear in table 2 of each Appendix in the second volume of the *Final Report*.
10. For a full analysis see Featherman and Hauser (1976b).
11. For a fuller discussion of the age/experience issue and of Mincer's specification and data see Bartlett and Jencks (1978).
12. For more details see chapter 6 and *Final Report,* chapter 14.
13. See *Final Report,* Appendix G.
14. For a more detailed comparison of the Talent sample to others, see *Final Report,* Appendix H.

CHAPTER 3

1. Taubman reports 18 percent nonresponse on the occupational item. He allocated nonrespondents their twin's occupation if the twin reported it. Otherwise he allocated nonrespondents the sample mean. If nonresponse had been randomly distributed, 0.18^2 = 3 percent of all pairs would both have been allocated the mean. Another (2) (0.18) − 0.18^2 = 33 percent would have had identical values other than the mean due to allocation. Even if there were no correlation between pairs with independent data, the expected correlation between all pairs would thus have been 0.33. Since the observed correlation between DZ twins is only 0.20, we infer that nonresponse was nonrandom. This leaves the correlation between pairs with independent data unknown. Taubman also calculated these correlations omitting men with allocated values. He reports that the correlations fell by about the same amount for both MZ and DZ twins, but he could not locate the exact values when we queried him.

Background explains less of the variance in occupational status than in ln earnings in Taubman's sample—a very unusual result. The SD of respondents' Duncan scores is only 21.4 points for Taubman's sample, which is lower than in any other unselected sample where occupations were coded into Census three-digit categories. We suspect some peculiarity in the coding of occupations, which was mostly done from a survey of these same twins conducted some years before Taubman's.

2. In addition to these five surveys, four others have come to our attention. Gorseline (1932) published data on economic resemblance between brothers in Indiana, but they are quite peculiar. The correlation between brothers' occupational statuses in Gorseline's data is close to zero (Chamberlain and Griliches, 1975). The correlations between brothers' educational attainments and their earnings, in contrast, are quite high. Hermalin (1969) collected data on occupational resemblance between brothers using a sample of utility workers. OCG asked respondents who had older brothers to report their oldest brother's educational attainment, but it did not ask about the brother's occupational status or earnings. Kohn (1969) asked respondents about their brothers' occupations but did not code the results in readily usable form. We obtained a number of tabulations from Kohn which yielded results similar to the NORC survey for men from small families. The results for men from large families are hard to interpret due to the way Kohn recorded the data.

3. The fact that Brittain's sample was surveyed in 1966 rather than 1972–74 may also raise R^2, since demographic background explained less of the variance in occupational status in 1973 than in 1962. We would, however, expect Brittain's coding scheme to lower R^2, since most alternatives to the Duncan scale seem to have this effect (see Featherman, Jones, and Hauser, 1975).

4. Chapter 10 compares the bivariate relationship of father's education, father's occupation, and siblings to occupational status and income in OCG, PA, and PSID, using common coding procedures.

5. For additional evidence on this point, see Featherman and Hauser (1976a, 1976b).

6. For a more detailed analysis, see Smith and Welch (1977).

7. We also tested for interactions by splitting the sample into whites and nonwhites and into men from white-collar, blue-collar, and farm fathers. Chapter 7 discusses white/nonwhite differences. Chapter 6 discusses differences in returns to education for men with white-collar, blue-collar, and farm fathers.

8. Bielby et al. (1977) estimated the reliability of March CPS occupational reports at 0.84 for nonblack males aged 20 to 64 and 0.75 for black males. The pooled reliability should be about 0.83. This estimate is biased downward by the fact that both the March interview and the fall followup asked respondents about their current job, and the followup did not ask whether respondents had changed jobs since March. Allowing for such changes, we estimate the reliability for all males aged 20 to 64 at about 0.85. The value for males aged 25 to 64 is likely to be marginally higher—say 0.86. Correcting for errors in measuring occupational status should therefore raise R^2 from 0.25 to 0.25/0.86 = 0.29.

Bielby et al. did not estimate the reliability of ln income, but the CPS-Census match for 1970 provides relevant data. If errors were uncorrelated with true values, line 2 of Table A2.13 would indicate that ln income had a reliability of $1 - (0.316/0.988)^2 = 0.90$ for CPS men aged 14 and over who reported positive incomes. Since negative incomes are allowable only under special circumstances, errors are probably negatively correlated with true values, and the CPS reliability is probably closer to the CPS-Census correlation (0.84) than the random error model implies. Restricting the sample to men aged 25 to 64 might reduce the variance of reporting errors but would also reduce the true variance. The effect on reliability would thus be unpredictable. If the reliability were as high as 0.90, accurate income data would give us an R^2 of about $0.11/0.90 = 0.12$. If the reliability were as low as 0.83, accurate income data would raise R^2 to 0.13.

Bielby et al. estimated the amount of error in OCG–II respondents' reports of their parents' characteristics by comparing a respondent's report in the OCG–II mailback questionnaire to his report of the same characteristic in a telephone followup three weeks later. A respondent's initial report of his father's education, father's occupation, and parental income correlated very highly with his report in the followup. Indeed, reports of parental characteristics were more stable than reports of the respondent's own characteristics. (Some of the relevant data appear in Tables A2.13 and A2.14.) Bielby et al. concluded that this stability implied very high correlations between reports of parental characteristics and the parents' actual characteristics.

When Bielby et al. combined father's education, father's occupation, and parental income with age and age^2 to predict the occupational status of nonblack males aged 20 to 64 in OCG–II, the observed R^2 for nonblacks was 0.176. Assuming their estimates of reporting errors in father's education, father's occupation, and parental income are correct, eliminating such errors raises R^2 to 0.191. The implied reliability of the predicted value of occupational status ($\hat{Y}$) for nonblacks is thus $0.176/0.191 = 0.921$. The analogous value for blacks is 0.838. If we combined blacks and nonblacks the reliability of $\hat{Y}$ should be around 0.91. We doubt that dropping men aged 20 to 24 would alter this figure appreciably.

Our equation is somewhat different from Bielby et al.'s, however, since our independent variables include not only parental income, father's education, and father's occupation, but race, mother's education, number of siblings, region of birth, farm upbringing, and a dummy for having a white collar father. In addition, we have tried to take account of the likely explanatory power of ethnicity and religion. Corcoran (1979) found that mother's education was less reliable than father's education and occupation in her PSID sample. Farm upbringing is also poorly measured in OCG–II (see chapter 2). Adding these variables is therefore likely to reduce the accuracy of $\hat{Y}$. But reports on number of siblings, region of birth, having a white collar father, ethnicity, and religion probably contain less error than the background measures in Bielby et al.'s equation. All things considered, if $\hat{Y}$ really has a reliability of 0.91 in Bielby et al.'s equation, the analogous figure should be at least 0.92 in our equation. The figure for our income equation is likely to be quite similar. These estimates of measurement error imply a "true" R^2 of about $0.29/0.92 = 0.32$ for occupational status and about $0.13/0.92 = 0.14$ for ln income.

We doubt, however, that respondents' reports of their parents' characteristics are as reliable as Bielby et al. believed them to be. Reporting errors are of at least two kinds. Some are due to random variation in the way respondents describe reality. Errors of this kind are not likely to be correlated from one interview to the next, at least if there is a reasonable interval between interviews. The correlation between successive reports is thus likely to provide a good estimate of the reports' accuracy when this is the only source of error. Bielby et al.'s data strongly suggest that respondents' errors in reporting their own education followed this pattern. But errors in reporting parental characteristics are also likely to take another form. Some men are simply misinformed about their parents' characteristics. When this is the case, they will repeat the same error in successive interviews. Bielby et al. could not investigate errors of this type for any measure other than the respondent's own education. The high correlation between successive reports of parental characteristics in OCG–II could therefore be partly due to correlated errors. Bielby et al.'s model would then overestimate the accuracy of reports on parental characteristics.

To test this hypothesis, Corcoran (1979) used white PSID fathers' reports of their education and occupation and mothers' reports of their education in 1968 to predict the education, the occupation, and the earnings of their 23- to 30-year-old sons in 1976. She then repeated the analysis using the sons' 1976 reports of their parents' education and their father's occupation when the respondent was "growing up." If Bielby et al.'s estimates of measurement error were correct, a son's report on his parents should predict his success better than the parents' self-reports do. In fact, parents' self-reports predict a son's success considerably better than do sons' reports of their parents' characteristics. Using a multiple indicator model similar to Bielby et al.'s, Corcoran estimated the correlation between sons' reports and parents' actual characteristics at 0.852 for father's education, 0.879 for father's occupation, and 0.815 for mother's education. For parents' self-reports the analogous values were 0.925, 0.912, and 0.933. Thus if sons' errors in reporting their parents' characteristics were uncorrelated in successive interviews, the correlation between successive interviews would be only $0.852^2 = 0.73$ for father's education and $0.879^2 = 0.77$ for father's occupation. Yet Bielby et al. obtained correlations of 0.94 for successive reports of father's education and 0.87 for father's occupation. The difference may be partly due to differences among samples, questions, coding procedures, and the like. But we strongly suspect that it is also partly due to a positive correlation of sons' errors in successive interviews.

When Corcoran used father's education, mother's education, and father's occupation to predict a son's economic success, the overall reliability of $\hat{Y}$ was 0.712 for occupational status and 0.690 for ln hourly earnings. Father's occupation and education exhibit more variance in her all-white PSID sample of men aged 23 to 30 than in our sample of PSID men aged 25 to 64, implying that $\hat{Y}$ might be even less reliable in a sample of 25- to 64-year-olds than in her sample. Differences between the OCG–II and PSID questionnaires could either raise or lower the reliability of $\hat{Y}$. Thus, if $\hat{Y}$ were as unreliable for our extended list of variables as for the three Corcoran studied, eliminating errors in measuring background would raise R^2 from 0.29 to $0.29/0.71 = 0.41$ for occupational status and from 0.11 or 0.12 to $0.11/0.69 = 0.16$ or $0.12/0.69 = 0.17$ for ln income. These estimates are probably too high, but they may be more realistic than those we obtained using Bielby et al.'s data.

9. In the Kalamazoo sample, R^2 was 0.125 for occupational status and 0.080 for ln earnings. The Kalamazoo survey did not measure parental income, ethnicity, or religion. These measures might plausibly raise R^2 by 0.03 for both occupational status and ln earnings. The sibling correlations are 0.309 for occupational status and 0.220 for ln earnings. The expected values of R^2, uncorrected for measurement error, are thus about half the correlations between brothers, which is consistent with the table in the text.

In the NORC Brothers sample, R^2 is 0.189 for occupational status and 0.045 for ln earnings. Had the NORC survey measured parental income, mother's education, region of birth, religion, and ethnicity, R^2 might have risen by as much as 0.04 for both occupational status and ln earnings. The sibling correlations are 0.371 for occupational status and 0.129 for ln earnings. The expected value of R^2, uncorrected for measurement error, is thus about two-thirds of the sibling correlation for both occupational status and ln earnings. This is a bit higher than the table implies, but the discrepancy could easily be due to sampling error.

Both Taubman's R^2 and his sibling correlations are higher than Olneck's, but the ratio of R^2 to r_{sib} in his sample is similar to the ratio in Kalamazoo.

10. Taubman (1976b) uses his data to argue that genetic factors could explain as much as 50 percent of the variance in earnings, implying that common environment must explain at least 4 percent. He assumes no assortative mating. If one allows for assortative mating, the genetic correlation between DZ twins can exceed 0.50, and Taubman's data can imply a "heritability" as high as 0.54. Misdiagnosis of MZ twins as DZ would have the same effect.

11. Some fraternal twins look very much alike and are often mistaken for one another. If these fraternal twins' earnings were no more alike than those of other fraternal twins, we could probably dismiss the first two alternatives. To test the "interaction" theory, we would need data on unrelated men who had been reared together. If genes explain the entire economic resemblance between twins and siblings, adopted

son's earnings should not correlate at all. Jencks and Brown (1977) provide a more detailed analysis of these issues.

12. Table A3.3 in the Appendix summarizes our regression results. For additional discussion, see the *Final Report*, chapter 12. For an analysis that reaches the opposite conclusion, see Gordon (1978). For empirical evidence of the extent to which parental status is a proxy for IQ genotype, see Jencks et al. (1972), chapter 3, and Scarr and Weinberg (1978).

13. The derivation is as follows. The standardized regressions of Q and Q' on F_Q are:

(A) $$Q = bF_Q + e_Q$$
(B) $$Q' = bF_Q + e_{Q'}$$

where b is the correlation between F_Q and Q. The standardized regressions of U and U' on F_U are:

(C) $$U = cF_U + e_U$$
(D) $$U' = cF_U + e_{U'}$$

where c is the correlation between F_U and U. If brothers do not affect one another, $e_{Q'}$ and $e_{U'}$ will not correlate with e_Q and e_U. Multiplying equation A by equation B, summing over all observations, dividing by the number of observations, and dropping zero terms will therefore yield:

(E) $$r_{QQ'} = b^2$$

A similar manipulation of equations C and D gives us:

(F) $$r_{UU'} = c^2$$

while equations A and C or B and D yield:

(G) $$r_{QU'} = r_{UQ'} = bcr_{FQ,FU}$$

Taking the square roots of E and F, substituting into G, and rearranging yields equation 2 in the text.

14. The correlations in table 3.2 all have large sampling errors. But because they have mean values well below unity, one must assume that their true values are also less than unity. This means that one must assume the existence of as many independent background factors as outcomes. One or more of these independent factors may fail to contribute significantly to R^2 in a small sample (see e.g. Chamberlain and Griliches, 1975, 1977; Behrman, Taubman, and Wales, 1977). But the fact that one or more factors is insignificant in a small sample does not mean that its contribution to R^2 is in fact zero.

15. This argument rules out Hauser and Dickinson's (1974) single-factor model. It does not necessarily rule out the models suggested by Chamberlain and Griliches (1975, 1977) or by Behrman et al. (1977). These models assume fewer independent background factors than measured outcomes and then use this assumption to estimate the effects of other unobserved variables (such as ability) or to estimate the correlations among unobserved factors. This procedure is perfectly legitimate so long as one has strong theoretical reasons for believing that there are fewer background factors than outcomes. It is not legitimate, however, if the only evidence for assuming fewer background factors than outcomes is the failure of additional background factors to provide a significant improvement in the model's ability to predict the observed correlations.

One cannot legitimately use the observed data matrix to determine whether a given parameter is zero, then convert this finding into an assumption, and "reuse" the same data, along with one's new "assumption," to estimate otherwise underidentified parameters of the model. When a model is underidentified, one must use *external* information to identify one or more of its parameters. In most cases one asserts that since there is no imaginable way in which A could affect B directly, the observed association between A and B must reflect their causal links to other variables in the model. In this case, however, the investigators wish to assert that since there is no imaginable way in which A could differ from B (where A and B are the background characteristics affecting two different outcomes), the observed associations among outcomes allow us to estimate the effects of other unobserved variables or the correlations among these variables. Unfortunately, we find it extremely easy to imagine background characteristics that would have relatively large effects on one outcome and relatively small effects on another outcome. We can therefore see no theoretical basis for assuming that there are fewer background factors than outcomes and would argue against using this assumption to identify an otherwise underidentified model.

16. For details see tables 5.7 and 5.8. The occupational preferences index used in these analyses predicted eventual status better than did a more conventional index based on the status of the occupation the respondent said he would prefer to enter.

17. On college students' ability to estimate one another's class background from speech patterns see Ellis (1967).

18. *Final Report*, Appendix H.

CHAPTER 4

1. See Duncan (1968), Griliches and Mason (1972), Bowles and Nelson (1974), Taubman and Wales (1974), Sewell and Hauser (1975), and Fagerlind (1975).

2. See, for example, Hunt (1961); Katz (1968); Jensen (1969); Jencks et al. (1972); Herrnstein (1973); Karier, Violas, and Spring (1973); Kamin (1974); Block and Dworkin (1976); and Bowles and Gintis (1976).

3. See Jensen (1969:109).

4. Table A4.2 in the Appendix summarizes these results. Taubman and Wales (1974, 1973) suggest that mathematical ability is a more important determinant of income than verbal ability. However, their verbal factor included substantial weightings for tests of mechanical principles, spatial orientation, and two-hand coordination, which may have reduced its ability to predict success.

5. Table A4.2 in the Appendix illustrates this for eight tests. The other tests in the Talent battery follow the same pattern.

6. See table A4.2.

7. Hauser (unpublished, undated memorandum).

8. McCall (1977) describes these results in more detail. The sample covers ninety-four males and ninety-six females. Female IQ's between age 3 and age 6 predict educational attainment considerably better than male scores at these ages, but the difference is not significant.

9. McCall (1977) found the same pattern for occupational status as for education in the Fels sample. Olneck reports that sixth-grade Terman or Otis IQ's correlate 0.491 with the current occupation of 35- to 39-year-old-Kalamazoo men. Tenth-grade test scores correlate 0.350 with the occupations of 31-year-old-EEO men. Eleventh-grade Academic Composite correlates 0.474 with the occupation of 28-year-old-Talent men. Eleventh-grade Henmon–Nelson scores correlate 0.376 with 24-year-old-Wisconsin men's occupations. These correlations do not suggest that tests given in late adolescence predict occupational status any better than tests given in early adolescence. This is consistent with the results when predicting education.

10. Test scores at age 10 correlate 0.220 with the ln earnings of Fagerlind's Swedish men at age 30 and 0.343 with ln earnings at age 35. Sixth-grade Terman or Otis IQ's correlate 0.319 with the 1973 earnings of 35- to 39-year-old-Kalamazoo men. Tenth-grade test scores correlate 0.070 with the 1969 earnings of 30- to 31-year-old-EEO men. Eleventh-grade Academic Composite correlates 0.203 with the hourly earnings of 28- or 29-year-old-Talent men. Eleventh-grade Henmon–Nelson scores correlate 0.163 with the earnings of Sewell and Hauser's 27- or 28-year-old-Wisconsin men.

11. Taubman and Wales base their findings on average IQ for high school graduates who did and did not attend college. To convert such means into correlations, we would need the means for high school dropouts, college dropouts, and so on.

12. OCG's demographic background measures explain a maximum of 30 to 35 percent of the variance in men's educational attainment. See Hauser and Featherman (1976).

13. See Jencks and Brown (1977) for a discussion of these issues.

14. Both the Wisconsin and EEO surveys have a measure of curriculum, but not in available samples comparable to Talent. See Alexander and Eckland (1974) and Hauser, Sewell, and Alwin (1976).

15. Rosenbaum (1976) and Alexander, Cook, and McDill (1978) argued that curriculum placement does affect test scores. If this is true, ability affects education by influencing curriculum placement less than the text implies. Rosenbaum's findings rely on a single school, which could have atypically large curriculum effects. With ninety-eight schools and better controls for background, Jencks and Brown (1975) find that curriculum placement does not appreciably affect test scores.

16. Also see Rosenbaum (1976) and Rist (1970). See Cronbach and Snow (1977) for a different point of view.

17. See Bowles and Gintis (1976) for a historical critique of the ideology which holds that a necessary connection must exist between academic ability and educational success.

18. The estimates of Jencks et al. (1972) in *Inequality* ranged from 26 to 38 percent.

19. We investigated the same twenty-eight interactions (including the test score by education interaction) in the Talent Survey for ln earnings that we described earlier for occupation. None was significant at the 0.05 level. Regressions for subsamples of Talent and Kalamazoo respondents who had blue-collar or white-collar fathers also showed no significant differences in the test-score coefficients. We also investigated the test score by education interaction in the PSID and Veterans samples. It is less than twice its standard error in both surveys. Examination of over twenty multiplicative interactions in the PSID and Veterans surveys shows no consistent pattern of interactions.

20. Sweeney's explanation of the effects of immigrants' low ability on their social character, taken from the appendix to the hearings of the House Committee on Immigration and Naturalization on January 24, 1923, is illustrative: "They think with the spinal cord rather than with the brain. . . . The necessity of providing for the future does not stimulate them to continuous labor. . . . Being constitutionally inferior they are necessarily socially inadequate. . . ." (quoted in Kamin, 1974). Also see Karier, Violas, and Spring (1973).

CHAPTER 5

1. See Korman (1968) for a review of longitudinal studies that relate managerial success to individual traits. Brenner (1968) related teachers' ratings of high school students to supervisors' ratings of these same students in later jobs as production employees.

2. See Heise (1972) for discussion of this coefficient, which he labels the "sheaf" coefficient. The composite is constructed in such a way as to capitalize on sampling error, so it is likely to have a small but systematic upward bias.

CHAPTER 6

1. See Levin (1977) for discussion of educational programs operating under the War on Poverty rubric.

2. See also Denison (1964) and Griliches (1970).

3. See also Becker and Chiswick (1966), and Mincer (1970, 1974).

4. For early attempts to calculate rates of return, see Houthakker (1959), Renshaw (1960), Hansen (1963), and Hunt (1963). More recent attempts include Weisbrod and Karpoff (1968), Rogers (1969), Hanoch (1967), and Hines, Tweeten, and Redfern (1970).

5. Economists have long recognized that some portion of the schooling–earnings relationship is spurious, but disagree as to how much. The data with which to study the question have been limited and can support widely divergent conclusions. For example, contrast Welch's (1974) comment that empirical estimates are "remarkably

stable," suggesting 10 to 15 percent of the apparent effect of years of schooling is spurious, with Blaug's (1972) assessment that Denison's (1962, 1964) original guess of a 40 percent bias is empirically justified. For technical treatment of the problem of bias due to omitted variables, see Goldberger and Duncan (1973) and Griliches (1977).

6. For technical details and fuller discussion of our procedures and choices, see *Final Report,* chapter 12. Note that we did *not* include a dummy variable for high school graduation, even though theory suggests that high school graduation could be as important as college graduation. This decision was based on the need for simplicity and preliminary earnings equations from the Census sample in which such a dummy was not significant once we controlled years of education. The dummy *would* have been significant if we had also included a dummy for *entering* high school, but we did not try this until our work was almost complete.

7. See Duncan, Featherman, and Duncan (1972, pp. 210–12) for a discussion of this item.

8. The linear regressions appear in table A6.1 of the Appendix.

9. The relevant regressions appear in table A6.2 of the Appendix. Educational differences probably explain more variance in status within the broad white collar occupational groups in which whites are often found than within the broad blue-collar groups in which nonwhites are concentrated.

10. The relevant regressions appear in table A6.3 of the Appendix. We excluded the PSID sample from this analysis because the PSID test cannot safely be viewed as a measure of initial ability. Including it would not alter our conclusions. One could argue for excluding Veterans on the same grounds.

11. The relevant regressions appear in table A6.4 of the Appendix.

12. For the relative value people assign to occupational status and earnings, see Coleman, Rainwater, and McClelland (1978) and *Final Report,* chapter 11.

13. See Solmon (1973) and Mincer (1974).

14. Mincer (1974) reports evidence that an extra year of elementary or secondary schooling is generally accompanied by an extra year of work, that men who begin college do not extend their working lives to compensate completely for their first years of college, but that men who remain in college do extend their working lives to make up for later years of higher education. Mincer's estimates appear to ignore the fact that highly educated men live longer than poorly educated men (Kitagawa and Hauser, 1973). Taking this into account, extra education does not appear on the average to shorten men's working lives at all. See *Final Report,* chapter 14.

15. For discussion of our method of measuring experience, see chapter 2 herein and *Final Report,* chapter 12. The measure of experience in the Talent 28-year-old sample is a direct measure rather than a construct (see *Final Report,* Appendix H). For discussion of the consequences of alternative measures of experience for estimating the effects of education, see Chiswick (1972) and Hansen, Weisbrod, and Scanlon (1972).

16. Table A6.5 presents the linear regressions.

17. The implied discrepancy between returns to secondary and higher education is consistent with the PSID and Kalamazoo results but not with the veterans results in table 6.3.

18. See *Final Report,* Appendices D, G, and I, table 9A.

19. The coefficient of years of higher education is always negative in table 6.3. The estimated return to four years of college exceeds that to four years of secondary school in PSID and Kalamazoo only because college graduation has a large positive coefficient with everything else controlled.

20. See Taubman and Wales (1974), chapter 9. If there are unmeasured occupation-specific skills, Taubman and Wales overestimate the impact of screening. If there are unmeasured skills of general applicability, they underestimate screening. Layard and Psacharopoulos (1974) reject the screening hypotheses, arguing that extant data do not evidence diploma effects. Our data imply a small college diploma effect, though our specification does not precisely measure its size. Blaug (1972) questions the screening hypotheses because the effects of education occur throughout the career.

21. See Olneck (1976), chapter 4, for analysis of measurement error in the Kalamazoo data.

22. See Olneck (1977) for calculations.

23. See table A6.6 in the Appendix for the relevant regressions.

24. There are few significant and no consistent interactions between level of schooling and test score in the NLS sample of young men (Link and Ratledge, 1975; Griliches, 1977), in Cutright's sample of Selective Service examinees (Cutright, 1973), in the follow-up of 1957 Wisconsin high school seniors (Hauser and Daymont, 1976), in the Wolfle Smith 1938 Minnesota high school graduates sample (Taubman and Wales, 1974), in the NBER-TH sample, using math ability (Taubman and Wales, 1974), or in the NBER-TH, Rogers, Talent Five-Year Follow-up, and Husen samples analyzed by Hause (1972). Hause interpreted his findings as demonstrating an ability–schooling interaction, but his evidence for the conclusion is weak and inconsistent.

Weisbrod (1972) called attention to the possible omission of measures correlated with both ability and schooling in Hause's analysis, e.g., motivation. In and of itself, this would not bear on the question of ability–schooling interaction. However, if an omitted variable bore a different relationship to ability across several levels of education, it could obscure an actual ability–education interaction. For example, if motivational differences between ability levels are greater among better-educated men than among less-educated men, and if, as Weisbrod suggests, motivation and ability are negatively correlated within educational levels, then the differences between the actual ability coefficients across educational levels would be larger than present data suggest.

25. Hauser (1972) divided OCG and Wisconsin respondents by farm vs. nonfarm background and by father's Duncan score. He found no consistent differences in the effects of schooling on ln income in the OCG sample or on ln earnings in the Wisconsin sample.

26. This conclusion is also consistent with Link and Ratledge's (1975) finding that controlling district expenditures per student does not affect the coefficient of education. Johnson and Stafford (1973) obtained similar results for state expenditures per student in the PA survey.

27. See *Final Report*, Appendix C, for a description of the index and the analyses on which our conclusions are based.

28. For a sample of those 1957 Wisconsin high school seniors who attended college, only 5 percent of the variance in 1967 earnings lay between twelve categories of college type. Controlling socioeconomic background and eleventh-grade aptitude score reduced the amount of unexplained between-college earnings variance to 2 to 3 percent. Moreover, the relationship of college prestige to earnings was not consistently positive (Sewell and Hauser, 1975).

Solmon (1973) and Wachtel (1975) found evidence of a significant college quality effect on earnings in the older NBER-TH sample. Solmon finds that various indices of quality, including teachers' salaries and average SAT score, add from 0.01 to 0.02 to R^2 for 1969 in earnings, after IQ, education, and experience are controlled. He warns that the effects of average SAT may reflect the effects of individual abilities not measured by IQ. Wachtel finds a positive effect of educational cost. But individuals who pay a lot for their schooling may be more highly motivated than others, or may both attend school and then work in areas in which both costs and income are higher than average. This last problem also constrains efforts to assess the effects of educational expenditures for elementary and secondary education on later earnings. See, for example, Link and Ratledge (1975), Johnson and Stafford (1973), and Morgan and Sirageldin (1968). Aiken and Garfinkel (1974) try to control market conditions, but they do not control for individual mobility status, which may reflect personal characteristics related to earnings.

29. For the relative earnings of high school and college graduates in 1967, 1968, 1975, and 1976, see U.S. Bureau of the Census, *Current Population Reports*, Series P-60, Nos. 60, 66, 105, and 114. Data on the effect of the 1975 change in procedures for estimating missing income data appear in No. 105. The change in estimation procedure raised the mean for all male college graduates aged 25 and over by about 6 percent. It raised the mean for male high school graduates aged 25 and over by about 1 percent.

30. See Featherman (1977) and Featherman and Hauser (1978). An alternative

explanation is that the distribution of earnings is exogenously fixed and that schooling functions only as a queuing mechanism (Thurow, 1975).

CHAPTER 7

1. Hamblin (1974); Schwartz (1975); Coleman, Rainwater, and McClelland (1978).

2. See also the discussion of education-by-experience interactions herein.

3. These findings also support our earlier argument that Census–PSID differences in sampling and coding have no important consequences for our analyses. For evidence that returns to higher education declined after 1969 for new labor-market entrants, see Freeman (1975). Smith and Welch (1977) use the same evidence (CPS) over a slightly longer period to dispute Freeman's conclusion. As we emphasize elsewhere in this volume, there is a general need to consider the possible effects of business cycles when comparing cross-sectional surveys.

4. Smith and Welch (1977) used a 1/100 1970 Census sample to estimate ln earnings equations within experience classes. They found greater returns to higher education than to grades 1–12 for nonwhites in each experience class. This suggests that our finding of lower returns to a BA (compared to other years of schooling) for Census nonwhites would not be replicated in the larger 1/100 sample.

5. For the evidence supporting these conclusions, which are derived from Census data, see *Final Report*, chapter 8.

6. The CPS tabulations for 1975, the first year when CPS published mean earnings as well as mean personal income by years of schooling and race, confirm this judgment.

7. It is tempting, and almost natural, to argue that the increase in returns to a BA for blacks is largely attributable to affirmative action programs which were most vigorously implemented at the turn of the decade. However, Smith and Welch (1977) correctly argue that it is unreasonable to assume that those changes in black earnings which cannot be explained by the independent (human capital) variables are attributable to government action. They introduce some evidence indicating that the direct effect of government legislation is small. Welch (private communication) has suggested that the changes in the returns to black BAs relative to less-educated blacks could be largely attributable to business cycle changes since 1967.

8. Thurow and Link both worked from published Census data in which both the education and earnings data are grouped. Weiss and Williamson (1975) argue that this has a significant effect on results. Weiss and Williamson (1972, 1975) included men without earnings in their samples, assigning them $1. As chapter 11 shows, including nonearners converts the dependent variable (ln earnings) into a virtual dichotomy between labor-force participants and nonparticipants. The determinants of labor-force participation are not the same as the determinants of earnings among those who participate, so the results from samples that include nonparticipants will be very different from results from samples that exclude them.

Weiss and Williamson's (1975) conclusions regarding the causes of differences between Link's analysis and theirs (1972) are also misleading. They group nonearners with low earners and conclude that since the result is much more similar to Link's, the use of grouped vs. individual data was the primary cause of the difference between their findings and Link's. They then find only a small effect when they exclude the nonearners (which, at this point, is equivalent to excluding a percentage of the low earners). However, had they excluded the nonearners and not grouped the data, we suspect they would have explained virtually all of the differences between their results and Link's. In short, we believe that their treatment of nonearners, either by excluding them or making them look like low earners, was the primary obstacle to comparability. As a general rule, multivariate analyses are *very* sensitive to the treatment of individuals who are more than a few standard deviations from the mean.

Thurow's results should be more nearly comparable to ours. Yet he concluded that the income elasticity of education was greater for whites than for nonwhites in 1959, whereas we found no difference in percentage returns or marginal utilities in 1961. Using similar methods, Link concluded that while the elasticities increased for both whites and blacks between 1959 and 1969, the difference between the two groups' elasticities was almost as large in 1969 as in 1959. While we cannot conclusively demonstrate that their findings and ours are simultaneously consistent with the available data, we note that *if* the "true" relationship between education and earnings is constant in either percentage returns or marginal utility, the elasticity of earnings with respect to education will increase at higher levels of education. Two conclusions follow: (1) Since whites are more educated than nonwhites, the overall white elasticity (as indicated by a regression coefficient) will be greater than the nonwhite elasticity. (2) Since the mean education of both groups increased between 1959 and 1969, the elasticities of both groups should also have increased. (The change in the difference between the white and nonwhite elasticities would depend on how the "true" elasticity increased at higher levels of education and how the distribution [not just the mean] of education changed over time.)

9. See chapter 2 for a discussion of this problem.

10. Fogel (1966) found that income returns were lower for minority ethnic groups and that even after a group (in his case, Japanese Americans) attained an average level of education equal to whites, it was more than a decade before they enjoyed comparable incomes.

11. Table A7.1 in the Appendix shows that using earnings or earnings$^{1/3}$ as the dependent variable yields similar results.

12. This finding is consistent with Duncan's (1968) results using OCG.

13. In Duncan's (1968) terms, the PSID data suggest that middle-class nonwhites were passing on more of their advantages to their sons in 1971 than in 1961.

14. Featherman and Hauser (1978) reach the same conclusion after comparing OCG and OCG–II.

15. Arrow (1972a:96) has suggested that since such traits as these are easily assessable after an employee is on the job, then, if there were no costs to the employer, he should hire all applicants and fire those who turned out to be unsatisfactory. However, since hiring and firing do entail administrative costs, employers have an incentive not to hire unqualified applicants.

CHAPTER 8

1. See table A6.7 in the Appendix.

2. These are weighted averages of regression results from the OCG, PA, PSID, and NLS surveys.

CHAPTER 9

1. The relevant regressions appear in table A9.2 of the Appendix.

2. The work of Tobin (1958) and more recently Gronau (1974) and Heckman (1974, 1976) demonstrate some of the methodological problems that arise when we restrict the analysis to those who work. Their basic argument is that the application of such restrictions creates a sample which is unrepresentative of either society or the labor market. This is because those who do not work would probably command a lower market wage than similarly qualified individuals who do work. The average market wage of those who work will therefore overestimate the average market wage of the total group. This is likely to bias regression coefficients as well. Models assuming truncated variables have been proposed in the econometric literature to deal with this and related problems.

3. Benham (1974), however, also finds that wife's education has a significant positive effect on husband's income. He suggests some mechanisms (such as improving the household's decision-making ability or helping in the acquisition and processing of information) by which the education of wives might affect their husbands' economic position. Benham concludes that when individuals live in families, human capital accrues not only to them but also to others in their family.

CHAPTER 10

1. We took these means from U.S. Bureau of the Census (1970) and from more recent CPS reports in the P-60 series.

CHAPTER 11

1. Compare, for example, the conclusions of Bowles (1972), Jencks et al. (1972), and Duncan, Featherman, and Duncan (1972), all based on data from OCG; or compare analyses of the Veterans Survey by Duncan (1968), Griliches and Mason (1972), and Jencks (*Final Report,* Appendix G). For other examples, see McClelland (1976) and footnote 8 in chapter 7.

2. For a full description of the problems involved in converting PSID labor income, see *Final Report,* chapter 16. The calculation of PSID earnings varies slightly from that used elsewhere in this volume.

3. Our inability to eliminate all the allocated education data from the PSID probably biases the PSID education mean slightly downward and results in underestimation of the true PSID–Census difference. See *Final Report,* pp. 732–33.

4. *Final Report,* chapters 13 and 16, by Jencks and McClelland respectively, present two different estimates of the reliability of Census data. Chapter 16 presents results corrected for unreliability (p. 740). In general, random errors in the dependent variable do not affect regression coefficients. Thus, if Census respondents made greater random errors in reporting earnings than PSID respondents, the Census correlation would be lower than the PSID correlation but the regression coefficients would be the same.

5. Reconstructing PSID self-employment income involved estimating some totals from grouped data. This procedure undoubtedly leads to some errors. For details see *Final Report,* pp. 743–44.

6. PSID respondents drawn from the Survey of Economic Opportunity had been followed for seven years. See Survey Research Center (1972:9–13).

7. For details, see *Final Report,* pp. 750–51.

8. *Final Report,* pp. 779–83.

9. The U.S. Bureau of the Census reports a similar finding in *Current Population Reports,* Series P-60, No. 74 (1970:20–22).

CHAPTER 12

1. One possible exception is Jencks and Brown (1975), but like most other investigators they were unable to distinguish the effects of high schools from the effects of local labor-market conditions.

2. Apparent discrepancies between our results and Mincer's (1974) can be explained in the same way. Mincer analyzed 1960 Census data on men 15 to 64. We analyzed 1970 Census data on 25- to 64-year-olds. Including men 15 to 24 increases the variance of ln earnings. It also means that experience explains more variance. Expanding the sample to include 15- to 24-year-olds does not, however, appreciably change the variance of the residuals.

3. These estimates assume R^2 (uncorrected for measurement error) is 0.30 in Kalamazoo, 0.26 in Talent, 0.20 in NORC, and 0.35 for Taubman's DZ twins. They assume that the standard deviation of ln earnings is 0.45 in Kalamazoo, 0.41 in Talent, 0.87 in NORC, and 0.57 for Taubman's DZ twins, and that absolute differences between brothers average 1.13 times the standard deviation of the residuals in all four samples. Nonnormality of the residuals and measurement error both tend to bias these estimates upward.

4. Featherman and Hauser (1976b) present equations for cohorts aged 25 to 34,

35 to 44, and 45 to 54 in 1962 and aged 35 to 44, 45 to 54, and 55 to 64 in 1973. The coefficients of demographic background characteristics and years of schooling show no consistent trend as these three cohorts age. Likewise, the 1962 and 1973 occupations of OCG-II men who had finished school and were working full time in 1962 had virtually identical correlations (±0.01) with demographic background and education. (We are indebted to William Bielby for making these tabulations for us.)

Bielby et al. (1977) present equations predicting both current occupational status and initial status after school completion for all OCG-II men aged 20 to 64. Their equations for initial status control labor-force experience (by constraining it to be zero), while their equations for current status control age. We can compare the two equations by assuming that age equals experience plus schooling plus six. If this is the case, substituting experience for age in the equation for current status will raise the coefficient of schooling by an amount equal to the average linear coefficient of age and will leave the other coefficients unchanged. After making this adjustment, the coefficients of schooling in the equations predicting initial and current status are virtually identical, at least for nonblacks. Once education is included, demographic background characteristics make minimal contributions to R^2.

5. We know of no systematic study of intragenerational mobility that would allow us to assess the likely importance of this bias. Spillerman (1977) reviews most of the relevant literature. Only 19 percent of OCG-II respondents aged 25 to 64 were in the same occupation in 1973 as when they finished their schooling.

6. After making the corrections in note 8, page 362, Bielby et al.'s (1977) results imply that reports of initial and current occupation are equally reliable, and that the reliabilities for OCG-II men aged 25 to 64 are about 0.86.

Miller (1977) found that retrospective Census questions on occupation in 1965 indicated less movement between major occupational groups than did NLS data obtained by following the same individuals for five years. Retrospective reports on occupation in 1965 do not, however, contain any more *random* error than current reports, since they do not correlate worse with other traits. Rather, appreciable numbers of respondents seem to report that they were in the same occupation in 1965 as in 1970 although they had actually changed occupations. This inflates the correlation between 1965 and 1970 status in Census data.

If this same pattern holds for OCG-II reports of initial and current occupation, we have overestimated the degree of occupational stability and the explanatory power of stable traits. But OCG-II respondents reported their current and initial occupations in different surveys, and in many cases the data on current occupations came from wives. We therefore doubt that the correlation between initial and current status is as inflated in OCG-II as the correlation between 1965 and 1970 status in the Census.

7. If we follow men initially aged 41 to 45 from 1951 to 1955, for example, the correlations between their earnings in adjacent years average 0.82, while the correlations for three-year intervals average 0.75. If we follow a cohort of the same initial age from 1956 to 1960, the correlations between adjacent years average 0.90, while those for three-year intervals average 0.83. (To increase comparability, both cohorts were restricted to men in continuous, covered employment from 1937 to 1940 and 1947 to 1970.)

The change in estimation procedures also lowers the correlation of pre-1956 earnings with post-1956 earnings, because it changes the shape of the distribution. If we look at men aged 30 to 34 in 1940 who were in covered employment from 1937 to 1940 and 1947 to 1970, their 1939 and 1940 earnings correlate 0.53 and 0.55 with their 1950 earnings. The correlations hover between 0.53 and 0.55 from 1950 to 1955, drop to 0.45 and 0.46 in 1956, hover between 0.45 and 0.46 from 1956 to 1969, and then drop to 0.43 in 1970. The drop in correlations involving years before and after 1956 is also about 15 percent for men aged 25 to 29 in 1940.

8. Restricting samples of men aged 55 to 64 in 1970 to those with covered earnings in every year from 1957 to 1970 has virtually no consistent effect on either the correlation between earnings in adjacent years or the correlation between earnings over ten year intervals. Restricting such a sample to men who also had covered earnings from 1937 to 1940 and 1947 to 1955 eliminates those who were self-employed at any time during the earlier years. This restriction raises the correlation between earnings

in 1959 and 1960 or 1969 and 1970 from an average of 0.87 to 0.90. It raises ten-year correlations from an average of 0.69 to an average of 0.74. Excluding the self-employed has roughly similar effects in PSID. The upward bias could be even greater for longer intervals, but we have not yet had time to investigate this possibility.

9. This judgment is based on preliminary comparisons between PSID, NLS, and Social Security correlations. Since we have not yet eliminated all the possible sources of noncomparability between these three series, the conclusion in the text is tentative. The results for ln earnings are clear, however. Taking logarithms has no consistent effect on interannual PSID correlations. It lowers Social Security correlations by a tenth or more, presumably because Social Security records contain more spurious low earners and taking logarithms inflates their importance.

10. This assumption is so consistent with conventional sociological thinking that it may not strike most sociologists as potentially controversial. Indeed, Coleman (1973) criticized *Inequality* for even entertaining the naive hypothesis that income inequality is an endogenous byproduct of the degree of inequality in individuals' personal characteristics.

BIBLIOGRAPHY

Aiken, John S., and Irwin Garfinkel. "Economic Returns to Educational Quality: An Empirical Analysis for Whites, Blacks, Poor Whites, and Poor Blacks." Madison, Wisconsin: Institute for Research on Poverty, University of Wisconsin, Discussion Paper no. 224-74, 1974.

Alexander, Karl L., M. Cook, and E. L. McDill. "Curriculum Tracking and Educational Stratification." *American Sociological Review* (1978), 43:47–66.

Alexander, Karl L., and Bruce K. Eckland. "Sex Differences in the Educational Attainment Process," *American Sociological Review* (1974), 39:668–82.

Alexander, Karl L., Bruce K. Eckland, and Larry J. Griffin. "The Wisconsin Model of Socioeconomic Achievement: A Replication." *American Journal of Sociology* (1975), 81:324–42.

Andrisani, Paul J., and Gilbert Nestel. "Internal–External Control as Contributor to the Outcome of Work Experience." *Journal of Applied Psychology* (April 1976), 61:156–65.

Arrow, Kenneth J. "Models of Job Discrimination," in Anthony H. Pascal, ed., *Racial Discrimination in Economic Life*. Lexington, Massachusetts: Lexington Books, 1972a.

———. "Some Mathematical Models of Race in the Labor Market," in Anthony H. Pascal, ed., *Racial Discrimination in Economic Life*. Lexington, Massachusetts: Lexington Books, 1972b.

Bartlett, Susan. "Education and Economic Inequality," unpublished Bachelor's thesis. Wellesley, Massachusetts: Wellesley College, 1975.

———. "Education, Experience, and Wage Inequality: 1939–69." *Journal of Human Resources* (Summer 1978), 13:349–66.

Bartlett, Susan, and Christopher Jencks. "Returns to Schooling, Experience, and Age in 1959 and 1969." Harvard Department of Sociology, offset, 1978.

Becker, Gary. *Human Capital: A Theoretical and Empirical Analysis with Special Reference to Education*. New York: Columbia University Press, 1964.

———. "A Theory of the Allocation of Time." *Economic Journal* (1965), 75:493–517.

Becker, Gary, and Barry R. Chiswick. "Education and the Distribution of Earnings." *American Economic Review* (1966), 56:358–69.

Behrman, Jere, Zdenek Hrubec, Paul Taubman, and Terence Wales. "Inter- and Intra-Generational Determination of Socioeconomic Success with Special Reference to Genetic Endowment and Family and Other Environments." Dept. of Economics, University of Pennsylvania, 1978, offset.

Behrman, Jere, Paul Taubman, and Terence Wales. "Controlling for and Measuring the Effects of Genetics and Family Environment in Equations for Schooling and Labor Market Success," in Paul Taubman, ed., *Kinometrics: The Determinants of Socioeconomic Success within and between Families*. New York: North-Holland, 1977.

Benham, Lee. "Benefits of Women's Education within Marriage." *Journal of Political Economy* (March/April 1974), 82:557–74.

Benson, Viola E. "The Intelligence and Later Success of Sixth Grade Pupils." *School and Society* (1942), 55:163–67.

Berg, Ivar. *Education and Jobs: The Great Training Robbery*. New York: Praeger, 1975.

Bielby, William, and Robert Hauser. "Response Errors in Earnings Functions for Non-black Males." *Sociological Methods and Research.* (1977), 6:241–80.

Bielby, William T., Robert M. Hauser, David L. Featherman. "Response Errors of Black and Nonblack Males in Models of the Intergenerational Transmission of Socioeconomic Status." *American Journal of Sociology* (May 1977), 82:1242–88.

Bishop, John. "Biases in Measurement of the Productivity Benefits of Human Capital Investments." Madison, Wisconsin: Institute for Research on Poverty, University of Wisconsin, Discussion Paper no. 223-74, 1974.

———. "Reporting Errors and the True Return to Schooling." Unpublished, Madison, Wisconsin: 1976.

Blau, Peter, and Otis Dudley Duncan. *The American Occupational Structure.* New York: John Wiley and Sons, 1967.

Blaug, Mark. "The Correlation between Education and Earnings: What Does It Signify?" *Higher Education* (1972), 1:53–76.

Block, N. J., and Gerald Dworkin, eds. *The IQ Controversy.* New York: Pantheon Books, 1976.

Bloom, Benjamin S. *Human Characteristics and School Learning.* New York: McGraw-Hill, 1976.

———. *Stability and Change in Human Characteristics.* New York: John Wiley and Sons, 1964.

Borus, Michael C., and Gilbert Nestel. "Response Bias in Reports of Father's Education and Socioeconomic Status." *Journal of the American Statistical Association* (December 1973), 68:816–20.

Bowles, Samuel. "Schooling and Inequality from Generation to Generation." *Journal of Political Economy* (May/June 1972), 80:S219–51.

Bowles, Samuel, and Herbert Gintis. "IQ in the U.S. Class Structure." *Social Policy* (December 1972–January/February 1973).

Bowles, Samuel, and Herbert Gintis. *Schooling in Capitalist America: Educational Reform and the Contradictions of Economic Life.* New York: Basic Books, 1976.

Bowles, Samuel, and Valerie Nelson. "The 'Inheritance of IQ' and the Intergenerational Reproduction of Economic Inequality." *Review of Economics and Statistics* (1974), 56:39–51.

Brenner, Marshall H. "Use of High School Data to Predict Work Performance." *Journal of Applied Psychology* (1968), 52:29–30.

Brittain, John A. *The Inheritance of Economic Status.* Washington, D.C.: Brookings Institution, 1977.

Chamberlain, Gary, and Zvi Griliches. "Unobservables with a Variance–Components Structure: Ability, Schooling, and the Economic Success of Brothers." *International Economic Review* (June 1975), 16:422–49.

———. "More on Brothers," in Paul Taubman, ed. *Kinometrics: Determinants of Socioeconomic Success Within and Between Families.* New York: North-Holland, 1977.

Chiswick, Barry. "Schooling and Earnings of Low Achievers: Comment." *American Economic Review* (1972), 62:752–53.

Coleman, James S. *The Adolescent Society: The Social Life of the Teenager and Its Impact on Education.* New York: Free Press, 1961.

Coleman, James. "Equality of Opportunity and Equality of Results." *Harvard Educational Review* (February 1973), 43:129–37.

Coleman, James S., et al. "White and Black Careers during the First Decade of Labor Force Experience. Part I: Occupational Status." *Social Science Research* (September 1972), 1:243–70.

Coleman, Richard, Lee Rainwater, and Kent McClelland. *Social Standing in America.* New York: Basic Books, 1978.

Conlisk, John. "A Bit of Evidence on the Income–Education–Ability Interrelation." *Journal of Human Resources* (1971), 6:358–62.

Corcoran, Mary. "Measurement Error in Status Attainment Models," in Greg Duncan and James Morgan, eds., *Five Thousand American Families,* vol. VII. Ann Arbor, Michigan: Institute for Social Research, University of Michigan, 1979.

Corcoran, Mary, Christopher Jencks, and Michael Olneck. "The Effects of Family Background on Earnings." *American Economic Review* (May 1976), 66:430–35.

Cronbach, Lee J., and R. Shaw. *Aptitude and Instruction.* New York: Irvington Press, 1977.

Cutright, Phillips. *Achievement, Mobility, and the Draft: Their Impact on the Earnings of Men.* Washington, D.C.: Social Security Administration, Office of Research and Statistics, SSA 73-11854, Staff Paper no. 14, 1973.

Denison, Edward F. *The Sources of Economic Growth in the United States and the Alternatives before Us.* New York: Committee for Economic Growth, Supplementary Paper no. 13 (January 1962).

————. "Measuring the Contribution of Education (and the Residual) to Economic Growth," in Organization for Economic Cooperation and Development, *The Residual Factor and Economic Growth.* Paris: O.E.C.D., 1964.

————. "Reply," in Organization for Economic Cooperation and Development, *The Residual Factor and Economic Growth.* Paris: O.E.C.D., 1964.

Duncan, Otis Dudley. "A Socioeconomic Index for All Occupations," in Albert J. Reiss, *Occupations and Social Status.* Glencoe, Illinois: The Free Press, 1961.

————. "Ability and Achievement." *Eugenics Quarterly* (March 1968), 15:1–11.

Duncan, Otis Dudley, David Featherman, and Beverly Duncan. *Socioeconomic Background and Achievement.* New York: Seminar Press, 1972.

Eaglesfield, David. "Family Background and Occupational Achievement." Cambridge, Massachusetts: Ph.D. dissertation, Harvard Department of Sociology, 1977.

Eckhaus, R. S. "Estimation of the Returns to Education with Hourly Standardized Incomes," *Quarterly Journal of Economics* (1973), 87:121–31.

Elder, Glen. "Achievement Motivation and Intelligence in Occupational Mobility: A Longitudinal Analysis." *Sociometry* (December 1968), 31:327–54.

Ellis, Dean. "Speech and Social Status in America." *Social Forces* (1967), 45:431–37.

Fagerlind, Ingemar. *Formal Education and Adult Earnings.* Stockholm: Almqvist and Wiksell, 1975.

Featherman, David L. "Achievement Orientations and Socioeconomic Career Attainments." *American Sociological Review* (April 1972), 37:131–43.

————. "Has Opportunity Declined in America?" Madison, Wisconsin: Institute for Research on Poverty, University of Wisconsin, Discussion Paper no. 437-77, 1977.

Featherman, David, and Robert M. Hauser. "Changes in the Socioeconomic Stratification of the Races, 1962–1973." *American Journal of Sociology* (November 1976b), 82:621–51.

————. "Design for a Replicate Study of Social Mobility in the United States," in Kenneth C. Laud and Seymour Spilerman, eds., *Social Indicator Models.* New York: Russell Sage Foundation, 1975.

————. *Opportunity and Change.* New York: Academic Press, 1978.

————. "Prestige or Socioeconomic Scales in the Study of Occupational Achievement." *Sociological Methods and Research* (May 1976c), 4:403–22.

————. "Sexual Inequalities and Socioeconomic Achievement in the U.S.: 1962–1973." *American Sociological Review* (June 1976a), 41:462–83.

Featherman, David, Lancaster Jones, and Robert Hauser. "Assumptions of Social Mobility Research in the U.S.: The Case of Occupational Status." *Social Science Research* (1975), 4:329–60.

Final Report. See Jencks and Rainwater, 1977.

Flanagan, John C., et al. *The American High School Student.* Pittsburgh: University of Pittsburgh, Project Talent, 1964.

Fogel, Walter. "The Effect of Low Educational Attainment on Incomes: A Comparative Study of Selected Ethnic Groups." *Journal of Human Resources* (1966), 1:22–40.

Freeman, Richard. "Changes in the Labor Market for Black Labor." *Brookings Papers on Economic Activity* (Summer 1973).

————. *The Overeducated American.* New York: Academic Press, 1976.

————. "Overinvestment in College Training?" *Journal of Human Resources* (Summer 1975), 10:287–311.

Gasson, Ruth M., A. O. Haller, and W. H. Sewell. *Attitudes and Facilitation in Status Attainment.* Washington, D.C.: American Sociological Association, Rose Monograph Series, 1972.

Gintis, Herbert. "Education, Technology, and the Characteristics of Worker Productivity." *American Economic Review* (1971), 61:266–79.

Gocka, Edward F. "Coding for Correlation and Regression." *Educational and Psychological Measurement* (1974), 34:771–83.

Bibliography

Goldberger, Arthur S., and Otis D. Duncan, eds. *Structural Equation Models in the Social Sciences.* New York: Seminar Press, 1973.

Goldfeld, Stephen M., and Richard E. Quandt. *Nonlinear Methods in Econometrics.* Amsterdam: North-Holland, 1972.

Gordon, Roger. "The Influence of Class Background on IQ Scores." Princeton, New Jersey: Princeton University, Department of Economics, Offset, 1978.

Gorseline, Donald. *The Effect of Schooling upon Income.* Bloomington, Indiana: Graduate Council of Indiana University, 1932.

Greeley, Andrew. *The American Catholic: A Social Portrait.* New York: Basic Books, 1977.

Griffin, Larry. "Specification Biases in Estimates of Socioeconomic Returns to Schooling." *Sociology of Education* (1976), 49:121–39.

Griliches, Zvi. "Estimating the Returns to Schooling: Some Econometric Problems." *Econometrica* (1977), 45:1–22.

———. "Notes on the Role of Education in Production Functions and Growth Accounting," in W. Lee Hansen, ed., *Education, Income, and Human Capital.* New York: Columbia University Press, 1970.

Griliches, Zvi, and William M. Mason. "Education, Income, and Ability." *Journal of Political Economy* (May/June 1972), 80:S74–S103.

Gronau, Reuben. "Wage Comparisons—A Selectivity Bias." *Journal of Political Economy* (November/December 1974), 82:1119–43.

Hamblin, Robert. "Social Attitudes: Magnitude Measurement and Theory," in Hubert M. Blalock, ed., *Measurement in the Social Sciences.* Chicago: Aldine Publishing, 1974.

Hanoch, Giora. "An Economic Analysis of Earnings and Schooling." *Journal of Human Resources* (1974), 2:309–29.

Hansen, A. Lee. "Total and Private Rates of Return to Investment in Schooling." *Journal of Political Economy* (1963), 71:128–40.

Hansen, Lee, Burton Weisbrod, and William Scanlon, "Schooling and Earnings of Low Achievers." *American Economic Review* (June 1970) 60:409–18.

Hause, John C. "Earnings Profile: Ability and Schooling." *Journal of Political Economy* (May/June 1972), 80:S108–S138.

Hauser, Robert M. "Socioeconomic Background and Differential Returns to Education," in Paul Taubman and Lewis C. Solmon, eds., *Does College Matter?* New York: Academic Press, 1973.

Hauser, Robert M., and Thomas N. Daymont. "Schooling, Ability, and Earnings: Cross-Sectional Findings Eight to Fourteen Years after High School Graduation." *Sociology of Education* (July 1977), 50:182–206.

Hauser, Robert M., and Peter Dickinson. " 'Inequality' on Occupational Status and Income." *American Educational Research Journal* (Spring 1974), 11:161–68.

Hauser, Robert M., and David Featherman. "Equality of Schooling: Trends and Prospects." *Sociology of Education* (1976), 49:99–120.

Hauser, Robert M., William H. Sewell, and Duane F. Alwin. "High School Effects on Achievement," in William H. Sewell, Robert M. Hauser, and David L. Featherman, eds., *Schooling and Achievement in American Society.* New York: Academic Press, 1976.

Heckman, James. "The Common Structure of Statistical Models of Truncation, Sample Selection and Limited Dependent Variables and a Simple Estimation for Such Models." *Annals of Economic and Social Measurement* (Fall 1976), 5:475–92.

———. "Shadow Prices, Market Wages, and Labor Supply." *Econometrica* (July 1974), 42:679–94.

Heckman, James, and Solomon Polachek. "Empirical Evidence on the Functional Form of the Earnings–Schooling Relationship." *Journal of the American Statistical Association* (1974), 69:350–54.

Heise, David R. "Employing Nominal Variables, Induced Variables and Block Variables in Path Analysis." *Sociological Methods and Research* (November 1972), 1:147–73.

Hermalin, Albert. "The Homogeneity of Siblings on Education and Occupation." Princeton, New Jersey: Ph.D. thesis, Princeton University, 1969.

Herrnstein, Richard J. *IQ in the Meritocracy.* Boston: Little, Brown, 1973.

Hines, Fred, Luther Tweeten, and Martin Redfern. "Social and Private Rates of Return to Investment in Schooling by Race–Sex Groups and Regions." *Journal of Human Resources* (1970), 3:317–40.

Hodge, Robert, and Paul Siegel. "The Classification of Occupations: Some Problems of Sociological Interpretation." *Proceedings of the Social Statistics Section, American Statistical Association* 1966, pp. 176–92.

Houthakker, H. S. "Education and Income." *Review of Economics and Statistics* (1959), 41:24–28.

Hunt, J. McV. *Intelligence and Experience.* New York: Ronald Press, 1961.

Hunt, Shane J. "Income Determinants for the College Graduates and Return to Educational Investment." *Yale Economic Essays* (1963), 3:305–58.

Jencks, Christopher. " 'Inequality' in Retrospect." *Harvard Educational Review* (February 1973), 43:138–64.

Jencks, Christopher, and Marsha Brown. "Genes and Social Stratification: A Methodological Exploration with Illustrative Data," in Paul Taubman, ed., *Kinometrics: The Determinants of Economic Success within and between Families.* NY North-Holland, 1977, pp. 169–233.

———. "The Effects of High Schools on Their Students." *Harvard Educational Review* (August 1975), 45:273–324.

Jencks, Christopher, and Lee Rainwater. "The Effects of Family Background, Test Scores, Personality Traits, and Schooling on Economic Success." Springfield, Virginia: *Final Report* under National Institute of Education Grant #NIE-G-74-0077, National Technical Information Service, 1977.

Jencks, Christopher, Marshall Smith, Henry Acland, Mary Jo Bane, David Cohen, Herbert Gintis, Barbara Heyns, and Stephan Michelson. *Inequality: A Reassessment of the Effect of Family and Schooling in America.* New York: Basic Books, 1972.

Jensen, Arthur R. "How Much Can We Boost IQ and Scholastic Achievement?" *Harvard Educational Review* (1969), 39:1–123.

Johnson, George F., and Frank P. Stafford. "Social Returns to Quantity and Quality of Schooling." *Journal of Human Resources* (1973), 8:139–55.

Kamin, Leon J. *The Science and Politics of IQ.* New York: Lawrence Erlbaum Association, 1974.

Karier, Clarence J., Paul Violas, and Joel Spring. *Roots of Crisis: American Education in the Twentieth Century.* Chicago: Rand McNally, 1973.

Katz, Michael B. *The Irony of Early School Reform.* Cambridge, Massachusetts: Harvard University Press, 1968.

Kitagawa, Evelyn, and Philip Hauser. *Differential Mortality in the United States: A Study of Socioeconomic Epidemiology.* Cambridge, Massachusetts: Harvard University Press, 1973.

Klatzky, Sheila R., and Robert H. Hodge. "A Canonical Correlation Analysis of Occupational Mobility." *Journal of the American Statistical Association* (March 1971), 66:16–22.

Kohn, Melvin. *Class and Conformity.* Homewood, Illinois: The Dorsey Press, 1969.

Korman, Abraham K. "The Prediction of Managerial Performance: A Review." *Personnel Psychology* (1968), 21:295–322.

Layard, Richard, and George Psacharopoulos. "The Screening Hypothesis and the Returns to Education." *Journal of Political Economy* (1974), 82:985–98.

Leibenstein, Harvey. "Economics of Skill Labelling," in Joseph A. Lauwerys and David G. Scanlon, eds., *The World Year Book of Education 1969.* London: Evans Brothers, 1969.

Levin, Henry M. "A Decade of Policy Development in Improving Education and Training for Low-Income Population," in Robert Haveman, ed., *A Decade of Federal Antipoverty Policy: Achievements, Failures and Lessons.* New York: Academic Press, 1977.

Link, Charles R. "Black Education, Earnings and Interregional Migration: A Comment and Some New Evidence." *American Economic Review* (1975), 65:236–40.

Link, Charles R., and Edward C. Ratledge. "Social Returns to Quantity and Quality of Education: A Further Statement." *Journal of Human Resources* (Winter 1975), 10:78–89.

Lohnes, Paul R. *Measuring Adolescent Personality.* Pittsburgh: Project Talent, University of Pittsburgh, 1966.

Lorge, Irving. "Schooling Makes a Difference." *Teachers College Record* (May 1945), 46:483–92.

Masters, Stanley, and Thomas Ribich. "Schooling and Earnings of Low Achievers: Comment." *American Economic Review* (1972), 62:755–59.

McCall, Robert. "Childhood IQ's as Predictors of Adult Educational and Occupational Status." *Science* (July 29, 1977), 197:482–83.

McClelland, Kent. "How Different Surveys Yield Different Results: The Case of Education and Earnings." Cambridge, Massachusetts: unpublished Ph.D. dissertation, Harvard University, Department of Sociology, 1976.

McNemar, Quinn. *Psychological Statistics.* New York: John Wiley and Sons, 1962.

Miller, Ann. "The Measurement of Change: A Comparison of Retrospective and Panel Surveys." Philadelphia: Population Studies Center, University of Pennsylvania, offset, 1977.

Miller, Herman, P. *Income Distribution in the United States* (A 1960 Census Monograph). Washington, D.C.: U.S. Government Printing Office, 1966.

Mincer, Jacob. "The Distribution of Labor Incomes: A Survey with Special Reference to the Human Capital Approach." *Journal of Economic Literature* (1970), 8:1–26.

———. "Education, Experience, and the Distribution of Earnings and Employment: An Overview," in F. Thomas Juster, ed., *Education, Income and Human Behavior.* New York: McGraw-Hill, 1975.

———. "Investments in Human Capital and Personal Income Distribution." *Journal of Political Economy* (August 1959), 66:281–302.

———. *Schooling, Experience and Earnings.* New York: Columbia University Press, 1974.

Morgan, James, et al. *Five Thousand American Families,* vols. I–VI. Ann Arbor, Michigan: Institute for Social Research, University of Michigan, 1974–78.

Morgan, James, and Martin David. "Education and Income." *Quarterly Journal of Economics* (1963), 77:423–37.

Morgan, James, Martin David, Wilbur Cohen, and Harvey Brazer. *Income and Welfare in the United States.* New York: McGraw-Hill, 1962.

Morgan, James, and Ismail Sirageldin. "A Note on the Quality Dimension in Education." *Journal of Political Economy* (1968), 76:1069–77.

Morgenstern, Richard. "Direct and Indirect Effects on Earnings of Schooling and Socioeconomic Background." *Review of Economics and Statistics* (May 1973), 55:225–33.

Moynihan, Daniel P. "The Schism in Black America." *The Public Interest* (Spring 1972), 27:3–24.

Olneck, Michael R. "The Determinants of Educational Attainment and Adult Status among Brothers: The Kalamazoo Study." Cambridge, Massachusetts: Ed.D. thesis, Harvard Graduate School of Education, 1976.

———. "The Economic Effects of Cognitive and Educational Differences among Low-Ability and Blue-Collar Origin Men: A Comparative Analysis." Menlo Park, California: Stanford Research Institute, Research Note, EPRC 4537-22, 1976c.

———. "The Effects of Education on Occupational Status and Earnings." Madison, Wisconsin: Institute for Research on Poverty, University of Wisconsin, Discussion Paper no. 358-76, 1976b.

———. "On the Use of Sibling Data to Estimate the Effects of Family Background, Cognitive Skills, and Schooling: Results from the Kalamazoo Brothers Study," in Paul Taubman, ed., *Kinometrics: The Determinants of Economic Success within and between Families.* Amsterdam: North-Holland, 1977.

Olneck, Michael, and James Crouse. "Myths of the Meritocracy: Cognitive Skill and Adult Success in the United States." Madison, Wisconsin: Institute for Research on Poverty, University of Wisconsin: Discussion Paper no. 485-78, March 1978.

Project Talent. *The Project Talent Data Bank: A Handbook.* Palo Alto, California: American Institute for Research, 1972.

Reed, Ritchie, and Herman Miller. "Some Determinants of the Variation in Earnings for College Men." *Journal of Human Resources* (Spring 1970), 5:177–90.

Renshaw, Edward F. "Estimating the Returns to Education." *Review of Economics and Statistics* (1960), 42:318–24.

Rist, Ray C. "Student Social Class and Teacher Expectations: The Self-Fulfilling Prophecy in Ghetto Education." *Harvard Educational Review* (1970), 40:411–51.

Rogers, Daniel C. "Private Rates of Return to Education in the United States: A Case Study." *Yale Economic Essays* (1969), 9:89–134.

Rosen, Bernard C. "Industrialization, Personality and Social Mobility in Brazil." *Human Organization* (Summer 1971), 30:137–48.

Rosenbaum, James E. *Making Inequality: The Hidden Curriculum of High School Tracking.* New York: John Wiley and Sons, 1976.

Rotter, J. B. "Generalized Expectancies for Internal versus External Control and Reinforcements," *Psychological Monographs* (1966), 80:1–28.

Scarr, Sandra, and Weinberg, R. A. "The Influence of Family Background on Intellectual Attainment." *American Sociological Review,* (October, 1978) 43:674–92.

Schoenfeldt, Lyle. "Hereditary–Environmental Components of the Project Talent Two-Day Test Battery." *Measurement and Evaluation in Guidance* (Summer 1968), 1:130–40.

Schwartz, Joseph E. "Theoretical and Methodological Issues Relating to the Study of Income, Income Distribution, and Inequality." Cambridge Massachusetts: Harvard University, unpublished, 1975.

Schultz, Theodore. "Capital Formation by Education." *Journal of Political Economy* (December, 1960) 68:571–83.

Sewell, William H., and Robert M. Hauser. *Education, Occupation and Earnings.* New York: Academic Press, 1975.

Shaycroft, Marion F. *The High School Years: Growth in Cognitive Skills.* Pittsburgh: American Institute for Research and University of Pittsburgh Project Talent, 1967.

Siegel, Paul, and Robert Hodge. "A Causal Approach to the Study of Measurement Error," in Hubert M. Blalock and Ann B. Blalock, eds., *Methodology in Social Research.* New York: McGraw-Hill, 1968.

Smith, James P., and Finis R. Welch, "Black–White Earnings and Employment 1960–1970." Santa Monica, California: Rand Corporation, 1975.

———. "Black–White Male Wage Ratios: 1960–70." *American Economic Review* (June 1977), 67:323–38.

Snedecor, George, and William Cochran. *Statistical Methods.* Ames, Iowa: Iowa State University Press, 1967.

Solmon, Lewis C. "The Definition and Impact of College Quality" in Lewis C. Solmon and Paul Taubman, eds., *Does College Matter?* New York: Academic Press, 1973.

———. "Schooling and Subsequent Success: The Influence of Ability, Background and Formal Education," in Lewis C. Solmon and Paul Taubman, eds., *Does College Matter?* New York: Academic Press, 1973.

Spence, Michael A. *Market Signalling.* Cambridge, Massachusetts: Harvard University Press, 1975.

Spilerman, Seymour. "Careers, Labor Market Structure, and Socioeconomic Achievement." *American Journal of Sociology* (November 1977), 83:551–93.

Stice, Glen, and Ruth B. Ekstrom. *High School Attrition.* Princeton, New Jersey: Educational Testing Service, 1964.

Stinchcombe, Arthur L. "On Curvilinearity in Regressions Involving Age and Social Status: A New Approach to Cohort Analysis and to Social Mobility Studies." Chicago, Illinois: National Opinion Research Center, 1976, offset.

Stolzenberg, Ross M. "Education, Occupation, and Wage Differences between White and Black Men." *American Journal of Sociology* (September 1975), 81:299–323.

Survey Research Center. *A Panel Study of Income Dynamics: Study Design, Procedures, Available Data; 1968–1972 Interviewing Years.* Ann Arbor, Michigan: Institute for Social Research, University of Michigan, 1972.

Taubman, Paul. "The Determinants of Earnings: Genetics, Family, and Other

Bibliography

Environments: A Study of White Male Twins." *American Economic Review* (December 1976b), 66:858–70.

―――. "Earnings, Education, Genetics, and Environment." *Journal of Human Resources* (Fall 1976a), 11:447–61.

―――. "The Relative Influence of Inheritable and Environmental Factors and the Importance of Intelligence in Earnings Functions." Philadelphia, Pennsylvania: University of Pennsylvania Department of Economics, offset, 1977.

Taubman, Paul, and Terence Wales. *Higher Education and Earnings: College as an Investment and a Screening Device.* New York: McGraw-Hill, 1974.

―――. "Higher Education, Mental Ability, and Screening." *Journal of Political Economy* (1973), 81:28–56.

―――. *Mental Ability and Higher Educational Attainment in the 20th Century.* Berkeley, California: Carnegie Commission on Higher Education, 1972.

Thurow, Lester. "Education and Economic Equality, *"The Public Interest"* (Summer 1972), 28:66–81.

―――. *Generating Inequality,* New York: Basic Books, 1975.

―――. "The Occupational Distribution of the Returns to Education and Experience for Whites and Negroes." *Proceedings of the Social Statistics Section, American Statistical Association,* 1967, pp. 233–43.

―――. *Poverty and Discrimination.* Washington, D.C.: Brookings Institution, 1969.

Tobin, James. "Estimation of Relationships for Limited Dependent Variables," *Econometrica* (1958), 26:24–36.

Treiman, Donald, and Kermit Terrell, "Sex and the Process of Status Attainment: A Comparison of Working Men and Women." *American Sociological Review* (April 1975). 40:174–200.

U.S. Bureau of the Census. *Current Population Reports,* Series P-60, No. 74, "Annual Mean Income and Educational Attainment of Men in the United States for Selected Years, 1956 to 1968." Washington, D.C.: 1970.

―――. *Current Population Reports,* Series P-60. Washington, D.C.: 1967–1975.

―――. "Estimates of Coverage of Population by Sex, Race, and Age: Demographic Analysis." Washington, D.C.: *1970 Census of Population and Housing: Evaluation and Research Program,* PHC(E)-4, 1973.

―――. *Public Use Samples of Basic Records from the 1970 Census: Description and Technical Documentation.* Washington, D.C.: 1972.

Wachtel, Paul. "The Return to Investment in Higher Education: Another View," in F. Thomas Juster, ed., *Education, Income, and Human Behavior.* New York: McGraw-Hill, 1975.

Weisbrod, Burton. "Comment on Hause's 'Earnings Profile: Ability and Schooling.'" *Journal of Political Economy* (1972), 80:S139–S141.

Weisbrod, Burton A., and Peter Karpoff. "Monetary Returns to College Education, Student Ability, and College Quality." *Review of Economics and Statistics* (1968), 50:491–97.

Weiss, Leonard, and Jeffrey G. Williamson. "Black Education, Earnings and Interregional Migration: Even Newer Evidence." *American Economic Review* (1975), 65:241–44.

―――. "Black Education, Earnings and Interregional Migration: Some New Evidence." *American Economic Review* (1972), 62:372–83.

Weiss, Randall D. "The Effect of Education on the Earnings of Blacks and Whites." *Review of Economics and Statistics* (1970), 52:150–59.

―――. "Measurement of the Quality of Schooling." *American Economic Review* (1966), 56:379–92.

Welch, Finis. "Black–White Differences in Returns to Schooling," in George von Furstenberg, Anne Horowitz, and Bennett Harrison, eds., *Patterns of Racial Discrimination, Volume II.* Lexington, Massachusetts: Lexington Books, 1974.

―――. "Relationships between Income and Schooling," in Fred Kerlinger, ed., *Review of Research in Education.* Ithaca, Illinois: Peacock, 1974.

Winsborough, H. H. "Age, Period, Cohort, and Education Effects on Earnings by Race: An Experiment with a Sequence of Cross-Sectional Surveys," in Kenneth Land and Seymour Spilerman, eds., *Social Indicator Models.* New York: Russell Sage Foundation, 1975.

Wolfle, Dael. "To What Extent Do Monetary Returns to Education Vary with Family Background, Mental Ability and School Quality?" in Lewis C. Solmon and Paul Taubman, eds., *Does College Matter?* New York: Academic Press, 1973.

INDEX

academic ability: of adolescents, 86, 87, 97, 108, 109, 112, 120; of adults, 97–99; and age tested, 96–99; and aspirations, 106; and curriculum placement, 108, 112, 114; and earnings, 85–86, 115–21; and economic success, 85, 87, 90, 91, 98, 104; and educational attainment, 86, 101–04, 106, 108, 109, 110, 115, 119; encouragement of, 86, 106, 108–9, 123; as factor, 88–89; and life chances, 91; and occupation, 114; tests of, 87–88, 90, 91

adolescents: academic ability of, 86, 87, 97, 108, 109, 112, 120; cognitive skills of, 85–86; college plans of, 106, 108, 109, 110; earnings of, 101, 117, 120, 220–23; educational attainment of, 101; environment of, 98; occupational advantage of, 101; personality and effect on earnings, 222–23; personality and effect on occupational status, 222–23; personality traits, 11, 14, 75–76, 122–24, 130, 132–38, 221–23; scores and effect on educational attainment, 96; scores vs. adult scores, 97–98; test performance of, 106, 112, 117

adults: academic ability of, 97–98; status and test performance, 91, 93, 97, 98; success of, 85, 97–98; tests, 98

affirmative action, 79

age: and earnings, 45–47; and education, 45; and occupational status, 44–45; and race, 45, 46; and status change, 45

Alexander, Karl L., Eckland, Bruce K. and Griffin, Larry J., "Wisconsin Model of Socioeconomic Achievement," 93

Andrisani, Paul J. and Nestel, Gilbert, "Internal-External Control as Contributor . . . ," 124

"appearance," 152

Armed Forces Qualification Test (AFQT), 22, 42, 48, 95–96, 98

Army Alpha, 95

Army General Classification Test, 95

Arrow, Kenneth J., "Models of Job Discrimination," 211; "Some Mathematical Models of Race in the Labor Market," 211

aspiration: educational, 77, 86, 106, 123; occupational, 51, 77, 86, 123

Bachelor of Arts degree, 161–64, 172, 195–96, 224; "bonus," 172; and "credentialism," 163; and earnings, 177, 192–200; of nonwhites, 174, 192–200; of whites, 174, 192–200

Becker, Gary, Human Capital, 159; and Chiswick, Barry R., "Education and the Distribution of Earnings," 185

Benson, Viola E., "Intelligence and Later Success of Sixth-Grade Pupils," 100

Bielby, William T. et al., "Response Errors in Earnings Functions . . . ," 185; "Response Errors in Black and Nonblack Males," 185

Bishop, John, "Biases in Measurement . . . ," 36, 185

bivariate relationships, 25–31, 236–37, 261–68; and education, 265–67; and family income, 236–37; and father's education, 263–65; and father's occupation, 261–63; and occupation, 267–68; statistics of, 25–26, 28–31

Blau, Peter and Duncan, Otis Dudley, American Occupational Structure, 4

Bloom, Benjamin S., Human Characteristics . . . , 109–10; Stability and Change . . . , 97

blue collar: children, 186; fathers, 33, 175, 224, 228, 253; returns to education, 33, 175, 186, 224, 228; sons, 175

Index

Index